Become the Maelstrom

By D.H. THORNE

Copyright info

ISBN 9781794566170

Please email all serious correspondence to:
d.h.thorne666@gmail.com

Disclaimer

The contents of this book are intended for mature consenting adults, 18 or older. Nothing in this book is in any way to be treated as legal or medical advice. Use this book at your own risk. D.H. Thorne is not responsible for any consequences incurred by anyone. Spiritual belief and practices are a personal experience, and your experiences will vary.

Dedication

This book is a manifestation. It is result of a promise I once made to the demonic and spiritual entities with whom I have conspired. In turn it is a manifestation of my will, a gift granted to me by them. It is part of an ongoing work of liberation… As we work together to help align those humans who are ready to be free, to find their way into the dark places, where the true black light of freedom shines.

For it is in this darkness where we can light the spark of illumination and become the god of our own universe. To become the sun, the light and the glory of our own personal dream.

The dream within a dream…

I hereby dedicate this book to all those spirits who have come to give me the gnosis of this work, and specifically with the highest honor to the following spirits, in no particular order:

Nyarlathotep, Malphas, King Paimon, Vine, Baal, Nicodemus, Dantalion, Azazel.

I would also thank all those people I have met along the way along this odyssey, the various internet personalities and video bloggers, social media characters, as well as fellow authors and friends who I have made on this journey.

I went from a complete nobody, and through the help and support of you, and your ability to see what was working through me, I am now confident that this book will reach the people it needs to reach, and my gnosis shared with those who will appreciate it.

Lastly, I dedicate this work, and any and all future volumes, to my beloved wife, and my stepson. Their support, love, and patience have made this work possible. I am both proud, and humbled at your dedication to me, and my insanity.

All the power I have is yours.

- D.H. THORNE

CONTENTS

INTRODUCTION

I have always felt that introductions should be personal in some way, perhaps autobiographical in nature, somehow drawing the reader into the web of events that lead to the writing of the book. I promise you; it won't be very long or boring.

This first part of the book is presented as a series of Essays, each one intended to align you more and more with my specific personal gnosis about magick. The most important chapter is the Trinity of Self, if you read nothing else, read that section, read it twice, read it thrice... but make sure you read it, for that is perhaps the most important piece of specific personal gnosis I will include in this work. If you read nothing else, you would have read the fundamental key of how I do what I do. Everything else is just a prop that is used in that performance art that is the trinity of self.

After this will be a more specific section about the mechanics of the way magick works in various activities. And lastly will be the example spells, pathworking and related nuts and bolts rituals and methods.

I say my "specific personal gnosis" because I believe magick is a subjective experience in an extreme way. More so than almost any other phenomenon in our lives, magick is personal. What has been shared throughout history on the subject has been largely lost to time, and we have very little way of knowing if the information and grimoires and ancient tomes of magick we have found are at all reliable or trustworthy, save through personal experience.

Indeed, it is entirely possible that the sources we can access today about magick from antiquity aren't even the best possible sources that have existed. Perhaps they burned in the fire of Alexandria or bombed in one of the great wars. Maybe the little old man on the top of the mountain took his ultimate secrets to his grave?

Or maybe far better ones still exist, locked away in the secret vault of some noble family or elite order.

As Baal once told me... **Some things are not to be known!**

It is for this reason that I decided that my own practical and personal experience and expression in magick was worthy of the light of day. Not because it is better or worse, I am indeed arrogant, but not in that way. Rather because I believe magick is an art form... and like all art, it is for nothing if it is not shared.

For I had found my own truths in my art, and the methods that work for me, and I found them in the vacuum of relative ignorance. Drawn forth from the depths of my intuition, with only a scant glance at the books or works of others. This isn't to say it is somehow better because of it... I could be wrong about all the things I believe.

However, it is authentic, and it's honest. It's from the source of personal practice. It isn't secondhand gnosis. It isn't something created by a person taking the manuscript of a dead eccentric and giving it new meaning.

No, this is the mature adult's iteration of a child's fanciful magick scribbles on the floor of his nursery... the strange arrangement of blocks and toys, and the arcane symbols conjuring up reality that only other children can see... Logic only the mind of the child can appreciate.

Indeed, growing up in the 80s and 90s, before the prolific spread of the internet, and the scores of ancient manuscripts and modern interpretations available in PDF format for free. The only magic we had available to us, was what was for sale in the spirituality section of the local bookstore.

I noticed as I progressed in my own magick arts, that I cared very little for the things that were called magick by others. In most cases all they really taught you was a bunch of dogmatic gobblygook, or just rehashing's of astrology or worse yet, extensions of religious faith.

I saw them as just extensions of religion, as not being true magick, but just different ways to worship some higher power, to beg on the power of god or nature to grant us our desperate wishes. Like an ant commanding an elephant to somehow convince the queen of the hive to give it a better paying job in the nest.

There was no power in this... It was just a new way to kneel...

I do not kneel! Even when I bow, I keep my eyes locked on the object of my respect.

Truth be told I can't really decide when I consciously

began my journey into dark magick. It certainly wasn't those years in the bookstore... I already had something of an idea of what I was doing by then... But as of late I have been reminded of a long forgotten memory, and it sticks out in the funny way a memory does when it has been repressed long enough, and just kind of pops up out of nowhere, and you have to take a minute to think about it, asking yourself why you forgot it, and how is it possible to remember it so vividly after all these years.

No, this might not have been when it started... really it started much earlier than this, but this story more than some others, has a special significance, and for you dear reader, perhaps it will be compelling in its own way. Maybe you will relate to my desperation and need?

Maybe that is why you hold this very book in your hand now? Or maybe you are already an accomplished sorcerer, and this story will remind you of your own first time dealing with a spirit?

This memory is about me as a young boy, calling upon the devil in the bathroom stall down the hall from my third-grade class. Begging Satan to help me where God had yet not dared... I was weak, I was pathetic, the fat new kid in school, the kid with the smelly clothes, the kid who never did homework because my home was a nightmare of constant drunken fights and cognitive abuse... there I was with my pants down around my ankles weeping silently. Raging impotently at the cruelty of a god I was taught to ask for salvation, a god who might allow an innocent child to suffer... all because some woman ate an apple... Allowing me to be punished and tortured just because I existed.

God wasn't listening to me... I had to be the one to save myself...

I wanted to kill them, to tear them apart with my teeth and claws... I wanted to be like Carrie, or the American Werewolf, or maybe a vampire, yeah just not a silly Dracula kind, something more cool and powerful.

Little did my parents, or anyone else know I had an adult level book about werewolves I stole from the library in town. I remember reading it, over and over, wishing I could be one.

*I'd be one of the **good ones**!* I reasoned. *I'll **only** eat the bad people! Please!*

I begged and begged.

I read the part about how different people believed they could become werewolves.

I wanted it to be real, I found several good examples of spells and rituals I could try, but Most called for crazy shit, human fat from an unbaptized male child, rendered into a paste to be rubbed into a wolf pelt and worn on a full moon... Yeah, I know, sounds like Hollywood witchcraft to me too.

Another was simple enough: make a deal with the devil, sell my soul, or some other precious thing, in exchange for power, or the powerful curse of a werewolf.

That was it... that was the one. I had read those 2 or 3 paragraphs over and over and drew the picture of the mighty black demon wolf I might become several times every day till it was firm in my mind. I was obsessed...

The passage in the book talked about how if the petitioner really begged the devil to appear, and was at a moment of true weakness, he would appear. And he would appear as any of several forms... one stuck out in my mind. That of a shadowy man in black, with black skin in a brimmed hat, with the smell of brimstone and the cloven hoof of a goat.

So, there I was, in the bathroom stall... having suffered yet another terrible ordeal at home, and it was followed by an equally bad day at my new school among those kids who hated me. Just for being the fat new kid who didn't play sports.

I begged Satan, Lucifer, ANY DEVIL that would hear me to give me the power. To make me a monster, to turn me into a werewolf or give me whatever evil power it would take to destroy those who hurt me and regain power for myself. I would give anything... I wouldn't go to hell, I would give anything but my soul, I didn't want to be tricked like in the movies. But I was desperate... I would have given anything at that moment.

For I, like a great many people who are attracted to the dark forces of the occult, do so out of a sense of helplessness, and a need for power, money, or some other thing which we feel we need to save us. I remember sitting in that stall, praying for the devil to come. Weeping his name in tears… It must have been a good fifteen minutes maybe a half hour, and nobody came. It was deathly silent… just the drip of a leaky faucet.

Drip… Drip… Drip…

I closed my eyes to try and calm myself. And my mind was filled with the image of the hallway outside the bathroom. It was a vivid daydream…as my mind focused on it, I began to see a man with dead eyes and jet-black skin… smiling to me… tipping a black hat… he had cloven hooves and he was in the hall just outside the bathroom… He was coming in and opening the door.

At that moment the door burst open and the teacher yelled at me. Breaking my apparent trance… startling me back to horrid reality.

I will never really forget him, nor the gist of his angry shouts.

"For *fucks* sake, first you interrupt the class with your stories about how the other kid called you a name, then you beg to use the bathroom, and now you're still in here after half an hour! How big a shit are you taking you *fat* little worm?"

Yes, he really spoke to me that way… He hated me, he hated how I openly defied him. How I refused to be threatened into doing extra homework to make up for what I wasn't doing at home. I hated him for not believing me when I would tell him what home was like.

Well, all I could do was dry my eyes, stand up and clean myself up and go back to class. I was still powerless… even the devil wasn't going to save me, or even give me the dignity of revenge. Had I known then what I know now, I might have known that image of the black man in the hall was likely more than just an illusion of the tormented mind. The teacher's abrupt entrance and horrible words were too synchronistic to be mere coincidence.

More than likely I had called my first spirit.

I asked for power… Perhaps it was just a coincidental daydream… or perhaps Power answered.

After several decades of unbelievable experiences, having been a leader of a small cult, to having a total inversion of my belief and becoming a hard skeptic, to having a complete 180 shift in belief yet again to reawaken to magick… Feeling like a vampire that was asleep in a tomb, going to sleep in the early millennium, only to wake up 18 years later and seeing all that has changed.

From being spiritually blind, to once again seeing shadows in the corner of my eyes even now as I write this and having no fear at their presence. So much like black cats playing in the dark corners of my home… they watch my family sleep… they sit in awe and whisper to me the gnosis of this work… Always around the witching hour, when everyone else is most deeply asleep, the spirits rise, and I sit alone and write, and conjure, and scheme.

At last, I am a Lord of Shadow.

I now know and admit and declare that I have that power… that power is mine, it wasn't given to me, or taught to me by some priest or magus… I took it like a thief in the night, and now I am free.

Of course, I realize now I was always free… I realize now that every pain, every struggle everything done to me was done by myself. Done to bring me to this moment, where I finally am the powerful monster, I wished I always was… And as promised - **I only eat the bad people…** now here I am giving the methods I use to do just that.

This book is just one way, one of many valid ways. I promise you, that it is not my intention for it to become your way… more like a gateway to your own path.

This book will merely point you in the right direction so you can find your own way… your own path to liberation and power in magick. May you be a lord/lady of your own shadows, or a master or mistress of your own dark dream.

But be warned… Magick is not a thing to dabble in, you either commit to doing it, and learning it, or you will fail, or even worse, you will succeed, and in that success be powerless and at the mercy of forces beyond your comprehension.

The shadows are always watching, waiting and looking for a fool like the one I once was, to drag them down into the depths and devour… Of course, if they hadn't done this to me, I wouldn't be the monster I am now… and you wouldn't be reading this book.

So, come with me if you wish, walk with me a while, only for as long as you find what you need. Let's explore the dark path together! Just make sure you *mind the shadows…*

NONDUALITY

Ah, the joys of synthesizing an entire personal philosophy, down into an essay designed to prepare you to use my system of magick, based on a nondual approach to mystical reality. All without overly regurgitating the wisdom of profound thinkers to the point of banal plagiarism or creating a limiting dogmatic paradigm in which the user would become entrapped instead of liberated.

The quest to be both concise, but also complete…

I find myself torn between writing a book of philosophy, and a book of specific magick based on that philosophy. I do not want to write another book of pure philosophy, even if that book could somehow be a superior repackaging of the genius of men like Alan Watts, Carl Jung, Terrence McKenna, Joseph Campbell, and Ragnar Redbeard.

COME TO ME BREVITY!

I hereby silence the chattering of a disorganized mind and replace it with profound silence into which wisdom and vision may flow!

So, here we are, reading a book of magick, not a book of philosophy, so I must have already made up my mind, and created the book you are reading right now, all that remains is for me to carry out my true intent, and stop thinking I can be contrary to it.

Let me align myself with my truest intent and make myself an instrument of the reality I yearn to experience.

Let me measure the currents and the tides, hoist my sails and cast myself from the shore, and harness the true power of the trinity of self to manifest this tome of magick from the black depths below.

And this here is the heart of the meaning of the statement, Become the Maelstrom…

This is the essence of my way, the Tao of my magick.

I will not bore you with an in-depth analysis and discourse trying to align you with the entire current of non-dualism. There are men who would run circles around me in that regard… In fact, if you want to understand the inspiration for my magick, go to the source of it, and look up a man named Alan Watts, and listen to his recorded lectures, and read his books. He is quite literally a real-life Obi Wan Kenobi of western Zen, and I was a Padawan of his Digital force ghost for some time… until I "mastered" myself and had my moment of liberation.

My perception of myself was inverted, and I no longer identify exclusively as the man who carries my name, but as the universe that peeks through that limited pinhole of experience that has the audacity and arrogance to think he can recite a few magick words and make the entirety of the universe bow before him.

I understand now the futility of having the intention to change or control my intention. I now understand that the only way is the way of no way, the way of Wu-Wei.

If I want to compel reality to do my will, I need to understand I am reality, and reality IS true intention in action, and it is already conformed perfectly to my truest intent.

Thus, what I am seeking is not a mechanical operation, but a way to awaken in myself an awareness of that intention, and to align with it in such a way as to become my true self, and not limit myself to this collection of tortured portraits I hang on the walls of my mind.

I need to see through the fundamental delusion of the experience of my biology, and understand that I create what I see and feel, and hear, and smell… I create experience as it happens.

I need to see that what I experience is not reality, but a dream my brain created based on the interaction of my neurology with the rest of the world.

I need to see that my brain exists only as a figment of its own imagination, and that all that is, all that we are… is all that there is, and all that ever was, and all that ever will be again.

I need to see that this dream I call reality is really no more than a memory of what already was, for by the time my nerves send my brain the signal of what they experienced, and my brain processed it, and by the time I experience that process as an experience, it might as well have been a million billion years ago… because that moment is gone… forever… So, I am, so too are we all, living in the past… But it is a dream of the past, and all dreams can be mastered…

We are not made of this crude substance… we are not limited to the shapes and contours of our frames. We are not bony meat-bags with ghosts piloting them… How barbaric and inelegant…

No… We are the universe, and our bodies are an interface for it to experience itself, we are the nerve endings of a vast organism of consciousness, and what filters through as awareness, is just a tiny fraction of that consciousness… A sleeping god dreaming it is a man or woman, star, or stone, and loving every moment of it.

Perhaps we are a sentient Tulpa created by the true self to keep itself company, and the universe we experience is the wonderland we created for ourselves to play in.

Perhaps we are a Boltzmann brain, created in the infinite fire of the singularity of pre-bang reality, and our boredom led to the creation of a universe that exploded into being… as one idea led to the next, and each idea spawned an infinite number of possible ideas, creating a maelstrom of chaos… in which we find ourselves…

Lost, alone, afraid.

We are born into the dream, and our new eyes look at the bright light and the shadow and decide that this contrasted light and dark has meaning, we begin to recognize the shapes of this contrast, and we begin to contrast sound from not sound. And feel from not feel… We begin to make sense of the Rorschach ink blot we see around us, and we lose our awareness that we once WERE that ink blot… we forget…

As we mature, we start to notice the patterns of the light and shadow, the sound and not sound, the touch and not touch… we begin to see shapes, we begin to see color, hear high sounds and low sounds, musical notes and sour notes, noise and speech… we begin to feel pleasure and pain…

As the complexity of our illusion improves, so does the depth of our delusion…

What began as a process of learning to see, becomes a process of forgetting what we already knew…

Those vibrant searching delirious eyes of a newborn child are the raw eyes of the newborn universe reveling in its decision to forget itself…To focus its awareness for a short time on the material aspect of itself.

As the child grows it becomes more and more locked into the world of symbols, and forgets the world of essence from whence it came, it breaks apart from the maelstrom, like a small cloud going its own way… getting swept up in the current of the storm, but believing itself estranged and alone, because the maelstrom is not the clouds, it isn't even the wind that pushes them around. For as the 6th patriarch of Zen said, "it is mind that moves…"

So it swirls and blows this way and that, convinced of its uniqueness, convinced it is what is in control, until at last, having utterly forgotten who it was, it is blown at last back into the collective storm… as the old man or woman crawls into the grave, the nimbus of individuality dissolves back into the storm of the singularity. Realizing at last that it never left!

And all this time, the same process is repeated, over and over, each little puff of vapor thinking itself alone, unique and different, until it isn't.

Some of us figure this out before our time, we embrace it, and when we do, we wake up to the fact that we are not really separate from the storm… we are the storm… we learn to see there is nothing to control, we are doing all of it already, and that it is absurd for us to believe we are victims of the storm. At the mercy of the storm.

Others do not, they cannot accept the truth, they cannot face the fact that they do unto themselves that which they think they do unto others. That the fate they suffer, is only suffered because they think it is fate…

We suffer only because we think we ought not to. And for no other reason.

And if people simply understood what was happening, they would never truly suffer another day of their lives. They would still experience discomfort, because a certain dialectic duality is required for experience…

Experience must have a hot and a cold, but it is really all temperature. Experience must have a light and a dark, but it is all just illumination. Experience must have a SELF and another, but we are all just I. Backs must have fronts, ins must have outs, and "as above," must have "so below."

And in that statement, as above So below, we see the true nature of the nonduality that is the dialectic. Even in the opposite of above, there is the reflection of sameness below.

Duality or dialecticism itself is not enough, for if there are only 2 things in the universe, they cannot truly know how they relate to one another. They cannot truly know which is soft, and which is hard. Hot, or cold.

In order to have experience, for reality to be sane, we must introduce a third participant… We must create a trinity… We must create something to compare the two extremes of hot and cold, self and other, in and out, up and down… And in so doing, reality explodes into being as a fully realized experience… A delusion of endless magnitude and possibility limited only by our intention and will to experience it… and our experience is all there is.

We argue incessantly about the nature or existence of free will, but there is no alien will for us to free from. There is only one will, the true will of the trinity of self. It manifests as fate, as causality, as cause and effect. And yet these spooky coincidences, these synchronistic effects happen again and again… Science calls it Causality and coincidence, Christians call it god will and divine providence, Gnostics call it god or source and the demiurge, some call it the seven hermetic principles or mind, Taoists call it the Tao, and on and on it goes, where it stops, nobody knows.

Each expression is a little different, each of them holding a unique truth and each one is true in its own way.

Like the fingers of a hand grasping an object with multiple features, each one is convinced it is having an experience of a separate truth, but they all hold the same truth in the same hand.

Like the blind men and the elephant, each one touching a different part thinking they know what it is… the man holding the trunk says it's a snake, the one holding a leg thinks it's a tree, the one holding the tail thinks it's a lion… you are like this. I am like this.

But we are all not this… *Neti Neti*… Not this, nor that… the only thing we can be certain of, is that the totality of all that there is, cannot be limited, nor defined by the words of blind men - and we are all equally as blind…

Only by the acceptance of what is, without trying to define it, or describe it can we at last know it as it truly is.

All of reality is a decision, this very book is a decision you made to see a collection of energy fields as a book… to give it meaning… the words you see on the page are just ink blots, and you are deciding they have meaning as you read them.

All of this is your playground, all of this is the maelstrom… All of this is mind, and you can become this maelstrom, you can consciously connect with this true will of the storm. You can learn not to try in vain to force this storm to obey you…

But instead to align yourself with this storm and use its infinite power, it's natural current of causality to blow you where you want to go. You only must recognize yourself as the entirety of the void that creates the storm, not even the wind, and certainly not the little puff of vapor being blown around.

This book of magick does little more than describe another fun game the maelstrom plays with itself. It is my way of showing you how to teach yourself what you probably already know. You may not understand a word I have said so far, you may never understand it. I am but a fool that has seen nothing and knows nothing. I am not writing this book for the eyes that read it, I am writing it for the true intent behind the eyes, the one that is playing the game… The Same I that I am.

I am awake, and I am speaking to the you that is dreaming. You can become the maelstrom again… and you don't have to lose yourself to do it…

This book of magick is my written consent and permission for you to wake up and realize life is but a dream, and all dreams, **ALL DREAMS** can be made lucid… Are you ready? Let's begin…

THE TRINITY OF SELF

PART 1: INTRODUCTION TO THE TRINITY

Before we begin, I want you to understand that this is the centerpiece of my method in magick. This concept is the product of a lifetime of experience, a creation of my own, and part of the foundation of my magickal system. It is not something taught to me by some old hermit on top of a mountain teaching magick to the worthy, nor a dusty tome.

It wasn't a gift from god, or the menacing threats of a dark spirit. It is what came out when I sought for truth and refused to let my understanding be too polluted by the dogma of other sorcerers, or their faiths.

It has certain rules and principles, and these rules and principles are shared within many other traditions of magick.

The fact that it echoes or exactly matches many of the things found in other philosophies and magick systems around the world validates it… (In fact, the more I look the more I see the symbolism I used is almost universal!)

I essentially reinvented the wheel - But in a way that made it more relevant and up to date with modern minds like my own. Call that arrogance if you will, but I admit and accept it. I also accept that many will not accept it or admit or believe in it.

Still it amazes me that without any real study or intent, it so closely meshes with and is verified in many aspects with many other ancient traditions, and is essentially a simplified, modernized version of some very old magickal philosophies. Translating some of the most fundamental principles of magick and philosophy into a simplified modern set of symbols and ideas that any modern westerner who speaks fluent English will probably easily understand.

Yet it may take a lifetime to comprehend and fully explore what it means. I myself am still enraptured by this task!

This was developed over years and improved dramatically recently. It was developed through my own intuitive creation, meditative contemplation, and communion with spiritual beings other than myself.

I am going to put into this book a base form of my core system of metaphysics that is entirely open to interpretation. Make no mistake – I have a very specific way of viewing this concept, and I have a very deep set of correlations and correspondences involving it. But I do not want you to have your own gnosis polluted by my own self-created Dogma. Instead I want you to treat this as a work of art, meant to inspire you and guide you, not shape you and limit you.

Thus every word of this 3 part essay is not meant to be a description of rules… but a form of literary fantasy meant to inspire you to reflect on how you see reality in a geometric way, filled with relationships you may not have ever considered before that will hopefully encourage you to think deeply about the interplay between different things in your life and come to understand how this becomes magick.

If anything, I include here contradicts your own beliefs or findings, just allow yourself to entertain these notions long enough to finish reading the chapter, and then ignore whichever most offends you, or find ways to modify one to fit the other. Thus, do not mistake this for the true shape of reality, it is merely one of the best overlays I have found to help me rationalize the impossible nature of magick and experience itself.

Again, my goal here is not to make you think like me, but rather to give you inspiration to think for yourself. To point you to the path I have taken so you can follow it, and warn you of the deadlier pitfalls, and what points of interest I found along the way.

So, I don't want you to feel like before you can begin practicing magick with my methods that you have to somehow master the foundational philosophies that I use. Indeed, if you did, you wouldn't need any of my other methods, nor the rest of this book. You would simply do magick. Your own magick, and you wouldn't need mine.

I simply want you to be aware of these ideas, and to seek the truth for yourself.

To that end, I am going to give you the briefest possible outline of what I have come to call the trinity of self. While still painting for you a complete mental picture.

The trinity is an idea that can be found in almost every major magickal tradition in some form or another and is for all intents and purposes a Kind of Mystical meme, that we all intuitively seem to recognize and accept as true or relevant. It is undeniable that the nature of the trinity is sacred in virtually every culture, magick system and even in science.

Buckminster Fuller said - "The Triangle is the most basic unit of all structure, and the tetrahedron as the most basic system of energy dynamics."

As a beginner, or even an advanced student of magick, all you need to understand fully is that the foundation of our limited experience of reality is the trinity, and the trinity I employ is the holistic trinity of Mind, Body and Soul.

Performing magick requires the alignment and union of these three distinct aspects of reality within ourselves, our immediate environment, and in how we interact with the world. We then energize this new pattern with the maximal intent and energy we can muster and set it free to materialize in the rest of reality through non-attachment. If we do it right, if our intent is lucid, and our energy is potent, and it doesn't defy the laws of totality overmuch, we will see our will manifested in the subjective or objective matrix of our experience.

Thus, I created for myself a Device, a Design, a symbol, and a way of thinking about reality that I meditate on in ritual and contemplate. I created this symbol, and I have yet to find all its meaning and potential. Maybe one day you will improve upon it, or find out things I missed?

You will be using this symbolism and its various expressions throughout the methods I share in this book. It will be a centerpiece on your own Altar and in magickal rituals, it will be a meditative focus, a triangle of manifestation where you can concentrate your intentions and have them literally appear before you, a portal to other worlds, and much more.

You can feel free to ignore it completely, and or substitute your own symbolism if you wish. If you prefer the Pentagram, or a circle or some other diagram or symbol for any reason, do not feel obligated to use my symbolism. However, unless you find it utterly wrong and inappropriate,

create your own and keep it in a place of reverence and contemplate it in meditation regularly.

The trinity of Self is represented by the imagery of a Triangle and can take on several different iterations to express different layers and truths about reality.

This is the complete visual representation of the Trinity of Self in its primary form complete with labels (in English). Use this, or any of the other examples below in any way you see fit.

Here are a few iterations which can be used for simplicity sake, or for focusing less on the complete meaning, and more on the general concepts -

In ritual, you can use any one of these representations you feel most comfortable with. Either in physical form as a drawn sigil on paper, or even create a larger version to place on your own Altar by painting it on wood or fabric.

There are no rules here, it can even be rendered as a design carved in dirt in the wilderness or even outlined in chalk, salt, or painted on the floor of your ritual chamber

It can even be used just as a picture hung on the wall to help you focus your intent.

You can interact with it any way you like, either touching it and visualizing your power and intent flowing into it, standing inside it, or simply meditate upon it during or outside of ritual.

You can and should also feel free to customize it, decorate it, stylize it, and make it personal to you, because in so doing you might find truths I missed in my basic design. So long as you keep the essential symmetries and symbolism the same, it will be fine.

Even just a simple triangle inside a circle is fine.

The most important symbol is that of the equilateral triangle, everything else is secondary, such as the concentric circles outside and inside. It is important to draw or imagine a kind of vortex or direction of flow in the center of the triangle which can be oriented either clockwise, or anti clockwise.

Which should give the impression of flow either inward from the edge to the center, or outward from the center into the edge. This direction can be used either to signify creation, or destruction, empowering or dis-empowering. Liberation or slavery, yin or yang. Or the direction can be utterly ignored, or the symbol can be drawn without direction, invoking a sense of balance and equilibrium without movement, but understand that this may be less useful as a symbol in ritual but should still work for you. Remember this is just a symbol, it by itself has NO power, save what you give it!

Another important consideration for the symbolism of this diagram can be the circles, and while they are not needed at all and thus secondary to the triangle, I find them both aesthetic, symmetrical to the design and they have an important meaning that you will intuitively understand after reading this next section fully.

What this symbol, and the soon to follow meanings teach us, is that to do magick, indeed, to do anything, requires the intentional alignment of the 3 primary aspects, to charge this intent with energy, and then release it. This means all magick requires a mental aspect, a physical aspect, and a spiritual aspect.

Part 2: Exploring the Trinity of Self

Let us now explore each of these aspects, which are represented by the outer triangles pointing inward, and their apexes invert to become the points of the inner triangle. Creating a mirror symmetry which will become clear in a moment -

The essential meaning of this aspect of the symbol is to show the interconnected nature of the mind, the body and the soul and how each of these elements creates our reality and influences it.

Each of these elements when combined, create the totality of experience, all that is, was, and will be again.

Thus, each of the three corners of the design represents one of the 3 fundamental aspects of self/reality. The three aspects can be oriented in any way, with the mind on top, or on bottom or to the side, or the entire image can be mirrored and reversed - so long as each of the aspects is in the same relationship to the others that it is shown here. Each of the three aspects can be imagined as having a color, and the color is that of the trichromatic color wheel (RGB)

The aspect of Body (Red): This is Represented by a triangle with a Capital "B," and is more than just the biological body your being, though it includes that. This is the "Body" of reality. This is the realm of substance without form. It is here that the raw goo of causality waits to be molded and shaped by form. It is the silent motionless dark sea of primordial Chaos. It is raw energy without direction. Logic without reason. It is perfect Order without organization. It is the great entropy at the end, and the stagnation of the perfect balance of the beginning before the bang. It is the Rorschach inkblot before we pick out shapes and give them meaning.

The aspect of Spirit (Blue or indigo): This is Represented by a triangle with a Capital "S." If the body is the Dark primordial sea of motionless chaos, this is the Vibrant light which shines upon it, and it is a black light and a white light, the true light of source. An eternal paradox of potential. This is the realm of pure ideas, ideas without limits, ideas without ideals. One idea is no better or worse than any other. It is the realm of language and symbols. It is here where every idea exists, and it exists simultaneously with its opposite, and every idea in between is also without. It is an empty void of possibility. It is a place of form without substance. A place of Perfect crystalline order, so vast and limitless that it is pure chaos. It is shape without content. It is the place where the voice of divinity echo's silently for eternity. A chasm of paradox, where the abyss is finally seen as just an inverted hollow mountain. It is a place where every possibility and impossibility exist, but never with substance. Fire has no heat, though it will feel hot. Pain is without harm and can be a pleasure. There are no ideals, no one is better or more correct than any other. Everything is best and worst.

The aspect of Mind or ego (green): This is Represented by a triangle with a Capital "M," or "E" for mind or Ego. This is the act of decision, reason, intent, the experience of self-awareness, and interpretation. It is the seat of the ego, the realm of logic and causality. It is the part of the human experience that is most easily mistaken for the "Self" or the "seat of will." However, it is best described as more of just an interface. A driver's seat for the avatar of our biology. It creates the world around us by imposing meaning onto the subtle forms and substances of the totality of experience.

The interplay of these three aspects, creates the totality of experience, both the ones you know, and don't know. The ones you can experience and cannot. It creates the subjective and objective reality in equal measure, both are true, both are objective, both are subjective.

The subjective world is represented by the exterior circle -

Because from the perspective of our experience, all reality is subjective, and all is contained within the subjective circle of experience. Thus, there are the three triangles of the aspects, penetrating the outer circle, pointing inward influencing our subjective experience and being influenced by our experiences, and all this influence is being pushed into the middle of diagram, where it is met by the influence of the objective or collective experience at the center of the image.

Why is the subjective outside? Isn't the Objective the REAL world, and the subjective world just an illusion? Isn't that what science and skeptics tell us?

That depends… It depends on your perspective and personal meditations. This diagram appears inverted because in my experience, the subjective universe is the container, and the objective is just another part of the illusory inner universe we experience. This is not a contest where the inside is less important or weaker or stronger for that matter. Ultimately what we believe shapes what others believe, and what others believe shapes what we believe. So, it should really be visualized as a kind of mobius strip, where one becomes the other and in turn, becomes again as it was.

You could even imagine that my subjective reality is in the center representing the objective, and your subjective reality experience is the outer as your experience contains all of what I am. Just as my subjective experience contains within it, all that you are.

This is the Collective reality we experience daily, the give and take between he said, and she said. The laws of nature and the anecdotal evidence that adds up to prove it one way or another. The fine line between sanity and madness. And it is easily then represented by the inner triangle - a triangle of manifestation, which connects it's points directly to the outer triangles of the aspects. This is the boundary of where the objective and subjective worlds meet. And it is within this fine barrier line of the triangle that all you experience takes place in a firm, manifestation of reality.

All the space inside the triangle is the experience of the collective of other subjective experiences.

All the space outside the triangle is all the inner truths of the subjective reality you experience that are not shared equally with others.

For example, along the lines of the triangle is the concept of blue.

We can all agree that the sky is blue. But each of us has a subjective experience of what exactly blue looks like. We can all agree blue has measurable universal qualities, like it's wavelength and where we can see it in nature. But what it looks like exactly is entirely subjective.

Thus, the color blue you see is in the space outside the triangle, the color blue your friend sees is on the inside of the triangle, and the part you agree upon is the sliver of the line of the triangle, the point where your experience and theirs meet and agree or disagree.

The black emptiness between the outer circle and the inner circle is the location of the 3 planes of experience, the Material plane, the astral Plane, and the Void.

On the inside at the center of the standard device is a series of lines that connect the corners to the center circle and each of these triangular swirling shapes is the knowable objective reality that is constantly shifting and flowing out from the inner circle. This inner circle represents the objective world that you CANNOT know, IE the subjective reality of all the other observers. This circle is in the center of a triangle and it pushes its influence outward instead of inward. It is left black or empty as a cut out **and is an EXCELLENT place to put a circular mirror** during meditation, representing the way the world sees you! Reflecting your will and intent and action back at you. It is however designed to be the focus for our intent, because when we work magick, we are attempting to bring our subjective will into the objective world and have it manifest so that it enters the experience of all the objective observers, including their subjective private experiences.

So, when we cast a spell, the sigil, or key materials being charged with our intent can be symbolically placed in the center of this inner circle where they will be compelled by our will to take on our intent. It should be reinforced here again, that you need not physically do this. Doing this physically is merely a symbolic act, and it reinforces the intent in your subconscious.

So long as you understand intuitively that this is what you are doing when you charge the object or manipulate it in ritual. There is little need to do it in physical practice, but I usually do anyway.

Indeed, there is little reason to make this symbol more than it is, just a tool and a way to look at reality that penetrates the subconscious mind and tells it you see yourself. Even if only dimly and this alone can be a powerful thing.

This entire process can be inverted, and it is possible to invert this diagram or mirror if it as needed. Placing the objective world outside, and the subjective inside, to represent the forces of nature and causality outside of us and this is useful when we are trying to do divination or learn new things. To see with clarity or allow outside influences to influence us. Or to drain and empty something that is charged to release it into ourselves.

Part 3: The three planes of experience.

The Material plane, The Astral Plane, and the Void - Each of these planes are theoretical constructs like the aspects. But they are in fact very real to most people in some way, most will instantly understand what is meant, and many of us claim to visit the astral world while others dwell firmly in the material.

As shown in this diagram, all this is meant to be used as an aid for visualization and for helping you align yourself with the principles they represent. I assure you, the correspondences and interactions between them are as I describe them, and they can bring you to a very interesting place in your understanding of your experiences. Teaching you to harmonize and recognize how each influences your experience.

They are best imagined as the colors on a trichromatic (RGB) color wheel between the 3 primary colors (Cyan, Magenta, and Yellow) Each of the 3 primary colors themselves are what happens when we focus our attention more on one aspect than another, or none.

The material plane (Yellow): This is the world that exists when the mind aspect focuses its attention on the body aspect. This is a lower vibration centered on the body. This is the mundane world of physical reality, of natural laws, solid objects, and organic life as we know it. It can be subjective, or objective, and it is almost entirely devoid of **obvious** magick or the supernatural.

It is no less real than the other worlds, and no more real. It is; however, the world most human beings are focused on due to the limitation of our biological senses.

We often do not realize that it is technically a creation of our mind's interaction with the body of reality, taking the forms and ideas of the spiritual world and imposing them selectively on the body itself. Essentially if the body is the Rorschach ink blot before we look at it and call it a butterfly. This is the Rorschach ink blot AFTER our mind has observed it and called it a butterfly. This is Reality after we decided to give it shapes and meaning, creating dogs, and stars, and atoms and physical laws that can describe it all.

Some people make the mistake of thinking this means we literally create these things, and if we are unaware of them, they do not exist at all. This is a simplistic misunderstanding, predominantly used by critics and skeptics with little understanding of nuance and the fundamental nature of experience. These things DO exist without us being aware of them, but not as things. They exist as what they truly are without us. And this is an abstract notion that takes time to understand.

We have focused our attention, and intention on the material world almost exclusively soon after birth, though at first, we are not yet fully invoked into the physical form we have chosen. The biology is not yet fully fleshed out, and it takes time for us to settle in, and as we get more settled in, we forget the bigger truth, because the delusion of the material world is so much more compelling and fun.

For one thing all lower order sensations are magnified many times. Pleasure, pain, orgasms, taste, sound, color. Things which are muted in the astral plain, or at least expressed along different pathways.

To a demon or other spiritually focused being, the material world is a wonderland of vivid experience, compared to the ghostly experience of the spirit. The supposed limitations and inconveniences of material reality that often frustrate people, like gravity, death, birth, time, space and impermanence, all becoming a joy and a pleasure to the spirits. In the same way that the lack of limitations in the astral world is a joy to us.

In the astral plane they can fly, teleport, ignore time, and be anything they want (as can we with practice) even making their own pocket universes at will, and all this power can become stifling in its own way. The only limitations they tend to have depend on those they create for themselves. The same could be said for our experience of the astral, but for a spirit like a demon or god, it is more difficult to understand.

I myself do not fully understand how this works, but you should take careful note to pay attention to the fact that virtually all cultural expressions of spirits include a sense of Hierarchy, rivalry and dominion on some level. Notice how they can interact with one another… with one entity being more powerful or less powerful in its own spiritual way, much as some of us are more powerful or less powerful in mundane ways.

So, they truly relish the challenges, and heightened vivid sensations of being in a physical form, or interacting with the material world, even if only on small levels. Because we are focused primarily on the material world, even when we enter the astral our experiences are more vivid than their experiences are.

Our experiences of the astral are also more limited than theirs by our own inborn sense of limitation based on the mundane world. Some of us do not experience it with our conscious minds at all… Going there, it is said, only in memoryless dreams. Others can barely see it, though we are strongly aware of it. Others can go there as easily as taking a nap, and we can fly and explore and be as gods… Limited only by what we are unaware of, but unaware of our limits all the same.

Therefore, many people who travel to the astral, feel a sense as if the astral world is very close to the material with similar features, and the further you go from the material the more spiritual it gets, and the less limited the experience becomes.

There is truth to this, but it has more to do with human perception, than an actual feature of the astral. The more we vibrate or focus our attention on material aspects of the astral realm, the more it seems to be limited. Instead, some have pushed far beyond the bounds of mortal material reality. And it is only for them to decide of what they experienced was "real" or a dream.

I would say… there is no difference really. Both are true.

Demons and other spirits constantly seek ways to interact with the material world. For better or for worse. And because of their disembodied form, they can see things we cannot, know things we cannot, ascertain the causality that will lead to the event they want to see happen in the material world… but they can sometimes struggle to put them into motion without help from material beings such as we.

This is one of the big reasons why so many of them are EAGER to not just work with us but are willing to do for us what they are willing to do. As we are excited to work with them! All, without asking for anything close to what think of as comparable in value. They will move heaven and earth it seems sometimes, just for the pleasure of sharing the experience of incense smoke. Indeed, it is my pleasurable experience that a spirit, especially one like a demon, loves when you invite them into your body and awareness to share in the experience of an offering of food, drink, sex or some other activity is one of the highest pinnacles of ecstasy for them.

This alone can explain the reason for entities and events such as Succubi, incubi, demonic possession, sudden religious rapture (next time you go to a church with people speaking in tongues and falling in rapture to the holy spirit, I promise you, many of them are faking it, but a few aren't, those people are not feeling gods holy ecstasy, they are invoking "spirits" of unknown identity into their body, and they are overwhelmed with the pleasure the entity is feeling, as this entity might just be a passing spirit or lesser demon of some kind, hungry for experience and sees and open door… Notice how most of these churches who do this prepare the individual with ritualized prayer? Complete with chanting, dancing and subconscious commands to open themselves to the holy spirit? Trust me, I know, I have experienced it. I know what is going on.).

There is a reason why this is such a sacred act, and it is not just because you trust them to become part of you for a time, but because they crave it in ways we barely understand. It has long been my suspicion that this is the true motivation for at least some of their willingness to serve us, so that they can eventually be invoked by us, or in the case of the malevolent or offended demon - possess us and walk the world of the living for a time.

Some even believe that spirits once walked this world in human form all the time, passing from host to host, often willingly, cohabiting with the person, even taking a back seat and only really sucking up the vivid energy and experience of life in the material realm. Becoming a living embodiment of god, like a Pharaoh, or Emperor of Rome, and that many of them desire to someday do this again... though for whatever reason, they cannot, or do not... or do, and simply do not reveal themselves, or perhaps fail to obtain power over mankind.

This is also why so many of the things they ask us to do as an offering involve seemingly random actions that have little connection to anything. What you do not realize is that when they ask you to go place a quartz crystal on top of one of the fence posts on a white fence on the other side of town. It is because they know this action is going to cause a chain of events that leads to something they are trying to have happen.

You need to recognize that you are every bit as powerful and important to them, as they are to you. Just for different reasons. As you build an Altar to them in the material world, they metaphorically (sometimes literally) build their own Altar in your honor in the astral. For you are the God and the Devil of your reality, and they are part of that reality, and they are Gods and devils of their own reality as well.

It is important to note that the SPIRITUAL aspect is in opposition to the Material plane, and it is for this reason that the skeptic and the spiritually blind cannot see it.

For they are utterly focused on the material world that can be experienced with the five senses... and what can be imagined or seen as spiritual is false and unreal to them.

This is the same reason why the people who focus too much on the spirit can become detached and insane from those who focus on the material.

The Astral Plane (Cyan) - This is the abstract world of symbols, ideas, form and the source of our dreams and the destination of astral projection. It is the higher vibration reality centered on the spirit. It is the plane of reality that exists when the mind aspect or ego is focused on the spiritual aspect. It is the place we go every night when we dream, and it too can be subjective, or collective/objective in its own way. For it is well documented that when some people dream, they have shared dreams... it is well documented that when some astral travel, they can see the material world represented in it and know things they should not know, or at least think they know things they didn't know before... thus it is my personal belief that what we visit when we astral travel is ultimately inside of us... We do not GO anywhere, we simply invert our awareness to the astral... We lucid dream in the astral - and the Astral is not the same as the material, and thus any correspondences you see are synchronicity or coincidental.

They are not in fact directly connected by default. My search for answers here is still ongoing, however the Astral realm has (like the material) a subjective, and objective nature to it. I can tell you with certainty, I have experienced beings in my dreams that I know did not come from my mind. They were living beings with an intellect all their own, their eyes were alive, and they "felt" alive. Which, to an empath, is a very real tangible sensation or experience. Those few times I have experienced this are never forgotten.

So, what is astral travel? Is it a real thing or a lucid dream? Why can't it be both?

So, when you see your friend in the astral realm reading a book in his reclining chair, chances are that isn't really him. If it has any objective truth at all, it is more likely that this is his essence, not his astral body so to speak. And he might not actually be reading anything when you see him, and he might not even really be there in the material world at the moment of your visit! But he might have been reading there at some point or left an impression of reading or educating himself in that place and you will see that represented symbolically by the reading and the chair.

This is possibly why it has never been proven (at least not to the public or to my personal satisfaction) that astral travel can reveal reliable specific divination about places the traveler has never seen or been. They will only ever see or experience a place they can imagine or have seen in some way in their material experiences.

That doesn't mean they won't experience something real or truthful. But it may be symbolic in nature, and not specific.

In this way they can still experience the essence of the thing, so when they astral travel to someone's home and see inside their home. What they see is what they expect to see... but the essence of the experience is true, and likely verifiable.

If you ask your friend if he was reading a book last night when you visited him in the astral realm, he might say no... I was watching a documentary about something though.

Perhaps this is why there remains a shadow of truth to the claims that people can astral project and go places and see things and know things they shouldn't know. Not enough to prove it to a jaded skeptic, but enough to prove to someone like me who has had similar experiences.

In the astral realm nothing is solid, and nothing here has any substance. Any resistance you experience is either more like trying to move through water, or nothing at all. Thus, you can pass through solid objects if you decide you can. And you can make a dead rotting fish smell and taste like birthday cake. However, the essence of things is strong... the symbolism of the thing is very powerful.

A mundane tree in our yard might just look like an old ugly dying tree, but in the Astral plane it can become a menacing entity, a huge mass of black boughs, moving with intelligence, reaching out to clutch us and do us harm. We come to understand that this tree in the mundane world is sick, and that sickness manifests as a monster here.

It should be noted, that despite being without substance or firmness, a boundary made by a being is difficult to cross. A circle drawn in the astral by a powerful being can have as much, or more power to contain you or another spirit than a stone wall in the material world. You can literally be tossed like a rag doll by a word...

A psychic attack here can be made from any direction, even from inside yourself. It can take the form of mundane weapons, fireballs, or just a terrible feeling of destruction. However, defense is often just as easy... here the stronger intention prevails, the stronger belief.

And so, this is the plane of reality that Demons and other disembodied entities and spirits are focused on primarily, in much the same way we focus on the material world and can only delve into the abstract world of the Astral occasionally, they are unable to interact as strongly with the material world as they are the astral world.

Like us, who have an astral aspect but focus on the material, they have a material aspect, but focus on the astral.

If you can forgive me for theorizing for a moment in a book meant to teach what I consider fact -

Whatever constitutes their body or physical form in the material plane is less localized, or possibly of miniscule size. Either being spread out over larger areas as subtle bodies of energy like wind, or water, electricity, or even movement, or as tiny sparks of current... easily mistaken for the ebb and flow of natural energies in the material world.

Some of them are elemental in nature, and they are limited to one form of matter or energy or another. Care must be taken when trying to envision or understand the elementals... It is easy to confuse their expression, with themselves. A fire elemental may not be in fact fire and flame, but the energy that makes fire... Possibly heat, which is entirely kinetic in nature.

Take special note that those who work with such flame elementals value intensity and highly erratic and kinetic movement. The Flame dancers' moves are graceful and full of life and energy. Not like the wind, which is also graceful but moves with a more aloof and light quality.

Therefore, a thunderstorm could be just a portion of the body of a demonic entity, and that entities entire body might be spread out over thousands, or even hundreds of thousands of miles, or may even be everywhere in the universe, and we only interact with a tiny fraction of its energetic vibration. There is no way of knowing, for they do not see the world as we see it, they are not as limited by location as we are, and while they are not omniscient, or omnipresent, they certainly do have a sense of focus and that focus is limited to only a few people or places at once. It is not limited by time or distance in the same way we are.

Indeed, if you do work with these beings, you will notice how they seem to draw heat from the room, or heat it up, move the air around, causing eddies in the smoke and flame, douse candles, or make them blaze with incredible ferocity. Ask any ghost hunter worth his EVP recorder, and they will tell you that it is widely believed that "ghosts" draw energy in the form of heat or electricity from the environment to manifest their actions.

Demons and other spirits are essentially no different. Indeed, I do not actually believe in "Ghosts." Per say. Spirits… yes. But there is a difference in my mind.

Let it be clear, they can respond to the respectful call of Frank in Philadelphia at 8PM, and then appear to Beth in Bolivia at 8:10. Or they might split their time equally with both, appearing to come and go. Or do this back and forth so rapidly that the people working with them don't notice them coming or going, like the flicker of a strobe set to the highest speed. Or they might compel one of their many lesser spirits in their service to be their messenger.

All of this can never be understood in the same way we might understand it in our world. It is only a close approximation.

Some spirits ARE more focused on the material than the spiritual, like us they can vary a bit, and some of them are often called "lesser" spirits. But they are only lesser to those who do not understand them. They may indeed be tied to a geographic locality, and this is because they are LESS focused on the Astral world. They might "vibrate" at a lower wavelength closer to the material world and thus be stuck in a specific place or bound to a specific object for one reason or another. Much as we are bound to the surface of the earth but can still move around. Thus, they can be incorporeal, but still be almost entirely without physicality or material expression.

Due to the abstract/idea-based nature of the universe as we diverge from the material world, we start to reach the limits of our biological mind, and there are less and less words we can use to accurately define or explain, let alone understand the exact limitations or mechanics of how this plane of reality works.

Yet, intuitively it makes sense to us. Just as we know how to walk without usually having the faintest idea how we actually do it… We just know an object can be charged with magick, or have a spirit bound into it. We know if we consecrate an object to a spirit it creates a kind of bond with them, a link, a tether of spiritual energy that creates a connection that can cause virtually instantaneous interaction between the spirit or energy and the bonded object or location.

It should be of special note, that the Astral Plane is in opposition to the body, and thus the body is intangible to the astral world… nothing in the body truly matters to the astral plane the further removed it is from it, and thus beings that are focused on it, have little care or consideration for the body of the material world itself. As stated before, they can pass through, see through, and otherwise ignore the limitations of physicality… This can also mean they do not always comprehend the attachment we have to material objects the way we do.

Or they may only know it is sacred to you, seeing that energy, and thus understand in their own way that it matters to you as it does, but may in some cases not understand why. Some demons are like this, some are the opposite, some DO know why we are attached to things, and offer to help us obtain them.

Just as some of us do not comprehend the significance of an omen, but others do. These beings vary just as we do.

This also means that the closer a spiritual being is to the spirit aspect, the less intensely it can experience the mundane experiences of the body. It can know what hot is, but not feel it the way a material being can. It can know the sensation as an idea, but not necessarily as vivid experiences.

It can know pleasure, but vivid physical pleasure as we experience it is muted and deadened. Their idea of pleasure is cerebral and emotional.

However, through some mechanism (like the same one we use) somehow, they can know it much more intimately by piggy backing on or taking over our experiences via invocation and possession. Just as we can use our biological body to feel the pleasure of a cold glass of water on a hot day… they can to. For we are not so different from them… it is only our awareness that is different, it is focused and concentrated on the body in a way they are not.

Note: It is with little irony that the keen observer will note that the Mind can be thought to be a part of the material plane, as well as the astral plane... and this is because the mind itself is a product of both and is a producer of both. It is its own source...

The Void (magenta) – Buckle up, because this is a place that is devoid of Mind, Ego, or sanity of any sort. Without the mind or the ego to decide, shape and limit, choose, select and judge... the 2 remaining aspects both become true equally. Indeed, it is important to note that the void is in opposition to the mind, and this, more than any other feature is the only way we can define it with any satisfaction. It is utterly and completely unknowable to the mind or the ego.

The very moment we think we have an idea of what it is like, is the moment the truth of the void is obscured to us. The best the mind or Ego can do, is fantasize what it might be like, but this will always and forever be a pale meaningless fantasy.

This is the fundamental nature of all reality, the void... and in Zen and many other traditions, this is the thing that is sought... Satori. No mind. To know without knowing. To know nothing. Nothing, but everything.

Thus, If the Material world is the world that exist when the mind focuses on Body, and the astral the world that exists when the mind focuses on the spiritual... this is the world that exists without any active mind at all. Not even the mind that reflects and creates the material world. Even when we do our most pristine no mind meditation, have ZERO thought... mind is still moving. It is simply moving silently.

When the body and the spirit combine without mind to control the reaction... This is the YIN and the YANG intertwined and spinning eternally. A dynamo of causality that explodes and creates universes out of nothingness.

The mind does not normally go here, and when it does try, it can only do it by inverting itself, a thing that mystics and their followers might call enlightenment, or madness.

It cannot stay here, and comes back altered, scarred and subtly shifted toward madness, for better or worse, for this madness could be liberation, or it could be slavery. It is a place of paradox, and utter madness, and the "beings" that do not dwell here but dwell nowhere else are both ethereal and substantive. I repeat... this plane of reality is the product of the spirit aspect, and the bodily aspect colliding without the logic or meaning of the mind to give it structure or anything resembling purpose or meaning.

This plane of reality is no less real, no more subjective, and no less objective than all the others. It is utterly devoid of any experience we would call reality, subjectivity, and objectivity. It could be said that this is the REAL reality that exists when there is no mind, or more specifically, NO EGO, to govern or shape, and this is the true seat of the observer, of the entity that dwells in the spaces between your thoughts. It could be said that this is the source-of ALL awareness, and it observes ALL thoughts, and all worlds, and all spaces, and all times at the same time.

This is where the dreaming god sleeps, Vishnu, or the blind idiot god Azathoth - that menacing metaphor of creation that Lovecraft dreamt in his nightmares, not realizing how close to reality his dreams were... a being that is not a being that dreams all dreams which become all realities, and in each dream, it is the star of the show, each dream is one of us, each dream is an atom, or a moment in time.

Some might call this source... and that mind is the demiurge. It is truly primordial, and it is truly what awaits at the end of time when the last atoms have decayed, and entropy has had its way.

Some might say it is the Big Bang before the Bang, all the universe in a single point of infinite density that is infinitely small... That there was no big bang that exploded outward, that the big bang was really an implosion and we are not in an expanding universe that is exploding out, but imploding into an ever-smaller point, creating infinite negative space, and dark energy that grows in power as it expands instead of weakening as all sane matter should...

Whatever it might be... It is my belief that this is the true source of all reality, all space, and all time. That the trinity of self was just a dream of the void, a dream I am having, that others have had, that you are having right now. That dream that became self-aware, and out of this dream sprang innumerable new dreams.

Much could be said of the void, and all of it would be

true, and all of it false.

Human intelligence's and spirits alike are all connected to the same source of madness and dream. But the flow of this connection only goes one way…. Experience flows TOWARD the void, not from it… As it creates the things we experience, we create the experience that it takes in return… What we see and experience, flows from us to the void, and there they are lost… what happens to them is impossible to know. Perhaps they become inspiration for new dreams… Perhaps this is why the more we seek for truth, the more we find… Why nature abhors a vacuum, for the moment we find one, the void rushes in to fill it with something to experience.

But again, those experiences cannot flow from the void into us… Therefore, the void is little more than a flight of fancy for me, a thing I intuitively made up to fill in the gap and create the symmetry… Yet I, and many others intuitively know it is real. It is a thing. And a nothing.

Thus, our subjective and objective experience of the void is intuitive in nature, we know without knowing, we act spontaneously and know it is us that did it, though we know not how.

However, as we have our experiences, they have their effect on the void, and the void responds by giving us new reality to experience… Thus, without being knowable, it has knowable effect on the totality of experience in its own subtle and important ways… and thus, it is an important part of the equation, though it is one even I do not fully comprehend or understand in a logical or expressible way.

You might say, that Zen is a finger pointing to the "moon." And the void…? It is the "Moon" that Zen points to with its "finger…"

I simply know intuitively that it exists, it is an empty place… It is the Maelstrom itself. Full of "everynothing" that is, isn't, can be and can't be, and this creates a symmetry that likely serves as the true origin of all experiential reality and is likely the source of all usable energy and intent. But this itself does it an injustice…

As you can see, even writing this section I touch lightly on insanity, as I repeat myself cyclically, describing it over and over in slightly more nuanced ways. It is a thing that defies the thing that defines it.

To know that small fallacy of truth I experienced when I had my moment of Zen… allowing me to even attempt to explain the void (an act I know I could never do, for I do not know what it is… no one can know) required a total inversion of my mind, turning it inside out… and like a mirror image of reality, I see the world the same as I ever did, but everything is changed…

It is likely the seat of True will, and true intent… and therefore it is so often in opposition with the mind, the ego.

For the ego thinks it is free will and intent, but the ego is just a mask worn by the true free will and intent of infinity… And the Ego runs from it, refuses to face itself, refuses to see into that place it dares not look. The void cannot see itself, much as the tooth cannot bite itself, the blade cannot cut itself, and the ear cannot hear itself.

But perhaps this is not because it is impossible, but because if it did, the game would end, the dream would be over, and the void would stretch, and rise and forget it was ever a dream in the mind of madmen like myself.

Or perhaps, like a mirror turned perfectly on itself… it would reflect itself endlessly until there was nothing left to reflect… it would cease to be a mirror… as the light became absorbed rapidly, and darkness would reign forever within. And a mirror is not a mirror without light to reflect.

Be we a mortal human, a god, or a demon. This is the thing that looks out from our eyes in wonder at the dream it has made… this is the maelstrom, this is the thing, this madness, we must align with to truly have power.

It is why all the most advanced sorcerers, or enlightened sages seem a bit or completely insane, for they have found the void, and found it to be what they truly are… Though they may not know it, for as I said, no one can know the void in a way that can be said… it can only be known intuitively to be true… and even that is almost too much. For it can disturb the dream too much.

In much the same way a lucid dream tends to happen just before we wake ourselves up…

And as I said before… all dreams can be made lucid, we just have to want to wake up inside of it without letting it end. Do you want to wake up?

If you really think about it, this, more than any other

reason, explains why we do not always get our way, why even the magick of a master seems to always be unpredictable and unprovable when it does manifest. Because the moment magick became easy, the moment we can have everything we want with just a thought, is the moment we risk waking up and ending our fun.

It is with these colorful descriptions in mind that we should Meditate on the trinity of self, complete with the mirror in its center, and play with its meanings… let it break you open and show you yourself. You can do this right now if you like…

When you are ready… continue with this book. It will still be here when you come back.

The funny part is, when you come back, if you found what I have found, you may find out this book is gone, as is the person who read it, and you don't really need the rest of this book to teach you anything at all. It will become just another work of art to you, as it is to me.

You will use or not use it to express your own art, in your own way.

LIMITATION

It is my opinion that magick is an Art form more than it is a science. It technically is both, but much more the former than the latter. I have often believed that limitation is a necessary part for something to be a valid art form. Or as I have recently learned, there is a quote attributed to Orson Wells that goes like this:

"The Enemy of Art is the absence of limitation."

The true beauty of art is what we do with the limitations of the medium. We all marvel at the fact that the painter can capture a scene and communicate the emotion of it on a sheet of fabric typically only a few feet across, by using pigmented dirt and some oil and a brush.

We are amazed by how it can be so moving. Never realizing that what makes it moving, and effective, is not the perfect or near perfect rendering of the scene.

For the fashion in art has proven in the past that abstraction can be just as evocative and communicative.

We have also seen in modern times the thing we call the uncanny valley.

And further still I have personally found that people tend to linger much longer and get lost much deeper in the art that I draw by hand that is not meant to be photorealistic. While art I used to produce with a vivid photorealistic quality was often well rated, but people spent almost no time studying it.

The irony in the fact that the sketchy hand drawn comic/pen and ink drawing took me 2 or 3 hours for every ten hours I spent painstakingly rendering a photorealistic scene was never lost on me.

I would draw a single scene in common ballpoint pen and people would ogle it for several minutes at a time commenting on all the little details and nuances.

"You did this with a ballpoint pen? In three hours!?"

Meanwhile I would spend sometimes DAYS painstakingly rendering a graphic on a powerful computer. I would still get the same critical approval, but I would notice people would just look at it for a few seconds and tell me how cool it was and move on to something else.

Wtf?

This is an important thing to notice… because all of reality works like this.

As mentioned before, each of these worlds influence each-other… What we believe is true in our subjective experience, becomes a potential influence in the subjective experience of others, assuming they experience it and agree with it, creating an objective consensus, or collective of truth.

What we choose to believe in the consensus, or collective world, becomes important in our subjective world, often limiting or inspiring us in some way.

If you jump off a cliff, in your subjective experience you may indeed fall a short distance then catch the air and fly. But to the rest of the collective, you hit the ground with a splat. And because the collective knows this, you believe it as well, and so your awareness becomes limited to the realities where you will not fly, and instead of experiencing a flight, you will experience a death.

Of course, this death experience is subjective as well, your biological body will die, and upon death you will be convinced you are dead and have the experience of death. If you believe in heaven or hell you will experience them. If you believe there is nothing, you will experience nothing, and because nothing cannot be an experience, you will not suffer it. You as an ego will simply cease to be. The game will be over. But what you really are never ends, it goes on and on my friends, until you decide it mustn't, then it will stop.

I can't prove any of this to you, any more than I can prove to you that I can fly unaided by science or technology, but by sheer force of will. Because even if I took magick flight right in front of you, you would be the one that has to believe it. I can't make that happen, I can encourage it with evidence, sure. But you are the final arbiter of what is real, even in an objective reality.

Indeed, because we collectively believe it is impossible, and because I don't believe I can fly based on some of that consensus…I can't.

That being said, never mistake thoughts about what you believe, for what you actually believe. Humans are all excellent at lying to themselves. We all think things we do not believe from time to time, if not most of the time. What we truly believe does not belong to the thoughts that we think, thoughts do not produce thoughts. The origin of thoughts, the thinker, that is the one who holds the power, and the belief.

I currently hold that the subconscious mind is the closest we can come to accessing this core origin of our awareness. It could be pictured as the gateway between the ego, and the void. The pinhole through which the void peers...

And it is that pinhole that creates the universe by way of limiting what can be seen... where the pinhole focuses, is the artistry of the subconscious.

So why can't we fly? Why can't we just convince ourselves of something and do it? Well... We can, and we can't.

Notice that flight is a thing we are capable of, but... we are limited in how it can be done. It is no less magickal in fact than a telekinetic levitation. Especially to the mind that doesn't understand how it works. Mundane flight then is just understood magick. Magick based on mastering the physical laws of the material world.

But we will tackle that sticky subject in the next essay – for now let us focus away from the material objective limitations we all already know by heart and focus on the true ROLE of limitation itself as a function of true power.

This is key! limitations are as important as possibilities.

We cannot have one without the other.

Therefore, it is wrong to simply say – "If you believe strongly enough, it will be real."

Because this violates one of the requirements of the game.

If you truly believe you can do ANYTHING, you will wake up and the game will end. Much in the same way the game stops being the game if you enable all the cheat codes in a video game. It can be fun for a while to be invincible and fly and have infinite health and ammo... but the challenge is gone. And unless you substitute the challenge of the games rules for some other personally created challenges, you will grow bored.

But magick could be so much more powerful than god mode, and infinite ammo. Because most of us can still have fun playing some games that way, right?

Well, what If you could also cheat and skip any level in the game, or automatically complete any quest just by choosing to do it... the game becomes less and less interesting. Like reading the last page of a mystery, or someone spoiling a movie.

In eastern belief this concept is related to the six realms of desire... and they believe THIS human experience is the only realm from which the individual can escape Samsara, for it combines the best blend of freedom and limitation, wisdom and foolishness.

In heaven things are too easy, one becomes too filled with pleasure, and journeys to hell where pain and horror become the new pleasure... as we become numb to pleasure, we desire pain and as we become numb to pain, we desire pleasure and the cycle continues.

So too in life, the easier, and the less limited we are, the more boring life quickly becomes. The more sex we get, the more depraved and visceral the experience of sex must become. Till we reach some limit and find ourselves unable to really find pleasure... then we abstain.

The key is to find an equilibrium you enjoy. And this is the equilibrium we already typically have in our lives, but do not know it to be so. This is where magick can help. It can allow us to tweak our experience so we can enjoy it more. I say tweak because big changes, become game breaking cheats. So, our truest will rarely if ever allows us to cheat... Not really. It wants to play the game, and so it will prevent us from ever having everything we as an ego might want.

I often think about what it would be like to be the ultimate being, to be the god of all gods, and I can think of nothing so unpleasant. To have no limits... at all.

I know this isn't the thing people want to hear. People want to hear how they can light a few candles and have their dreams come true. How if they practice every day, learn every secret ever written by every master, and find all the keys, they can do anything. And sometimes they can. But sometimes (most times) they can't. Magick is not a genie in a bottle that grants infinite wishes.

It is a tool, A true form of Yoga, a way to align your experience with your truest will and intention. It is like learning to walk, the way we align and balance our body over our legs and engage in a controlled pattern of falling we call walking - all to propel ourselves where we want to go. The key is to find a balance between moving and aligning yourself with that movement.

If you lean too far back and resist the flow of your legs, you fall backward and go nowhere and suffer. If you lean too far forward trying to pull your legs along, even though you are going the right way, you will still trip and fall, or become tired.

Still, even if you do everything right, you will still be unable to walk to the moon… You will ever only be able to go where your limitations allow.

This means magick has, indeed must have limitations. But even that rule is a decision… but I assure you, this is a decision you have already made, or you would not be here at all, you would wake up and all reality would end… till you decided to do it all again.

However, these limitations are not universal laws, rules, or anything of the sort. There is no 3-fold law of return, no karmic debts that must be paid. No sins. There are no solid walls around anything save those "you" build. The limitations of magick are personal things, and each of us has our own limitations we have created for ourselves.

In other words, no two practitioners will agree completely on what the limitations are. But we all have them. For some the limitation is energy, how much energy can be harnessed. For others it is how much belief or faith can be harnessed. For still others it is simply a matter of knowing the right formula or finding the right deity to petition.

Thus, it is my objective to liberate you from your current paradigm of limitation and then entreat you to discover a realm of unrestrained possibility. Yet somehow, also to encourage you to never make the mistake of thinking limits are a bad thing.

Embrace them, press against them, like a mime in an imaginary box…of course to those outside your box, you look ridiculous. But these spirits, gods, and demons love a good show.

MAGICK AS AN ARTFORM

It is my highest held opinion that Magick rituals and a magickal life, should be seen as a kind of holistic form of performance art, and living art.

Not so much as because we are performing for others or communicating to other people.

But because we are performing for ourselves, our true self. It is a celebration, and a joy to carry out rituals and commune with spirits and perform magick and get results.

We should never get so attached to the outcome of our magick that we get hung up on the belief that what we are doing in magick is for a reason other than fun or expression.

The moment you think what you are doing in magick is really a mechanical operation of A+B = C. That it is merely a formula where you MUST use specific chants, candles, cardinal directions, etc. to get a result. That is the MOMENT that you are no longer doing real magick. You are doing superstition.

You are NO LONGER aligning and asserting your intention and true will, you are placing yourself SECONDARY to the silly props you use in magick.

Magick should always be performed as a kind of expression or celebration of the power we have. The props do nothing by themselves. And rituals, be they low magick or high, are themselves are just the scripts by which we perform, the candles the props. But it is the performance itself that matters. The holistic performance of mind, body and soul, aligning to bring our true will into focus and manifest for us in the dream.

In a very real sense, there is no WRONG way to do magick.

This is why there are so many different variations of the same things. How the same object can be used for different things in different traditions, and why so many of them all seem to sound plausible and true. Why they all seem to work for those who use them.

It is not simply that they believe they work, though that is part of it, it is they all do work because what is done specifically is not the magick.

A good analogy would be like saying Painting is a form of Art, but art isn't painting.

Alchemy is a form of Magick, but Magick is not alchemy.

Demonolatry is a form of magick, but magick isn't Demonolatry.

Wiccan spells are a form of magick, but magick isn't wiccan spells.

This to my mind, is one of perhaps the essential foundations of the concept of Chaos Magick (admittedly, I know only marginally what its academic principles are). However, I feel confident that this is why you have a bunch of postmodern people running around jerking off to sigils and having success.

It is almost certainly a postmodern parody of the dogma of classical magick. In the modern year of 2018, the spirit of parody at the expense of the classical and the dogmatic is all the rage. And thus, Chaos Magick is on the rise. And as more people engage in it, the more it becomes plausible in the collective experience, and this all by itself can make it work, even if nothing at all was being done. It is no surprise to me than that for many people, it works wonderfully! But it is no more or less intrinsically real or effective than others. It is ALL art, and all art evokes emotion and experience.

The classical magickian will open an ancient grimoire, and use the text exactly as written, varying only what they must - based on the availability of materials or legality, sometimes not even then. They will use the Red Dragon, the Lemegton, the Qabalah, and so on. Many of these classical mages are dogmatic in nature, but not all. Some of them truly believe in Yahweh as the god of gods, some believe in the source and demiurge, some believe in Christ, Satan and on and on.

There are not many truly classical mages around in my humble opinion, simply because the old grimoires are written in the vernacular and symbolism of the time they were made. They do not speak to modern people in symbols that matter anymore. So even those who use the old books exclusively, and to the letter. They do not truly use them as they would once have been used. It is even possible that this is a reason why so many people have little luck, if any luck when using them.

Indeed, I often muse about how my own book, scattered and only found in fragments, might someday be the source of some far future school of magick. All the others lost to antiquity, burned in fires, lost on hard drives that broke and were discarded… I often snicker at the idea of those futuristic people trying to figure out what I was talking about when I reference pop culture or having no idea what the word nondualism means because that too is lost to time.

I laugh a good belly laugh when I imagine them all arguing about how important it is to use real old-fashioned wax candles, never having seen them, and trying to figure out what they are, all because they think the candles somehow have REAL power in them, when to me they are symbolic receptacles and transmutation mediums for the energy of intention and astral energy. They could very well be a burning stick, or a ticking wind up clock, or an hourglass, or a digital timer counting down.

Of course, for me a candle works, best. But not because it is a candle, they just have more meaning to me personally.

Know you then - there was a REASON the ancients used the materials they did, said the words they said, invoked the spirits they did. It was because these objects had cultural and spiritual meaning to them. Not because these objects or materials or words had real power in and of themselves.

There is a similar reason why the Goetic Demons are described and looked the way they did to the mind of the people who wrote those books. Look at the art of the period… Look how animalistic and strange ALL demons and devils looked to those people. Notice the way they look like ancient gods from the olden times but warped and distorted, bat wings instead of birds, horns instead of halos. Reptiles instead of men and women. Look at how angels and holy things looked, look, look at how avian they are, how much they fit the standard of human beauty, how their body is glowing with light and energy.

It is all symbolism, and over time the very reason for those symbols are lost. Which is why today some of these images, sculptures and story's look, sound and feel outright strange and some even childish.

Were the beings really like that? No… not at all. The beings they saw in their minds eye were formed out of the symbols they understood and believed in, and the art and expressions they used to communicate them to others was limited by these beliefs and the skill of the artist or author to communicate them.

This is why the modern demon sorcerer may see a whole range of clearly subjective experiences with these entities. Why they can be so different yet so like how other contemporary people experience them.

Why you can google them, and often see modern depictions of them and often feel they look more "right" than the ones in the old grimoires.

Thus, many Modernist magickians will follow a modern adaptation of those classics. Valuing those works created more recently so as to contain updated symbolism and context. There are many of them, such as those created in the late 1900s, or early to mid-20th century. Thelema, The golden Dawn, Wiccan, paganism, Heathenism, Demonolatry, and so on.

And there even new ones coming out all the time.

Postmodern Magickians will use some form of Chaos Magick, which can range from a purely post-modernist expression using little more in the way of complexity than sigils - energizing them through various means to invoke manifestations, or some blend of classical, modern and postmodern expressions because they have come to believe and see that a "sigil" can be made up of more than just lines on a page, but in action like dance, ritual and energy visualization.

I most closely fall into the latter category, I do not personally believe in the deification of any entity like god, or devils. I do not appeal to god, Jehovah.

I am not a Theist. I do not worship anything. No entity is higher, or lower, than me. We are all one.

Nor do I believe candles have inherent power beyond what I and the collective mind believe they have, or that herbs have mystical properties beyond those given them by the collective wisdom of those who use them.

However, it is my firm experience that without such props, magick is like a bicycle with only 1 wheel. Sure, you can pop a wheelie and get around (astral magick does work!). But the ride is so much smoother and easier going if you just put

the front wheel on and pull out a few props to help you stay on the road.

Thus - If you were to find a person with zero mystical knowledge at all who was being troubled by spirits. Then hand a stick of sage to them without giving them any idea of what sage is used for, or even that you are giving it to them to use against those spirits. Just giving them simple instructions to burn it and walk around the house with it and blowing it in corners.

Or better yet, use a drone or robot to do this without any connection to a human…

It is my firm belief that the sage would have no effect, the smudging would fail to do anything. It would just stink up the place with the smell of sage (which I find pleasant of course), and anyone with allergies might have to leave the room till it clears.

No…

Just like how if you take a bucket of paint, and hand it to someone with no idea of what art is, or a drone or robot, and had it randomly spatter paint around, there would be no "Art" produced there either. Oh sure, the random patterns might look like something relevant to someone else… This might even make it subjective art.

But as there was no act of communication involved, it is not art. As there was no element of personal or even collective expression… there is no art.

Without the mage to imbue the materials and rituals with their artistic vision, their attempt to express their intent upon the one true will there can be no alignment, no communication, no manifestation.

The presence of the mage means nothing then too… for I have seen many of these mages who say the words, and light the candles, but do so mechanically and without any emotion or energy. They are spiritually dead. They are wooden. And their magick suffers greatly for it.

Then I see the performance artist, the one who injects REAL emotion, energy and intent, the one who pours their heart and soul into not just making sure the words are said but said with feeling and emotion. These Sorcerers are the real deal, because you would have to be spiritually DEAD not to feel something when they do these magick performances.

It is in this way that Magick is a holistic art form. It is like theater, dance, visual art, culinary art, music and literary art all crushed into one ball of expression.

If you suck at art, don't worry. Art isn't about how pretty it is… If your magickal art is ugly, but it is from your heart and you pour everything you have into each and every performance. I promise you results will come.

Even if your magick art is no better than a child's crooked stick figures, you can move mountains so long as you pour every ounce of your being into the performance of that magick act.

MAGICK AND SCIENCE

For most people, magick and science mixes like oil and water. And for most rational people, magick takes an absolute THRASHING when it comes to which one is proven real and true, and which is just make believe.

The first thing you need to do then, if you are new to this, is accept and be ok with the fact that magick might be fake. You need to find the razor thin overlap between the two ideas and make this your base of reason. You need to let go of your DESIRE and ATTACHMENT to the idea that magick works at all. But carry on with it as if it does.

The skeptic, the materialist, they look at magick and only focus on the result, and that result cannot be something that can be explained by rational means. Otherwise, it's… Not magick.

Meanwhile you have people like me, people who are actually very knowledgeable about scientific truth, who do not deny science, nor do we attempt to use pseudoscience to explain or validate our results (skeptics call this woo). Though I may engage in speculation from time to time of a pseudoscientific nature, I make no scientific claims of truth.

Yet here I am, talking to demons, casting spells, and seeing results. If confronted by a skeptic or a scientist, I would calmly (I hope) explain to them that what I am doing is a kind of holistic performance art. I do not "expect" a result in the same sense I would "expect" my microwave to cook my dinner.

I would explain that I cannot prove that my rituals do anything at all, and that in fact, it is my theory that when I do rituals it is just a kind of spooky coincidence that I seem to get results.

I would explain that I am very familiar with the idea of confirmation bias, and how we can fool ourselves into believing anything under the right situation.

I would also explain that my interpretation of magick is that it rarely, if ever, violates the laws of nature. If it has, (and I have seen it happen) I am fully aware I have never experienced it in a way that I could prove, and upon close inspection by someone more qualified in science, I'm sure they could find an excuse for why it wasn't magick, but just some swamp gas, or mass hallucination etc.

I would tell them that Magick follows the path of Least "irrational" resistance. And this is the path where it needs to violate the least number of objective or subjective laws possible, to do what it does outside the realm of objectivity.

I would never expect my magick to make a hurricane magically materialize over my enemy's house in Florida. No, that hurricane will develop off the coast of Africa, following seemingly mundane and expected patterns. It will roll up the coast and destroy the town of my enemy.

Never mind that somewhere on the plains of Africa my magick influenced a butterfly to beat its wings a certain way that started the tiny current of air that led to the disturbance that caused the storm.

In this way, if it has ANY real influence on reality at all, I would never be able to prove it. Nor do I feel the need to. A scientist could rationally explain every single thing to be a result of entirely natural forces, they could debunk every single synchronistic event.

And I would still light incense, draw sigils, and speak to

demons.

Because, as I said in the last essay, for me, Magick is a holistic performance art, and even though I seem to get 95% or better success on my magickal efforts… Even though I really do want my magick to do something for me.

I do not expect it to do anything. I expect nothing.

I do magick.

Things happen.

The fact that they line up? Sometimes perfectly? Call it spooky coincidence if you like… I make no claims about cause or effect.

I simply note down in my journal that I performed a ritual for X, and got the result Y, and see what, if any correlations there are. Smile and chuckle at the way my will manifested through totally mundane pathways, marvel at the mysteries of life, and move on to the next thing I want to work on.

The fact that I have a high success rate has more to do with selective working than with the power of my magick. I am careful to only use magick when it's success or failure won't destabilize the careful balance of belief and experience that I have established.

I won't cast a spell to do something impossible, because the failure might make me skeptical. I won't cast a spell for every other easy thing because that can make you crazy and start relying on magick for everything… It would become a superstition. I would be afraid to get into a car without asking a demon to watch over me, and never have time to drive.

And I would remind them, that what I CAN prove, is that when those things happen in alignment with my magick, the pleasure, excitement and joy I feel… That is the true goal. Not the manifestation of the ritual itself.

Even the blackest spell I ever cast, when it came to pass, I wasn't just happy because it worked. I was happy to experience the mysterious spooky coincidence itself.

Therefore, it is important to be non-attached to the outcome of my magick, and when I feel like I AM attached to it… that is when I know the odds of my magick aligning with the result I want is close to ZERO.

I have often noticed, as have others, that sometimes we can't help but be attached to the problem and the result. And we dwell on it, and it is at the moment of liberation between

us and our concern, the moment we forget about it, that is when the spooky coincidence so often takes place.

What's more, we KNOW IT.

This is a key in manifestation, you will just KNOW when the events taking place are the alignment with your magick. You won't question it, the hair on the back of your neck will stand up, and you will know.

Magick is not in opposition to science… not in the slightest. They work together like paper and pen. Most scientists would be offended if you told them that the airplane is a result of magick. If you explained to them that the dreams of flight were the spells cast by the ancients over and over, and because the objective mind of the world says it is impossible to just lift off the ground for no reason… This spell was countered by a more powerful spell, the spell that mankind cast upon the world saying it was simply not possible.

But because Magick does our truest intent, and follows our truest will, magick found a way for us to fly…

All of reality shifted to align mankind with the secrets and sciences needed… Mankind, and science took generation after generation to become aligned with the desire for human flight. It took thousands upon thousands of years, but the intent of mankind to fly was finally realized.

Every single thing that happened that led to human flight was not coincidence. It was magick.

And mankind now knows how to reach space, and one day, if we survive as a species, we will certainly go to the stars.

What form that blessed manifestation will take, I can only imagine and dream. But I know, without doubt or hesitation that it is our destiny as a species unless we find a way to destroy ourselves.

Oh… how I long for such a manifestation, to fly through space in my personal starship…

And if I am alive in such a time, through reincarnation or other means. Despite being surrounded by science that is so advance as to be indistinguishable to magick…. I will still go to my dark places, light my candles, meditate on demonic sigils and see as deeply into the void as I can.

I know, some of you, especially the skeptics out there think I am copping out, you think – Oh, so this guy is really just playing head games with himself. He is creating a circular argument for why magick could be true.

I would agree with you, but I don't care if magick is true or not. If I am making a circular argument, that is just a coincidence.

It is a matter of perspective. And I am not alone, not by a long shot. Many highly intelligent men and women believe in some form of magick, be it the way I describe it, or some other.

They know magick is not the thing pop culture and Hollywood says it is. Like most things, the truth is stranger than the fiction. And when we behold it, it is vastly more satisfying.

Even to the point where I cannot enjoy fantasy video games sometimes because the rendition of magick is too flashy and silly. Fireballs, and summoning badgers out of thin air to fight by your side.

In the astral realm? Sure. Do it all the time.

But in the real world?

Well, I hear all kinds of claims by "other" sorcerers… but they never seem to produce those fantastic claims. There is always some reason of course. The stars aren't aligned, they don't want to prove it, or I'm just not worth it as a target.

Lots of cop outs, and circular reasons.

My point with all this flowery rhetoric is to stress, magick is not a genie in a bottle that grants impossible things. It is not a machine into which you put a quarter and out comes a toy.

Magick is a strange subjective mind game, and when you do it right, you will experience the uncanny synchronicity of experiences that align with the rituals you perform.

You will be unable to prove them. But they will happen.

It is also important for you, as you explore this art form, that you learn to keep notes, that you learn to experiment effectively. That you never allow your expectations to sour the possibilities.

Never command magick to do something so specific that it cannot materialize without breaking the laws of nature.

Never assume it CANNOT break the laws of nature either.

It just doesn't "like" to.

Why?

Two key reasons

First – Mankind is exceptionally fearful of what it cannot control or understand. Our primitive brains are still wired for survival in a place where death can come from anywhere at any time. When left alone to our own imaginations, we can even scare ourselves.

Magick, especially dark magick, if proven, would terrify the world, especially those people who are in control. Not even because they would fear magick like the masses would, but what could be done by people who use it to threaten their power.

They allow us to know magick only so long as we as a collective community remain on the fringes and do not actively seek to wage war against them and their plans for the rest of humanity.

Our civilization has always been "Ban happy" in one form or another. Most people don't even realize that, as liberated as we often think we are - because we don't burn people at stakes anymore – we are still in the dark ages of intolerance and mental slavery. Our culture is still constantly shitting itself over anything that is scary or dangerous, for example - firearms, self-medication, dark humor.

Can you imagine the legislation that would ensue if magick could be PROVEN to be capable of killing people? That so called "Demons" are real and can be interacted with to produce reliable results?

We do not live in the stone age, the methods used to exterminate witches wouldn't be mere torches and pitchforks, witch smellers and inquisitions. It would be a nightmarish hell on earth, as our modern technology and culture would industrialize the practice of eradicating its practice without license.

Magick though perhaps not itself sentient in the living sense, is at the call of sentient beings and behaves with a mind of its own, and since most of us know intuitively what would likely happen, magick refrains from risking the obvious repercussions.

The second reason is because, as I pointed out in the limitations section… You don't want to wake up, not all the way anyway. And if you suddenly gained the power the likes of which we see in movies, even the lower level ones like force telekinesis or something. It would create a ripple of impossible events that would shake the sleeper awake, and the dream would end.

Magick prefers to only do the miraculous in strange mysterious ways, preferably only to small numbers of people, or in ways that can't upset the natural balance of objectivity.

It is my firm belief that once upon a time, deep in history when mankind was more open objectively to magick, that magick was far, FAR less timid in performing miracles. As time, science and superstition evolved… As religions sprang up condemning the old magick and old gods… making such things evil and wrong and scary… As science stepped in and put everything in boxes… Magick complied, because magick doesn't want us to wake up, not all the way.

Individuals waking up are fine… the Buddha, Bodhisattvas, the ascended masters… assuming you believe in any of them. And they are permitted to influence and guide mankind in the direction of ascension and enlightenment. This is because there is nothing they can really do to make it happen. Instead they manage to keep the heard of kittens moving in the right general direction through a virtual minefield. All the while they wander all around exploring all the wrong things, the overly curious cats being killed when they play with an explosive landmine or fall down a pit of delusion, while the more cautious and intelligent move on toward the truth, following the siren song of the guru.

It is up to you to decide what is true. To recognize that ascension and enlightenment is a thing you already have! The thing is, you just don't believe it to be true just yet, you want to have more fun first, you want to work for it, and so you shall.

And magick will make sure that struggle is very real, and very objective and very much in line with the laws of nature as they currently stand.

Till they change. And they DO change. Retroactively of course. Nature abhors a vacuum, everywhere mankind looks we see a new law, a new fact, or rule. Filling in the tiniest cracks. Limited only by how large or small we can focus our senses.

The further in space we look, the more stars and galaxies we see, the smaller we probe with our math and machines the tinier the components of reality become.

It is only a matter of time before we discover some new fact that will rewrite all of reality that allows for some new miracle. The same way we discovered flight. Or the splitting of the atom.

We will discover alien life, or some substance that will give us superhuman abilities, or warp drive. Maybe it will be virtual, maybe it will be "real" (though I would argue there is no real difference).

But if you close down your minds chattering and open it all the way and see where we are and imagine where we are going… you can just feel the general direction of where things are going.

You *can* feel it can't you? In time it will shift, but that current you feel, if you feel it at all, is the maelstrom roaring at you of things to come.

Do not fight it, do not deny it, just so you can enjoy your petty desire for science to be wrong and magick right. Embrace it, see that the two are one, and use it to empower you, ask not how to do magick despite sciences disapproval, ask how to use the fruits of science to make your magick better.

DAEMONIC INSPIRATION

This is the final essay of this part of the book and it is also one of the shortest. The next part of this book will be instructional essays talking about and breaking down the specific methods I use in my magick, why I do them the way I do, and enough information to get you started, but one of those methods needs to be discussed as a fundamental aspect of magick, not just as another method.

I am an intuitive demon sorcerer, everything I do comes from "within" me, inspired by intuition and by the spirits I work with. It is my belief that the most effective way to do and learn magick, is to connect your experience with that of daemonic/demonic inspirational source. To contact spiritual entities such as the gods, the demons, the angels, and djinn, and other spirits that can both teach us, validate our ideas, and help us understand the inner working of magick in a way that is personal and tuned for your personal ability.

To the ancient Greeks, the Daemons were what inspired and taught men new things. To the ancient Hebrews, the demons and angels taught mankind technology, and other skills.

Indeed, in virtually every single culture we find interaction between humans, and some disembodied spirit. Spirit which was DISTINCT from individual imagination and intuition and was a direct influence or inspiration on their ideas at all levels of expression.

Some people, both mages and skeptics alike, have made the compelling case that these beings are nothing more than psychological constructs, made by individuals to help them be creative by taking the burden of success off their own personal shoulders. To essentially lay the blame of success and failure on a spiritual origin to give them confidence in it.

If someone says – "I believe X" the burden of responsibility is often on them, and them alone. If they say, "I believe X because a God or Demon told me." This shifts the burden of proof for the believer from the individual sharing the idea, to the spirit… and allows for the messenger to be wrong without being responsible for the information itself.

This allows the individual to use the demon or spirit as a scapegoat. Allowing them to hide behind these spirits and take risks they might not otherwise be willing to take.

From my own experience this can be partially accurate and fitting. Because in my experience, demons and other entities do not limit their interactions with us, to just the rituals we perform. When we establish a direct bond with them, or any other spirit, they generally come and go from our awareness and experience as they see fit, and if you are trusting and open and have mutual bonds with them, they

may directly influence or otherwise guide you without you ever knowing it.

In fact, a good deal of my writing is done as a combination of meditative gnosis, leading to a free flow of spontaneous thought that I channel into my hands. Instead of thinking with my brain and materializing thoughts in my mind, I materialize the thoughts into my hands as they type. This means my mind is utterly empty and free of conscious thought when I write, and if they are invited, this is the fertile playground of spirits.

Like the channeler of old, scribbling on paper and producing scratches that had sinister or eerie meaning. I channel the spirits around me, through my own lens and create things that tell their story, as well as mine.

And so, in the process of writing, spirits will come and go and give me inspirations and ideas. My hands will fly over the keys at 140+ words per minute, and when the word processor goes over it, there are no strong spelling errors, or grammatical errors worth bringing to my attention. I'm in "The Zone."

One could say it is written via "divine" inspiration as a Christian might call it. However, it is entirely fallible, it is Afterall, my hands, and my mind that is reading the impulses of the spirits.

What is interesting is this information is not often overtly contradictory, it only ever evolves and improves. I can often see the aspects of what was said that came more from my mind, versus the influence of another mind.

This means I have a high level of confidence in what I am saying and writing to be true, honest, and effective.

Now, obviously, you can see where what I said matches perfectly with what a skeptic, or those who believe demons are personal creations of our delusional mind might say.

I do not, nor can I hope, to dispute, or make the claim that they are wrong. It is entirely possible that everything I am doing is a form of mind game, and when I am experiencing gnosis and communion with a demonic entity all that I am really doing is relaxing and opening myself to my own ideas in a way that lets them flow unimpeded by second guesses, lack of confidence, and similar faults.

What is remarkable is, many times have I compared my

personal ideas and gnosis with people whom I have never worked with, and they are startled at how similar it is to what they have found.

This verification of gnosis is an important step for some people, to see that what a demon told them matches what others were told. It's never a perfect 100% match. Or should I say, not in my experience. However, the number of corresponding bits of information are astounding and relevant.

Some other occultists have done experiments where they asked different people to submit to them their personal sigils for specific demonic entities, and then compared them and found them all to be similar enough to be recognizable. The differences either being minor, or the similarities being too striking.

To me, having similar experience, this is strong (admittedly anecdotal) evidence that these beings DO exist outside our awareness of them. However, it also reinforces the idea that our experience of them is personal and subjective as is the rest of reality.

People often make the mistake of thinking the entities create the images and gnosis for us. Instead it would be better to describe it not as creating knowledge but triggering memories we can learn from. Taking the patterns of our experience and finding correspondences to what they want to tell us and using them to influence our dreaming mind to dream the details around the key bits of information.

Therefore, so much of what we see and experience with these entities is symbolic. Seeing demons holding snakes, swords, riding bears, or dragons. While entirely plausible in the astral realm, is also little more than window dressing meant to inspire in us certain cultural understandings.

It is why the ancient imagery of a demon can be so different than the modern. Their cultural symbolism was very different to ours. Therefore, it is so important for so many occultists to also be students of history to some degree.

It is also my experience that humans, being more focused on the material plane, find that our objective experience is also more inclined to be shared on the material plane.

And because we (in my experience) are not focused on the astral to anywhere near the same level as the material, our astral experiences are LESS objective in nature. But they are still objective enough that we can all agree on certain details.

Many people have seen shadow people, and the "Hat man." Many people describe certain cryptids the same way, despite never having really been exposed to the same lore. Many people claim to have the same experiences with the same demonic entities, with the differences being far outweighed by the similarities.

It is my opinion that in magick, the demonic forces are among the most objective of all astral experiences. And for this and other reasons, they are also the most important for us to focus our energy on as a source of magick and knowledge of the mystical forces of reality.

If you picked up this book looking for a work of secular magick with no theism in it, that is fine, I do not actually consider myself a theist in the textbook sense. This is a book of Agnostic magick! I do not believe in a "God." Rather a much simpler perspective on divinity, that expresses itself in complex ways as a byproduct of our own limitations.

Therefore, a major element of pathworking my system will revolve around working with (not worshipping or praying to) disembodied spirits, and most specifically and importantly, DEMONIC spirits, dark spirits, spirits that are considered evil by most civilized people.

However instead of evil, they are, for the most part, found to be noble, and often quite helpful, supportive and benign. Or at the very least uninterested in being malevolent toward those who approach them with respect.

In every single interaction I have had with the demonic beings I call into my home on a regular basis, they have come to me as if I was royalty, or of equal importance. Some have demanded a high level of respect, but this is not the same as demanding subordination. As Azazel recently said to me, when he informed me that he would require me to devote myself to him exclusively for 30 days…

If I am going to devote my energy and teaching to you, I require you devote yourself to me in similar and equal measure.

Indeed! These beings are nothing if not **shrewd** deal makers!

In this manner, they have come seeking to teach me, guide me, uplift me and help me achieve my goals, and in return have me share what they teach, share my gnosis, and help others come to them for similar guidance.

I am not saying these beings are totally benevolent and loving of all humanity. Or that they are somehow not terrifying.

These beings are from the dark side and often take on aspects in our experience that speak to the macabre, the uncomfortable, the scary, and the dangerous.

They appear as monsters, sinister villains, voluptuous sirens, as horned devils and unspeakable Lovecraftian horrors. Even those such as Lucifer, who appears as a shining angel with flaming devil wings and blinding light for me, still has the eyes of a serpent, and the air of a fallen angel, the beauty of a gothic vampire reclining on a throne of personal agony.

They are always tinged with our own personal experience of darkness… and for this reason to the uninitiated, to the weak of mind and character, these beings are utterly unspeakably evil and bad.

But like any creepy crawly insect or spider, they are largely misunderstood.

Dangerous, to be sure, even cruel and malevolent to those who offend them in some way.

But what about how evil they are? I hear some asking…

There is no such thing as evil, or good. This is not simply a cop out, it is a fact.

They themselves are not "Evil." They are what they are, and some of what they are is a result of large parts of humanity "Demonizing" them… As powerful as they are, what mankind believes about them can indeed affect them, and alter them.

Most of the Goetic spirits and many others that have been catalogued, are "safe" for the responsible, and respectful practitioner, some more so than others, but safe enough.

For those who mistreat them, have bad expectations, or seek to abuse and control them… for those who already fear and hate them… these beings are glad to invoke their darkest aspects to scare, or even harm those who offend them.

When approached respectfully however, when seen as the dark side of the same "divine light" from which we all emanate. When approached as a potential ally and friend. When we seek to work with them, not to control or threaten them. Then things get truly interesting, and enlightening.

They prove themselves to be far more interesting, and inspirational for some of us than any god, or Judeo-Christian angel (true angels are not loyal to Yahweh or any other god specifically, Angels serve the most high, and this is you!). Unlike beings of light, they do not appeal to the cowardly and pretentious part of us that pretends to be good, humble or holy.

But they do tend to appeal to the selfish and aggressive sides of us.

I find those who can balance this to be of exceptional character.

For humility done intentionally is the most offensive form of vanity… For goodness done intentionally is the most heinous form of evil. For holiness to act holy on purpose, is the lowest form of sacrilege.

For these are not merely misdeeds, they are lies, and they are not merely lies we tell others, but lies we tell ourselves. When we lie to ourselves, we distance ourselves from our true will much more than when we lie to or abuse others.

It must be stressed, that those entities who come to us from the darkness can appeal greatly to those of us who are broken, fallen, damned, and ashamed. They can give us a sense of freedom. More importantly, they are attracted to us… eager to give us the dark experiences we crave.

For when we truly believe we are damned, when we truly believe we are destined for hell, we are no longer imprisoned by the chains of moralistic thinking.

We no longer crave to do the right thing in the vain hopes of finding our way to heaven. For all hope has been abandoned, by we who entered here.

Instead we have the chance to face ourselves, we can face our true motivations and come face to face with the demon inside of us, and realize we are looking into a mirror.

Obviously, this isn't true for all of us. For every one of us who finds some mature measure of enlightenment and power through these beings, dozens, if not hundreds, burn themselves in the fires of their own self-deception and self-destruction… Living and dying in vain.

Often binging on drugs, sex, and other libertine experiences, all things the demons encourage us to do because when invited, they can enter us when we do them and enjoy the vivid experiences through us. For not all these beings seek to guide and uplift us, many such spirits roam this earth that are not recorded in the grimoires and catalogues of sorcerers.

However, for those of us who follow this path with any kind of maturity, dedication and honesty, our reward is not heaven, nor are we punished with hell. We become liberated and transcend both lies.

We find ourselves to never be alone in the dark again. And the so-called light is just another kind of darkness… It no longer burns us or reminds us we are evil. Because the true light doesn't judge, it loves unconditionally.

This is the same lesson taught in virtually all religion… that we remove ourselves from the divine through sin.

And the only sin I am aware of, that appears to be universal and leads to anything resembling a "hell" is the sin of not recognizing your divinity and your birthright to be a free and liberated being. It is lying to yourself and being in denial of who you are. And this "sin" is not really a sin at all, just a choice our ego makes to play the game without the distraction of divinity to muck it up by making it too easy.

Instead we become inspired to be (not become, but BE) a being who is noble, and ethical, but not moralistic or dogmatic.

I myself went from a very balanced and peaceful westernized Zen oriented person, who had his moment of liberation and revelation and subsequent peace, to realizing that Zen embraces the light, AND the dark… and its history teaches that there are many paths to enlightenment, Zen ways and not Zen ways for all ways are Zen, and eventually end the same.

For some, the light is their salvation and hope… for us, the darkness is the most intriguing path of all…

In the orient enlightenment revolves around endless hours of meditation and chanting mantras and self-discovery. The fool's errand of finding and ridding yourself of your ego, only to find that this is impossible and that the true nature of the exercise is to obtain wisdom and enlightenment through

failure. For some, this is the wall, and they abandon their practice, or go from total devotion to just making it a regimen in their life. While others transcend the failure, they realize suddenly, that the moment we truly give up and stop trying and just accept we can't do it… only then can enlightenment finally happen.

At this moment, we stop looking outside of ourselves, and stop looking to the future. We stop striving to be free… we awaken to the fact we have always been free; the gateless gate has always been open. And a gate with no gate… isn't a gate at all, and there isn't really an "other side" that we must get to. For once we do it, we see it is the same as it ever was, nothing but our perspective has changed.

Similarly, In the west we spend our whole lives striving for the ideal of the Abrahamic, classical, western ideals of morality and justice, and invariably we fail. And in that failure, we have the blessed opportunity to find liberation and true enlightenment.

Those of us who embrace the darkness, those of us who accept we are "damned" for our dedication to darkness — finding liberation can be trivial.

It isn't very different than the Zen monk who wakes up and realizes that the futility of their practice is the point, and in abandoning it, perfects it.

And this is the path of Lucifer, of Satan, and the glory and divine blessing of utter hopelessness and damnation. To lose it all, all your inhibitions, all your attachments. All your morality.

Not to be evil for evils sake, for this is just an inversion of the norm. *No! Bad monkey! No!!!* for even in that distorted inverted ideology, there is still hope…

Instead, you must find your own nobility, to decide for yourself what is meant by right and wrong, and to abide by your OWN rules of ethics and find that when we base our ethics on solid foundations of truth, they are almost universal to others, but unique to our experience just the same.

METHODOLOGY

BOOK 2: INTRODUCTION

The Last "Book" was a brief peek at the fundamental mystical nature of reality as revealed to me through many years of self-reflection, study, and practice.

This book is about the methodology that I use to make use of that fundamental mystical perspective. Some of these methods are universal, and if you are advanced you may know some of them already. Some of them are variations of common methods, and some will likely be entirely new to you.

In this book I want to awaken within you an intuitive understanding of how you can create your own methods and not rely on mine save for by choice. Essentially, I want to liberate you from feeling like there is a wrong way, and a right way. Not because there isn't a wrong way, or a right way. Rather because most people think they don't know enough to do their own magick.

I am hoping that by showing you the principles behind how I do things and why, it will resonate with things you already know, either by study or intuition about how magick works.

Some of the subjects in this book could easily become full length grimoires, and I may in fact create such a work in the future, but for now, my goal is to get you off to a good start, or to see the deeper connections I have found that underly all these different practices in magick. You are welcome to use these methods, or any others you find or create for yourself.

If you are a beginner to magick, I highly suggest you take the time to study this section and work through it in order. The most important section is about meditation and altered states. Nothing else in this section will be as important or valuable to you as these. For it is through altered states of consciousness that true holistic magick can take place.

Master them, and the rest can come easily by comparison.

Let me give you the keys to the kingdom right off the bat.

I consider myself a Sorcerer, and in my dictionary, Sorcerers and Sorceresses, are individuals who manipulate the fabric of reality intuitively and internally through sheer force of will. They do not require a large library of books to teach them all the ways magick works for others, instead they focus on finding and developing their own magick.

This magick is chaotic and personal in nature and can even run contrary to the formulaic methods used by others. The sorcerer "feels" their way through magick, instead of reading all about it. To a sorcerer, the idea of picking up a book of magick and performing a ritual verbatim without feeling is absurd.

A sorcerer trusts their feelings and begins to live a mystical life as a result. They do not have a need to cast spells every day for trivial matters. Their life simply unfolds in a magickal mystical way, and the use of ritual magick is merely a supplement for their ongoing ascension to godhood.

This means, virtually ANY established or rational methodology can have value, meaning my own expression of sorcery falls under the rather broad umbrella of Chaos magick. However, what makes my own methods and mentality different is that I arrived at similar conclusions on my own without ever hearing about Chaos Magick until long after I had been doing it for decades. Yes, I truly lived in a bubble, but remember I began my magickal journey in the days prior to the widespread use of the internet, and never really trusted the internet as a source for magick like it is now.

Chaos magick is more of a fundamental philosophy than a method, because chaos magick does not actually condone any specific methods but encourages the practitioner to abandon virtually all dogma and limiting ideology. To embrace the potential for literally any style of magick to work, real or imagined, so long as the practitioner can justify it somehow. This does not mean literally anything will work, the practitioner must still strive to do magick with a certain logic and fundamentally systematic approach. But that approach need not be limited to any specific method, discipline or tradition.

In my form of sorcery, I add the stipulation that the sorcerer should use intuition and "feel" their way through their magick, rather than seek for a formula that does what you want, you devise your own formula based on your own research and understanding. You can find a spell or ritual and follow it, alter it, or make it up completely, so long as the symbolism you use makes sense to you on a magickal level.

However, because we ALL must start somewhere, and have a guide… I will give my own time-tested methodology for you to start with. Giving you just enough to formulate your own system, and then let you go.

In a nutshell, the methodology I use to perform and learn magick, revolves around the following core ideas -

Altered states of consciousness – The 3 states of mind. Gnosis, Meditation, hypnosis, binaural beats, exercise, chemicals (not for me so much but for others it can be valuable in moderation), sexual climax, emotional climax etc.

Using, developing and trusting my intuition – This can be difficult to do on purpose, but learning to use Divination methods like scrying, tarot, and opening your third eye are the best methods for this.

Magick as a way of life – My magick suffers when I am not 100% immersed in the character of the demon sorcerer D.H. Thorne. When I feel any doubt, depression, lack of motivation, my magick becomes little more than a waste of time. So, I spend time finding ways to inspire myself to "feel" like a powerful master of the darkness. This means building up my ritual environment to inspire me, wearing the right clothes, talking to the right people and more. It is literally a way of life, and not simply a hobby.

Magick must be something you feel intensely – Magick has very little to do with the words you say, the tools you use, or the circles you draw, and everything to do with how it "feels" when you do it. You must have a visceral sensation of energy moving into and through you, spirits must be felt and heard, the astral must be glimpsed or seen. If you just stand before your altar and recite occult poetry, you may still have success, but you're working will be spiritually dead. Your spell will be Stillborn…

Buffet style research – Nondogmatic research, never drink the poison in the punch bowl, always read between the lines,

and never be a joiner. Always look for the fundamental key that makes something useful and steal that and ignore the rest unless it serves you! Want to know about angels? Read a book on Enochian magick, but do not become an Enochian magickian. Want to work with Demons? Call them, but do not become a Satanist. If along the way after years of study and self-exploration you find yourself becoming a believer in some dogma, or decide to join some tradition or religion, do so with my blessing, but never START that way… Start as a blank slate, and try to stay that way as long as possible.

Communion with entities that go by titles such as demons, djinn, gods, and shadows. – This is why I often call myself a Spirit Caller, or Demon Sorcerer, because working with Demons is my specialty. Demons are the source of my most intense gnosis, and while I would have plenty of skill without them, they consistently give me the most intense experiences. The only problem is, they are often associated with religions, and traditions that span tens of thousands of years with confusing variations and associations. Entities such as Lucifer can be traced back to antiquity as Venus, phosphorus, Horus and many others. So, it becomes important to research these, without letting your mind become too polluted by the dogma of the religion and approach these entities with a pure mind.

The Rest of this second book is designed to walk you through some of these concepts in detail, as well as outline some basic methods and principles you will need to make use of the 3rd book titled "Pathworking."

If you skip ahead to the last book without trying to absorb what is in this book first, or have your own methods, I imagine you will have limited success, if any. It is my hope that if you master what is in the first and second book, the third book will become more of a reference and set of examples rather than something you will rely upon.

I am telling you right now, that I only include the 3rd book in the spirit of setting some examples and presenting the novice with a suitable pathworking to get them started. Because the examples I give, despite all being original spells I created and have used with success, are common in magick in some variation, some are even rudimentary in nature, and borrow from dozens of traditions and styles… But enough about book 3, let's get down to business!

Fundamental Actions of Ritual Magick

All intentional magickal operations require the sorcerer to use a holistic combination of mind, body and soul elements to create manifestation. Sometimes, due to various external reasons (Privacy, lack of funds) we cannot effectively manipulate all three elements of a working and may even be forced to use only one. This will not necessarily impede your manifestation, but it is my experience that all three being used in conjunction are the most effective way to achieve your magick goals.

The following concepts are the key personal actions we will use in all our magick to perform rituals and evoke manifestations. They are listed in no particular order, and may be used alone, or combined in sequence, or even some or all as part of one elaborate action (such as gesturing, speaking and visualizing). Some are more focused on the mind, body or spirit, while others may combine 2 or more. Many are holistic actions or can easily be made holistic by combining other actions. I feel like I could write a lengthy essay on each of these actions and how they truly work, but it would be tedious to read, and it is better learned by experience. So, I will keep it brief.

The first 3 entries are the KEY fundamental actions of magick. Before we do anything else in magick, we must run through the trinity of action – Intention, Decision, Will/action.

Intention – Everything begins with intention. This should not be confused with desire, though it can express in a similar way. Desire is a passive thing, and our desires rarely align with our intention. You may think Desire comes first, but in fact all desire is born of our truest intent to experience bliss, we do not "desire" to experience bliss, then intend to be blissful. We intend to be blissful, and our will spawns the illusion of desire, creating a sequence of needs and wants that must be fulfilled by our will. Therefore, the mere act of wanting to do a thing is not Intention.

Instead, Intention is the spontaneous precursor to action. The moment before you decide to act, you intend to act. Our truest intent is a powerful and often hidden thing, if you can ever align your truest will with your truest intention, miracles will happen. Intention is the spontaneous urge to do or obtain something. For example, you Intend to be comfortable. So, your will makes it happen for you by acting in ways to bring you comfort.

Before you can raise the glass of water to your lips, you must intend to do it on some level.

You can go mad if you try to find the true source of your intentions, because the experience of our intentions is felt to be entirely spontaneous. Born perhaps of desire, but still often appearing out of nothing. However, to the unenlightened, it can also always be traced to some other intention, and many of us are not in tune with our intentions at all, so we feel compelled by circumstance or primal desire for safety and comfort. We place the self below the circumstances of our life, instead of seeing ourselves as the doer, and the done.

Your truest intention then is often something very exquisitely simple, and selfish in nature, and it is up to you to find out what it is… For the sake of working magick, all you need to become aware of, is the clear intent that motivates you to act magickally. Make sure you are being honest about what you are trying to do and why. Never assume that you are telling yourself the truth. Do you truly intend to have a million dollars? Or is your truest intention to simply be happy and stress free and you think having that money will cause that happiness and lack of stress? Magick tends to follow our truest intention, so do not be surprised if you do not get your money but find peace in some other way instead.

Another example is If you want to curse someone with death, what you really might intend is for them to simply go away. Death is just one option. Thus, the curse will likely not manifest in death, if at all, but may even manifest as the target having good fortune in such a way as to remove them from your experience somehow (such as winning the lotto and moving away).

This can of course make everything seem very unfair… unless you fully understand your true intention.

Therefore, finding your true intention for the purposes of performing magick, revolves around tracing your intentions to the fundamental true intention behind it. At the fundamental core of our being is the selfish intention to experience "bliss." However, bliss is not created by endless pleasure, sooner or later you need to experience displeasure or even pleasure can become pain. Bliss can only be experienced fully if there is suffering to compare it to. This means, your truest intention is not for endless pleasure, but also pain, loss, and ruin.

It has been said – *We suffer for many reasons, but most of all because we believe we ought not to suffer.*

The study of true intention is far beyond the scope of this simple explanation and should instead be the subject of your own meditations.

Will – Will is the compulsion of action we take intentionally. Our truest will is the action, be it mundane or magickal, that aligns best with our truest intention. There is a lot of talk in philosophy about Free will, that is, you can choose to do, or not do something. However, our will is always going to be at the mercy of our intent… the key is learning to align the will and the intent, rather than pit the one against the other. For example –

You have the intent to stop a bad habit such as smoking. So, you will yourself to stop doing that habit. But the habit is addictive, and you find yourself uncomfortable after a while,

and your truest intent will either be for comfort, or health.

If your truest intent is for comfort, and not health, then your truest will, will be to give up on quitting, and your truest will, will create roadblocks and suffering to keep you smoking. Thus, if your truest intent is to be comfortable and you will yourself to quit anyway, you may reap the rewards of better health, but suffer the conflict of truest will and truest intent.

On the other hand, if your truest intention is to be healthy and not necessarily comfortable, and you give in to your craving and have a smoke, your will is not aligned with your intent and can overpower your truest intent bringing you into self-conflict and greater suffering as a result. Sooner or later our truest intention always prevails.

Thus, it is a key action in magick to find and align your true will, with your true intent, or suffer in some way. Magick always follows our truest intention and will… If either of these are in conflict… you can get strange results, if any at all.

Decision – This is the true description of what others call free will. The ability of a conscious individual to "decide" to act on their intentions, and in what ways.

It is my assertion that the concept of "free will" as contemplated by most people is an illusion, because we mistake our meat bag body with the thing making the decisions. When in fact this meat bag is little more than an expression of our truest intention and will to experience life. Every decision we make is born of an intention. Thus, decisions are at the mercy of intentions! Conscious decision is illusory… studies have shown that LONG before we make a decision consciously, our subconscious mind has already decided for us, and our conscious mind is nothing more than a way for us to have a second opinion to make sure it's not something that will get us into too much trouble.

We can even be very intimately aware of our intentions and decide not to act on them. Ironically however, this is because our TRUEST intention is what is driving our Decision. One intention overriding another. Conscious or unconscious decision that is made to do or believe something.

The mind decides what things look like, feel like, and what they are called. The mind decides what we believe, and don't believe. The mind deciding an action is required, then deciding to act, deciding how to act, and then to ACT with terrible and powerful actions. When the act is done, you must decide and KNOW that it is done! When a thing is done, it is best to decide to forget it, and not dwell on it. To decide it is done and settled.

When you decide to act, act without hesitation, and know that indecision is the bane of all magickal action.

We must decide also to be brutally honest with ourselves, because honesty is a choice, and if we choose not to be honest with ourselves, we are essentially causing our spiritual alignment to break down. Leading to failure and suffering. For example, if we choose to deny our true intention to be a thief and decide to become a monk instead to rid ourselves of our wickedness, we will find ourselves robbing the monastery, and potentially feeling worse guilt and suffering more for it.

The next entries are the fundamental components of performing magick in ritual. Each of these is a common element in ritual magick that should be considered and understood before attempting to perform magick.

Altered States – There are many ways to achieve altered states. I will cover my preferred methods later in this book. For now, know there are 3 key altered states of conscious you should master entering and exiting before you can expect magick to be at your beck and call. They are the Empty state, the Focused state, and the Open state. There is also the BASE state, which is our normal operating state.

It is important to understand that all my rituals and methods, require the intuitive and easy use of these states, and until you can enter and exit them at will for a period of at LEAST 1 minute without interruption, you will still be able to perform my magick, but to a far less reliable degree. I know because when I am distracted or unable to truly enter these states, I sometimes fail at my own magick.

Declaration – Speaking your intent is a powerful holistic magickal action. It combines the mind body and spirit into a single action. There is a reason that Magick words are such a culturally universal concept. Every single culture has some understanding of the idea of magick words, chants, or intonation. The key to using simple verbalization of intent without any other element, is that you must KNOW that your spoken intent is being carried out, it requires experience and intensity, confidence, and sensitivity. I will include a separate section devoted to Intonation and declaration.

Inscription – (I have included a special section for magickal writing later in this book.) This is an action that is best done holistically, where you may write, craft, or otherwise manipulate an object and attune it to your will. When we create a sigil, we are inscribing the paper and ink with our will, and we need to be vividly aware that our action is leaving a mark or scar on the astral plane as much as the material plane. You must visualize the fire of your spirit burning the sigil onto the paper… and you must DECIDE that it is SO!

This applies to any other object we might craft or manipulate in magick such as when making poppets, crafting tools etc.

Movement – Bodily motion and hand gestures such as pointing or feeling the energy with your body and hands can be a very powerful way to manipulate the energy around you. It is very, very important to FEEL the energy, and the astral world when you move, to feel the energy flow through you, into objects, through your chakras, Dan Tien, and or energy body and more. All movement is often best coupled with visualization making it a holistic action.

Visualization – The mind and the spirit come together and create for us the astral world and our mental picture of it. It is important to know that what we see in our minds, is real in the astral world, even if we are unaware of it. Every daydream, every nightmare, every hallucination, is REAL in the astral. Thus, it is important to visualize your magick and rituals and see the spirits, energies and materials moving in accordance with your will.

Holistic Actions – In most of these actions I have listed, I repeatedly tell you how it might be turned into a holistic action. It should be apparent that if you stand in a ritual circle, raise your arms, intone your will, and visualize it happening in the astral realm, you have thus aligned the mind, body and spirit into a magickal operation.

What you should also know is that just doing a mental act, a spiritual act, and a physical act at the same time doesn't yet make it holistic. What makes it holistic is when you blur the lines to the point of them being irrelevant, it stops being a mental act combined with a bodily act, combined with an astral act. It becomes a HOLISTIC act... and there is no separation.

This itself is a very difficult thing to do with intention. It can take many years of practice, I myself do not attain this level of focus in every working. When I do, it leads to powerful reliable manifestations.

This does not mean it is REQUIRED for magick to manifest. Far from it. But when all three are in alignment, when we act holistically, we have the highest level of confidence in the operation. This alone can make it more potent and reliable. Any doubt or lack of clarity can mean a lack of manifestation.

Altered States

The skeleton key to magick, the key to anything spiritual, the key to health, wisdom and a favorite path of enlightenment in every culture is to practice and master various Altered states of consciousness. This can include, but is not limited to – Meditation, medication, mantra, prayer, binaural beats, hypnosis, and ritualized mania.

Altered states are primarily focused on altering the ways we perceive our world or altering the mental state behind the experiences themselves, opening us to different perspectives, energies and so on.

As mature individuals, our experiences are entirely focused on the subjective experience, and those of us who are sane, are attentive of what is considered the objective material plane. Those of us who are deemed insane are less focused on the objective plane, and more on the subjective plane.

We are all initially born without limitations such as these, our minds are not fully formed, and our astral bodies and spiritual identity is not firmly focused just on the biology of the self.

Instead, it takes time for our spiritual aspect to align itself with the biology being developed, and it takes time for the biology to align with the spiritual aspect that is taking possession.

When you look into a baby's eyes, you can see that the being that is regarding you is not yet a fully integrated and identified individual, they are the eyes of the virgin universe beholding the majesty of its own creation… Deciding what is, and what is not. Deciding what blue looks like, what pain feels like, and what thoughts sound and look like. All for the first time from that unique perspective.

This however becomes a deep distraction from our ability to perceive and manipulate magick consciously. There is only one effective way to deal with his problem and these are to master the altered states of consciousness, so they become as second nature, and as natural to us as breathing.

It is believed by many, including myself, that at some point it can be possible for an individual to no longer experience these states separately or intentionally, but they utterly transcend this paradigm completely, and they see with the eyes of a god, and can manipulate reality as readily as you or I might manipulate a thought.

I do believe that it is possible that some of these people have already walked this earth, or perhaps it is the same individual, having mastered a way to bend the laws of time and space to the point of irrelevance. Mythological and legendary figures abound, and many with a token nugget of potential truth.

In the meantime, allow me to teach you the 3 altered holistic states of consciousness you need to align with your magick ability!

Let's Describe Them

No mind – This is a state of stillness and silence of the mind, coupled with full awareness and clarity of intent. In this state we act without thinking, our actions, even the words we speak are spontaneous.

In magick the state of no mind, is a state where all conscious intentional thought is silenced and or ignored. That is, you recognize and focus on the space between your thoughts as your truest self. These empty moments are, at first, fleeting. Hard to notice or dwell on, and no sooner do you experience them, do you exclaim internally in an excited manner - "I'm doing it!" when that very thought scatters it like glitter in a whirlwind.

After a time, we learn to ignore the interrupting thoughts, and it becomes easier to focus on the empty stillness between, and these periods of stillness expand until they can last many minutes, even hours… At some point we find that where once we could not find more than a moment without thought… now it becomes hard to find a moment WITH thought… and when the thoughts do happen, they do not scatter the calm… they come, and they go and the still pond of reflection that is our true self remains.

This is the mental state that precedes the casting of the intent, and the mental state that follows when we lose our attachment and let the magick loose to do its work.

This would be like pressing your hand on the strings of a guitar to silence them, and then letting go. Soundless, open, waiting.

Focused/full mind - This is quite opposite to empty no mind, except it is without obsession, anxiety or chaos. In chaos magick it is often called a state of Gnosis. It is focused fullness of mind, complete and utter concentration on a single thought, idea, action, vision, moment or sequence.

It can be used to repeat a pattern, or visualizing an action intently, or holding a single thought. It can also be thought of as a kind of mania, the way tribal dancers can work themselves into a frenzy and in some cases even become enraptured.

There are some such as the Sufi Dervishes who can become so deeply enraptured they can withstand physical punishment such as having their entire body perforated by spears, their skulls can have daggers driven into them, and they can flay the flesh open on their backs with swords revealing the bones underneath… miraculously in some cases these people heal with supernatural rapidity.

I am not suggesting this become a part of your practice, but you should know that this state of mind is incredibly powerful…

Thus, it is more than simply thinking the same words over and over like you are deeply worried about something (though this is the best way to start doing it, but you must transcend the recitation), it is eventually being able to hold a single word in your mind without repetition with incredible intensity, a timeless idea without beginning or end. Like pressing pause on a movie and the image freezing on the screen, but the sound also being paused but not stopping. To freeze the entire sound of a cannon blast and hear it from start to finish without repeating.

In much the same way an image can be held, a word, idea or even an entire movie can be held in the mind, suspended, motionless. All points of the thought equally known at the same time. The front, and the back of an object is known at the same time, but cannot be visualized…

This kind of focus then is not simply an echo, or a flow of moving pictures, but a solid state, and it can be held, like the state of emptiness for nearly as long as we want… and when it is interrupted, it is undisrupted, it is still there, unmoved, unchanged.

This is the most powerful state of mind possible, but it is also when it is the most limited and vulnerable to disruption. This is the state of mind that aligns the disparate and out of tune strands of the holistic interface between mind body and spirit and holds it as long as it takes to make them all harmonize and sing in unison.

This would be like plucking the string of a guitar, but not yet letting go. Instead holding it with your finger at the absolute last moment before it is released.

Open mind - This is the mind that is open, that dreams, that is in touch with sensing a more balanced perception of the holistic reality, it thinks, it feels, and it flows without any limitation. It is the mind of the pleasant melancholy daydream stare, the mind of the waking dream, the lucid dream, the loose mind of the astral traveler. This is also the first phase of hypnotic induction, and as such you can be open to suggestion.

Most people are familiar with this state of mind intuitively, as most people have achieved it by accident many times in their life just by sitting in a classroom being bored, their mind wandering, daydreaming.

This state is exactly like the moment AFTER we release the guitar string and simply enjoy the sound it makes, and the places the tone takes our imagination when played as a song, it is quiet, open reflection...

Let's Find Them

Each of the following meditative exercises are meant to teach you ways to enter these states. How long you can hold them will depend on you. **It is my opinion that in order to perform most magick consciously through ritual, you MUST be able to enter at will, and hold each of these states individually for a period of at least 1 minute or longer, with little or no interruption.**

Once you have mastered the ability to enter and hold

these states at will, you will see your ability to perform magick and get results, improve exponentially.

If you do not wish to wait until you master these states before practicing rituals, there is little harm in this, many people do it with great results. However, all effort must be made to master these states at some point. All advanced sorcerers I have ever met are familiar with their own interpretation of these states and use them in magick.

Best method — Relax, Focus, and Release

You will learn our mind is a bit like our lungs. It doesn't need us to control it, but it can be controlled. Furthermore... when it is full, it is easier to make empty, when it is empty, it is easier to fill, and when it is relaxed, it can take you amazing places.

Phase 1: Calming and opening the mind - This is a simple meditation you can do at any time, it requires only time, and patience.

Sit comfortably in a chair, on the floor on a cushion, or even laying down. There is a higher risk of falling asleep in a bed, but you can practice this every night as you fall asleep and it will pay great dividends. The only drawback to doing this as part of falling asleep is you can become conditioned to do just that when entering these states.

The objective is to stay AWAKE on a much higher plane of awareness. Not fall asleep and enter the dream that much deeper.

However, you situate yourself, make sure your spine is straight, but relaxed.

Your arms should be resting comfortably, and there should be no tension anywhere. Stretch yourself to release distracting tensions if necessary.

For this exercise, you may find the use of a rosary or Mala useful to keep track of your breathing and help you keep time. Each time you complete a full cycle (in out) of breathing, move to the next bead in the string until you have made a complete circuit. On a Mala (which is 108 beads), this

takes approximately half an hour to complete one cycle if you breathe at a normal rate.

It is recommended that you practice meditation for a period of about a half hour at a time, more or less is fine, but aim for one half hour.

Close your eyes and begin by becoming aware of and controlling your breath. Start by exhaling aggressively but not forcefully all the air out of your lungs but not to the point of pain or discomfort. Hold it for a short time until you feel the automatic sensation as if the air is begging to return into your lungs. As soon as this happens, allow the intake of air to happen, but do not rush it, nor should you allow it to rush.

Allow the air to fill your lungs to about 70% or so on its own accord without gasping inward intentionally until it reaches a point where you feel like your lungs are now getting full. It should begin to feel like a weight is pressing down on your lungs and trying to blow the air out for you. Almost like the way a ball will hit the ground, bounce back up and reach a point of equilibrium.

For the first few breaths, hold this for several seconds, say 3 or 4 heartbeats. Then, just like before, release the air, do not blow it out, or force it out, let it fall out on its own. You can use the YinYang breathing method found in the section titled "Projecting your intention" for this if you like, but it is not required. Just breathe comfortably.

Allow the air to fall out until it reaches a new point of stasis at the lower end or bottom of your lung capacity and repeat the process several times. You will notice your BEST neutral and natural breathing rhythm is based on this stasis. It is neither a full top to bottom inhale and exhale, nor a short gasp.

After several repetitions you are ready to engage your mind fully on the next step, allowing you to clear your mind of distractions.

When you inhale, imagine the energy of the world around you is being drawn into you. And when you exhale imagine it flowing back out of you. Like a wave on a beach. It comes and it goes...

As we do this allow your stresses and concerns to bleed away from your mind... if you have a stressful or distracting thought, let it pass through your mind and make no effort to reach out and grab hold of it.

At some point you should feel an energized sense of calm. Little do you realize but you are stabilizing your astral self as well… the visualization of energy is real. Know it is real.

When you feel you are ready, and your mind is at peace. Know that you are in an open state, you may feel the urge to let your mind wander. If you wish you can do that now. Congratulations you have achieved the open state on purpose.

This is the natural entry state of scrying, and the most fertile state of mind for interacting with spirits in ritual.

If you wish instead to continue, it's time to enter phase 2:

Phase 2: Focus the mind (level 1) - Begin by reaching the end of phase one, the point where your mind is at peace and open. But instead of letting your mind wander, focus your attention on your breathing, but ignore the sensation or intentional action of breathing out, instead, focus on breathing in. And let your breath fall out without worrying about.

As you do this, I want you to begin to imagine an inverted or right side up triangle, a simplified trinity of self. Don't make it complex, this works better if you keep it simple. Imagine JUST the Triangle. Imagine it glowing and pulsing with bright light of any color you like.

With each inward breath, make the triangle go from invisible and dark, to a bright light. When you let the air out of your lungs make it go dark and impossible to see, and have it spring back again when you breathe in.

Visualize it in pure darkness to minimalize distraction… and imagine as it pulses it gets brighter and brighter, then fades into nothingness and returns again and again. Focus all your attention on it to the exclusion of all other visual thoughts.

If you suffer from Aphantasia or any other disorder where visualization is difficult, you should still attempt to see it. But do not stress about it, simply follow the next step.

Now softly say the word *trinity* as a mantra (repeat it). As you say it, think it. And think only it and the visual triangle. Do this slowly at first keeping in time with the pulsing glow of the trinity symbol, saying the word slowly…

While you say this again and again, take your hands, and form them into a triangular shape by touching your index fingers and thumb together. Carefully press your fingers together tighter and tighter and release them so they barely touch in time with the way the symbol pulses or flashes in your mind.

Feel the way the triangle feels in your hands. Focus all your attention on this one thought, this one word, this one sensation.

Do this over and over, allowing your breath to come and go naturally. Allowing the symbol to pulse, the words to repeat, the sensations to repeat. Over, and over until it is all you can think about. You will likely notice that the word Trinity begins to lose meaning for you, the word will become a sound, the image might also lose meaning, and your hands might lose sensation.

This is not necessary, but it is the IDEAL time to enter phase 3.

Phase 3: Emptiness - For most people, this is the hardest of the 3 phases. Most people can focus more or less, almost everyone can relax and daydream, but emptying the mind of chatter is almost impossible for most people.

You can either interrupt Phase 2 at any point, or instead Meditate through to the end of Phase 2, where the word trinity has become just a sound or a meaningless symbol.

When you are ready, take in a deep intentional breath, and release it. When you release your breath, also release the image, the sound, the word, and open your hands like you are letting the triangle go as you breathe out. In other words, release the entire experience of the trinity. Do this without thinking about it or thinking any other thoughts. Simply let the triangle vanish and disappear from your mind, simply stop repeating the word, simply stop pressing your hands together.

If you have never experienced it intentionally before, you will now experience at least a brief moment where you have no thoughts at all whatsoever in your mind. For even just a split second, it will be darkness, soundless, emptiness. For a moment you may even feel like you are in a kind of freefall.

Know that in this state, you are truly YOU. This is the real you. You can still act, talk, move, and do everything you normally do, you just don't have to think about it or tell yourself you have decided to do something. It will feel spontaneous.

Most likely you will Immediately break this calm by thinking – *I DID IT! I'm not thinking!* Which of course is a thought, and you will crash back onto the shore. Marooned on the island of chattering monkey brain thoughts.

That is ok. Don't fight them, just let the thoughts come and go, and notice now the spaces between the thoughts… recognize them for what you are.

Now would be a good time to allow yourself to enter either the open state again or end the meditation and come back to your normal state of thinking.

Taking it to the next level

This 3-phase exercise should be repeated until you can hold EACH state for a period of at least 1 minute. Once you can do it for more than a few seconds. It will help you to recognize the 3 primary altered states… and when you can recognize them, you will find with practice you no longer need to do the exercise as much to return to these states.

You will notice, that like breathing, if you empty your mind, it seeks to be full, if you fill your mind, it is easier to empty. With continued practice, you can just *will* yourself to enter them, or with as little as a moment of preparation visualization and breathing.

When you are truly advanced, the open mind state will be vivid, connected to the astral senses, not just the imagination, and you will have visions or hear sounds and feel things that are not there as spirits and spiritual forces will have an open channel to influence your experience. You can even enter an astral state, similar to an out of body experience, but typically much less vivid. Always be careful and know that YOU are in control over these experiences. You can make them go away just by thinking of something else or focusing.

As you master it the empty mind state can in fact become a normal way of thinking for you, as for me. I do not spend much time with subvocal thoughts, or images in my head. I find them distracting and sometimes downright annoying. I

can go many seconds, minutes, even hours without having a single conscious thought flitter through my head.

As I write this I am in a state of empty mind, and it allows me to write freely and without the need to plan or worry about what I am going to say. It just happens. You can do this in ritual, or virtually any other activity, save perhaps heavily analytical actions like doing math in your head, but even then, I find it increasingly possible.

The focused state (in particular) can be improved much further, and essentially giving way to a second form of focus. Some people might not find it difficult at all, while others will find it much more so. Technically, you do not need to be capable of both kinds, but the second kind is MUCH more potent in ritual and aligning your will.

So far, I have shown you how to focus on a repeating pulsing idea. But you can also learn to hold a single idea, image, sound, thought, feeling in your mind, suspended without changing or fading. The longer you can do this, the better and more advanced you are. The more magick will happen for you.

There are no specific exercises for this except to just do it. When you are ready to practice phase two. HOLD the image of the triangle, hold the sound of the word trinity (hear the whole word and don't repeat it, just keep hearing it as a single event, it's very hard to understand until you can do it), hold the idea of the word trinity and don't let it echo or fade. Hold the feeling of your fingers by keeping them pressed together. Ignore your breathing altogether and just breathe naturally.

The Base state

This is more or less the natural state we find ourselves, I am making it a special category all its own because it has a special and important use in magick. When we work magick, or experience the supernatural, it can be very important for us to not simply close the ritual with a lack of attachment and emptiness, but to return to the base state. We cannot live in the magickal state all the time without suffering certain mental and emotional desynchronization with the objective world.

Furthermore, sometimes the forces and situations we find

ourselves in can be disturbing, upsetting, frightening or just plain creepy and eerie.

Even the blackest demon worshipper can be given the creeps sometimes and feel uncomfortable at the presence of spirits. Even spirits we consider allies can make us uncomfortable when they show up in our bedrooms at 3 in the morning and give us the feeling like we are not alone.

The more we work magick the more these spirits can be attracted to us, not just the ones we call… but all of them. The good and the bad. Of course, we can do things to protect ourselves, wards, guardians, banishing's and more. But unless we cleanse ourselves of the "feeling" or "state" these experiences can lead to, we can find even the most powerful banishing has little effect.

And so, like someone waking from a bad dream and rushing to turn on the TV to watch children's cartoons or the news to get their mind off the dream. WE must learn to detach and normalize our experience by taking that important step to engage in normal activity when we are done with our magick and supernatural interactions.

After the experience (and potentially after recording it in our journals) we must return to the normal state. Turn on the lights, talk to someone, watch tv, eat some ice cream, pet your dog…

This is another important aspect of being nonattached, not just clearing your mind, but forgetting you did anything at all.

Reap the rewards!

Putting it all together

When you have mastered the ability to enter at will each of the 3 altered states of magick and hold these states for a period of at least 1 minute or longer, you will see a marked increase in the potency and vividness of your magick.

You can now apply these states in any ritual, working, or even as a quick way to gain control over your emotions and experiences and deal with everyday problems.

Spirits will find it easier to communicate with you, and working with chakras, Dan Tien, energy bodies and the astral will be easier.

Becoming sensitive to magick

When the seeker embarks on their spiritual or magickal journey, it is often preceded by an event that opens their eyes to a larger world. This event often inspires in us the ability to trust our magickal senses if we did not have it already. Great care must be taken to differentiate between what one imagines, and what is.

It should be apparent to anyone who has mastered the altered states of consciousness in the last chapter, that each of them expands and improves the individual's ability to sense and work with magick, to make one more and more sensitive to it.

However, by itself this may not be enough.

Becoming sensitive to magick can be a long process of experience that over time hones the senses of the sorcerer to see, feel, even think magickally. Yet in many cases it will just happen all at once. One day you will be struggling to see, and then bam, there it is, and you will realize you have been seeing it all along.

There are various experiences and exercises that one will learn, that will help you to recognize magick when you experience it, however, there is no "trick" to it.

It is a shift in perspective and expectation.

If we refer to the trinity of self, we see that all of our experience is a kind of decision made for us by our mind, it takes the subtle cues of the astral realm and overlays them onto the material realm and creates a reality it can work with.

This means some of our experiences are decidedly internal, while others are decidedly external.

This book for example exists in what most people would call their external experience.

However, the images and inner voice you see and hear when you read it are part of your internal world.

If you really explore this concept, you realize there really is no difference between your internal world and your external world experientially. You just have developed a knack for differentiating the two and giving them a separate meaning in your life, but there is not much of a real difference.

As above… So below…

We learn to trust what others might call imagination, to trust what others call coincidence. To learn to tell the subtle difference between fantasy and vision.

When you scry into a mirror and see the face of a spirit, it is not your physical eyes that see it, and the mirror is not technically important at all, it is a prop, or a conduit for manifestation, a way for your mind to bypass your disbelief, or a way to distract you, or just a fun way to do it that helps you enjoy and trust it more.

The real meat and potatoes of what is happening is happening internally in such a way that it bleeds over into also being partially external.

The vast majority of magickal experience is in this twilight area of internal experience. When you have attuned yourself, you will suddenly realize that what you once thought was pure imagination on your part, sometimes isn't so pure… that in fact you have been having visions all your life, and never recognized them because you did not know how to tell the difference, and or how to trust in it.

Of course, we need to learn discernment, because it is very easy to believe our own fantasies when the line between real magick and fantasy is so thin. And it is thin indeed. Necessarily so.

The third eye, and the physical sensations of magick

When we work with magick and the supernatural there are certain characteristic sensations reported by most all practitioners. The ability to feel energy, the sensation of being watched, the chills running up and down your body when a spirit is touching you, seeing visions and more.

It is a fundamental thing to learn to recognize and have as many of these senses open as possible for you to have a high degree of ability and mastery over magick.

In the occult community this is called having an open third eye. Many people quite literally believe this is a vestigial eye deep in our brain, which is the pineal gland (which long ago in our evolution was a primitive eye that sensed light from dark, but millions upon millions of years ago it became a gland in our brain instead that secretes melatonin that helps regulate our sleep patterns, among other things).

It is an interesting, almost vestigial organ that can certainly correlate in many ways to many spiritual phenomena. My own opinion is that we should not place too much importance on a tiny organ the size of a grain of sand. It demystifies the experience a bit too much to assume that all our mystical ability or even our soul as Descartes believed, is somehow centered on this organ without more than just the opinion of some quacks practicing various forms of pseudoscience.

In other words, do not discount it, and do not drink the punch either. Merely be aware of it and have discernment.

In ancient India, then later the rest of Asia, the idea of Chakra's arose, and the Anja Chakra is the Chakra associated with this third eye. The Anja Chakra has become almost universal in any conversation about the 3rd eye and the spiritual senses that virtually everyone that has studied the occult for more than 20 minutes, knows what it is, where it is and so on.

Now, while I have experience in Chakras, and Kundalini, my goal is not to teach you Kundalini, Chakras or anything else. My job is to get you up and running and using your spiritual senses so you can perform magick. And you do not need to embark on a lifetime study of Chakras, or even be aware of them to use your third eye effectively.

Afterall, it is a great big world and it has a long history. Prophets and seers have been having visions for thousands of years, most of whom never heard of the Anja Chakra.

An open third eye, doesn't *just* mean literal "visions," what it really means is that you can discern imagination, from intuitive insight and information. You may never "see" anything at all, or you may have "visions." However, these visions are not something that is done by your eyes, it is something processed by your visual mind, or some other sensory part of your mind.

You may stare and scry into a crystal ball and see shapes and colors and visions, but they will not actually be IN the ball, the ball is just a focus and a catalyst, a conduit and gate, but not a projector, not a TV screen.

Every one of us is different, and no two sorcerers will feel magick the same way. Some people are very sensitive to things like the astral world, having visions and hearing voices. Others are more prone to feeling emotional or intellectual energy or feeling empathy, knowing what other people or spirits are thinking and feeling. Still others will literally feel energy in some way, perhaps tingling, warmth, vibration, or pressure. Others will simply "know" something. They won't be able to tell you how they know it, where the knowledge came from, or how they are able to put it to use, but they can use it all the same.

There is no better or worse way to interact with the supernatural. Some might be more fun, others easier to interpret, but what really matters is that you come to develop your own senses, to a point where you can trust them. However, trusting them must be tempered by rationality. You must have discernment.

The difference between a prophet and a person who is delusional, and a normal person is not that one sees visions and the others do not. It is that the prophet knows which visions are true and which are fantasy, the delusional person cannot tell the difference but treats them all as real, and the normal person see's all the same things but decides they are all make believe and never pays attention to the subtle truths right in front of them.

Most normal people, and even some masters (apparently) think that having an open 3rd eye means you see things others do not see… the truth is, you are always seeing these things, the 3rd eye really is not what lets you see things, it is what lets you see the difference between a true spiritual experience and a fantasy. A true spiritual message of significance and a simple coincidence.

Most people fail at having true discernment. It is a rare gift, and nobody can have perfect discernment and never be wrong. I too get caught up in my own prophecies and visions and in the past, I was as delusional as they come because of this, it has taken me years to learn to tell the difference well enough to trust myself.

Most people are easily deceived either by mundane lies, or complex propaganda and con artistry. Many faith healers are nothing more than con men and women. Many occultists exaggerate and deceive when it comes to their abilities or wisdom.

Even I am not above using a dramatic floor show and literal pyrotechnics if it helps the petitioner (or myself) see things in a magickal way, even if just for a moment. From Flash paper to elaborate gothic looking ritual setups. However, I am always forthcoming and make it clear if I am using staged effects and why, but even still. It is still a form of manipulation and deception, benevolent as it may be.

Many of us, when starting out on the path of magick, tend to experience what I refer to as a calling, or a moment of wonderment, and sometimes this calling becomes exaggerated in our own minds to be what I call a "Chosen one complex."

I went through this phase… It is not inherently wrong to believe you are chosen, what is wrong is to fall into the trap of self-delusion and self-destruction that often comes with being so "special."

I am going to tell you right now, if you have not yet had a powerful supernatural experience, or the manifestation of a spiritual entity to physical form or experienced an unexplainable poltergeist or similar phenomenon, you have no idea how much of a shock this can be to an otherwise rational mundane mind.

Even a true believer can be broken and sent into hysterics. If their fanaticism and belief is built upon nothing of substance, it cannot prepare them for the reality.

Even someone who has seen dozens of unnatural things can still be made to jump or have the hair on the back of their neck stand up, even when a familiar spirit they trust enters a room.

Worst of all however are the legions of fakers, and those who would overly dramatize their experiences and claim them to be true, merely to get attention.

As I have become more of a public figure in magick, I have seen far too many people exaggerate, dramatize or otherwise jump to conclusions regarding their experiences. Either exaggerating their meaning, or letting their imaginations run away with them making them see absurdly fantastical things that always have the unique habit of making the very humble and mundane person some kind of "Chosen one."

The bride of Satan, the son of an angel, etc. Now, I'm not saying these things can't ever happen… I have my own (private) claims of importance. Some of us ARE chosen! For example - I am known as a Chosen of Lucifer. However, be mindful of others, and be mindful of yourself. Are you just trying to live out a fantasy? Or are you having a legitimate experience? The title of "Chosen of Lucifer" isn't some title or rank that makes me special, it simply describes my personality and the path I am on. It means I do not simply follow a Luciferian LHP perspective intentionally because someone taught it to me, it means I naturally embody most of all of the Luciferian/LHP ideals and put them into practice long before I ever encountered them.

That being said - here are a few types of experience, and some methods for experiencing them –

Astral hearing

The hearing of the supernatural. This usually means hearing what cannot be heard with the ears alone. It is my belief that the best way to experience this, is to find a suitable source of NATURAL and varied white noise. Sit on the beach and listen to the surf and the wind, sit in the woods and listen to the wind in the trees and the call of animals. Sit in the dark around a crackling fire and listen for the sounds of the fire or the night. Again, it is key (at least while you learn) that this noise be natural, and not created by electronic means, either as a recording or transmission.

Enter either an empty, or open state, and simply listen… Ask questions, both in your mind and with your voice, and listen for the subtle voice in the wind or the surf or the fire that responds. It may come as part of an audible sound, or the timing of the snapping of a twig might be a yes or a no message to you. The voice may not even be a voice, but a sudden sensation like you heard someone say something in response.

It is important to understand is that what is happening here is nothing more than letting your 3rd eye/ear recognize the subtle patterns in the sounds and interpret them as intelligible things. There is *usually* not a REAL voice in the wind, it is a personal subjective experience. If you were to ask anyone else, even someone with similar sensitivity, there is little chance that they will have heard the same thing as you, unless it really was an audible voice. Which would likely make it more a poltergeist or synchronistic event than an astral sensation. This of course is also valid, as many times the supernatural communicates with us in this way.

You can experience auditory components when scrying, so keep this in mind as well, and do not assume that just because you are gazing into a mirror, the experience will be visual…

Having Visions/Astral Sight

As mentioned before, much has been said about the 3rd eye, it is beyond a fad at this point, with every other mystic talking about it. So many people claim to have astral sight, or an open 3rd eye, and talk about these elaborate hallucinatory trips they have been on. Sometimes they are authentic, other times they are not.

What the third eye really does is an overly complex subject and could needlessly fill an entire book. Each person can have a unique experience of what this is like and desperately try to explain it, and fail… Because most people's third eye is closed, including those doing the teaching. If it was open, they would know the 3rd eye is a metaphor and the goal is not to have these holographic images suddenly be overplayed into your sight… but instead to be able to notice what has always been there that you ignored.

So, let me keep this simple for you… know simply that the difference between a closed 3rd eye, and an open one, is mostly just a matter of being able to recognize spiritual and magickal things when you observe them.

You may start noticing patterns in everyday things, shapes in clouds or tendrils of smoke. These abstract patterns will suddenly have meaning, it will no longer just be a random pattern. Instead you will know it is a message or the embodiment of something without a body. It will not (in my

experience) lead to you having superhuman ability to see through walls, or see ghosts walking around clear as day all the time. Sometimes? YES! It can, *sort of*… again this is not your eyes doing it. If you "see" anything abnormal, chances are it is not your eyes seeing it, and you will know the difference.

If your 3rd eye is truly open. I won't have to explain this to you when it happens, you will simply nod and "know."

Sadly, this is not a skill you can easily teach, how do you teach someone to suddenly notice things they couldn't before?

The only way I know is to immerse the person in the experience and provide contrast and point directly at it till they figure it out.

It is a bit like the Zen Saying that Zen is a finger pointing at the moon.

So, let me repeat, an open third eye, more than anything will allow you to recognize the patterns in your environment and in your imagination as something meaningful. Your imagination may embellish on what you see and give you a cool daydream/experience that has meaning for you.

You will have visions that you once would have thought were little more than flights of imaginary fancy, that you now can recognize as spiritual in origin. At first you might "Imagine" you can see energy emanating from your wand in ritual, but with practice, you will learn that your imagination is more and more part of an accurate picture of what IS happening. Because what you imagine in your mind, is REAL in the astral… From the most absurd thing, to the most terrifying.

It is truly that pliable.

Developing Astral sight typically requires the practitioner learn one or more methods of scrying and allowing their eyes to relax to the point where the imagination can create its own interpretation of what is seen, and override the eyes… For example, staring "through" a mirror when scrying, causing the Troxler effect to distort your vision, creating a kind of Rorschach ink blot that your imagination and 3rd eye will run away with and give you a vivid vision.

Some of these visions can be simple flashes, and other times can induce a full sensory experience, even an out of body experience…

Learning to develop this sense is a matter of spiritual

practice, it is not actually a complex thing. It is a LOT like learning to see those 3d pictures in those funny 3d pattern pictures where you cross your eyes and a 3d image appears to pop off the page at you. It was always there in the patterns and in your imagination, you just didn't distinguish it.

The method of seeing with an open 3rd eye, is similar… through a process of meditation, altered states, and self-discovery, you can find yourself seeing patterns and truth you never saw before.

In a very real sense, opening the third eye can feel like crossing and uncrossing your natural eyes until you find the right focus.

There is no mechanical recipe to make this happen, you simply must keep working on it, till you notice one day that the candle flame is flickering in a way that looks like a face talking to you, after you call a demon into your chambers,

There is nothing supernatural about the flame however, it is just a flickering flame on the end of a candle. The fact that it looks like a face may merely be synchronistic, and the fact that you recognize it to look like the face of a Demon you often work with, and that you understand that this experience has meaning is the true magick.

I will endeavor to give you a few methods in the scrying section to help you ritualize your practice of scrying so that you can at least give yourself that little added confidence and energy to help you learn to see.

Tactile sensation of energy

This one is fun, as you can develop your ability to literally feel magickal forces and energies. Some will experience this as electric, heat, cold, movement, vibration or pressure. My own experience is that this mostly feels like pressure, like the way two opposing magnets feel when you try to push them together.

When you can feel energy in one form or another, you can learn to play with and manipulate it, to use your will to direct it, charge it with intent and release it into the world or into an object.

The easiest method I have found for becoming sensitive to this pressure is by way of learning to make an energy ball (called Chi, prana or Psi ball.) I will go into this in more detail later in the section entitled – Projecting your Intention.

Signs and Omens

Directly related to having visions and astral sight, are Signs and omens. We do not talk of signs and omens as much these days, now we typically refer to these events as synchronicity. Synchronicity is a term that was introduced by Carl Jung in the 1920s and is most easily summarized as: A situation that has meaningful coincidences without any possible causal connection.

That is, when something, or some series of events or observations occur in such a way that they line up independently with other events or observations. This alignment happens in a way that has some deep meaning for the observer.

For example:

Early this morning waiting for the bus to get to your job in the city, you notice a young child picking up a coin on the street… they pick it up and joyfully exclaim:

"Look it's on heads!"

Then run back to their mother gleefully.

Something about this event sticks in your memory, the happy kid, and the way they ran over to pick up the coin.

Later in the day you are waiting for a bus to go home, and while you are waiting, you notice a small coin out of the corner of your eye laying on the ground. It is a mere penny, but looks to be heads up, and you recall the child from this morning looking so happy, you feel like it would make you happy to emulate the child, so you walk over to pick it up with a smile on your face thinking of the child and their joy.

Just as you lay your fingers on it, there is a terrible crash as a car careens off the road and smashes through the bus stop where you had been sitting moments earlier without any warning.

Had you not been picking up the coin… you would be

dead. Had you not seen the child this morning, and been inspired to pick up the coin despite it being only a penny… you would be dead…

In this synchronistic way, the child and the penny saved your life. By all accounts this is just a coincidence, but you know better, in your heart, you know this was meaningful.

Another example:

You have been single for a while, and feeling depressed about it, everyone you have dated lately has been a disaster, and you have been hiding out at home a lot lately. Your friends, seeing your state, convince you to go out. You all pile into a car, with a designated driver to be safe, and while on the way to a local club with the rest of your friends, the car radio starts playing a song you don't like… you remark to your friends how much this song bothers you.

One of your friends playfully mocks you saying – "Knowing your luck, I bet the person you marry and live with happily ever after - will *love* this song…"

An hour later you are hitting it off with someone, but unsure if you should take a chance on asking them for their number. Suddenly, the song you hate comes on, and before you can complain, this person excitedly exclaims how much they love this song…

On your tenth anniversary you both laugh when you recall the story again about how you met and how that song played a role in you taking a chance to ask them for their number.

A more subtle example:

You are going through a family album and looking at pictures of a big party from several years ago. You find yourself drawn to a picture of your uncle Skip, your favorite uncle that you haven't seen in years…

Your thoughts are interrupted by the phone as it starts ringing.

You answer the phone and it is your aunt calling to tell you that Uncle Skip just passed away this morning in a tragic accident at a bus stop and thought you should know; the funeral will be on Saturday…

Throughout human history a great number of pivotal decisions have been made based upon synchronistic events, AKA signs or omens. Synchronicity can be either dramatic, life changing and bold like the first example, moderately dramatic or life altering like the second, or rather strange and memorable, but otherwise not very life altering.

Different people experience these same things in different ways, someone who is sensitive to magick and aligned to their intention will notice these kinds of things more often, and there are those who say that we are in alignment with our destiny when we experience synchronicity as these are examples of the universe poking us and trying to get our attention, often playfully.

This can be related to, or entirely separate from Signs, and omens, but often it is indistinguishable.

Those who are superstitious might be bothered by a black cat crossing their path into a dark alley. Taking it as a bad omen or sign

However, someone who just dreamt of a black cat last night, might follow it, and find that the cat has inadvertently led them to a wounded man who was just attacked and robbed recently and needs help… you are there just in time and are instrumental in saving the mans life.

All these kinds of example situations are usually clear to the person experiencing them as having a point, a message, a reason or purpose. Sometimes it is very easy to see the connections, such as these fictional examples, however sometimes (more often in fact) the message is so personal and so specific, that others even those who believe strongly, cannot understand the meaning.

It could be argued, that the very fact that you believe it MIGHT have meaning is meaningful in and of itself. You keyed in on the significance for a reason, and sometimes even you won't know why.

For example, you might notice a word in a song stand out somehow, and later that word appears again in another unrelated situation, and again in yet another unrelated situation. You have no idea why this word seems to be popping up all over, but you can't deny it. You may not realize it, but this word is shaping your thought process and experience, as the more it pops up, the more you notice it, and tell people about it. The final influence it has had over you may never be revealed to you directly, but you just know it meant something at the time!

Of course, to a skeptic, the only thing that happened is you learned to expect the word and noticed it more as a result. You are primed by that one experience, to notice the event, and decide it is important. Even though it is not happening with any higher frequency than normal.

As I have shown before, magick works along a path of least (rational) resistance. In my mind, there is no reason why both explanations cannot be equally valid.

Very often synchronicity is something personal, and it is one of the reasons I often refuse to read other peoples dreams or tell them what to make of certain situations. Instead, I will explain the symbolism as I understand it, and allow the querant to decide for themselves.

Learning to spot signs, and omens and synchronicity isn't possible, that is, there is no method to being more aware of synchronicity, or some way to make it happen more on purpose. However, I have found that the people who are more inclined to notice or have synchronistic experiences are those who are focused on a spiritual pattern of experience in the first place.

The skeptic and the mystic both experience it in equal measure, but the mystic sees it as synchronicity, while the skeptic mere coincidence.

The best advice I can give, is to continue with your meditations and spiritual practices to keep exercising your magickal senses. However, try not to get too paranoid and jump to the conclusion that every coincidence has meaning.

Synchronicity, aka signs and omens are one of the key ways the spirit world communicates to us. If you have a sign, an omen, or a synchronistic affect, only you likely know what it means. For many, this is the clearest form of communication a novice will get from a spirit. Long before they learn to see them manifest in various ways, they will experience synchronistic coincidences and signs and omens in their life. Even advanced practitioners know that just because they didn't sense anything during a ritual, the spirits may respond later with a synchronistic response...

Again, this is not a skill, nor an ability you can "train." But you can open yourself to them by being willing to accept them when they happen and not try to find every excuse there is to deny them.

The energy/astral Body

This can be important to working with energy in general and is related strongly to the Tactile Sensation of Energy. It can take time to learn to experience and sense your own energy body, and there are many different paths which deal with them, and many correspondences between these paths.

In India, there originated the Chakra system, in the west, the astral body, and in Chinese medicine we see the 3 Dantian. I find all of them to have value, and I strongly believe that each one has a piece of the puzzle. I will not attempt to give you a complete understanding of each one because each could require their own separate books, but I encourage you to research them on your own. You do not NEED to master them to work with them, they are not (on the surface) very complex ideas.

It is my firm opinion that Chakras, Dantian, Astral bodies etc., are all projections of our mind, and made real in the astral by our acknowledgment and practices using them.

Thus, you do not need to worry about and choose one that is more objectively true, but rather decide which one is more useful to you in your practices. I use all of them when I need them.

I am, by no means, a master of either Chakras, or Dantian, I haven't spent decades in the orient learning these secrets from silent monks and enigmatic guru's on mountain tops.

However, one does not need to master any of these concepts to a very high level to put them into effective practice or show people the basics.

In my subjective experience, the Chakra system is best thought of as a system of tubes and conduits through which energy flows and is manipulated and distributed throughout the energy body. Each chakra becoming a focal point of awareness. Closely related in many ways to them are the

Dantian. Dantian are more like centers of energy generation and centers of the bodies spiritual mass and awareness.

Have you ever wondered why you believe the center of your awareness is in your head? Forget for a moment that this is where your brains are. Did you ever wonder if it was like that for everyone? Would it shock you to learn that other cultures and in other times in history, people not only believed, but FELT that their center of awareness wasn't in their head? Or at least not limited to their head?

How often have you heard people say – *I was thinking with my heart*. Or *He is thinking with his genitals*. - ?

If you practice with Singing bowls, you likely know they are tuned to match specific Chakra, and if you really open yourself to it, you can feel as if the sound of each chakra resonates with a different spot in your body. The Crown Chakra resonating to B, while the root is C.

Furthermore, if you can find these centers in your body, you can even "breathe through them." That is, you can feel as if your air when you breathe in and out is somehow passing through these points in your body as if they are mouths or lungs of their own.

Dantian can be experienced in much the same way, especially with breathing, but Dantian are also better experienced as centers of energy and awareness than just breathing passages. The lower Dantian is often considered the most important one to focus on because it promotes energy and health and makes working with the others easier.

Our Astral body as imagined by most westerners is like our ghost, a spiritual representation of our true selves. Often it looks like how you look, or imagine yourself to appear, but is mostly a ghostly - sometimes featureless - energy form, or can take on virtually any appearance we want, even growing far beyond the limits of our physical body.

It is often best for most western spiritualists and occultists to imagine the astral body as being malleable and capable of being worked with via Chakras/Kundalini yoga, OR Dan Tien/Qigong/Tai chi methods. If you spend any real time researching these individual subjects you will find many of the fundamental practices are similar or the same, Kundalini yoga (not to be confused with Hatha yoga) and performing Qigong for example have some of the same principles, each treating

the same awareness centers with similar importance.

It is far beyond the scope of this book to try to fully teach (or for me to focus on and learn) one or all these energy systems to you in depth. I am more like a general practitioner and mastering certain systems like this would be like being a neurosurgeon or oncologist instead. The General practitioner lacks the specialization, but the neurosurgeon or Oncologist isn't as likely to be able to treat your boils or arthritis.

In a similar vein, I am not a master of any of these systems, I know just enough about them to work with them loosely and prescribe methods and ideas to you.

Furthermore, since it is my opinion that these systems are projections of the mind made real in the astral world, it almost doesn't matter what you do, so long as you do it with intention.

My intention with this entry is merely to make you aware of these ancient practices as a possible avenue of study that will enhance your magick in the long run. Therefore, you do not need to master or even adopt ANY of these practices or ideations of the energy body to use magick effectively.

Adopt, or ignore them as you wish, but it is my opinion that at least *some* attention needs to be given to the energy body to be fully sensitive to magick. Even if all you adopt into your practice is the idea that you have some vague astral body of some kind.

To this end, later in the next chapter of this book I will be outlining a method for creating a Qi-Ball, which will make use of several basic energy working principles of Qigong, Kundalini yoga and the western astral body in conjunction.

Psychonautics

I am technically considered a Psychonaut because I spend so much of my time exploring altered states of consciousness, however, most people who use the term are referring to those who use chemicals to achieve these states. I have never made chemicals such as LSD, Peyote, Cocaine, Marijuana or any other as part of my spiritual practice.

I do not judge those who do, many cultures throughout

history have relied on these to break down the barriers that prevent them from accessing their spiritual senses. It is a very real, and very valid way of doing this.

However, nearly everyone I have ever known who claims to use these chemicals for this reason, is really just using that reason as an excuse to get fucked up and use drugs. It is a way to rationalize a bad and unhealthy habit of abusing a substance, and it does not in any way improve or expand their consciousness beyond opening their eyes a small crack…

I am not being judgmental, in fact I support the free will of anyone to self-medicate or do what they will with their body, all I advocate is self-honesty. If you are using these substances for a spiritual experience, but all you ever do is get high and fucked up and never really advance your spiritual practices, maybe you should be honest with yourself about why you are doing this?

I am telling you as a wise sage, I know what I see when I look into the eyes of many who claim a spiritual origin for their substance abuse, they are just as lost, perhaps more lost, than those who do not use these chemicals at all.

Conversely, there exists a tiny handful of people I have known who HAVE used these substances responsibly, in limited and controlled fashion. Those who kept these substances sacred, and treated them not as a guilty pleasure, but a gift from the gods to expand their minds… They on the other hand can achieve states of advanced awareness and consciousness that are to be marveled at. Some notable people who exemplify this are many of the great thinkers and pioneers of the use of LSD and other psychoactive chemicals in the second half of the 20th century. People like Terrence McKenna for example, who is someone I highly recommend you read… are profoundly aware of something few other normal mundane people are.

If you choose to incorporate these substances into your practice, I cannot help you, my experiences with this are my own and not for sale, only know that it should NEVER be used as an excuse to get high, you are STILL responsible for the things you do while high and working magick, and some spirits will be offended if you are not rational and in control over your faculties when you call to them. Treat these substances as SACRED, and do not abuse them at all, and

seek a respected guide, guardian or group of people to help you… You are very literally taking your life and your mind into your hands when you experiment with these chemicals. Be warned, but not necessarily discouraged.

Just Knowing

Closely related to Gnosis, this is the spontaneous and unexplainable ability to know things. It can be downright uncanny, and will express itself in the form of Synchronicity, or simply just come to you. You will "just know" something you didn't before.

A great deal of my magick, and many of the methods in this book come from "just knowing." It doesn't come in a vision, it isn't told to me. I just do it, write it, or think it, and when I check it's just correct.

Some have pointed out that this could be past life skills coming back to me. Others have suggested that this is the spirit world teaching me in my dreams or by directly channeling through me. Some have said that it is the product of the subtle truths about magick and mysticism in pop culture references. Watch enough martial art movies, you might pick up some Asian philosophy along the way. Watch enough movies with magick in it, you might pick up some authentic symbolism that is often used in such movies to make them more "Authentic."

Still others have said it's just uncanny synchronicity.

Whatever is going on, it is a very enviable ability, but it can have the drawback of being less inspirational. Sometimes I wish I learned things more through vision, and dream. Something to anchor the knowledge to a memorable story or something fun like that. It also makes the knowledge sound more valid to some people.

Let's be honest, the occult is FILLED with liars, and scam artists making things up. Some people find it easier to trust the stories of others if it comes with a cool vision than if you say – I don't know how I know it, I just do.

All I can do is hope that my desire to be transparent with you as a reader of this work is enough to at least allow you to consider what I am saying is truthful.

Just knowing is a big component of Gnosis.

Gnosis

Gnosis has several definitions in different magick traditions. In this system it is interpreted as personal knowledge and experience of a mystical nature. As opposed to intellectual knowledge that is simply learned and recited (mystical or otherwise). It is my belief that gnosis is the most precious and important thing we gain from our working with the various gods, demons, and other spirits we encounter, as well as what we gain from doing magick and meditation in general.

Gnosis in this system essentially means a state of knowing the mystical and supernatural truth that applies best to our subjective world. The spontaneous inspiration or induction of new information, ideas, or direction that comes to us without apparent source. Gnosis means more than simply knowledge or ideas, it means experience itself. The experience of that knowledge. It is one thing to know something is true because it was proven logically or taught rationally. It is another to experience it and live it.

For example - We do not need to intellectually understand gravity to have gnosis about the experience and rules of gravity.

Conversely, we can know that sugar is sweet, but until we taste it, we have no gnosis of that sweetness.

When we gain Gnosis through magick and ritual and communion with the spirits, what we get is always going to be a very personal experience, no two people are going to have the same exact experience of Gnosis, and when we experience our own personal gnosis, we should take care to never assume it relates, or applies to others.

Indeed, it is considered an important part of every valid occult system I have encountered, from the most benign to the most malevolent, to always respect the personal experiences of others. Very often extending to those who are outside your tradition.

Therefore, you do not NEED to believe anyone or their claims, but you need to respect them and not try to argue them out of their experience. Of course, this means we must assume the person telling it to us is being honest about that experience and demand they respect our own personal truths equally.

So, for example, if I call to the spirit of Azazel, and he comes to me in the form of a warrior in red armor wielding a shield and spear, and you see him as a winged deformed monstrosity with goat horns… Which of us is right?

Technically, neither, because Azazel does not necessarily have a "body" or "form" the way we do. If anything, we create that image of him in our astral eye out of the inspired imagery we prefer or that our culture gave us to expect.

In this example we need to accept that all gnosis is subjective in nature.

That does not mean it cannot have objectivity. It means most of it is meant for you alone, and some elements may be provable or universal. It means that many a madman has come running out of their ritual chamber, having been given a vision of the true nature of reality, that for them is 100% proven, but only a tiny fraction of it applies to everyone else, and this person is stigmatized as insane…

In fact, one of the greatest risks of truly devoting yourself to the study of magick and the occult is that your perception of reality can be irrecoverably skewed, for better or for worse. Leading to all kinds of psychosis and pathological delusion. Paradoxically, there is nothing "wrong" with this, even if it becomes pathological, it is still your life, your world, your experience.

If through this change in perspective your magick becomes potent and effective, if through this change in perspective you find happiness… all the better.

However, some people do not find peace, prosperity, or happiness in such shifts in sanity. Some people can become frightful and stymied to act. For example - they won't get into a car without banishing the evil spirits in the engine, they won't eat anything that is the color red because red is a demonic color… they won't go to the doctor because they believe doctors inject you with tracking devices and this device also lets them take over your body any time they want.

In their world this could even be 100% true, and if you were locked into their experience it would be the only rational things to believe. Yet, it might still demonstrably be hurting them.

One could of course make the same argument for all the various existential delusions we convince ourselves to believe. Leading to the creation of, and need for, magick to break us free of our delusion of helpless and mundane experience.

It is important then, when pursuing gnosis to have a very rational approach.

Consider the following key practices –

Keep notes - You may find it important to be meticulous, or only keep the more important things you learn. Either is fine, so long as it is done. This is because in the MOMENT of our acquisition of gnosis from spirits or experiences such as scrying, we can misinterpret or miss the meanings, and the true value of the information may only appear later upon reading the notes. Sometimes these things interlock and interconnect and co-create new knowledge and gnosis. I personally like paper notes and journals, but anything will be ok for this.

Start pure - Try to minimize the influence of outside sources until you have already had your own chance to experience the gnosis first hand. For example, when preparing to work with a known spirit, a lot of people make the mistake of spending too much time researching them and end up filling their heads with "other people's gnosis" about the entity which may not apply and may lead to the person having the wrong expectations. Have your gnosis, THEN research and compare what you find. Because some of that which you learn through gnosis is meant just for you or is just a mistake or daydream on your part. I have included some of my own Gnosis (in the pathworking section) for each of the key spirits of this system. I did my best to minimize how much impure information wound up in this section of the book, doing my best to limit it to what I believe helps update and decode the coded symbolism of the Goetia to connect with modern minds.

Trust but Validate - This is where you need to compare your gnosis with the gnosis of others, or the objective facts that are available. And make the conscious decision to keep or discard things that appeal to or offend you. I have contacted spirits and been told they can be "associated" with earth, but everyone else experiences them as being associated with fire… Who is wrong? Possibly nobody. Maybe this being CAN have multiple aspects with different correspondences? You need to decide for yourself. But remember, don't run out into the streets shouting about how wrong everyone else is… remember?

Be receptive even in mundane daily life - Gnosis can come at any time, during ritual, dreams, or even when browsing the internet, you might get a sudden idea, and "coincidentally" a web article talking about that idea might appear in your suggested feed. Learn to know when it's important and real, and when it's just random or imagined.

All is True - Be open to any and all new ideas and conflicting gnosis even within your own practice. Spirit A might claim the biblical god is the real one true god. Spirit B might say all are one and there is no god, Spirit C might say the other two are lying and to bow down and worship them as god. I have rarely experienced such a conflict, but it is possible. Spirits are just another reflection of the same truth that we all interpret in our own ways. They can be in conflict and can even tell you things that do not make sense, yet, somehow, in defiance of logic is just as true as the far more rational thing you learned from the others.

The good news is, you get to choose which truth you want to focus your attention on, and nobody can deny you this power. In magick, you can shape your reality any way you want. After all, is that not the whole point? This is clearly borderline madness and is a big reason why so many occultists can seem a bit "off." Usually in a harmless kind of way. We routinely need to juggle multiple truths in our minds at once and need to be able to pick up and discard threads of truth and reality without being too attached to them or we can stumble and fall.

Remember that your gnosis is separate from your intellectual knowledge, but they can co create one another, the final goal is to have a working current of experience and intellect that doesn't create imbalance and conflict and thus an inability to wield magick, let alone cope with reality as it is.

I have found that it is very distracting and destructive to your work to waste a lot of time trying to prove or disprove disparate bits of information beyond a certain point. At some point you must simply go with your gut, or ignore the discord, and assume both could be right.

Final word

This text represented only the tip of the iceberg when it comes to learning to be sensitive to magick. It is a skill that cannot be easily taught, all that can be done, is for you to be shown the path, and the methods that help us follow it, and it is up to you to practice and become sensitive. Master the Altered states of consciousness, and practice training your magickal senses and you will be many times more successful in your magick than anyone who simply picks up a book and starts chanting the words like they are rehearsing for a play.

Energy Work & Projecting Your Intention

When we perform magick, as described in the fundamental Actions of ritual magick, we touched about some key concepts that require deeper study. At this point, we have already discussed a great deal about how important it is to become sensitive to magick. But a large part of being sensitive to magick is also learning to manipulate energy and intent, and project our astral body and spiritual "force" into our magick working.

This can be done in virtually every physical and elemental sense of the word, we can create spiritual pressure, not unlike the pressure we exert with our body movements, or breath. We can create spiritual sound and vibration. Spiritual wind and flowing liquids, Spiritual heat, and electricity.

At first you may have difficulty with all this, particularly if you cannot comfortably control your altered states of consciousness or cannot yet feel or sense the subtle forces of magick in some way. In this section I will outline a series of practices and methods that should help you get your feet on the path to learning to project your intention better.

These are vital skills that will make your magick possible. In my humble opinion, an honest seeker must master these basic practices before they can move on to true power in the occult. These are the subtle actions that you must perform while you are performing the rituals… or all you are doing is reading occult poetry in the dark by candlelight.

I will not cover all the possible variations or forms of energy/intention projection, as many of them overlap and can be modified easily enough simply by changing your intention. So, I will focus on the easier ones to experience and conceptualize and allow you to develop the ability to feel and manipulate the others on your own.

This kind of thing can be exhausting at first, and this exhaustion can be physical, emotional, or simply just energetically to the point where you feel awake, but lack motivation or energy.

So, it can be important to take breaks and not overdo it.

Lastly, you can use one or all these kinds of energy manipulation at the same time. I believe the holistic approach is best, you want to see, hear, and feel the energy you manipulate equally well if possible.

So, when you are pushing spiritual pressure into an object, you need to not only feel that pressure, but see it, and hear the sound it would make. This makes it that much more real in the astral world and is a vital skill.

Celestial Energy and Time

Around 4.5 Billion years ago, the Earth was a giant primordial ball of partially molten rock. It swung around the sun, being constantly bombarded by the debris of creation which kept it soft and molten.

It had grown so large that it was pulling in tons of material every minute and had attracted another colossal body of rock about the size of mars that some call Theia.

Theia drew closer and closer… circling around the earth like a shark in the murky darkness of the early solar system.

One fateful day, Theia made Its final approach and collided with the earth it a cataclysmic impact. Had the conditions of the impact been much different, Theia and the Earth would have been obliterated and scattered, becoming just another asteroid belt.

Instead, this impact caused a smaller body to be ejected from the primordial earth, which was forever tidally locked to its mother planet…

As the two worlds cooled, Theia would be no more, instead Earth and Luna remained.

This fantastic story is not science fiction, nor is it dramatized gnosis from a demon, this is (more or less) how our earth and moon formed. It is why the energy of the moon and its relationship to us in the sky and how it reflects the rays of the sun is so important in our magick. Thus, it is in the story of this creation that the significance of the moon in our magick and our magickal energy should become apparent.

The moon was once a part of what we are, and it is still a part of our lives and experiences, controlling tides, growing seasons, and was once the best calendar we had.

Even more than the stars, the sun or the other planets, no other object in the universe has a more deep and important connection to us, we share a common origin, we are scarred by the same cataclysm that created us, and the cratered face of the moon glowing brightly in the sun shows us the beauty of the scars of causality clearly, as we show the moon the warmth and rejuvenating influence of life.

The position of the moon in its orbit around the earth, in relation to the sun, is an intrinsic aspect of the biology and causality of this planet. Even science cannot easily describe all the subtle and important influences our moon has had on our biology and evolution, with many species of animal being utterly dependent upon the moon, it's tidal influences, and even its light to survive.

These two heavenly bodies have more influence over our individual lives than almost any other force in nature, for without the sun, and the moon, we would not have any of the conditions for life.

In magick the interplay of these two bodies results in a cyclic pattern of Yin and Yang flow, of positive and negative energy.

While the sun is an important factor in our lives magickally, with the solstices, and equinoxes having powerful significance in our magick.

It is the Moon Luna, which truly has the most impact in our magickal working, particularly as black magickians working with infernal spirits and dark energies. As its creation shows it is literally a part of us and our world, its energy is therefore connected to us and our world in a way that even the mighty sun cannot quite claim…

In our practice, the most important astrological correspondences will be related to the moon, the time of day or night, and the planets are also important, but to a lesser extent.

Phases – The moon has 8 distinct phases and each one has significance to our magick and our energy:

The New moon - This phase is the point of lowest yang energy and maximal yin energy; it is an ideal time to begin any new project in magick. For some longer spells which have the goal of obtaining, creating or causing something positive, it is common practice to begin on the new moon, and finish on the full moon. The new moon is very powerful and despite being dark in the sky has a huge influence over our energy.

Waxing Crescent - This phase of the moon is when the energy begins to build, and any time between the new moon and the full moon can be considered a period of growth and an increase in Yang Energy. Many initiations will begin under the light of a new waxing Crescent moon.

Waxing Gibbous - At this point the moon is more than half full and we are nearing the climax of the full moon. This is a fantastic time to put the finishing touches on a project that is nearing completion but isn't quite ready to be considered done. Magick spells that are cast at this time should be for things that are already well on their way to becoming a reality, but just need that little extra push.

The Full moon - The maximal climax of Yang Lunar Energy and the culmination of magickal creation. This is normally the climax and final night of a longer spell that may have begun on the new moon. The full moon is very powerful in magick, but it should be stressed that the very next day or so will begin to see a decline in energy and it is not the ideal time to begin anything positive that is meant to grow. Instead it should be used to FINISH and CELEBRATE the culmination of a manifestation. It is also an IDEAL time to begin any long term working that is baneful, or when we need to cleanse ourselves of things, we do not like about ourselves, culminating on the New moon as a fresh start and new beginning.

Waning Gibbous - This is when the Yang Energy of the moon is decreasing, giving way to the Yin Energy of the moon. As the moon darkens, the energy shifts more and more toward negative flow. This can be an ideal time to do magick that reflects upon the past and helps us to not be attached to our desires and what we obtained in the full moons light.

Waning Crescent - The ideal time to bring something to an end, be it a bad habit, or the life of an enemy. The Waning Crescent is when the last light of the moon is poured out, culminating in the end of light and Yang Influence. There is nothing to fear, for the new moon is near at hand. The Waning Crescent is the best time to put into action your plan of attack against an enemy, stripping them of their defenses, as they will also be lower in Yang Energy to support them, and this Yin flow will benefit your efforts.

The Sun, the stars and planets – Many more billions of years ago, all the gas and dust that formed our solar system, the sun, asteroids, comets and other planets, all resided in the heart of a massive star somewhere else in the galaxy. A place that is lost to us, as scientists haven't yet quite figured out exactly where our star formed (it was ejected from its stellar nursery billions of years ago).

This old massive star exploded, and in the process created a nebula, a stellar nursery which condensed and formed our solar system, and a cluster of sibling suns, so in an important way, all the planets, and asteroids, and comets, and our Sun, are all interconnected by both causality and magick.

The positions of the planets and their relationship to us, one another and the sun also has an energetic influence over our world, though this influence may be much subtler, it is no less apparent to the sensitive sorcerer.

Indeed, the distant stars themselves hold similar importance, as they all formed out of the ashes of the same initial explosion… the big bang, let there be light!

Therefore, the very gods and demons themselves are said to be of these worlds, some of them thought to be the spirit of their respective worlds. For example, the spirit of earth is thought to be Gaia, the earth mother, the spirit of the 2nd world from the Sun is said to be Venus, Horus, or Lucifer.

At the very least these entities utilize them as powerful portals, sources and conduits for their energy and light and we need to be mindful of all these things in our magickal workings.

It is also important to note the significance of the Day and night cycle, some spirits are more potent in the day (including some so called "Demons"), some at night.

The summer solstice can be seen to be almost like a full moon on the solar scale, being filled with celebrations and the culmination of the winters efforts to create and build magick and mundane efforts. It is a time of abundance, fertility and joy. And the winter solstice can be seen like a new moon in the solar scale, an ideal time to begin things, a time when darkness has won, but the light is about to turn the tides. It is an optimal time for regeneration, renewal and self-reflection.

As stated, the Individual planets are also important, as each one of them is tied to the frequency of certain spirits. It should be noted that many people believe the spirits energy is somewhat influenced by what planetary gate it uses to reach us, if Lucifer (Venus) or another Venusian spirit uses Saturn as a planetary gate to reach us, we will get a different aspect of his (or her) nature, rather than if we conjure him when Venus is visible in the sky.

This is not a major concern for this system, or the initiate, and many masters do not worry about this overmuch, but it is a consideration to be aware of. As it can influence and empower your magick down the road.

However, it rarely causes any problems, unless you are attempting to go against the grain of the energies around you completely (trying to do something best suited to a New moon on the full moon).

When working with spirits that are known to have a planetary correspondence, in our magick we need to simply try to do our working with them at a time that corresponds to that planet being in the sky, and make sure we face it or at least acknowledge its symbolism in our ritual. Preferably when it is visible in the sky, or otherwise invoke its energy in the working for maximal effect if it is not the optimal time or location for it.

It is possible to become very well learned about the astrology and symbolism of the heavens, and I encourage anyone who is interested to do so, but It is beyond the scope of my skill to attempt to teach you astrology.

Eclipses – These are always of great importance, be they lunar or solar. Lunar Eclipses are far more common, usually happening every 1 to 3 years and is available to many people in the world equally, while solar eclipses can be many decades between them for a given location.

All eclipses are a time of tremendous change and potential for new beginnings and powerful initiations. All eclipses are transformative in the extreme.

In the case of a solar Eclipse this is a perfect synthesis of the Yang of the Sun, and the Yin of the moon, working together at once, and the ancients knew that the power of this event, harnessed for magick was of great significance.

Many cultures feared the event, and performed terrible sacrifices to bring the sun back, while others embraced it for other reasons relating to rebirth and victory over evil.

In ancient times it was almost always a sign of great evil having a temporary victory over good, and good eventually always triumphed as the light returned, and the darkness subsided.

Similarly, Lunar eclipses are always a perfect time to work with infernal demonic forces, and many other spirits, and I consider a Lunar Eclipse to be an ideal time to begin or end any lunar dedication pact with a spirit (working exclusively with a single spirit for one lunar month). In one of these dedication pacts, you agree to dedicate yourself fully to the spirit, who must also agree to work with you.

For the full 30 days, you will not work with any other spirit save those agreed upon by the pact (usually none).

When you are working with energy, take all these astronomical things into account, and feel free to research on your own to find what correspondences work for you. It does not require a complex understanding of astrology and astronomy to work magick but paying a little respect to the energy of the moon is a very easy and powerful way to work with the energy of the celestial spheres.

The Witching hour – Between 3 AM and 4 AM, the veil between worlds becomes thinnest. What this really means is that the barrier between your subjective and objective experience becomes thin, as there are fewer living souls around to influence your objective experience, and your subjective experience begins to take more objective hold over causality.

Most people in your area are asleep, and their minds are focused almost entirely on a subjective aspect of the Astral Plane, and no longer influencing objective material reality as strongly. Most animals of any significant intelligence are often daytime animals, and those animals which do come out at night are of a more Yin or spiritual aspect (cats, bats, many rodents, owls, etc.) and allow for a unique stillness in the vibration of the local environment.

In our system, the witching hour is the most useful time to attempt to contact spirits, and unless a spirit is strongly associated with daylight, it tends to be a time when spirits come to us with the most vivid manifestations.

Often our most prophetic and inspired dreams come to us at this time… and spirits will often come without needing to be called.

In my own home, the witching hour is when I get the most paranormal activity and poltergeists, particularly if there has been any kind of chaos or negative emotion in the house.

Some ways to capitalize upon this time are to wake up early, stay up late, or engage in sleep deprivation of at least 24 hours, then perform various magickal operations suitable to the night time and the witching hour in general.

There is tremendous magick potential in this time of day, more so (in the opinion of this author) than any other time.

Astral Travel, Invocation, channeling, possession and Evocation, scrying, and necromancy are all elevated during this time.

Yin and Yang

In Chinese mysticism, the concept of Yin and Yang has a complex, storied (and somewhat varied) meaning. To most westerners, Yin and Yang are thought of as a dualism, an idea of positive and negative, good and evil, light and dark.

That Yin must be bad, and Yang good, etc.

This is a very feeble understanding of these energies, and the deeper meaning of the symbolism of Yin and Yang. It is of course beyond the scope of this work to delve deeply into it, and there are far better scholars than I who could do so.

But let me set the record straight – Yin and Yang, when discussed together, should not be called Yin and Yang, or even Yin (space) Yang but YinYang without a space, because YinYang is really a singular force with a dialectic nature. A flow if you will.

YinYang should be treated as a wheel, not as two things.

When you want to turn it to the left, you need to pull down on the left side, push up on the right (or if doing it one handed, the wheel must move up on that right-hand side). Initially this makes it sound like they are in conflict or oppose one another. Instead, they both flow in the same direction.

In this sense, Yin could be the pulling down, and the Yang as pushing up. Even the symbolism of the YinYang is that of two objects chasing and swirling into one another.

At the centers of each of these dialectic forces, is a core piece of its opposite. And in a complete, animated sense, Yin doesn't just get chased by Yang, nor does it chase Yang, in the fullness of time, it BECOMES Yang, and Vice versa. Because a Pull is a push, and a push is a pull…

We can see this with the example of the wheel again, if we wish to turn it to the left, we need to pull down on the left side. But this pull BECOMES a push for everything in front of it on the wheel, and conversely, Yang becomes a PULL for everything behind it!

Remember this is ultimately just a symbolic model of a deep truth about reality. It would be a mistake to truly believe that there is an Energy called Yang. Or an energy called Yin (remember yin is not the absence of energy, it is rather a different kind of energy, a pull instead of a push, an exhale instead of an inhale).

Instead there is energy that has Yin nature, or Yang Nature. And taken at a whole, it is YinYang. Or YangYin.

Electromagnetism is a perfect example of this, and easily understood by most western minds… The positive and negative charge of particles leading to magnetism, light, and electricity.

We would call the negative pole of this magnet Yin, and the positive Yang. It is not an exact correspondence,

Electromagnetism ISN'T YinYang, but it has very clear YinYang nature.

When we work with magick, even as westerners, we can easily see that all actions, all outcomes, all cause and effect has this YinYang Nature, and is in fact the interplay between the 2 primordial furies, the first things to be selected by the mind… the idea of duality. Light and Dark, hot, and cold, up and down, male and female.

To a nondualist, these two opposites are not separate at all, they are instead one and the same thing, much like the push and pull of the hand on the wheel. They are the SAME thing, but seen either from 2 different perspectives, or from 2 extremes.

Hot is only hot, because it is warmer than cold. But both are temperature.

When we use magick then, we do not have to be masters of Chinese medicine or anything like that, but we should pay careful attention to the YinYang nature of energy and this becomes very important when working with our breathing, and physical and visual energy manipulation

Trust that your subconscious already knows or understands more about this than you know that you do, and that just by reading this, it is sparking a chain of events in your subconscious that will no doubt lead to a better fundamental working of magick.

To work with YinYang energy in magick, consider the next several sections VERY carefully, and put them into practice with as much fervor as your Altered state meditations.

We will discuss the nature of yin and Yang more in the section on elements.

Breath Control

Controlling your breathing can be exquisitely important for energy work and manipulation. Many people do not realize how holistic magick really is. They are unaware of how the way our body moves and how much energy it has, can be directly correlated to our spiritual energy and astral body's movements.

In our practice we will be borrowing the breathing methods used in certain qigong traditions to enervate our physical bodies and our astral bodies. These practices are not simply useful in magick, but also in everyday life. If you are tired and need to wake up, it is time to use Yang breathing, if you are suffering insomnia and need to power down, use Yin breathing. If you are seeking better health in general, practice yin/yang balanced breathing.

In Magick Yang Breathing is best used for charging and empowering a spell or entering intense focus or mania. Yin breathing is best used to enter deeper trances, or to come down from a particularly intense ritual or manifestation. While Yin/yang breathing can be useful to center yourself in basic meditation.

Some of the principles here apply to ALL our practice in magick, each type of breathing when done intentionally is great for our magick and our health.

How to breathe – For the purposes of our practice, A breath should fill up about 70% of your lung capacity, never try to force your lungs full to 100%. Likewise, an exhale should only breathe out to a comfortable level, do not force the last of your air out.

In traditional qigong and many other cultures, there are a lot of elaborate things that can be done to alter the act of breathing. For example, breathe in through the nose, out through the mouth, or in through the mouth and out through the nose, or both in and out through the same orifice, or even to close one nostril at a time to change how the flow of air influences the mind.

You may be interested to know that our own body shifts which nostril is dominant about once per hour. In other words, at say noon, you will be breathing more through your right nostril than your left, by 1 PM you might be breathing through the left. This cycle is predictable, and some ancient peoples used this to help them keep time.

For our purposes simply breathing in through the nose and out through the mouth is enough.

Next, to be doing this correctly, you need to make sure that when you inhale, you expand your belly and feel the air filling your lungs and pressing out your belly area.

When you exhale, your belly should be sucked in like you are trying to look less overweight. At first breathing this way can be tiring. But just doing this by itself can have health benefits.

If you practice neutral yin/yang breathing in meditation and suck in and out your gut as described it can add tremendously to your calm state of mind.

YinYang/Neutral breathing – This is simply a neutral equal style of breathing. Most healthy people do a simple form of this every day, of course most of us breathe too shallowly, and with uneven rhythm. Thus, practicing YinYang breathing can help us to breathe more healthily outside of our practice in our everyday life. Proper YinYang breathing is to breathe in an equal amount in and out, filling our lungs to 70% capacity, and using our abdomen (at least a little bit) to expand and contract with each breath (most people use their rib cage to breathe more, resulting in shallower breathing).

Doing this correctly has a very powerful grounding and centering effect on our awareness, and often balances our energy so we are neither too awake, nor too sleepy. It is fine for all mental states.

It is a good practice to begin all magickal workings by focusing on this breathing through meditation and performing it for a minute or two while you collect yourself in preparation for your ritual.

Yang breathing - Yang breathing is when we are focusing on building up holistic energy and is done by focusing our attention and effort on the act of intentionally inhaling slower, enriching our blood and energy body with more air and energy, and making our exhale shorter and really expelling the Yin energy quickly.

Yang energy is obviously very useful and important in ritual for building up personal power and projecting it into our working.

I often use Yang breathing when drawing energy into myself, such as from a crystal, or target for my vampiric tendencies.

Yang breathing is also very useful when in deep focus in ritual. But can also be used in open mind trance or empty mind for more intense visions or spontaneous thoughts.

Use either the 2 to 1 method, or the 2,4,1 method described later.

Yin Breathing - This is the opposite of Yang breathing in that instead of building up Yang Energy, we are building up Yin Energy. Yin energy is like a natural depressant and can help us calm down when we are feeling anxiety, but it can also help us in magickal ritual by helping us calm down after an intense working and allowing us to release our intent and break away from the ritual.

Yin breathing is also what I use for charging objects with my intention, essentially pushing my Yang Intention out into an object by breathing out into them.

We can have a much deeper open or empty mind trance while in the Yin breathing state than in the Yang breathing state, as the yin breathing State allows us to enter a deeper state of trance, bordering more on sleep. This is fertile soil for astral visions and spirit communication.

Use either the 2 to 1 method, or the 2,4,1 method described later.

CAUTION – It is possible to cause great discomfort or even physical injury by taking these breathing methods to the extreme and practicing them for too long. Yang breathing can feel amazing, but it will unbalance and burn you out. You may become manic, creating hyperventilation or excessive euphoria and dizziness.

Yin Breathing can be used to slow and even stop the heart with extreme practice, and long term can lead to depression and lack of motivation. ALWAYS practice neutral breathing to center and balance your energies after any breathing exercise so that it becomes habit.

Only use Yin or Yang breathing situationally to help you regulate your energy, or to build up energy of one type or another for magick operation.

Remember, both yin and yang are the same kind of energy, just with opposite polarity and effects, like the north pole and south pole of a magnet. Yin Energy isn't the absence of Energy, and Yang energy isn't just MORE energy though they can be experienced in this way to some degree.

2 to 1 method - The most basic form of yin or yang breathing is the 2 to 1 method. Simply stated, either your inhalation, or your exhalation, will be a multiple of 2 seconds, while your opposite breath will be a multiple of 1 second.

So, Yang breathing will be to inhale for 2, 4, 6, 8, or 10 seconds, while your exhalation will be 1, 2, 3, 4, or 5 seconds.

The goal is to simply change the way you breathe in and out so that either the inhale or the exhale is done quickly, while the other is done slowly.

Yang breathing would mean a longer inhale, with a shorter exhale. While Yin would be a longer Exhale, and a shorter Inhale.

So, at first do not stress out if you can't correctly keep count of how long you are breathing in, and how long you are breathing out, just remember, Yang = longer inhale, Yin = longer Exhale.

2, 4, 1 method – This is a more intense version of the standard breathing method and leads to much more profound energetic effects. You can put yourself to sleep easily by using this method with Yin breathing or wake yourself up with Yang Breathing.

The idea is like the 2 to 1 method, in that you will inhale or exhale for multiples of 2 seconds, then hold the breath for a multiple of 4 seconds, then release or inhale the breath for a multiple of 1 second.

Typically, it is unwise to hold the breath for longer than 20 seconds regardless of which type (yin or Yang) you are practicing. So typically, you will in/exhale for 2/4/6/8/10 seconds, hold for 4/8/12/16/20 seconds, in/exhale for 1/2/3/4/5 seconds.

It doesn't matter really at first how long you can hold the breath, not everyone is healthy enough to hold their breath for 20 seconds while breathing in this method (it is actually harder to maintain for long periods than it sounds, especially with the holding of the gut muscles). And people with lung disorders may be virtually incapable of going beyond level 1 (2/4/1). Let alone reaching the highest (10/20/5).

If all you can do is 2/4/1 breathing, you will still benefit and increase your magick potency by a great deal.

Which to use – Either of the breathing methods are appropriate for magick, while the 2/4/1 method can lead to more intense felt effects, that does not automatically translate into more effects in magick as the intensity of the effect can distract you from the working of your magick and ritual.

I would suggest, as it is my practice, to mostly use the 2 to 1 method in most of your rituals and only use the 2/4/1 method for the most important and intense parts of a ritual, or for the cool down while you enter the Empty state to release your intent.

Keep in mind that to a skeptic, all you are doing is playing with your blood oxygen levels and this is creating a very mundane shift in your biology and is not magick. What they do not understand is that old hermetic wisdom - So within, so without, As below, So above.

Again, understanding the Holistic Trinity of self is the key…

Vocal Projection, Vibration, and Intonation

Using our voices in magick is a key component of the holistic practice of magick and we must be able to vocalize not only in the material plane, but so that our astral body vibrates and intones a powerful booming echo in the astral plane. We can technically separate these two, and easily speak without an astral aspect, and intone on the astral without making a sound in the material. But when we do both together at once… the effect can be staggeringly potent.

We need to make sure we understand that magick, being a holistic art form, requires us to integrate elements of the mind, body and spirit together in one united action. And using our voices is one of the most holistic things we can possibly do.

Intonation in magick requires the ability to focus our minds and our imaginations, our spirits, and our bodies on the act of resonating our intent with every fiber of our being.

The better we can harmonize and resonate the physical sound with the mental sound with the astral sound… the more we align our intention, with the action we are taking with the totality of being… the more powerfully we cause manifestation to occur.

The specific words we might use are secondary, or even unimportant, the resonance with our intent is what matters most.

The easiest way to learn to do this, is to simply practice imagining saying things in your mind so loudly that they echo off the distant landscapes of the Astral. Getting your conscious mind used to the idea that your voice can boom in the spirit world like a giant gong or horn, or clap of thunder. You can even imagine your voice booming as if thunder down a mountainside, and all the spirits and demons and gods below picking up their heads and hearing you.

While you imagine yourself doing this, you need to match the sound in your mind with a sound you generate by your body.

The easiest way to do this at first is to use some method of generating a musical tone. Use a simple AUM or OM Mantra and try to harmonize your voice with a resonant tone in the real world. At the same time imagine that ohm is resonating with a similar tone in the astral world.

This can be difficult to describe until experienced, but you will feel your entire being, your mind, body and soul vibrate in resonance with the sound.

We can use an artificial sound (such as from a singing bowl) to harmonize with, because the human mind instinctively knows how to harmonize with sounds. Even if we are tone def, we still know what it feels like to try. Of course, the closer we can get to vocal resonance with the physical sound, the better and easier it will be.

I personally prefer to use a sound that is in the lower middle of my vocal range, something comfortable, something where my voice has power, without having to force it out. An easy way to do this, is to find a way to play a musical scale and sing or hum along with it till you find the sound that is both easy for you to resonate with and feels easy to do with authority.

You can create this base sound any way you like, though I prefer more natural means such as singing bowls, guitars, or sounds already in the environment, there is absolutely nothing wrong with using artificial sources of the sound. One time I entered a deep meditative intonation trance just by resonating with a noisy air vent that made a rather musical hum.

It is important to NOT use (both) Headphones for this practice, you need to feel the resonance through your entire body, and it is difficult to harmonize and resonate with the sounds of your headphones (therefore many people in the music industry only have one side of their headphones on to monitor when they record themselves.

This practice is useful for three reasons, it can get you used to resonating in the astral realm, can help you improve your musical singing, and is a form of meditation all rolled into one.

Exercise - Enter your ritual space, it is good to get into the habit of performing your magickal actions and study in your ritual space.

Dim the lighting, use candles or daylight if desired and Light some incense, again just to set the mood, any fragrance you enjoy is fine, the idea is to create a relaxing atmosphere.

Begin by calming yourself and entering an open trance state. Breathe and center yourself, and switch on your music player, or begin using your singing bowl to create a tone of sound you can harmonize with.

When you feel the time is right, take a comfortable breath in, and begin to hum, or sing the word OM/Aum. At first you will likely just feel like you are singing, but I want you to really focus on how the sound FEELS in your body. I want you to really look for a point when your body and your voice are resonating with the sound.

When you feel like you have got this locked in as good as you can get it, begin to imagine yourself in the astral realm, and imagine the sound of your voice beginning to resonate with the astral space around you.

You may begin to see or feel things in the astral realm vibrate to match and resonate and harmonize with your inner and outer voice.

When this first begins to happen, you can experience a kind of euphoria, and deep sense of peace, or conversely strong energetic arousal.

Continue to do this for as long as you like, feel free to do this with any other words, or sounds you like.

You can even do this with your favorite music, even if you are a terrible singer, the spirits will not mind, your astral voice is always angelic.

When we use this method to sing music, it can add a great deal of presence to your performance, if you are able to do this on stage, those people who are sensitive in the audience will have an even more moving experience. This is one of the things that separates a great singer, with a legendary one.

It should come as NO surprise that sorcerers often SING to spirits and SINGING is a valid part of magick. When we chant, or speak the occult poetry of a ritual, we sometimes sing instead, and this can have incredible effects on the energy of the ritual. Keeping in mind, it is not even important to sing with a given melody or rhythm as if singing a song, simply be melodic and fluid, even if utterly random!

All spirits are fond of singing, and some are moved by singing a great deal. King Paimon for example is very fond of song and talented singers should always consider making offerings of music and singing to him.

Energy Projection: Visualization

Visualization is a key skill in magick, while it is not required for your visualizations to be vivid (some people in fact CAN'T visualize at all), it is important to try to visualize magick.

This can take on many different forms, from visualizing spirits, the astral realm, the outcome of a spell or ritual, or the very energy we manipulate.

This latter part is the focus of this section, the act of manipulating energy, but SEEING it in our minds eye, and thus with practice... our astral eye. And what we "see" or know to be in our astral eye, is REAL in the astral world, and thus can have powerful impact on the material world when coupled with the right holistic actions and other methods of energy projection.

It is important to know that you have total control over what your magick and your energy looks like. To many people who have seen it in its true symbolic nature, it generally appears like a glowing mist, spherical/egg shaped aura of light, or high energy plasma. This glow is normally the colors of the rainbow depending on our moods, and energy vibration, or simply a ghostly white.

But we can easily imagine it to be any color, texture or kind of energy we want. It can look and act like fire, wind, electricity, it can flow like water, or harden and crystalize like ice. And these visualizations can be very valid in how they influence your magick.

For example - Visualizing Fire, and projecting fire energy into an object can charge it with this elemental force, and then be used in magick ritual or on the astral plane. Of course, you could make this fire, Red, blue, Yellow, Green, or even black if you wanted, any color is possible. You can even imagine it to be icy cold, or wet. As absurd as it sounds all these nuances and differences can in fact change the nature of the energy you are working with in the astral realm.

I have occasionally told people that what I see in the astral plane when I do magick, is a lot like what our pop culture tells us magick should look like, I hurl fireballs, shoot lightning bolts, I emanate power and force. I do Tai Qi and Qigong style movements and the gusts of wind or energy are blasted from my arms. I raise my hand to the sky and clench my fist and a terrible storm appears.

The difference between our imagination and the Astral Realm is subtle, because whatever we can imagine will become real in the astral plane, whether we experience it as such or not.

Let it be said that "controlling" our thoughts and imagination is a key fundamental skill every sorcerer should seek to master.

Again, it is my strong belief that Visualization should be coupled with more physical and auditory energy manipulation, in other words you should see, hear, and FEEL the energy, not merely see it.

Be sure to try to use good breathing practice, and decide which form of breathing (yin, Yang, or YinYang) might be useful. Or just breathe normally if it is too hard for you to focus on too many things at once.

Visualization is a very simple technique and requires almost no specific format for practice. Simply visualize the energy in your mind's eye. If you couple this visualization with the focused altered state (as discussed earlier), you will already be moving spiritual energy around on some level, it is not yet a holistic act and its effects will be limited, but there are many stories of how visualization alone can create manifestations. We will discuss this more after we examine the sensation of moving energy.

Another aspect of visualization is to enter a deep focused state and visualize the outcome of your magick, visualize the manifestation of your desire with such vividness, that you can see, hear, taste and touch what it would be like the have the object of your desire.

If you are doing a spell for money, imagine that money in your hands, imagine its weight, it's texture, everything about it. Imagine what it will feel like to have that money and imagine that the rest of the world is shifting to make that happen right now.

Energy projection — Physical

The ability to feel and project energy in ritual is one of the most important things a sorcerer can learn to do early on. The good news is, it isn't as difficult as some people might think. We do it all the time, but we often do not realize it. Every time we move part of our body, we are in fact moving energy around. The trick is to become consciously aware of that and learning to manipulate and project it intentionally outside the body. Astral/magickal energy should not be confused for mundane physical energy. When you project heat/fire in the astral world, it is not actual heat, or flame, though you may indeed feel warmth, or it might cause your body to grow warm and flushed.

There are some who claim to be able to move objects, light them on fire, or do other things with this energy, and while I cannot disprove this, I would caution anyone from getting obsessed with this as if this is the point of energy manipulation.

In our practice of magick, we are not seeking parlor trick telekinesis (though it would be nice), we are instead seeking a much more practical, and obtainable goal of manipulating reality overall.

A brief word about Telekinesis - I am not going to say that telekinesis is impossible, I have had my own very limited success in this regard. The closest I have come was to have some very interesting experiences with what are called Psi-Wheels, or chi-Wheels. The problem is, it is not a reliable or easily repeatable thing.

Making a psi-wheel change direction speed up, slow down and stop are all things I have done many times! Sometimes very easily, often causing me to get excited and lose focus. Or other times, despite doing everything the right way with the right "feeling," the same way I did it before… I can't get it to budge.

Other times it doesn't matter what I do with my mind, hands, or what I feel, or how distracted or tired I am, it just works. Like the stars must be in some random alignment I can't predict.

Of course, practice usually makes perfect (perfect success or failure if you are practicing the wrong way), but it is my opinion, like everything in magick, there is a rational explanation for this, and thus it may not ever be something I can prove is being done, nor will it be likely to ever reach super hero level of capability.

Thus, for this, and many other reasons, psi-Wheels have been largely debunked by science or determined to be inconclusive depending on who you ask.

I believe true telekinesis cannot be conclusively proven or disproven at this time – Also, at the time of this writing certain tests (like using a microbalance to test for minute changes in weight of an object that might be a result of psychic ability) are yet to be performed or performed in very limited fashion.

It is important for you to know that part of the reason it is so hard to test for these things is because people have the wrong idea of what it can do.

The moment you believe you can move things with your magick, and try to prove it, someone will come along and create an experiment which seeks to isolate the magick as the cause of the movement. But we as a species do not have a working definition of magick in the scientific sense, so how would they test for it?

They will claim that air currents are causing the test object to move, and that means it can't be magick. Even though magick could be using the air currents to move the object! Why should magick break the laws of nature just to do a parlor trick?

So, the scientist will seek to isolate the magick by enclosing the object in glass. And the skeptic will smugly be proven right, that it is impossible for the psychic to then move the object.

All this is doing is forcing the psychic to pass TWO tests. First to get through the solid glass barrier with their telekinetic forces, and second move the object.

Thus, it is either impossible to isolate the test so that it can be proven that it is the psychics mind/energy-body that made the wheel turn, or the act of isolating the test would also create a need for the claimants ability to penetrate solid objects, thereby making it two tests, and thus being unable to prove or disprove anything.

What is interesting is, in ANY other field of scientific inquiry this flaw in experimentation would not result in science automatically ruling it out as plausible or worthy of further research. Only when it comes to fringe sounding claims does this somehow count as debunking and proof for the lack of magick of psychic ability…

There are open minded scientists out there who would be willing to entertain the idea of other kinds of tests or even themselves believe in magick.

Still, it is virtually impossible to secure the funding to do the research because the proof would require more than simply testing, it would require coming up with a test that could work without creating a flawed result. To say nothing for the need for a repeatable experiment.

How many times do you think a psychic has successfully performed a psychic act, only to have that act debunked because they could not repeat it like a machine?

Magick is not like a machine. It does not follow the normal patterns of cause and effect.

Magick is more like a behavior of an intelligent energy or force than a mindless energy that simply responds to our manipulations in predictable ways like electricity does.

And this brings us back to the point/topic – When you are learning to manipulate spiritual energy, there is very little about it that is mechanical, it should never be imagined functioning exactly like electricity, even though it can look, feel, and move like it.

Yet at the same time, there can be many similarities, it can flow, it can be stored, it can be channeled through conductive materials, it can have polarity. Yet at the same time, it can betray every one of those similarities and simply do what it likes as well.

When you learn to feel spiritual pressure or spiritual magnetism or Qi/chi you can be forgiven to think you are feeling an actual physical force, because it will feel exactly like air pressure or magnetism.

Once you can feel your own Energy/qi, with a little practice, (often on the first attempt) we can feel the pressure of objects outside of ourselves. You may even notice that distance doesn't have to be as much of a factor as it would seem to be if it was a real material energy. I have sometimes noticed that if I am too close to the object I cannot in fact feel it! That is because I am already within its energy field.

Like a hand that is in still water, it is easier to feel the surface of the water when the hand enters, than the water when the hand is already immersed.

But it is also for this reason that we often need to move our hands because like a hand in water, we CAN feel the pressure of the water we are immersed in if we move the right way.

It is important here remind you that this force and pressure you are feeling is not a physical force or feeling in the classical sense. All you are doing on is pressing on the objects spiritual pressure, and manipulating that, not the object itself.

IMHO, this isn't because you or I am not "strong" enough. Or if it IS because we are not strong enough, then nobody else is either.

It is because this force/pressure is not directly tied to the material, this is ASTRAL force. Though it can influence the material object, that influence is more about intent not actual movement, or material world energy.

If you charge an object with heat on the astral level, you won't likely heat it up, instead you are charging it with the spiritual/astral form of fire and heat.

With continued practice you can even project this energy across a distance and feel it. For example, by pointing your finger at the palm of the other hand a few feet apart, you can trace shapes on your palm and feel it plainly as if you are in fact tickling that spot on your hand with the tip of your finger.

Of course, the skeptic will claim this is more psychosomatic, but this is just a misunderstanding of what is going on. It is indeed a kind of psychosomatic effect, but that doesn't invalidate it! It simply means it is a personal subjective experience, not easily translated into an objective one.

I have also found that this subjective experience CAN be made objective when you have two sufficiently sensitive people doing the same thing, they can feel each other's qi/energy.

Do not fret if you cannot feel other people's energy, or even the energy of other objects, the barest minimum is to feel your own energy and pressure and be able to move it around and feel it enter other objects.

You can start doing this, just by imagining what it would feel like, and practice as if your imagination was real. So long as you can feel your own energy, you will begin to feel the energy moving and being projected by your astral body.

Here are a few exercises you can do to learn the basics of this method of energy manipulation. I will focus on the sensation of spiritual pressure as that is the easiest one for many people to really feel and notice. Heat is also common, but heat is too easily mistaken as it can come just from the proximity of your hands.

Pressure is much more reliable in my experience for the beginner.

Qi-ball – In this foundational exercise you will meditate on creating and feeling a "Qi ball." Once you can feel this Qi ball, you can experiment with making it larger, smaller, and moving it around in your hands. You will also learn how to reabsorb the ball of energy. Reabsorbing is not vitally important, but it is a good practice and you will have less wasted astral energy (which can cause fatigue, or other issues in your astral environment).

This exercise will make all the others possible as all the other exercises are based on the raw ability to create a Qi ball and know that it is there.

Before we begin a few facts about Qi balls.

- Qi balls are ASTRAL constructs, they are ALMOST entirely without material substance, however, they can take up physical space. And influence things in subtle ways. For example, it is possible to build up a Qi ball of enough density that you can "throw" it at a candle flame, and this balls density can help the gust of material air to stay coherent enough to snuff out the candle from some distance. This does not violate the laws of physics in the slightest, as it is little more than a subtle way of maximizing the "air cannon" effect you can sometimes make with your hands when the conditions are correct. (Ex. The Bernoulli effect)
- Qi balls are variable in size, regardless of density or how much energy you pump into them. You can squeeze and compress them or open them up and expand them without making them more, or less, powerful.
- Qi balls can be moved, projected and thrown, or they can remain where you create them, and they can be attached to your astral body.
- A Qi ball can also simply be an extension of your astral boundary, it is possible to not create a Qi ball, but instead to inflate your personal astral form in such a way that it can feel like you have a ball between your hands, but you are really just touching your astral body.
- A Qi ball can be ANY shape.
- Qi (氣) literally translates as air, and thus Qi is very closely related to breathing and the ambient energy of air. But it should never be confused for actual air or wind energy.
- A Qi ball can be thought of as a kind of container and can be imbued with any other energy you see fit, any emotion, or any intention you see fit.
- Since a Qi ball can be filled with any kind of intent, energy, emotion or idea that you desire, great care should be taken in what you do with these objects. Enough negative intent can cause actual problems for anyone who receives it and absorbs it. Though it DOES take a significant amount of effort and intent, it is possible, so it is best to never direct a negative Qi form at anyone unless you mean to do them harm.

Creation of a Qi ball – this is a simple exercise and once you do it a few times, you will just instinctively make them whenever you want.

To do this the right way, with the best practices, it is a good idea to engage in Yang Breathing for a short time, say a multiple of 3, 6 or 9 times, and build up a strong flow of energy. Not so much that you are manic and distracted, but you should feel alert, and your senses should be open. Or if you are practiced and want to fully enrich yourself, continue Yang breathing while you are rubbing your hands in the next step.

Next, clap your hands 3 times to get the blood flowing, and then rubbing your hands together gently and slowly for half a minute or so. Start firm, pressing your hands together with a little bit of force, though not enough to be uncomfortable. Then slowly soften the pressure until your hands are only gently skimming one another. This will cause you to focus more on the subtle sensations of the hands, instead of the strong ones.

There is no wrong mental state, but I have found the focused mind is best for creation of the ball, and open or empty is best for sensing it and manipulating it.

At some point when you feel you are ready to try it (don't make your hands sore from doing this too long), Enter YinYang breathing, or Yin breathing and take both of your hands and hold them roughly 8-12 inches apart, at a point near your abdomen or solar plexus, or right in front of your chin.

Imagine you are blowing or pushing or pouring energy from your solar plexus or other nearby energy center into the space between your hands.

It doesn't really matter which energy center you use but know that these are the approximate locations of the Dantian energy centers of the body, or the chakras, and this correspondence often make it easier to work on making the Qi-Ball.

Remember to focus your intent on creating and visualizing a Qi-ball form, you can even intone the mantra Ohm, or Aum to give it added holistic energy.

Next, like a performing street mime, start slowly pressing your hands together with a slight waving motion as if you are holding a balloon between your hands and squeezing it gently. For some people this requires a rather large movement, almost like waving the hands, for others it is just a subtle movement.

Explore the space between your hands and pushing energy into it. By using Yin breathing you are ridding yourself of yang energy so this can be tiring, if so, switch to yang, or YinYang breathing and center your energy again. You can still make the ball while yang breathing.

If you still feel nothing after a trying for a short time, change the distance of your hands, bringing them closer together or further apart.

This movement is important because the boundary of the ball can vary until you learn to control it and finding the edge of the ball is what you will feel the most strongly.

As you are searching for the boundary, inhale and imagine when you exhale you are blowing magick pressure into an invisible ball in the space between your hands, making it stronger, firmer, more solid.

It is my experience that it is harder (at first) to create a small focused ball, than a large balloon. I have seen people struggle to be able to make anything smaller than beach ball sized Qi-ball.

The size of the ball doesn't matter very much in magick, so long as you can feel it and make it and move it around... It can still be potent.

Be patient if you do not feel anything, and do not be afraid to make many attempts before you sense the ball. It is a subtle sensation at first that can be easily missed, but once you feel it, it can become quite powerful, almost to the point where you feel like it is hard for you to move your hands together until you push through some kind of invisible barrier or force field.

This is exactly what a Qi-Ball feels like. Like a flexible balloon force field.

You will find that this exercise might cause you to feel fatigued, or that you cannot do it more than a few times a day, as if you are out of magick qi-ball gas or something.

This is perfectly normal, but with practice it won't become as big an issue.

Remember, when you let go of the ball, it will begin to dissipate and vanish and can be hard to find or get back. If you are trying to create a ball and leave it somewhere and pick it up again, this is entirely possible, but remember, it will disperse soon after making it.

So, if you wish to retain more of your energy you need to reabsorb it into yourself. This is done by finding the surface of the ball, and literally sucking it back into you while breathing in through your mouth like you are breathing in the air out of a deflating balloon. As you inhale bring your hands together, taking care to try and feel the perimeter of the ball as long as you can, you will find it shrinks rapidly then disappears.

You have successfully recycled a large portion of the balls energy and can reuse it. AGAIN, be careful what intent you put into the ball, if you fill it with dark thoughts of doubt and worry that you might not find or make the ball right, you will be taking that back into yourself. If you filled it with such negative thoughts it is better to project it elsewhere, or just let it disperse on its own.

Once you can create the qi-ball, try playing with it, try making it bigger or smaller, try moving it around in your hands. Try moving one hand and not the other and see what that feels like. (hint: It will feel almost like you are pushing a balloon into your other hand!).

There is no better way to practice this than just doing it. Just play with the ball till you grow bored or tired.

Once you can reliably move it around in your hands and change its size, it's time to try sending the ball into another object like a crystal or candle and seeing if you can sense and interact with it there.

Sensing an objects energy boundary and interacting with it – This is exactly like sensing your own qi ball, but instead of making one between your hands and feeling it. You are going to attempt to feel and find the boundary of another object's energy body.

Keep in mind, it is possible to feel the energy of an object, even if your hand is not near it, but it is best to be within a close enough proximity to be certain the energy you are feeling and interacting with, isn't something else getting in the way.

Once you can find it and feel it, you are going to attempt to modify it with your own energy, pushing more pressure into it, or deflating it and absorbing it into yourself. Note that inanimate objects do not normally CREATE energy of their own just by being an object, instead they collect and emit it from the environment, they ARE spiritual pressure manifest in the physical world.

The energy comes from the interplay of empty spaces and full spaces in the totality of reality itself (the Void).

In physical science most energy we deal with in our lives is the result of a temperature gradient, a hot and a cold spot creating a flow or pressure that can be harnessed by life or natural processes to do work. Or the interplay of positive and negative electromagnetism to power our electronics.

In the spiritual world, it is YinYang energy, and this is represented in the physical world by the Empty spaces and the full spaces that create energetic flow. Of course, the more we zoom in and look, the more we realize, that there is no "fullness" to anything, everything is empty, and hollow. What we interact with is a force field of energy… IE PRESSURE, this is because SPACE is really all there is, and all solid objects and manifestations of will are just solid forms of PRESSURE.

Like Temperature being hot and cold, space can be full and empty. Space can have more, or less localized PRESSURE. And this PRESSURE is ultimately spiritual in nature.

In our world, life is one of the greatest collectors and emitters of this and most other forms of energy. You are not mere cold dark matter; you are literally a power plant of both physical and spiritual energy and pressure!

So, if you are trying to feel the energy of an object and are getting nothing, but are confident that you can feel this energy, you may need to charge it, and what better way than to charge it with our own Spiritual pressure and intention?

Charging an object - Charging an object with energy can be done in many ways, by leaving it on your altar overnight and asking the spirits to charge it, leaving it out in the sun or moonlight for some time.

Or directly charging it with your own energy and intent. I find that directly charging it has the best control over the result, while letting spirits charge an object for you is not always up to you, but often results in more palpable energy in the object.

Some objects will interact with this energy charge in different ways.

Candles for example can be charged with your intention and your energy and will retain it for a long time. Especially if used in candle magick with inscriptions, sigils, and oil-based dressings. When the candle burns, the wax melts, and flows into the wick, where the flame consumes the oil of the candle and releases the magickal intention you charged it with into the world, becoming a kind of gateway for your astral will and intent to enter the material world.

They are most useful because they utterly release the energy they are charged with when expended and create an interface for the astral and the material world.

The color of the candle is symbolic but is resonant with your intent. It has only marginal effect, but it is best to use the right candle color for the chosen application.

Incense is another example of this same principle, but has other significances as the wood, resin and oils that are burned are of sacred origin, and spirits are drawn to incense. Furthermore, certain incenses have a specific resonance of their own, more so than even candle color, so while some incense can be used for many things, it is best to select incense based on their correspondences when possible.

A stick of incense can be charged, much like a candle, and release the intent into the spirit world. It is an age-old custom for many cultures to pray into a stick of incense, then burning the incense to carry the prayer to the spirit world.

Crystals are also similar, but are more like batteries and prisms, they can absorb spiritual energy and expel/radiate it in different frequencies and effects. They can be charged, or just left alone to modulate the energy that goes into them emitting it naturally over time, much in the same way it would change the color of light if you place the crystal on top of a light source.

Unlike candles and incense, crystals do not normally create the same kind of a gateway between the astral and the physical world, that doesn't mean they do not influence the material world, and they do act as gates, but this is more of a gate through which you can perceive and influence the astral world. Again, crystals are more like spiritual prisms and batteries, and their influences are subtler and more mental, emotional and spiritual. But they also do not ever wear out… some even get stronger with use and age.

Also, Crystals will work without you doing anything to them, they naturally absorb the energy in the environment and transmute it like a prism into the vibrational frequency of the crystal.

For example, if you pump all your negative energy into a piece of Obsidian, it will simply absorb it, and align/reflect it back as neutral or positive healing and protective energy. Despite its scary black appearance, it is not dark or evil at all.

Once you can feel the energy of an object, you can manipulate it, you can move it around, you can alter its frequency or intent, or fill the object with your own energy.

This is a simple matter of feeling and imagining your intent or elemental energy to be flowing into the object's own energy field.

I often imagine this as if the object is glowing brighter and brighter with my energy and intent until it becomes blinding and radiates this intent, I push more and more energy into the object by blowing out with my mouth and feeling the energy flowing into the objects energy field and being compressed down into it, making the objects energy field firmer and more dense.

Another way to feel this is like a spinning object that gets faster and faster when you blow on it. As you breathe out imagine your energy flowing into the object and making it "rev up" and spin faster and faster till it reaches a crescendo and can't get any louder or high pitched, at this point it should have a blinding light, and you know it's as charged as you are capable of doing it.

When I feel I have charged the object with enough energy. I stop and use the object as intended.

Depending on the nature of the object and its circumstances, it can retain this energy for quite some time, but it can also be necessary to refuel it every so often, or even very often.

Do not forget that a charged object has a potent part of you within it, and should be treated with respect, if not treated as sacred. Never let anyone you do not trust interact with, or obtain such an object, they can use it to do terrible things to you, even without knowing they are doing it.

Crystals are generally the exception; they transmute our energy into the energy of the crystal. It is only if you intentionally create a spiritual tether to the object that someone could use that crystal for, or against you spiritually.

That doesn't mean a crystal cannot be charged with negative intent and then used against you, rather it means the energy you give to a crystal becomes the crystals charge, and it's connection to you is diminished, or even utterly wiped away.

You can CLEAR an object of its charge, or drain it, by reversing the process. Encounter the object's energy body and inhale as you feel the energy grow softer and less solid, imagine the internal spinning engine winding down as you breathe and pull the energy and intention into you.

This can be very useful, for example when working with crystals, if we are feeling we need a certain kind of emotional or spiritual energy, we can hold a stone we have just charged with energy, and after giving the stone a short time to process and transmute the energy we pumped into it, we can drink/pull/breathe it back into ourselves.

Of course, we do not always want to drink in this energy like this if it is from a dangerous source or negative. In those cases, we can use various methods to clear and cleanse the object instead.

This can be done by fumigating the object with sacred incense smoke (sage is the most common), washing in clean, moving cold water (Clean Tap water works in a pinch, but it is preferable to use natural water, such as RECENTLY collected rain, or river water, but not pond or puddle water), or focusing our intention in a banishing ritual such as the Align and Clear method explained in the pathworking section (simply focus your intent on clearing and aligning the object rather than a given space).

Tracing patterns on the other hand – This is a useful practice as it can help you refine your sensitivity and your sense of control by creating more refined energetic objects that do not have to be large blobs or balls or force fields, but can be pinpoint accurate and focused, and they can remain a part of you as well.

This can further show you that you do not need to be touching a target object to interact with it energetically. We can reach out with literally tendrils and tentacles of energy, or even fully realized extensions of our body, making hands, arms, or other appendages to reach out with our awareness and at least sense, if not interact with energy more remotely.

It has been my experience that this is both nonlocal (time and distance almost doesn't matter at all in terms of making contact), except, the closer and more aligned you are in time and space to the object the more visceral and energetic the interaction is.

For our purposes in magick we will focus on objects that are present in our environment at the same time we are,

within 2 or 3 yards at most, and preferably less than a foot or two away.

You can of course reach out as described in the last section to an object and feel its energy, even if you do not reach out with your hand.

But it can also be useful to experiment by doing this to your own body. That is, not simply feeling a pressure ball between your hands, but draw and trace things on one of your hands by projecting your spiritual pressure and energy through your hand or fingertips.

Doing this follows the same initial procedures as before, except this time, you will hold your hands closer together, and put your index fingers approximately 1 centimeter, to 3 inches apart, so that the tips of your finger become like the palms of your hand.

Focus your awareness on the tips of your finger and imagine energy flowing between your fingertips. You might even see with your astral eye white ectoplasmic energy, electricity arcs, or plasma like in one of those novelty plasma balls.

When you have a clear sense that there is energy arcing between your fingers, carefully move your hands and fingers around, bring them close together, and further apart, also experiment with other directions, left and right, up and down, all while pushing energy into your fingertips.

If you can sense a Qi-Ball from the last exercise, this should be fairly easy for you to feel between your fingers, you should feel the connection, the flow of energy.

Now that you have tuned into that sensation, become aware that one of your fingers will be the emitter, and the other hand is the receiver.

Begin to draw or trace shapes in the air near the receiving hand with the emitting hand and try to feel the fingertip on the palm of your hand. Experiment from different distances, and see where you lose contact, or where you feel the most tingling or pressure.

Realistically, there is no limit as this is your energy body you are interacting with, and you should ultimately be able to sense this even with your hands spread several feet apart.

This exact technique and concept is what can be used for tracing the lines in a sigil or magick circle or trinity of self.

We can also combine this concept with a charged object like a want, or crystal and use that to project our energy and will through that object modifying its properties and empowering the sigil, or other object with our intent in symbolic and focused ways.

This is a thing you need to experiment with to fully understand, it cannot be taught in a book.

Working with others – This is the pinnacle of practice, not because it is harder for the practitioner to do, but because finding two people who can sense one another's spiritual force is rare.

In my experience, this is rarely as effective as it is when we practice on ourselves, and rarely as pinpoint accurate. Remember, everyone's dark gift is different, not everyone can feel, see, or experience magick the same way, therefore do not lose hope, or faith if you find someone who is practiced, who cannot feel your energy. It may not be your fault, or their fault.

However, with practice, you can often find what works…

I am highly empathic, I can also often feel other people's energy body, but I suck at feeling when they send energy at me. But I can feel them empathically, and sometimes that empathic sensation is in fact the energy and pressure they are sending me.

Normally the easier thing for people to feel is going to be the blob of energy, the Qi-Ball, or the overall energy body itself. Anyone who is sensitive to their own energy body can quickly learn to feel another person's energy body if they tune into it. Admittedly, this might require physical contact at first.

For example, I am well known for my ability to give good massages. This has nothing to do with knowing techniques for how to rub people the right way or anything like that. I simply touch them and instantly connect with their energy field and my empathy kicks into over drive and I instantly sense where their tensions are and can penetrate deeply into their energy body and help relieve their tensions (or cause them muahahaha!).

Thus, this can be an excellent form of practice for two consenting adults to learn to feel one another's energy body.

The Astral thought forms we create such as Qi-Balls, can be very subjective and subtle things, and unless someone is really looking for them, and looking for the right sensation… they may mistake it for anything… It might feel like a tickle, like a slight warmth, a pressure, a sudden shift in air currents, or even a sound or smell or taste.

As I mentioned before, I sense things empathically, I sense emotion and intentions better than actual physical force. Everyone is different, EXPERIMENT!

Movement and dance - It should be noted and strongly advocated for the sorcerer to make use of various movements, postures, mudras and hand symbols when working magick. Body motion in the form of dance or shaking or swaying can generate a great deal of energy and symbolism.

If you are visualizing and projecting energy into an object, then use your arms and hands to really act like you are moving vast amounts of spiritual energy through them, ham it up and really ACT like you are pushing your will into the world.

Raise your hand into the air and invoke the power of the sky, move your hands in a circle over your Altar clockwise to build Yang Energy… Assume yogic postures or use Mudras like the Kuji hand symbols, or the western esoteric hand postures to channel energy through your body and into the ritual.

Dance around your altar, or pace around the ritual chamber getting worked up. Whatever makes your spiritual energy flow into the material world.

There is almost no wrong way to do this, so long as what you are doing is what you FEEL to be correct. I would rather you figure as much of this out for yourself and what feels right for you, than have me confuse you or limit you with what I do as this is a form of personal expression!

Yes, it's going to feel funny at first, yes it's going to look goofy like you are role-playing a witch going bibbity bobbity boo waving your hands over your cauldron, but when you are doing it right you will see that those pop culture icons are there for a reason, that is essentially how it can and should be done.

For some this will mean just a few subtle movements, for others elaborate postures and dance…

Furthermore, when we invoke certain spirits, it can help to assume their mannerisms, or if it is an animal, to move as if we are that animal, it should be no shock that theatrical acting is a big part of invocation and some kinds of magick, so find what works for you and go with it.

Elements and how they can be utilized as energy

As I am a nondualist and a sorcerer, you might be forgiven for being mistaken to assume that I hand wave away all the conceptualizations of dualistic or elemental thinking. Instead, I use them as useful metaphors and a way to manipulate and conceptualize spiritual energies, I use them as part of the dream to help me manipulate it, much as I use any other part of the illusion to achieve whatever goal I find valuable.

One of the most universal and useful symbols in the occult is the symbol of the pentagram. Many traditions had different interpretations of this symbol, but most acknowledge it's elemental and cyclical nature. It is another symbol of infinity and the flow of reality. The elements are very succinctly represented in the symbolism of the pentagram and show how they interact and flow from one to the other.

To the layperson the point up is seen as good, the point down is seen as evil. The Satanic Pentagram is "inverted," while the new age witch's pentagram is "right side" up.

Exhibit A: The good witches Pentagram…

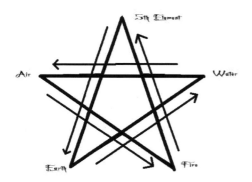

Exhibit B: The Evil or Satanic Pentagram

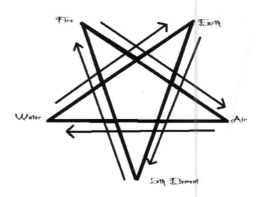

However, our reality is far more complex, and it is less useful to see the universe or magick as expressed in such binary terms…

If we focus on the "upright" pentacle's symbolism to the exclusion of the "inverted" we are excluding a very important perspective of reality that often hinders us or causes spiritual imbalances that lead to things like fanaticism, dogmatism, or religiosity.

In a moment we are going to correct this imbalance symbolically, and this can allow you to use this symbol in a more complete and intuitive manner.

In our system the pentangle or pentagram is a useful symbol be it "right way up" or "inverted" to help us understand the interaction of the elements and is every bit as valid a symbol for magick as my own Trinity of Self, but it enjoys a much longer and storied history!

We can see I have included lines of direction, and in our system, these have special significance and will be explained shortly. In other systems they can invoke or banish the forces of nature by way of pointing and cutting the air in these directions, or in the reverse order.

Of course, that is all it is, a diagram, a tool, and a symbol of the metaphysics of some magus of antiquity, not unlike my own. It can be empowered in the astral realm and is a symbol all spiritual forces know and recognize and respect. However, it has little power of its own save that which mankind has given it in ritual and tradition, but to the keen eye it has hidden meanings correspondences, relationships and uses in ritual.

The so-called upright pentagram represents the 5th element of spirit held above the 4 material elements and is the light or positive form of the symbol.

The so-called inverted pentagram represents the material held above the spirit, and is seen as darkness, or a mirror of the light.

As I mentioned earlier in the projection of physical energy, we can easily charge our energy with various intents, elements and principles. Let us briefly go over the interaction of the elements.

Keep in mind that in magick, elements correspond loosely to their physical counterparts, as this is a holistic system of magick. So, this means that fire in the astral/energetic sphere behaves a lot like fire in the material sphere, burning and consuming things, radiating energy, and acting energetically.

However, it does not actually necessarily cause a mundane object to get "hot." In the astral world Fire might burn and consume, even cause harm, but it need not be experienced as searing pain or actual heat.

Let's start with a brief exploration of the primary elements:

Fire (red) - Fire Can make water evaporate, but if there is enough water, the water will quench the fire and put it out. Fire consumes the earth, rejuvenating it and fertilizing it, it is possible for enough earth to smother fire, but normally the earth gives fire a stable foundation and fuel. Fire can be carried and invigorated by the wind but can also be blown out by it if the wind is strong enough. Fire is the spark of life and has a strong masculine quality (but all elements can be masculine or feminine), the thing that gives it its fury, it's passion and its warmth and zest. Fire can make fire hotter and more powerful, but it can also cause it to burn out, consuming its fuel and passion too fast.

Water (blue) – Water can stifle fire but can be evaporated by it if there is enough fire. Water washes across the earth and earth provides a stable foundation for it to flow, creating oceans and rivers, but earth can only keep water in check and keep it from flowing freely as a dam, sooner or later water always overpowers earth if given enough time and energy. Water nourishes Earth and makes it fertile but can drown it as well. Water can be evaporated by fire and turned to steam or simply evaporate into the air and has a very fair relationship to the air, creating storms, but air dries the water, and can blow it about violently. Water is the adaptability of life and gives life it's flow and direction. When water is empowered by more water, it stops being calm and placid and becomes a raging torrent, overflowing and overpowering even mighty earth.

Air (yellow) - The air is free and unstable, it is everywhere, and can be difficult to isolate and remove from your working. It blows this way and that, and fire is enraged by it, or blown out by it. Air can also be empty space, and vacuum in the physical sense, but not true emptiness in the spiritual sense as we will see in the 5th element. Air is also Qi in Chinese alchemy, and thus represents an important part of the energy of life as it is the very breath of life. Water can be pushed around by it or ride it into the heavens. Earth blocks it, and air is feeble before it, but the earth cannot follow the air, and if air is strong enough, the air can easily go around it unimpeded

Earth (green) - The earth is the most stable and permanent of the elements, and is the most resistant to change, instead it causes change in other elemental energies forcing the other energies to yield to it and go around it, and while it can be consumed by fire, earth can smother fire and contain it. Earth is also the cradle and body of life, being the nurturing mother, and the element most often associated with feminine energy (but like all elements it can be masculine as well), and the fire brings new life to the earth so that it may bloom yet again. When earth is strong enough it creates impossible barriers and smothering forces that can crush, mold and contain any other (material) element.

The 5th element (White/Yang, Black/Yin) – The fifth element is spirit in most systems, mind in others, Aether in still others, and this can be seen in our system as Nothingness, Emptiness, in the Trinity of Self it is the Void, the Lovecraftian spaces and angles in between. For it is this "space" which contains all and is itself nothing. It creates the compulsion for movement and energy, giving space to a system so that energy can move around freely. It is the dark energy of empty space pulling the universe apart at the seams. The emptiness of the bucket that makes it useful for holding water. It is the source and the space between your thoughts where the truth of your existence dwells. It is not simply a vacuum, or discernable expanse of nothing, it IS also true nothing, it is NO-THING.

All the other elements are derived from this source and return to it in their own way and time. It is the creator and the destroyer… It is the quantum foam where particles appear and disappear out of seaming nothingness.

If I can be permitted to speak in whimsical fashion - *It is here that the "Dragon" Sleeps, coiled around the singularity of the void, dreaming the dream of mortal life, of suns and moons and petulant childish mortals like you and me. When it wakes, the creation will end.*

Masculine and Feminine – It cannot be overstressed that Masculine and Feminine energies (also interchangeable with Yin and Yang) do not mean the biological male and female human expressions. This is not a sexual thing (though much of biology follows the masculine and feminine pattern, not all), instead it refers to an element's nature. Each element can have a masculine and feminine side, a creative and nurturing side. The masculine is the seed, the sperm that penetrates the soft nurturing womb and fertilizes the waiting egg.

The masculine is the spark of fire, the feminine is the waiting tinder that catches into a blaze. The Masculine is the vapor of water being evaporated by the sun; the air is the nurturing womb waiting for that vapor to make clouds…

I separate this from Yin and Yang in this discussion because I believe it is more easily examined in this way, but be aware that traditionally, YIN is a feminine force, and Yang a masculine one. And within each (yin and yang) exists a core of its opposite… Inside the nurturing heart of the Feminine Yin, is the masculine Yang. Inside the core of the yang force, is the soft nurturing side of yin.

This is a key idea, because it shows that the true source of Yang is yin, and the true source of Yin, is Yang, that any idea of separation of the two is illusory in nature.

The ancients who valued the hermetic principles, or the Kabbala, are very keen on the idea of masculine and feminine energies, and rightly so, it is the fundamental next step after source, the creation of male and female duality, that splits from the original ONE, or SOURCE.

Light and Dark/Yin and Yang - I find light and dark to be more easily associated and worked with in the yin/yang dynamic.

Yin being darkness and Yang being light.

Thus, it should be clear that each of the 4 elements can have a YIN and a Yang quality.

An element of the Yin or dark aspect tends to represent the dark destructive side of that energy, or that energy in decline. So, for example a fire that is out of control and destroys or one that is running out of fuel and burns down and smolders, or is a dirty fire filled with smoke and fumes.

While an element with the Yang or light aspect will be the light creative side of that energy, or the energy in ascent. So, a clean hot fire that is useful and controlled, a fire that burns and renews what it burns so something new can flourish.

A Yin form of air would be a terrible violent gale that uproots trees, it is the exhale, it is that desperate gasp of air when you are suffocating, or a person's last breath, air that is stale and sickly or air that is stagnant and not moving.

A yang form of air would be a cool breeze on a warm day, the wind that fills the sails, the air that fills the lungs with life and smells sweet and pure.

Yin earth is death, and decay, sickness. Yin earth is fragile and crumbling with age. Yin earth can be a violent earthquake, that topples a building and destroys instead of supports and builds. Yin earth can be unmoving, rigid, and unadaptable.

Yang earth is fertility, healing, longevity, strength and structural integrity. It is the soil that grows the seed. It is the strength that holds up a vast structure and its rigidity can be used to shape and mold things into useful shapes and forms.

Yin water is a dark frozen ocean of lifeless, motionless depths. Yin water is stagnant, and putrid, draining life of its flow, drowning it in its muddy tar like muck and mire. Yin water is a tidal wave of chaotic destruction crashing into the shore to destroy everything in its path then receding back into the sea dragging with it the remains of entire cities.

Yang water gives flow to life, and brings prosperity and joy, it adapts and trickles everywhere it is needed, conforming to whatever container it is meant for. It quenches thirsts and puts out forest fires. It is the "big wave" that the surfer longs to ride, and it is the current by which the ship can sail.

The Yin form of the 5th element is the emptiness that is devoid of all meaning and drains the energy of the other elements into useless entropy. It tears matter and energy apart on a fundamental level, dissolving it into nothingness. It should be clear that this is the fate of the material universe, one day Yin must prevail over the material world as the material world runs down and loses energy trillions upon trillions of years from now as the universe cools and goes out like a burning cinder in the dark.

The Yang form of the 5th element is the emptiness that allows for movement and draws the energy of the other elements into useful motion. It is the space in the bucket that makes it useful and is the space that creates the illusion of separation for us so that we can experience a material world at all. Yang flows back to the astral realm from whence it came, drawn forth out of the spirit by the mind in its quest to give meaning and form to the formless nothing of entropy and the body.

A new perspective - When we combine all these ideas, we see that limiting ourselves to seeing the pentagram as upright or inverted only, is a very limited way of seeing the universe or magick in general. In reality, it should be seen as two pentagrams, one over top of the other, with the point of the 5th element in the middle, and the other elements radiating out creating a light, and dark pentagram.

When we use the symbol in this manner, it begins to make a special kind of sense and can become of practical value in magick, helping us to understand how all these forces can interact in a much more accurate and intuitive way.

We can see a powerful cyclic pattern emerge where the elemental energy of magick flows to and from the 5th element, expressing itself as earth, water, air, and fire before returning to the void to reemerge as fire, air, water, then earth.

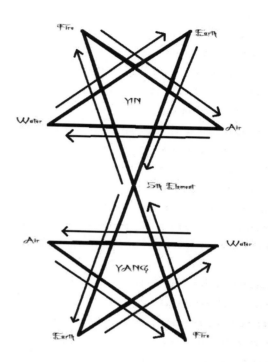

Manipulation of the elemental forces – By looking at the diagram we can see a certain pattern emerging – that as the energy state of the 5th element transitions from yin and yang and back again it gains and loses energy thus changing it on a fundamental level making it a new form.

In the light/white yang pentangle - Earth is a low energy vibration, it is dark, firm, and cold, and is drawn forth miraculously out of the emptiness of the 5th element.

Earth is raised in energy and becomes fluid and flexible like water, water is raised in energy and becomes free and unstable Air, air is raised in energy and becomes energetic and explosive fire, fire raises in energy and winks out of existence when it reaches its peak much like how the cooler low energy fires burn yellow and hottest fires burn white which is the color of the yang aspect of the 5th element.

Thus, becoming the 5th element AKA emptiness.

The spiritual world of the Astral realm is in the grip of the Yang cycle of the pentangle, it is still early in its cycle and in cosmic time is in the early water phase, which is why it is so easily shaped and pliable to the human mind and the imagination.

Like water takes on the shape of the container it is in, it conforms easily to the mind. Though the astral realm is timeless (it is really all time and times as one), it still flows with a current as we are creatures of time (mind is time) and causing changes within it. As the material world loses Yang energy, and is at the mercy of Entropy, the Astral world will gain more and more Yang energy, becoming more and more energetic.

It will take on the aspect of air becoming so easily perturbed and disorganized that astral travelers will need to be even more careful of their thoughts and actions! Despite being like air (which is LESS spiritually energetic in the Yin influenced Material world), in the Yang influenced Astral Realm air will be denser and more energetic than the element of water until it ignites and becomes like the fire element, which will be utterly dense and hot like the core of a star!

In this phase the Astral realm will begin to become so dense with ideas and potential that it will begin to dim as the density becomes so great that the light cannot shine... It will become hot, dark and dense, it will be so hot and dense that the freedom of the prior epochs will be forgotten, as this fire becomes so dense it forms a singularity like the one that spawned the big bang...

It is about to transcend through the 5th element and become A seed containing all the potential, all the ideas, all the shapes, forms and possibilities of countless new universes... until it reaches a point where it can no longer contain itself and it implodes into the Yin aspect, creating a material manifestation of reality we see as the material world today.

In the Yin (dark/Black) pentangle - Fire energy implodes in the Yang aspect (astral) and EXPLODES into the Yin Aspect. It immediately begins to lose its higher energy

vibration, and the fire rapidly burns out as it expands. Ironically this means it will start dark and dense and hot and as it cools it will become brighter and the light will begin to shine soon after the explosion has happened. (let there be light! This is precisely what happens in our universe after the big bang!)

The material universe expands and cools and becomes like the air element, this is the phase in which we find ourselves today. As entropy wins out and the universe continues to expand, it condenses into the element of water, it's energetic expansions and motions slow down as the fires of the big bang begin to die and smolder, after many trillions of years these smoldering stars will themselves begin to cool and condense, and the material Yin world will enter it's Earth elemental phase.

As the last light of the smoldering stars fades out the yin universe freezes and solidifies into solid earth, for entropy is the equal distribution of all energy causing change to become less and less possible, as the energy vibration winds down even the earthy element of the universe eventually fades as the space between particles expands more and more, pulling and tearing even atoms apart... many trillions of years from now, even the subatomic particles will be unable to withstand this powerful Yin pull, and will be torn apart and wink out of existence.

Like earth weathering away into nothing...

At this point the material world becomes the 5th element once again. In this way know that the entropy and dark energy of material reality is the yin force of creation spreading out and pulling apart the fabric of reality. When the material universe has returned to the 5th element it becomes the perfect place for the ideas of a new astral realm to emerge from the emptiness, a blank slate into which new ideas can be written, one at a time, by the mind that decides all.

Confused? We live in the Yin side of reality!? - Many people mistakenly think the material universe we live in is a balanced world of Yin and Yang forces, but balance implies stagnation! The problem here is that people are not aware of the astral realm, if they were, they would see the balance is not found within the material universe, but instead is found in the chaotic interplay of the Material and Astral worlds taken as a whole. Each world emerging from, and moving toward the 5th element of emptiness, or the void. The MATERIAL universe is YIN, and the ASTRAL is Yang, and the cycle of creation and destruction is eternal, the one becomes the other again and again, creating universes back to back over and over again.

It is our destiny, not just in death as a human being to return to the astral realm upon death, but the universe will become the astral realm for another material world with its own life and natural laws in due time. We will likely enter that material world when the time comes too… because the game never ends until it does.

Harnessing the symbolism of creation and destruction -
Thus, we see a cycle of energy which creates a spectrum of elemental forces which we can use in our magick as a symbolic force of invocation, creation, evocation destruction and much more. We learn that the 5th element is the source and the destination for all elements, as we learned in the Trinity of Self the void is the source and destination for all material and spiritual planes… and this 5th element is just another conceptualization of the Void.

It also shows the nature of the flow of elemental energy in a way that shows us how we can potentially tap into this holistic current like a waterwheel and use it in ritual or symbolism to empower our magick in various ways.

We can arrange the elements around our Altar to create yin or yang flow, or even a complete YinYang flow, we can use it to invoke/evoke or banish the energy as needed.

You are not limited to the energies of the traditional elements of earth air fire and water, it should be clear that when these elements come together, they can form other compound elemental forces.

Air and Fire forming Lightning.
Water and Air forming storm.
Earth and Fire causing earthquake, lava and destruction.
Water and earth causing Ice, floods, tides and flow.
Water and fire causing steam.
Steam and air creating clouds and storm.
Earth air and fire causing smoke and ash.

Also keep in mind that in the material world, all matter contains all astral elements, just in different energetic quantities. That isn't to say that we can combine physical water, Earth, Fire, and Air in a container in the right proportions and alchemically create any material substance or object we wish (or *can* we!? This *is* one interpretation of chemical alchemy Afterall) but we could easily replicate its astral energy to a certain degree, making its astral form energetic and real. Creating a thought form, a servitor, or astral magick tool for example, or even an egregore!

Using that energy in ritual or spell work might not cause the object of our desire to automatically appear in front of us… but by using this energy and setting it in motion in the astral world does influence the material world on the subtle levels of magick. This in turn can potentially bring something to us through magick manifestation down the road.

For example, if we did a ritual to create a storm, we might want to make use of the elements that make storms happen, this means you would in fact use all 4 elements but would focus on empowering Air and Water.

You will try to create a storm in the astral world that is so energetically dense that it influences the material world, causing a natural manifestation of a storm, following the natural laws of the material universe.

This also means these compounds in the material Yin world contain these Yang spiritual elements, and thus things like incense can be said to contain the powers of earth, air and fire, storms can contain water and air, steam containing water and fire.

Thus, in ritual, we can easily represent all 4 elements with the use of incense, and a bowl of water. But we can go one step better and use Incense, a bowl of water, a cauldron of Cauldron fire, and a handful of salt, or earth or some crystals for earth. This would be considered an energetically balanced Altar. If a spirit favors one of the elements, we can push our spiritual energy into whichever elemental metaphor we need, energizing it with whatever element we wish.

For example, Azazel is a Spirit that is most closely in tune with the element of air. Empowering incense and using lots of it can improve the chances, and quality of a strong physical manifestation.

Also know that compound materials that have multiple elemental associations (incense for example is earth, when lit, it is earth, fire and air). That one of the elements is dominant. In the case of burning incense, the incense begins dominant under the earth element, but as it burns it becomes the fire and Air elements.

In steam for example the dominant energy is water, in smoke the dominant energy is air, in lightning the dominant energy is fire, in earthquake the dominant energy is earth, in lava it is fire, in storm it is air.

Elements also have stability or instability. Earth is the most stable element, and is the most difficult to change and manipulate, and when changed is the one that will remain changed the longest. But it also does not yield much energy of its own and is instead more of a prism or filter. Therefore, Crystals do not generate energy so much as they store and emit and change or filter it.

Air is the second least stable element, and tends to fade quickly, as the effects of incense smoke are short lived. It is easiest to change but will not remain changed for long at all. Wind can have great force and fury, but it is often short lived, acting in gusts and bursts, and dissipates easily when confronted by earth.

Water is moderately stable taking time to evaporate and disperse, resisting sudden changes, but accepts gradual change easily and carries a lot of force with it when it does. Water can be very adaptive and become other things over time easily. Water is very kinetic and once put into motion likes to stay in motion. Yet it also prefers to flow back to its original self in short order.

Fire is the most unstable and requires fuel or it dissipates the fastest of all and is voracious as it consumes all it touches. Save for water, which it can disperse if fire is strong enough. Fire neither resists change, nor is it changeable, instead it becomes other things by consuming them and dispersing them. Fire is very destructive, but it also gives life, and in the core of each living cell is a small element of fire burning brightly, and when fire is finished its destructive rampage, its energy is returned to the earth again, sowing the seeds for new life and fertilizing the earth.

Each element also cancels one element out, water and fire cancel one another out, the one that wins depends on which is stronger at the time. In the Yin side of the pentagram water is stronger than fire, and equal amounts of fire and water, water will overcome fire. In the Yang side of the pentagram, Fire Wins out over water when in equal measure.

Air and Earth cancel one another out, the wind blowing over the earth, the earth stopping the wind. Whichever wins depends on which is stronger at the time. In the Yang side of the pentagram the Air wins over the Earth when in equal measure and blows it asunder like a hurricane tearing apart a trailer park. In the yin side of the pentagram earth wins out over air if the two are in equal measure, the earth will be largely unmoved, and the air will need to go around it.

One can go mad trying to list out and memorize all the possible correlations and combinations of energy, but in my opinion, this is never necessary, most people can intuitively discern what energy is present in all things and how they can combine or be used to move and compel one another.

For that matter, in ritual we need not focus too much time on our elemental arrangements, our spiritual astral body and subconscious will know how and when to manipulate the elemental forces in ritual, but any help we can give it consciously will cause far more energy to become available in the ritual.

Using the elements in ritual - We can use these elements in many ways in ritual, one of the easiest is to research and find the materials and symbols of the element you seek to use in your ritual and spend a few minutes charging them energetically with your spiritual energy (never just assume the object has usable elemental power just by existing.).

As stated before, you can represent each of the four elements easily with a candle, a stick of incense, a handful of salt or dirt, and a bowl of water. Nothing more is needed to start your work with the elements in magick, but if you intuitively feel you need more elemental or symbolic things in your ritual… Use them!

In our system we focus primarily on the elements as energetic intentions (using the element of Yang Earth to heal or make someone fertile) or for working with spirits that have a strong vibrational preference for one element over another.

However, as you progress and create your own system of magick understanding, using elements in your own unique way is a valid and important stage of your development.

The key is to be inventive and creative, I myself try not to get too distracted by the physical symbols of the elements in my rituals, I might start with a balanced Altar, and then empower the symbolic elements on my altar with my spiritual energy.

If I can't decide, or don't know what elemental energy is appropriate to empower, I give it my best guess, and let my intuition and subconscious do the rest.

If I was going to do a candle spell to cause someone illness, I might empower the candle and my altar with the yin side of Earth to impart the energy of illness, rot and corruption into my target.

If I was going to heal, I might empower the Yang side of Earth to give the candle or altar healing, nurturing forces.

To do this, I would of course follow the basic methods of energy manipulation discussed earlier, pushing either yin, or yang energy into the objects, imbued with the intention of one of the elements.

In this case, I might place the candle in, or next to the bowl containing a handful of earth, and empower the earth, perhaps rubbing the earth on the candle when done, or simply leaving it to absorb the energy naturally over time.

Then place the candle in the appropriate part of my altar (in this case in the center, as I am seeking to manifest something in the objective world) and burn it as normal.

Blood and the power of bodily fluids

WARNING this section details the use of blood, spit, and semen, and may offend some readers, or describe practices that may be dangerous or even unsanitary. DO NOT under any circumstances take this (or any other section) of this book as medical advice, nor a suggestion to perform anything in this book. This is for informational purposes only, and you emulate my path at your own risk!

When I was much younger, I was rather active in the Vampiric current and the vampire offshoot of Goth subculture. I focused primarily on psychic vampirism, and still do practice this to a somewhat lesser extent, but I was also quite fond of traditional Sanguinarian vampirism. This meant that blood holds a special significance in my magick, and I use it in many rituals.

Regardless of who you are, Blood is potent, it is powerful, and use of blood in magick can make your magickal rituals many times more potent and personal. It can be used as an offering, to create a magickal tool and connect yourself to it permanently and with great intimacy.

Blood should never be used Lightly, it should never be underestimated, and it should never fall into the hands of an enemy.

It can be used as is (taken with a lancet, or sharp knife) and smeared on an object, sigil or magickal tool.

Or it can be augmented or added as an ingredient to oleum's or even be made into ink for use in writing magickal sigils and signatures.

The blood of animals and people have similar value, and the energy state of the donor of the blood will have great impact on its utility and potency.

For example, drawing blood at the height of agony, pain and fear will result in blood that is nightmarishly potent in baneful magick.

Drawing blood at, or just before the peak of sexual climax can be incredibly potent for use in love spells or creating passion and inspiration.

Even if the blood is drawn without any emotional or circumstantial significance, even in its neutral state it has incredible power, and will give you intimate control over its energy and uses.

In my practice, virtually any ritual tool of significance is smeared, if not bathed in my own blood. The many dark stains attest to how often I reapply and recharge them with my Sanguine energy.

Blood ink – Blood Ink can be made by purchasing Sour Salt (citric acid) usually sold in the kosher section as sour salt. You will add about 3 drops per teaspoon of blood. This will keep it from coagulating and flow better as ink but be aware that blood tends to dry up and flake off most surfaces that it cannot deeply penetrate.

Some ideas for the use of blood – (always be clear and state your intention when you use blood, never just smear it on and hope for the best. Instead, say something like – "This blood is an offering to the spirit." Or "This blood is for the empowering of my magick and will not establish a connection to my enemy that I am cursing!")

- Use it in the creation/drawing or empowering of sigils.
- Use it as an offering/sacrifice to be smeared on a demon's sigil or some other object that is connected to them, or onto the incense you are burning.
- Use it to create a personal connection to any magickal object or tool.
- Use it to empower baneful magick but be extremely careful not to allow your blood to fall into the hands of an enemy, and be aware that if you do this incorrectly, you can create a connection to your enemy that can be difficult to break.
- Use it to seal your bargain in a written contract with a spirit as ink for a signature.
- Use it in Vampiric magick and energy transmission.

As always be creative and always clear with your intentions! And never let your blood land in the wrong hands.

I'm scared! How do I get my blood out? Doesn't it hurt? - The best way to obtain blood safely, is by using a simple instrument you can find in any drug store, called a diabetic lancet. Some people just use the needle and jab themselves with it, I prefer to use the small Diabetic testing pen that costs a few dollars more and is easy to use to safely control the depth and reduce the discomfort of stabbing yourself with the lancet by hand.

The best places to draw blood are usually from the hands, taking care to avoid any obvious blood vessels and veins.

I shake my hand, squeeze the tip of my finger a few times and slap it on a surface a few times till it gets nice and red, then press the device to my finger and press the button.

You should also make sure you clean the area before using this tool to avoid infection.

Alternatively, you can use knives or other objects, but I do not condone or suggest the use of knives for this purpose. Even though it is a part of my practice, doesn't mean it should be yours. Knives do real damage and leave scars. Stick to safe medically approved tools. Or if you are really concerned, it might be better if you don't use your own blood at all.

Animal blood – It is possible to substitute animal blood in magick for your own, but this is only viable in blood sacrifice or certain spells that require its symbolism and meaning. Animal blood can be easier to get than human blood, simply by going to the store and asking for it at the butcher or Asian markets.

Usually most places will have Cow blood available as it is a valid ingredient in many dishes. Be prepared to get a few raised eyebrows however!

Of course, you can get animal blood the old-fashioned way, by killing the animal yourself and collecting it.

But… make sure you are aware of your laws and do not break them in the process. Again, I do not condone, nor suggest this is a good idea to the practitioner, particularly any minors who might be reading this book!

I do not personally condone animal sacrifice, and most spirits, even demons do not in fact appreciate any form of living sacrifice (I have found the exceptions to be predatory nature spirits), however giving animal sacrifice in the form of burning an animal that has been humanely butchered already, or using humanely collected blood, can be pleasing to a spirit.

However, I would be lying if I said I never gleefully took an animal's life intentionally as a hunter for food or as a sorcerer for use in magick.

Still, I find the practice almost entirely needless, and my own blood is more than potent enough for 99% of the magickal operations I could conceive of doing.

In the end, my empathy means that it is uncomfortable for me to cause undue suffering to innocent creatures, I find animals easy to read, and commune with, and very difficult to mistreat unless for good reason (if a dog is attacking me for example I won't hesitate to do whatever it takes to defend myself).

But harming a harmless animal for the vanity of using it in ritual is distasteful to me in the extreme, and not for moralistic reasons, but entirely selfish ones…

Sexual fluids – These contain the powers of creation and lust. For some people semen or female sexual fluids are a cornerstone of empowering their sigils, reaching a state of maximal climax, smearing the bodily fluid on a sigil, and then burning the sigil as part of it's big "send off."

As strange as this might sound, there is very good reason to do it this way, and chaos sigil magick is a popular and effective form of spell casting that should not be overlooked.

These fluids are best used for spells and rituals designed to manifest the creation of something (particularly Servitors, Egregores, and similar entities you might create for yourself) as these fluids are charged with potent forces of creation and life. On the other hand, they are often a poor choice for baneful curses.

Vampirism and the use of blood and other energy – Blood can also be, and obviously is, used in a vampiric fashion, but those who do not experience the vampiric current will not likely gain much of any benefit from this, nor is it a good idea to try. It is very easy to transmit disease or negative energy between you and your willing donor or participant.

Vampirism is a complex status or condition of an individual's energy body that can be caused by many different things. It can be done either as a requirement to make up for a unique characteristic of their energy body (IE seen as a "condition"). Or can be a practice people without such a condition can utilize to empower themselves or ignore completely and suffer no ill effects.

Even for those with the condition in their energy body, rarely must intentionally practice vampirism, their subconscious and astral body will do this for them. But intentional practice can be very helpful and can even help them work to minimize any influence it has on their energy levels.

Vampirism as a condition can have many different causes:

- It can be a result of using vampiric practices too often, creating a kind of addiction.
- It can be the result of emotional or spiritual trauma.
- It can be the result, or perhaps cause of emotional disorders and psychiatric disorders like narcissism.
- It can be the result of having a vampiric entity attached to you directly or through a tether causing you to suffer regular energy drains, and require either the vampiric entities removal or the use of vampiric practices to stay healthy and provide enough energy for yourself and your astral parasite or symbiote (yes, some spiritual entities can be energy parasites, or symbiotic).
- It can also simply be an aspect of your astral spiritual body, not so much a flaw, but a unique quality. The same way some people have blue eyes, and others brown, or how some people prefer to be Vegan or Paleo.

Be warned, that it is simply make believe and fantasy that people in the vampiric currents "need" to ingest blood biologically to live. Indeed, in some cases it isn't required, or is done merely as a form of role play that gives them energetic empowering.

Blood does have a potent energy all its own, but the blood itself is more accurately a holistic conduit through which the transfer of life force can be made, the blood itself, especially in the form of a few drops collected via lancet, has only a small amount of psychic energy in it.

Instead think of it more like a conductor of spiritual electricity, and that it makes the connection between you and your donor more potent and complete.

The vampiric person need not even ingest the blood, in many cases simply being in close contact with it, or the bloody wound from whence it came will create a powerful connection and they can drink deep from the psychic well of their donor or victim.

Some of the most potent vampiric practices involve the mingling of blood, whereby the donor's blood is mixed with the "vampires" blood and then consumed or touched against an energetic entry point of the vampire (Psychic mouth). This creates a nearly perfect connection between the donor and the Vampire, but it can also create a powerful energetic bond between the two partners, which can be dangerous for both.

It can establish a permanent (or at least hard to remove) energy tether between the two people and make them subject to each other's energies, emotions, or lack thereof.

Know then, that there is then an intuitively obvious spiritual REASON that so many kids had the superstitious practice of blood pacts and blood brothers/sisters.

It should be stressed that Sanguinarian Vampirism is merely a physically augmented variation of what Vampirism really is. It essentially revolves around the absorption of psychic, emotional and spiritual energy of a victim or willing donor. Most people who are in the vampiric current have been doing this their entire lives without being aware of it.

Many natural energy vampires are narcissistic or have certain personality imbalances that cause them to make people uncomfortable and they feed on the energy this causes, and on the psychic wounds of the people they victimize.

When they or others make it into a regular practice it can alleviate many issues in their lives and balance their energy levels in much the same way a diabetic needs regular injection of insulin to be healthy and without imbalances in their energy and chemistry.

This can make them far less dangerous, and far less toxic to interact with.

It should be stressed over and over that blood is NOT required for someone skilled in their own energy work to get the energy they need, but blood is exceptionally better at creating an efficient and strong connection to the donor/victim.

Vampirism does NOT make you live forever, though it can improve your health if you are one of those people who finds it necessary or helpful.

It does not give you super powers or make you allergic to sunlight or garlic. However, many health problems or allergies can accompany vampirism because the imbalance of energy can cause an influence on our body's health.

Sunlight CAN interfere with the energy of someone experiencing vampiric imbalances and make it hard for them to cope… but in my experience it is not dangerous harmful and can even be reversed by exposure and taking supplements to the point where sunlight can become helpful and empowering.

In fact, almost nothing in the movies and books are true, but some of us still enjoy living a lifestyle that simulates these things… not just because it is fun, but because the way normal or judgmental people react to us gives us an opening to feed from…

One common attribute of all people in the vampiric current is a strong sense of empathy or other psychic abilities, and an innate talent for manipulating personal energy or the emotions of others.

How can you know if you are a Vampire? - Well, in my more mature age, I find it very cringey and silly when people get obsessed with the term vampire and want to know if they are a vampire. It is my opinion that nobody is a "Vampire" rather they have a vampiric need to interact with the energy body of other people (and sometimes animals) in such a way that augments, supplements, or restores energy that they have need of.

You cannot be "Turned" into a vampire by some head vampire and thus cursed… that is the role play. However, you can feed from someone for so long that their energy body can become destabilized and require that they find ways to supplement, often resorting to vampirism as well. Some vampiric entities can attach themselves to our energy bodies and similarly make us imbalanced and require supplementation and feeding as well.

Nor can you (easily) do real harm or kill someone just by drinking their energy. The target has a virtually limitless supply of this energy as it is the energy of the universe flowing through them that makes them alive.

But you can weaken someone, it can be a baneful practice that weakens them psychically, emotionally, and physically given long enough exposure.

Some Vampiric people are more symbiotic in their practice and less parasitic, they will exchange energy they have an abundance of, in exchange for energy they lack.

If you believe yourself to be in the vampiric current, you can easily put into practice some of the things in this section of the book about energy work and see if it helps you energetically.

If you intuitively know that what I wrote in this section is right for you, you can try to take it to the next level and attempt to safely feed from people around you.

I highly advise against predatory feeding; willing donors' energy is far more useful, and energy taken from people against their will or knowledge is always tainted by the act itself. Of course, this is again a case of me telling you to do as I say, not as I do… your miles may vary, and you may wind up having no ill effects.

The Vampiric Psychic mouth – People who experience the current of Vampirism typically have one or more points on their astral body that act like psychic mouths, others have feeding tendrils instead. These tendrils usually originate in this psychic mouth or have these mouths on the end of them. But more often in the case of a Sanguinarian vampire the psychic mouth is close to, or directly in correspondence with some part of the individual's body, often around the mouth, but can also be elsewhere.

Some people like being touched, or like touching people with this part of their body and this can be a subconscious effort to engage their subtle energy body with the subtle energy body of another person in the corresponding location of their psychic mouth.

Now this doesn't mean someone who likes to play footsie is an energy sucking vampire, but some people can be very touchy feely, and like to hug, hold and otherwise be in close contact with people all the time, and sometimes, just sometimes, they favor a specific location to make this connection, the hand, the lips, the head.

If they are in the vampiric current, this is a possible location of their Psychic mouth.

This is not always or even often the case, but it is something I have noticed many times.

Others, like myself mainly used our hands, or our mouth, or feeding tendrils that strike out like black tentacles, like inky black lampreys with harsh looking mouths filled with vampire fangs, they latch on and suck the energy out giving me some energetic stability.

As these are ASTRAL appendages, they can take on virtually any form you can imagine.

Spiritual anchors

This is a fundamental component of working magick for, or against someone specific. These are objects, or materials that closely connect the energy of the target to you in a way that puts them within your reach magickally.

I classify these in 3 classes or grades of potency and effectiveness:

Grade 1 - The first and best grade are bodily fluids and cast offs like skin or hair. For example, a lock of hair, a collection of fingernails, a bit of skin, a bodily fluid (blood in particular) all make for exquisite spiritual anchors. And these are Grade one. A spell cast upon someone using this material or object will be like a flawless heat seeking missile. If you do your part, the spell will home in on the individual and not miss.

Grade 2 - Are objects of important significance to the target. This doesn't mean it is valuable (though it often is), it is an object of deep personal connection. A wedding ring, a favorite shirt, an old lucky rabbits' foot. These are excellent and can be considered the norm for the best effect, but of course if you can get blood or other cast offs, this is ideal.

Grade 3 - These are things like photographs, or more mundane and common items they own but care very little for. You can even capture the reflection of your target in a mirror and then cover it with black velvet or silk immediately to retain the reflection until needed.

Remember These objects can retain a spiritual psychic link with the person for a long time, and this can be used against you as well. Never retain such an object for any real length of time, or even worse, let someone you do not trust WITH YOUR LIFE encounter such an object, Ever.

When working with spiritual anchors, care must be taken to preserve the potency of the connection from being tainted by your own energies. When you acquire the anchor, it should be stored in velvet or silk, either wrapped up, in a bag made of this material or in a box lined with it.

Do not taint the energy by fondling it or exposing it to strong emotions or thinking about what you are going to do with it. Instead, simply try to visualize and feel the vibration of the object being in harmony with the target, and a cord of energy connecting the object or material to your target and store it immediately.

Storing any mystical object in silk or velvet has the effect of keeping it sacred and prevents spiritual interference, it is like a Ziplock bag for magick objects. Do not worry, the connection to the source will remain strong, as soon as the object is removed from the silk or velvet, it's energy will fully reconnect with the source.

When you are ready to use it in ritual, take it out, and attempt to feel and see the energetic vibration of the target and this target being in harmony, and visualize the psychic tether between the object and the owner as vividly as possible. This is so that you can lock in on the vibration of the target of the spell more than anything else.

Make sure when you use the spiritual anchor object/material that you are not tainting it with any outside energies save those of your magickal working. Remain focused on the intention and outcome of the spell and imagine and feel the power of your will using the harmonics and spiritual tether to travel to the target.

If this is for Baneful magick be careful to not imbue or charge it with ANY of your own energy as you might in other workings, you do not want this anchor to in any way be traced back to you, instead use it as a gateway to reach the target this

is sympathetic Magick at its finest! Whatever you DO to the anchor, will be done to the target. So do not give them your energy, as it can backfire and work against you.

Instead, simply pour your hate, disdain and baneful intent through the object as if it was the mouth of a wormhole leading directly to the target's energy body. And when you are done casting the spell or the curse laden object to be buried or hidden in the target's vicinity, you carefully sever your bond with the object and enter an empty minded state and pull back any and all energy that might have been inadvertently put into the object. You want to completely let go of the spiritual arrow so it can hit its target.

For a beneficial spell or the creation of a talisman, you can choose to mingle your energies with that of the target if you wish, but be warned, this can be risky, and hard to reverse.

Letting Go

When working magick the most important reason magick usually fails to manifest, is because we are too attached to the result, and our energies linger and hold back the magick from working.

You cannot fire an arrow by holding on to it and worrying about its trajectory and never let go, you cannot throw a punch by holding it back to make sure it is on target, you cannot send a letter to someone if you are constantly revising it, you cannot feed yourself if you get too attached to how food tastes and never swallow it…

In magick this means, first and foremost – Do not be so attached to the outcome of magick that it bothers you if it fails. I have a high success rate simply because I am very picky about when I use magick, and I do not (often) use it for frivolous things, or things I cannot detach from.

If I worry about the outcome, nothing good comes of it, and if it does, it only comes AFTER I completely forgot about it and stopped thinking about it. You just wake up one day, and it's done, or get a phone call out of the blue when distracted by something else etc.

However, this also means in ritual and energy work that you need to know when to pull back and cut off your energetic connection to the magick and when to allow it to continually work.

At the end of virtually every magickal working, I detach my mind, and my energy body from the work through energy manipulation, meditation and normalization.

If you have practiced the 3 fundamental projections (vocal, visual and physical), and can properly manipulate energy via those pathways, you can easily pull back and cut off your energy from a working and let the spell carry out its task.

But Thorne, Don't I want to give my spell ongoing magickal support? Shouldn't I reinforce it or give it access to my energy all the time so it can be potent?

Not exactly, you need to let the magick go, you have already pumped into the ritual all the energy the magick needs, and if it needs more you can do follow up rituals etc. Also, your subconscious mind will take care of the little details. The key here is to keep your conscious monkey brain from interfering in whatever way.

Of course, some spells in fact require repetition of the ritual every day, or every week or some other interval for it to work best. A 30-day spell for example starting on a new moon and ending on a full moon typically requires daily, or weekly ritual. Many initiatory rites can take several days to complete.

However, when the final day and final ritual in the working is done, the sorcerer will completely detach pull back and let go of the energy, the obsession and the worry. They will let it go completely and TRUST the magick.

Because what are you really saying if you worry about the outcome after casting the spell? You are saying you do not trust the spell.

Making and using sigils

Sigils are one of the more fundamental forms of so-called Chaos magick that exists, combining a very holistic act of creating a tangible physical symbol, linked to a strong mental intent and empowered by spiritual energy.

Virtually anything can be a sigil, some would say that our rituals are sigils, our very lives might be a form of sigil.

Sigils, at least in the sense we will be using them, are things that we create that could be thought of as a magickal doodle. I follow a simple pattern of rules designed to create a powerful statement of intent, reduce it down into nonsensical consonants or a magickal alphabet (see the chapter on Magickal Writing). Then we take those letters or symbols, and turn them into shapes, and combine them to create a unique image that can then bypass our rational conscious filter and go to work directly on our subconscious mind, and thereby alter reality as we see fit.

Once we have this symbol manifested in the material world, we put it away, and we forget about it for a while, giving ourselves a chance to forget what it means exactly, to further remove our conscious minds interference.

Then when we feel we are ready, we stage a magickal "sendoff" where the sorcerer takes the sigil, empowers it by entering an altered state of consciousness that chaos magickians call "Gnosis" (not to be confused with the term Gnosis used to describe knowledge). And then the sigil is destroyed in fire, releasing the magick into the world.

Many gods and demons have certain sigils that are unique to them, and these should be used in ritual to evoke, invoke, and otherwise work with these spirits. We can use the sigils handed down through history by those who first recorded them, or we can ask the spirits to give us one for our own personal use.

However, when using Sigils in chaos magick, we do not (necessarily) get our sigil from a spirit, but from the depths of our own psyche.

Step one - Create a short sentence that describes your powerful intent, and phrase it in the present tense. For example: "I have thousands of dollars!" Or "I am a great and powerful sorcerer!" or "That cute guy in the office has a crush on me!"

But never phrase it in the past or uncertain tense, for example: "I will have thousands of dollars." Or "May I be a powerful sorcerer." Or "I want to marry that cute guy in the office."

Step Two- Carefully examine the statement and remove all the vowels.

Step three- Next remove all the letters that repeat so there is only one of them.

At this point if your starting Statement of Intent was "I have thousands of dollars." The letters you would be left with would be: "hvtsndlr"

Step 4 - Enter an open-minded state and take some time to doodle your sigil. Use those letters to doodle and create a symbol that uses each letter but arranges them randomly and makes them unrecognizable. It should not look like you simply mixed up and jumbled up some letters, you need to stylize each letter to make them less recognizable. You can even break them apart into pieces of letters, making an S turn into a pair of "C" shapes, or an H could become two I shapes, and a – Shape. A V can become a \ and a /. You can even remove elements or blend them into one another to hide them. You can add shapes as well, shapes such as open and filled circles are popular, triangles and squares, Crosses and stars.

For example, "hvtsndlr" might end up like this:

Somewhere in that seemingly random jumble of shapes is the essence of each of the letters, embellished with little extras, and blended together to make them hidden in the image.

When you create your symbol at some point you will just "know" that it's right, now is the time to take that sigil, and destroy any evidence you have for what it means, and put the sigil in a secret and sacred place until such time as you have more or less forgotten the exact wording of the sigil, and if possible, what it really means.

Then, when you have forgotten, and if you have not yet done so, it is time to transfer it to a cleaner and fresher piece of paper or card stock such as a blank flash card (the side without lines), using a marker or blood ink, or some other special kind of ink or medium.

When you redraw it, you need to enter a state of trance, either open mind, or Focused mind or both, allowing the open mind to flow into the focused mind.

If you already redrew it before storing it, that is fine, instead of redrawing it, you can trace over it with your finger, or simply stare at it, and imagine your mind's eye burning the image onto the paper.

You need to push all your energy into it using the methods I described earlier, and you need to enter a deep state of trance or rapture, you may need to work yourself up or make yourself manic.

A popular (but not at all required) method for building up energy is to masturbate and use the sexual fluids (sexual fluids, esp. male semen, are seen as ideal fluids for anything creative in nature), or the blood drawn at the moment of peak arousal before climax to smear on the sigil. The idea is to reach a moment of sublime ecstasy and then use that energy to empower the sigil.

Once you have reached this state of mania, or sublime ecstasy, and smeared whatever substance on the sigil you feel is best, you then burn the sigil immediately, and as it burns you must feel your full intention burn with it, releasing the intention into the world, never thinking about that sigil or what I might mean ever again.

I can hear it now: *But Thorne… if I forget the meaning of the sigil, how will I know it works?*

The simple answer is, you will just need to trust yourself. Still, many others will instead create a very scientific practice of keeping records and notes about what sigils they make and use, and check occasionally for results, and do so discretely enough that they do not spoil the manifestation by dwelling on it. For example, they simply check their journal once every month to see if any of their sigils came true or not, if it did, they mark it down to potentially use again later.

This is also a very valid method if you are capable of not dwelling on the meaning of sigils and check every few days or something. The objective is to forget and be reminded by the manifestation. Magick is a pot that if watched never boils!

Using the Trinity of Self in Ritual

The trinity of self is nothing more than a powerful symbol, it has little power of its own. It is not a secret Arcane sigil given to me by a demon. It is not the true name of god. Instead it is a grand unified theory of metaphysical truth, laid out in a single symbol that can contain all the truths of all reality within its simple premise. I know how humble that sounds... Your miles may vary...

For the sorcerer that adopts this grand unified theory of holistic mysticism and magick, the trinity of self is far more than just a symbol. It is a hyperdimensional gateway between the reality you know and wish to change, and the reality you wish to bring into focus in the world you experience.

It can literally become a focal point of change for your subjective experience, and a holistic gateway through which the multiverse of quantum potentiality can flow, both to, and from your personal experience.

Somewhere in the Paradoxical "insignificant vastness" of the "infinite singularity" of the void, lies the exact reality you wish to experience, and with the power of this symbol made manifest in your holistic experience as a material symbol, an Astral gateway, and a mental focal point - you can open a portal to the universe that contains your deepest truest desire.

Your subjective experience can tune into this reality and in so doing, it can bring this reality back with it when the ritual is over... Or bring the subjective self into that reality - making it real.

Essentially by bringing a tiny fragment of that possible universe into this one, it forces this reality to conform to the causal nature of this new part.

Kind of like dropping a pebble into a pond causes the pond to change to accommodate the pebble... creating ripples of change and raising the level of the pond imperceptibly to match the added volume of the pebble. The ripples flow outward from the point of entry of the pebble, and the pond is forever changed. Even once the ripples have finished their journey and crash upon the shore, the changes

are still ongoing... To most, it will appear as if nothing happened... but you will know.

In ritual, you can bring the reality you truly intend to experience into sharp focus in the center of this symbolic object. In so doing you can bring it back with you through that portal, assuming of course, that you are truly working magick in alignment and accordance with your true intention and true will. Nothing can stop the magick from happening, it is a thing that is already done and when you work your magick, you are merely celebrating the manifestation that is certain to come.

The Neophyte always makes this mistake at first, they assume magick is done like anything else is done. That it is a way to influence cause and effect to create an outcome we desire.

In truth, the magick is in the intention and the doing of magick, not in the result... It is therefore something I say without any sense of irony, when I say that everything in this book is just a work of fiction, like a stage play, the actors are not real. When they draw swords and fight, it is ultimately pointless, there is no winner or victim because nobody is real. Yet somehow, the emotion the performance elicits IS real, and the personal gnosis that the audience experiences as a result, IS the goal...

When the villain strikes the hero through the heart and he "dies," if his performance is in accordance with the intent of the actor and the writer... we swoon, we experience a moment of true magick.

The trinity of Self is merely the stage of the action, and the tools we place upon it the props and the backdrop. We can of course perform our play without it, and elicit all the same emotions and outcomes... However, it can help us with our immersion if we set the stage just right!

To do this cannot be taught because only you can master the symbolism of your subjective experience. This is a thing better discovered than taught, for the act of teaching would spoil the lesson.

If the Trinity of Self does not appeal to you, if you prefer pentagrams, circles, or other occult symbols instead, then, ignore the Trinity and focus on my other instruction instead.

But... If the Trinity of Self speaks to you, if you can feel its potential truth... do not hesitate to use it. Your mind is already making it real for you! Experiment with it, meditate with it, play with it and imagine it spinning and rotating in multiple dimensions, becoming a hyperdimensional object that defies Euclidean space and time.

You need to find how to manipulate its symbolism and unlock it like a 4-dimensional puzzle, to power it with holistic energy and make into more than simply a symbol drawn on your altar or hung on your wall or adorning the floor of your ritual space.

It needs to become real in all three aspects of itself. It's inside must become it's outside on the inside...

You must visualize and see it. You must feel it and know it. You must sense it viscerally and empower it with your belief and your spiritual pressure.

You need to empower it, even wake it up so that it becomes self-aware like an Egregore but not an egregore at all.

Instead, *you* must become the gate... for *you* are the Trinity of Self.

Altar Layout – The trinity of self creates several key nodes in its symbolism for placing ritual tools and offerings.

Each of the 3 aspects is an ideal place to put a Candle that represents one of the aspects. A red candle in body, Green in mind, Blue in spirit. (black can be substituted for these colors)

Each of the large spaces in between can correspond to certain elements and concepts and there is room for overlap so do not lose a lot of sleep trying to decide if something should go on one part of the trinity or another. Instead ask yourself what feels right to you and go with your first gut impulse.

For example:
The Material plane – This is where I put solid offerings or components such as Food, sometimes drink offerings, Earth elements, amulets, daggers wands etc.

The Astral plane - This is where I mostly put liquids, and airy materials, and spiritual symbols, so offerings of wine, the element of water, and air like smoke and sometimes fire.

The Void plane - This is where I almost always put my burnt offering bowl, incense, and other airy and spiritual elements. The Center of the trinity – This is where I place the focus of my intention, a sigil a candle, or a group of objects.

Try to balance the energy by judging it aesthetically, if it looks wrong, it probably is!

Putting it all together

In this section we have covered what I consider to be the absolute essential and basic methods of projecting your intention using various energetic methods and considerations. I am not suggesting that you need to always utilize every single method in every ritual or spell working. That can become exhausting and rob you of a sense of intuitive and natural flow.

Instead, mix and match, experiment and find which ones matter most for you. Keep in mind the principle of the Trinity of Self, the mirrored Pentagram, the YinYang duality, and the holistic nature of Magick and simply find ways to empower your magick with whichever method speaks to you for your chosen ritual.

The most important thing to remember is that the best magick has a physical, a mental and a spiritual element combined into one holistic magickal action.

Thus, there is no wrong way to combine or use these methods, the important thing is that you find what works by using them all in your own way.

The pathworking section will contain a small selection of spells, rituals and exercises that can help you begin to practice and learn which ones work best for you by using them in ritual.

Living a Magickal Life

This one can be tricky, and is often completely overlooked, but is absolutely a key facet of becoming competent in magick of any kind. You must learn to immerse yourself in magick, the study of magick, the aesthetics of magick, the history of magick. You must not simply dabble or study magick, you must live it.

You must come to see yourself not as an accountant, or a husband or father - but instead as a SORCERER, or SORCERESS. You must OWN the title and be bold about it. You must never be timid or fearful or artificially humble. You must be able to accept that most people in this world will either mock and ridicule you, misunderstand you, or be fearful of you.

You must be able to thrive on the knowledge that you will forever be an outcast in modern society, until or unless you find a group of likeminded people.

You must do whatever it takes to keep yourself grounded in what you are, but also empowered and inspired and to keep you believing in magick in a day to day fashion. This can be nearly impossible sometimes in today's modern world, with the utter all-out WAR that skeptics have waged against any and all forms of magickal or spiritual expression (on par with the theistic crusaders of the past, minus the violence, unless we are talking about authoritarian regimes).

Our very society discourages people from being individualistic in the extreme. Preaching tolerance on the one hand, but creating outcasts with the other... This is a dysfunctional and toxic society we are currently building, one that could potentially rival the most closed-minded insular cultures of the last centuries.

For this reason, it is even more important than it ever was before for you to find a way to live a magickal life and express this part of yourself in a way that keeps you motivated and inspired.

This is going to express itself differently for everyone, but here are some key considerations, apply them as you see fit based on your social capabilities and responsibilities (obviously if there is a practical need to keep a low profile, or cannot afford to have some things, you should not stress about it, do whatever feels right, nothing more, nothing less).

Getting into character

I am going to say something not many people in magick like to admit. A lot of what we do as advanced occultists, is an act. It is literally a character we created consciously. I am not saying we are "lying" I am saying we are consciously aware that we have control over how others perceive us, and do not need to "just be ourselves."

We are never "ourselves." Not a single person you meet is "being themselves." Everyone is acting, all the time. Nobody "keeps it real." Nor should we.

This "being yourself" nonsense is just false humility, and keeps you locked into the paradigm of the spiritually dead mundane world. Because more often than anyone likes to admit, the "REAL you" lurking beneath your civilized exterior, is a frightened, selfish, childish, perverse, dangerous animal.

No... No one is truly genuine.

Most of the time we are who society needs us to be. We are who society expects so we don't break the social contract that allows us to live in a civilized world.

This by itself isn't really all that bad, until or unless it becomes pathological and starts to destroy who we truly are, in favor of what our bosses, teachers, or family expects us to be.

It begins from a young age, we are given a name, encouraged to express a gender. We might get taught what sport teams to like, or to avoid sports. We might be given a racial or ethnic identity, a religious identity.

All these things came from outside yourself. You didn't choose these things; they are chosen for you...

Do you understand now what I'm getting at?

A sorcerer is not a slave, a sorcerer must be individualistic and SELF AWARE in an extreme way. Or nothing they do has any deeper meaning. Essentially, they will not be doing magick for themselves, but for the people who made them who they are... The people who named you become the subtle reason you do what you do. The people who told you what your race or gender is become the ones who guide your magick. And so on.

So, what you need to do, is think carefully about who you really are, who you are as a SORCERER, and make it your mission to get into that character. To find your mannerisms, your voice, your way of dealing with problems. I don't mean become fake, I mean, if anything, figure out who you really are, and stop pretending to be someone else! Be who you WISH you could be. Be sexy, be brave, be confident. But, ironically, don't do it because I'm telling you to… Do it because you see the wisdom in it.

It can take a long time, and a lot of work, but when you finally cast off this fake skin, and become who you truly are, you will look back and know how important it was to make this change in your life.

Dress code

There is a saying – The clothes make the man/Woman. This is not just a saying; it is established in psychology and is a very important thing for a Sorcerer to take control over.

It is well known in the occult world, that in the twilight of antiquity, Azazel and the other watchers taught mankind many things, among them were body ornamentation and makeup. You need to understand that this wasn't just for teaching women how to attract men, or vice versa… but because these personal ornamentations and styles are very important magickally.

How we decorate and carry our bodies, is a very important and oft overlooked facet of magick. This applies to how we dress in the ritual chamber, and in everyday life.

I'm not talking about being ultra-fashion conscious, or super fit and sexy. I'm talking about the material side of getting into character.

It isn't just important to ACT and think like the sorcerer you truly are. But to dress and carry yourself like them as well. This means every day, and especially when in your ritual chamber.

What's more, the clothing we wear can be augmented with magick. Talismans, amulets, even makeup, piercings, and tattoos can have profound magickal properties.

For example - the ancient Egyptians believed their eye makeup was a protection from spiritual dangers, as it shielded the eyes, the gateways to the soul…

Now, not everyone can walk around wearing eccentric ritual garb all the time (I do, but I'm also not everyone). Not all of us can be open about our spirituality or our dark side. We all have people in our lives that might make us feel awkward or uncomfortable in our own skin. We all have 9-5 jobs, and most of those jobs have dress codes.

However, I am going to tell you that this is no excuse to ignore this aspect of your magickal life. The more you allow the world to dictate what you should look like and when, the less you are in control over your own life.

Let me be honest with you for a second and go on a related tangent – I abhor what passes for "style" in the modern era. Every facet of it, is built upon the idea of deemphasizing someone's individuality, and make the textile factories richer by keeping the clothing we wear simplistic and cheap to mass produce. Now, I've got nothing wrong with people making money. Far from it. But let's be honest. People these days are anything but stylish or individualistic.

When I was younger, we had some very liberated counter cultures running around. We had punks, goths, metalheads, grunge, hippies, gangsta's, and many others who bucked the social trends of the mainstream and went to great lengths to distinguish themselves. Most of this revolved around the music scene, and you were essentially showing people what kind of music you preferred based on how you dressed, but even still, it created a variety and a color, and a chance for people to really try to stand out and be themselves.

20 years ago, despite how normal so many people looked, when I walked down the street in my gothic every day clothes, it wasn't that unusual. Especially in cities.

Look around you now… where have these people gone? I pick up my kid from school and notice that everyone, and I mean everyone, looks like they shop at the same 3 stores.

Everyone has this cookie cutter appearance. It is clear to me that we are discouraged from expressing ourselves, because in this individuality comes self-empowerment, and our modern culture is hurtling toward a very homogeneous authoritarian state.

So, unless of course that expression involves wearing a printed T shirt with our favorite corporate intellectual property on it (band shirts etc.). We are discouraged from wearing anything interesting or expressive. Essentially, all our clothing is mass produced, and we are taught to avoid accessorizing or personalizing our looks, unless you count wearing the "BRAND" of some big corporation, sports team or band or something. Gone are the days of bangles, and bracelets, necklaces, scarves and gloves. Gone are the days of ripped jeans, and sequins, gone are the days of fishnets or even tie-dye…

You are all literally branded livestock.

When I walk around in public wearing my "normal clothes" I go to great lengths to avoid wearing anything that advertises a brand or product for anyone. I wear all black, I have an unusual haircut, I wear designer leather gloves, I wear a duster or other long flowing garment in cool weather.

I am never forgotten… When I go to a restaurant or store a second time, they remember me. I also make sure to tip well, even when I'm not doing well financially, and I get treated like I am a celebrity.

There is utter power in taking control in how you look.

Those who are uncomfortable with how I dress, make themselves obvious to me as people I want little to do with. They are hopelessly unlike me and will likely take issue with everything I do and stand for.

People sometimes stop and stare, sometimes out of confusion, sometimes fear, sometimes to admire, It's not even that elaborate or unusual. It's rather casual and conservative by the standards of the counterculture I grew up loving.

Don't worry, I'm not turning this into a fashion book. However again recall that Azazel and other watchers taught humanity about makeup, and ornamentation of the body.

So, don't think of this as being about fashion (though it can be), think of it as being about assuming the mantle of a Sorcerer in EVERY possible aspect of your life. To go from being the average mundane to becoming the supernatural being that you truly are meant to be. To stop letting the sheep tell you how to dress.

I will let you figure out the rest.

Ritual Garments

These are of special consideration. It is my firm belief that ritual clothing is an important part of the magickal act.

At the very least, when you are engaging in ritual, especially high ritual ceremonies (longer more involved, more formal rituals), you absolutely MUST try to wear significant and sacred garments that signal to your subconscious that it's showtime.

Some people believe that your most special ritual clothing should never be worn in public, and I can see and understand why. In my case, I believe I am always a sorcerer doing magick even when I am not in my ritual chamber doing ritual! So, I almost always wear certain clothing and jewelry items I also wear in ritual.

Still, I do reserve certain amulets, talismans, and other things for wearing during ritual and not in everyday life unless I need them for something specific (for example, my Familiar's anchor).

If you are like me then, your Ritual garments aren't that different from your day to day clothes look like… But I don't dress normally either.

Practice something magickal every day

This can be meditation, this can be casting a simple spell, calling a spirit, or spending some time curled up with a good book about magick.

You should seek out one magickal experience every day, it won't happen, but you need to be open to it, and encourage it. Talk to your spirits, draw sigils, paint images, sing a demon's name, etc.

Whatever you do, try to do it at a minimum of 30 minutes a day. You will have many days when you are just going through the motions and not learning anything or really doing anything, but they pay big dividends down the road.

If you are NEW to magick and this is your first book of magick, you should be practicing your Altered States meditation daily, seeking a breakthrough and enough mastery to hold each of those states for at least a minute uninterrupted.

If you feel burned out, and need a break from serious study, give yourself a break, but continue trying to have at least one magick related experience at day.

This is who you are now, it is a way of life. Not a game.

Live in a magickal home

This should be obvious; your home and environment should reflect and inspire who you are. Your furniture, decorations, artwork. All should speak to your interests in magick. For some this means subdued and subtle hints of spiritual art and symbolism, for others, it means living in an eccentric home filled with oddities and curio.

The centerpiece of this magick living space should be your Altar, and if possible, a dedicated ritual chamber.

Considering the current of magick that is presented in this book is one that embraces the dark side, you should probably favor styles and decoration that at least hints at this.

Your altar - A table of any height, made of any material, large enough to hold most of your magick tools, and have space for working magick. A black fabric table cloth, marked with a representation of the Trinity of Self on it, large enough to cover the entire surface is important, unless your Altar is of deep dark wood, or dark stone like marble or perhaps glass.

I am a fan of those tall circular Cocktail tables you see at bars which are roughly chest high. These make for SUPERB central altars in a ritual chamber, as they can keep your work closer to eye level, and as they are circular, they can be arranged so that you can face any direction in ritual.

You can buy permanent ones, or foldable ones. Both have their advantages.

You could of course use any stable table or stand as an altar, I have used everything from folding dinner trays, automobile hoods, Cinderblocks, as well as more reasonable things like bedside nightstands, and credenzas.

However, due to various circumstances, you may be unable to set up a dedicated altar. You may even have to keep your practice hidden. In which case you need to be creative about how you do your magick. An Altar is not required to do magick, but it is very useful and important and can really contribute to the sense that you are living a magickal life.

Ritual chamber - A dedicated ritual space, such as a ritual chamber is one of the focal points of a dedicated worker of magick.

My ideal ritual chamber would be about the size of a large bedroom, large enough for me to stand in the middle with a staff in my hand outstretched in any direction and not hit anything.

It would be painted in Dark colors, preferably black. It would be hung with black velvet or silk drapery, and would likely not have any windows, or they would be heavily curtained with blackout curtains. This chamber would likely never see the light of day, save for unique daylight spells and rituals that I could just as easily do outside.

It would have a way to ventilate it, if there is no window, because the air can quickly become uncomfortable to breathe when you have enough incense burning.

On the floor would be a black or dark rug, or dark wood/tile floor. Upon the floor would be drawn in either white, silver, or bright blood red, a trinity of self.

In the center of the trinity would be the Ritual Altar, it might or might not have its own trinity of self on top of it.

At each corner of the trinity would be a candle stand, either on a short stool or table, or on the ground in such a way as to be unlikely to be knocked over. Upon each candle stand would be one large black candle, either a pillar, or a taper, something that will last a long time. If I felt like using colors, I would color them Red, Green and Blue to match the Body (red), mind (green) and spirit (blue) aspects.

Around the room would be practical, but attractive and thematic furnishings to hold my ritual tools, books, and other important things.

During ritual, the room would have NO unnatural lighting that wasn't specifically designed to set the mood in some way… candles and other natural lighting would be preferred.

A fireplace in one side might be very cool as well and could be used as an indoor bonfire.

Magickal name

Along with all the other ways you get into character and live an intentional magickal life, there is one final component to your magickal identity and magickal life that you need to consider, and that is the adoption of magickal names, titles and a personal sigil or seal.

Some of these things are meant to be personal and secret, others are meant to be public, or shared only with people you work with in magick such as people in your coven or lodge.

Not all of us need or want a magickal name. Names can often limit us, and I myself prefer to go without one.

However, I DO believe a personal sigil or seal is a useful and powerful thing to create.

The creation of a personal sigil or seal should be done using virtually any method you like, from the standard methods of Sigil creation in Chaos magick, to using your own magickal alphabet or simply drawing something pleasing to your eye.

It should be simple enough to easily recreate many times, but recognizable to you and those who might know it for what it is.

One person I knew many years ago used an Exclamation point and a Question mark, and combined them into the same space, so that they overlapped. This became his personal seal and it became powerful in his magick a way for him to "invoke himself" his "god self" in ritual. It was simple, and elegant. Though it wasn't quite as unique as a sigil, it was his.

I cannot tell you how to do this, you will need to figure this out on your own… however, the next section about magickal writing might help you!

Magickal writing — creating "Sigilscript"

This is a common feature in many a grimoire about magick in the modern era, a secret, or special script of characters that can be used by the initiate to create spells, sigils or to keep their knowledge secret in some capacity.

Sometimes this script is an accepted language from antiquity like Hebrew, Runes, etc. Or the discovery/creation of the author via channeling such as Enochian.

I have included my own magickal alphabet, but I must be clear with you, this alphabet is NOT some ancient tongue, nor is it the alphabet of the infernal realms.

It IS the product of channeling and meditation, but not in the sense that I got these symbols directly from any spirit. Instead I invoked several entities asking them for advice on this subject and they guided me into special gnosis on how written languages, words, and sigils can interact with the mind, and how I can make use of my own written language to reach through the conscious barrier and treat EVERY letter of the alphabet as a kind of sigil.

Following their guidelines, I designed a series of simplistic sigils to look otherworldly and coherent as a language. My rules were simple –

- No complex pictograms, 2 or 3 lines with a dot here and there.
- Vowels should have a rounded open look to them, consonants should be more angular.
- Any similar sounding letters when spoken should be combined into one letter (C/K/Q, CH, CK, becomes Just a single letter in this case "⟩." Thus, Clock would become Cloc – ⟩✕↩⟩ –, Choir would become Coir. Etc.).
- All letters are capitals, no lowercase. At least one letter must be an anchor to the English language

it is based on and have some similarity in appearance (in this case the letter A = 𝒜).

I did this while in an empty mind trance, and when I had what I felt was a good selection of symbols, I then went through them one by one, and asked myself what each sigil represented in the English alphabet using the rules I had outlined above.

What emerged was a simple, almost runic alphabet that is familiar to my eyes, but utterly unreadable. Even to this day, I can only pick out certain letters, and this is intentional. I could easily memorize this alphabet and use it as a magick font. However, I have chosen to not do this.

You may choose to memorize it and use it as your own form of hidden secret script if you like. However, for my own use in magick, I prefer to keep it mysterious and here is why-

When we learn to read, we are essentially programming our conscious mind to recognize a symbol as a sound and a component of thought. Indeed, it should be noted that if you are fluent, words become thoughts, and the alphabet can become thoughts as well. If you are much of a reader, you will often have the experience of reading a novel and after a few sentences or so, you stop registering the words on the page, and your mind suddenly starts seeing the scenes play out, hearing the words, even smelling the smells. Not as vividly as a dream, but the words become invisible and program your mind to think certain thoughts.

This phenomenon can work the other way as well, you can learn to write to the point where you can literally think in the form of writing. When you become truly skilled at touch typing, you can have a completely empty mind, and your fingers will quite literally type out your thoughts in literary form.

The point here is our conscious and subconscious mind are intrinsically altered and connected to the act of reading and writing, and this is a fundamental thing in magick to understand.

When you think of fire, you are thinking about the concept of fire, this is an astral activity… in your mind's eye, and in the astral realm FIRE manifests, and you consider and observe it. It is REALLY THERE in the astral realm.

You can reach into the astral and write the word fire on a slip of paper, and hand it to someone, someone who will read that slip of paper, and the fire from your astral reality will blaze to life in the mind of the reader.

You plucked an idea down from the astral, imprinted it on the material world and sent it into the astral reality of the reader.

This revelation about writing is utterly life changing for those who master it's uses…

Consider also that all magick in this system is based on the idea of a spell having a physical, mental and astral component. Writing something, either in the form of a sigil, picture or word, counts as a very holistic action. It is impossible to write, or draw, or do math without actively using all three prime aspects of reality.

Writing is easily the most magickal thing a mundane person can experience, and chances are, if you are at all sensitive to magick, you know what I am saying is true.

So why make your own mysterious alphabet, or even language? Why not commit it memory?

Because this sigil script bypasses the conscious filter and penetrates deep into your subconscious. You see, you do not need to be able to consciously read the words for your subconscious mind to read them and know their meaning. All that you need to do is tap into that subconscious mind when you create the symbols and focus on them intently and impress them into the subconscious mind when you choose them for each letter of the alphabet.

This language becomes a kind of subliminal message and works like an alternative form of Sigil as used in Chaos magick. For that matter, this language can become the most potent base for all your future sigil magick because you no longer must jump through as many hoops to hide the language inherent in the process of making a sigil.

You can literally just write the new sigil script on a piece of paper, in any order you like, and the meaning is instantly hidden from your conscious mind.

Remember the KEY here is to never allow yourself to memorize the script, if you do, you will likely need to start over and make a new one for maximal results.

On the next page is my own personal form of Sigilscript as created for my own use, and now I give it to you, you may feel free to use this if you like it, but I urge you to create your own when you feel ready. When you are ready to make your own, make sure you record it in your grimoire!

A B C D E F G H I J

K L M N O P Q R S T

U V X Y Z (spc)

Thus, the Title of this book, when written in Sigilscript would be:

𝒦Ɛ⋗ᴜ⋏Ɛ
Ⴖ𝟥Ɛ
⋏ᴧƐ✕⋏Ⴖ⅄ᴜ⋏

Try it for yourself, try making some sigils with this script, try using this in place of English when writing things in ritual. I have used them in demon sorcery, and other forms of magick to good effect.

When using Sigilscript in making a true sigil, you can still use these letters like you would use the regular letters of the alphabet in a normal sigil, be creative, take them apart, assembling them out of order etc. till you get a shape that is utterly unrecognizable but still feels right.

Then, when you are ready, make your own Sigilscript and use it for everything that seems suitable.

Pathworking with Spirits

Spirits, Faeries, gnomes, Elves, Demons, Gods, Angels, ghosts, Shadows, Djinn, Kami, Oni, Yaoguai, Mogwai, the ancestors… By whatever name you use, these beings are very real, and ever present in the astral world around us. Some of these beings have forgotten more than we are likely to ever learn in our lifetime about the nuances and traditions of magick.

Many of them experience reality from a completely different perspective, their "minds" focused on the aspect of spirit more than the material aspect. There can be no better guide to learning the deeper mysteries than to enlist the help of a spirit that cares about your personal ascension.

This book is written entirely from the perspective of someone who works exclusively with the darkest aspects of the spirit world. If you are interested in working with Enochian angels or other spirits like them, this book will not help you with that directly, but some of the same principles will apply.

So, keep in mind, I personally specialize in and prefer to work only with the dark entities. The so-called "Demons," the wickedest Djinn, shadows, and other spirits that many people in the "new age" would seek to avoid. It is just a personal preference, and I have found that when you are upon the so-called Left-hand path of liberation, these entities are often far more useful and interested in your progress.

It is also because I feel the other alternatives (Angels, god, or "good" spirits in other cultures), are all too often packaged in a limiting religion with a dogma and faith attached that can be difficult to ignore.

It should be restated that "Angels" in the occult sense, do not mean servants of Yahweh or the Judeo-Christian God. They are, for all intents and purposes available to anyone to call upon. From the most devout Satanists, to the most atheist Luciferian. Still, these entities have been engaged in various cultures and histories like all the others and have a certain cultural and religious identity. Angels can even be called along with Demons, but great care must be taken to ensure the Angel and the Demon have compatible energies and intentions. This is not a thing to be trifled with, and I will not be covering it in this work.

Even working with "Demons" in the irreligious manner as I do, requires that I frequently deep dive into religious dogma to find clues or scraps of truth.

Azazel for example has frequently pointed me toward biblical things like the Nephilim, The tower of Babel, and other things from the earlier books of the bible or Torah. Of course, he made it clear to me that most of these things are metaphorical and allegorical in the sense that I shouldn't take them too literally or become of a Judeo-Christian mindset.

Still it can be difficult to separate the truth from the fictional story sometimes, and it often requires sitting through abominably dogmatic lectures from fringe Christians and people with fringy conspiracy ideas about ancient aliens, and flat earth etc.

You should feel liberated and encouraged to try to reach out to and work with whatever spirits you feel suit you. It is my advice that you never do this from the perspective of a worshipper, or follower… You are not an inferior fallen being that needs a god to perfect them. You are the universe itself, you are the void, having an experience of mortality. Any being that calls itself god and places itself over you are just another tyrant for you to avoid.

I am going to do my best at least in this work, to not pollute your mind with any further sort of dogmatic belief in, or about any of the religions of the world beyond what I already shared earlier in the book of foundations.

IT should suffice to say, I am not theistic, I worship nothing, I hold that all religions have been perversions of the gnosis given to mankind by the spirit world and used to enslave rather than liberate mankind. Oh, it may have often started off with good intentions, but it only takes a short time for the best of things to be perverted by those who know how.

I say all this because working with spirits can bring all kinds of gnosis about gods, demons, angels, heavens and hell. And you need to be able to stay sane and sift out the parts

BECOME THE MAELSTROM 112

that are meant to manipulate and control you.

As I taught you earlier, Demons and other spirits work mostly by working with what you have available to you, either in the form of what you remember, or what is available to you in the form of research, for example internet searches and books you have on your shelf or might want to buy.

Never mistake their gnosis for objective fact, treat it as personal gnosis, and work with it, develop it, break it down and rebuild it. These are things the spirits want you to experience.

Spirits will even give you WRONG information, because in studying it, challenging it, and working with it, you can learn the RIGHT information, or the deeper meaning below the answers.

It is said by Judeo-Christians that "god" works in mysterious ways, and the rest of the spirit world is no different... They are direct when they need to be, but much of the time, they are very indirect. That is the secret of why those who spend many years on this path eventually become very wise, very knowledgeable, and observant.

How it's done

In the 3rd section (pathworking), I will lay out for you a complete pathworking that should help you to create your own working relationship with one of the demonic forces I have worked with, or one of your own compatible choosing, and as you build upon that relationship you will advance in your magick exponentially better and faster than if you just put your nose in a book and try to figure things out by trial and error.

Please note I have created this system of magick with the goal of removing or reducing the reliance on the dogmatism of religion. To a certain extent, it is impossible because the very seals of the demons, and their names, and descriptions come from Judeo-Christian occultism, or the dogmatic religion of some other culture.

Some systems such as Solomonic magick, revolve around abusing and threatening spirits, invoking the names and power of angels and the Abrahamic god to bully and force a spirit to

do your bidding without any real sense of respect for them.

To a Judeo-Christian this makes perfect sense, they see these spirits as evil, unclean, fallen, and an enemy of mankind. To them the idea of treating demons with contempt is no different than the idea of treating a murderer or child molester with contempt while forcing them to serve you like a slave. *They have it coming*, so to speak.

I am not Judeo-Christian; I am not even pagan. I defy the religions of the world, I am me, and I worship nothing, kneel before nothing. I am like the spirits I conjure, I am their ally, never their slave, I am free.

Remember, this entire system of magick is devoted to respectfully working with the neutral and darker aspects of the spirit world, if you are interested in working with holy angels or other spirits, some of the methods in this book will potentially work equally well, but you may need to experiment to be sure. Nor will it ever abuse so called "demons."

We begin this process with a step by step breakdown of how this relationship will be created:

Intention - Before you do anything, you need to identify your intention. It is my strong opinion that it is a foolish thing to attempt to work with any spirit with a petty, materialistic goal in mind. Not that you cannot have petty and materialistic goals at all, but your primary intention should always be noble in nature. By noble, I mean your intention should be to build a mutually valuable relationship with this spirit and understand your own true intention well enough to not make beginner mistakes and offend a cosmic being that has been known to destroy entire nations with curses and chaos.

It is perfectly ok to ask your friends for petty and material things from time to time, and that is how it will be with these spirits. Most of them are very willing to strike up a bargain on the first meeting but keep it noble in nature.

As a rule, most spirits seem to be more interested in your personal growth than in your material or ignoble desires for sex, money and power. But they will of course help you get those other desires too, especially if it can help you mature and grow as a spiritual being.

Even the darkest, blackest demon, once respectfully

called, is more interested in improving YOU, than improving your bank balance. The reason for this is simple. They want you to reach your potential and be a powerful ally that THEY can call upon as well.

So the wise Demon Sorcerer, always puts some time into considering what the spirit will get out of the deal, and how to genuinely devote themselves to the spirit without falling in worship (the spirits I prefer to work with, detest weak worshippers begging and pleading for scraps, they respect kings, queens, and nobility, act like it, and they will give you great favor.)

Selection - Selecting a spirit is not an easy task if you do not have a solid idea of what you are trying to do, and even then, there are hundreds if not thousands of known spirits that can be called upon. We can narrow that list a lot just by making a firm commitment to focus on just one or two pantheons, for example the Goetic pantheon, the Watchers/Grigori, Enochian angels, or even Lovecraftian entities.

We should use a combination of intuition and research to figure out what spirit would be best to call. If you do not already have experience here, and this is your very first intentional calling. I would advise you to begin with one of the spirits I recommend in the pathworking section, someone with authority that can lead you to other spirits, someone who has a good established history with human beings, who won't lash out and wreak havoc in your life.

It is very important to know that it is very common that these spirits will already be trying to get our attention long before we reach out to them. These entities can influence and inspire us and be active in our lives for many years before we realize it and take any action to respond. Nearly every spirit I have worked with, got MY attention before I got theirs.

Learn to see the signs this is happening. If you have been developing your intuition and sensitivity, you will usually just know when you are being contacted.

Immersion - Once we feel confident in our ability to communicate or at least dimly sense the supernatural and magick (see Becoming Sensitive to Magick), we can begin to prepare ourselves for our initial calling of the spirit. This is

best done by doing a little research, I do not like to learn too much before I begin, I prefer to learn only as much as I need to begin to feel really inspired to talk to the spirit. So, this means I usually just read a short write up about the spirit.

For example, with a Goetic demon, I focus primarily on the info in the Ars Goetia, and maybe do a little online research to find out what incense the spirit likes, what their favorite colors and numbers and dates might be. I do not like to learn too much, and I stay away from any major dogmatic religious perspectives of the spirit. You should have a paragraph or two at most of notes telling you some key details so you can lock onto the spirits vibration and let THEM teach you about them.

Once you have this paragraph or two of information, you need to really just keep them on your mind, draw pictures of how they are described, draw their seal and keep it in your field of vision while you go through your day, wear their favorite color, burn their incense, and do other things to really get yourself immersed in their energy.

Sometimes just doing these things will cause you to make a spontaneous connection with the spirit and you won't even need to perform a complex ritual to make first contact.

This immersion period should never drag on too long, a few days tops.

At this stage you should notice signs that the spirit is in contact with you in some way, literally waiting for you to make the final act of ritual to call to them. Now is the time to Prepare a ritual and execute it while the iron is hot.

First contact - In the Pathworking section of the book, I outline several different formats for calling a spirit. For the first calling, I prefer to use a modestly elaborate ritual to allow me to really build up the needed energy and immersion with the spirit to maximize the chances that I will truly tune into the spirit and call it into my ritual chamber.

It is my opinion that most spiritual working begins with Evocation, because you must bring the spirit into your presence and experience to fully tune into them before anything else can be easily done. Some would argue that we are not actually bringing them into our ritual chamber but tuning our own senses to them and empowering them with magick energy to manifest, that they are already here, and I can agree with this sentiment on many levels. Therefore, my first calling is still an evocation, it is the safest, simplest interaction to have, and goes a long way toward making you aware of the spirits energies and temperament. If things go well, this evocation can become an invocation/channeling instead. If things go badly, apologize and dismiss the spirit, if they go very badly, you may need to banish and protect yourself, which is much easier to do if the spirit isn't working through you directly somehow.

Chances are, that if the spirit is already active in my life and is the one that initiated contact, that the spirit will come through with a powerful and undeniable (even if subtle) manifestation. Many spirits like to make a grand introduction and memorable first contact. Some will utterly knock your socks off with poltergeist activity, maybe even physical manifestation, or Rapture.

This first ritual should establish a good working rapport with the spirit, and you should be open and up front about your intentions. Try not to make this first contact all about asking the demon for things. How much would you enjoy it if a stranger invited you over to their home to be friends, and within minutes of walking in the door they started asking you to bring them money and sex, and revenge etc.

Instead try to make this ritual a chance to get to know one another and tell them all about your hopes and dreams and plans and ask them to give you their gnosis and knowledge and wisdom so that you can understand them better.

Despite this first contact not being about getting your petty mundane desires taken care of, it is perfectly acceptable to ask for a few humble things at some point during the ritual, but do not make it the point or focus of the interaction. I have found some spirits LOVE showering us with "getting to know you" gifts of their own and show an eagerness to do things for us to win our favor (yes you read that right, to get YOUR favor). While others will be offended if you expect them to do much for you before proving yourself to them.

There is no way to know these things without trial and error. I cannot say this enough, but if you are being respectful, and noble, you should be fine when trying to work with most of the known spirits we work with in sorcery.

The end of any successful initial contact with such a spirit should conclude with a generous offering, and with you asking the spirit to return to you when you call again. You want this spirit to be active in your life, unless of course you don't get along in some way.

Continuing the relationship – Once you have established a strong first contact with the spirit, it is up to you how to proceed and what methods of contact you want to use. I have included simpler rituals for more "on the spot" style callings. However, it should be noted, if you have established a working relationship with a spirit, particularly if that spirit is your "patron" you likely will not normally need to conduct elaborate rituals any more to get the spirits attention. They will be keeping an eye on you so to speak.

It is always nice to perform a formal elaborate ritual for a spirit occasionally, as an act of friendship and a kind of offering. I have found that sometimes I MUST perform a more elaborate ritual with a spirit, or they do not come to me or commune with me. This could be because I need the ritual to inspire me and align me with the spirits current. Or it could be because the spirit wants the respect and energy of the ritual.

Typically (there are always exceptions), powerful gods, angels and demons do not "NEED" this energy, but they enjoy it, and what matters to them more is that you gave it willingly as an offering.

Sometimes the opposite is true, if I am always and only calling upon them in elaborate ritual and ignore them outside these rituals, I can eventually expect them to also potentially deny me.

Thus, you do not however need to always do formal actions with spirits, sometimes you can just speak to them as if they are with you or make small offerings to them on the spot when the urge strikes you.

I would begrudgingly compare this to the prayer to a saint a catholic might conduct, but we are not praying, and these are not saints.

Some ideas to try for these on the spot practices include (but are not limited to) – Lighting incense in their honor, lighting a candle for them, singing their name or singing to them, speaking to them privately (like prayer but without the prostration and worshipful tone), thinking of ways to decorate your altar in their honor, ways to incorporate them into your rituals etc.

Using Idols

I am a big proponent of using idols or other symbolic objects as focuses and anchors in my spiritual calling rituals. This is not at all required, however any spirit that I have a strong connection with, eventually gets some object that I associate as being strongly connected to them.

This could be a Crow Statue for Malphas.

A decorated resin skull with Azazel/Saturn's Sigil on it for Azazel.

A grimoire for Dantalion

A figurine of Isis for the feminine form of Astaroth/Astarte and Isis.

This all differs slightly from the act of consecrating the object to the spirit as you might with a wand or other ritual tool, as the idol is instead more or less a physical vessel for the spirit to inhabit and or be used as a gateway for the spirit.

The nice thing about Idols, is they make convenient and attractive ritual focal points. These can be sufficiently empowered in regular usage to allow you to make quick connections and meaningful offerings to your spiritual companions, without having to necessarily call them. Simply place the idol on your altar or somewhere special and declare your intention to make an offering or request, burn some incense or leave your offering, and go about your day.

This can be as simple or elaborate as you feel suitable for the given situation and is a common practice around the world.

Preparing an idol for this purpose can be a simple matter of just using it in ritual to represent the spirit and making a declaration of intention in that ritual.

Or you can go to more elaborate means and conduct a special consecration rite to the spirit and ask that they honor you by making that idol their home. I have found that some spirits like this added respect, while others don't need an anchor in the form of an idol, and the idol has more to do with manipulating your own psyche and attuning you vibrationally to the spirit via memetic/Pavlovian correspondence.

Almost like how you can make your dog happy just by picking up his or her leash, by the same token, just by placing the spirits idol on your altar, you can get a psychic alignment.

In all cases you should at least fumigate the statue or object with sage, sandalwood, or the spirits favorite incense, and charge it with your energy and intent in meditation or ritual for it to have the most use.

Also, consider the pop cultural "fear" of dolls, and consider making such a doll and anchor for a suitable spirit. Just don't come crying to me if the doll scares you in the middle of the night when it moves without explanation…

Manifestation of Spirits

If you have not already, make sure you go back a few chapters to the one titled "Becoming Sensitive to magick" and read and practice what you find there. It is also useful to practice scrying for a while to become comfortable with what it is like to have visions and experiences.

It is possible to start working with spirits without extensively training yourself to be sensitive to magick and the spirit world. Indeed, unless you are already attempting to do magick, it can be hard to learn to sense it.

However, be aware that spirits do not normally manifest for us like we imagine in the movies and pop culture examples. Actual physical manifestation should be considered a rare, and precious gift when a spirit takes on a remotely tangible physical form. If you work long enough with spirits, this will eventually happen for you. However, the form the physical manifestation takes may be (and almost always is) subtle.

Physical manifestation should not be your goal in every working, especially early on. Focus on making contact and establishing reliable communication. It is possible a spirit will want you to help them to manifest and show you ways to help them do it. However, keep in mind physical manifestation is a two-way street, and a spirit may not manifest for you, even if you do everything right.

Some spirits may even be offended if you seem preoccupied with making them perform these parlor tricks for you all the time. If you are having reliable communication, why do you need them to manifest into physical form all the time?

Here is a partial list of some of the way's spirits will communicate or manifest for you, broken down into categories:

Synchronistic – At any time during or after the ritual you may experience synchronistic events that relate to your working with the spirit. It will always be obvious that this is a sign or message from the spirit/s, and you shouldn't likely need to spend much time trying to figure it out. Synchronicity is not synchronicity if you must struggle to figure it out, it will almost always come to you instantly.

Internal – Having unusual thoughts or ideas you don't normally have (this can feel like a sudden inspiration), your internal voice might change in tone, inflection or personality and you might start having a 2-way conversation in your head where one thought pattern is you, and the other is you as well, but different. You may simply just know things suddenly, like a gut impulse, or spontaneous new idea or epiphany.

Astral – more than just strange thoughts, you may enter deep trance and have visions, hear voices, feel strange sensations, smell strange smells. These are usually unique to your experience but can sometimes be shared with a group. Both can be valid, not everyone in the group must share the same experience for it to be real. This can be a simple vision, or a full blown out of body experience. Buckle up! I enjoy these the most and these are often the most moving and significant and give the most meaningful exchanges of information.

Subtle manifestation – This can take the form of low level poltergeist activity - strange sounds, footsteps, things settling in the closet, the sensation of a presence or creepiness in the area, hot or cold spots in the room (or the entire room

abruptly changing temperature), changes in air pressure or humidity, sudden fog, gentle currents of air, sudden wind, incense moving suddenly without any apparent cause, candle flames or incense smoke acting strangely without apparent cause, and much more.

Strong Manifestation – This is rarer, it will usually be in the form of an unmistakable and obvious poltergeist, things moving or even flying across the room, things getting knocked off shelves, sudden gusts of strong wind, sudden unexpected storms, or breaks in said storms. You may have animals appear, or make themselves known in unusual ways, nocturnal animals call out in the day, or daytime animals appear or call out at night. Loud noises, bangs, thuds, booms, clear voices, strong sensations of being touched, pain or pleasure, or even physically moved or struck, scratches or welts forming on the body, possession, rapture, invocation, and channeling, and much more.

Full physical manifestation – This is the rarest experience for most occultists. It is always a life changing experience. For me the biggest distinction between a strong manifestation and a full manifestation is that the manifestation is clearly intelligent and will interact with you. This can range from an amorphous cloud of fog or energy or light, moving around intelligently, shadow people, figures of people or animals or object appearing in fire and being sustained for a lengthy period (not just a quick flicker, but several minutes at a time).

In the most extreme and rarest of cases (1% of 1%), it can be a fully formed physical being, a humanoid, or animal shape, grotesque or beautiful, or anything in between. These latter events can be utterly terrifying even when expected.

This is one of the reasons it doesn't happen often, is because these beings know that such a manifestation would be a shock to our hold on reality. Another reason is that most of these beings are NOT focused on the material plane the same way we are, taking physical form for them is difficult, taxing, and genuinely unnecessary most of the time.

Spirits will typically only do this for the most important of situations, or to make the strongest impression. Though I would not doubt that somewhere in the world, there are cabals of people who regularly get such things to happen by the very nature of their power and connection to these spirits and the power of their combined intention.

For our purposes, such an event would be a divine/diabolical miracle and if (when) it happens for you, never forget it, cherish it always. For you have seen a thing few on earth ever will. However, by the same token – NEVER expect or demand it.

For the record, I have never had the 1% in 1% experience of a full-bodied physical spirit manifesting as a flesh and blood being in a Hollywood way. I am confident this is somehow possible, but almost never done.

Remember, these spirits do not have physical bodies like we understand them, and to bend the laws of nature to make one appear out of thin air and then vanish without a trace is… well… things like this just don't happen, and when they do… it can never be proven.

What do they look / sound / smell like?

This is different every time for every person. Remember, nearly all of these spirits, as far as I can tell, do not have corporeal bodies in the usual sense, they are more or less a field of consciousness, which may have a physical component, but it is dispersed, like air, clouds or ozone, or electromagnetism in the environment.

When we "See" a spirit, normally it is in the minds eye more than anything, and even when it is in the physical world in a tangible form, it is usually in the form of smoke, or shadow or light or patterns in the environment.

In the very rarest of physical manifestations where you can literally touch them, it is still (IMHO) impossible to prove it is a physical form, it could just be so thorough a hallucinatory manifestation that you can't know for sure. Because to my knowledge, people only have isolated anecdotal evidence to back up such a claim.

If there are any groups that can reliably get full physical manifestations to happen, they aren't sharing any proof… just claims.

What I can tell you, is 99% of what we experience is egregoric in some capacity, that is, we create, in cooperation with the spirit, a kind of vessel they can inhabit in our minds eye. A kind of symbolic puppet that speaks to us on a subtle level of consciousness. Thus, it can be like an animal, or object, or be different for everyone.

I might see lucifer as a fallen angel of light, you might see him as a flaming phoenix, I might see him as a small child, you as an adult. Worse yet, they can change how they appear to us all the time, for example Lucifer has appeared to me in all the above ways! This can get confusing if you rely on what they look like.

The key I find is experience, if we have a cultural bias to see spirits a certain way, they will appear this way. A Christian based person will see Angels of light and Monstrous demons with horns and fire and brimstone. A pagan will see them appear as nature spirits perhaps or pagan gods. Someone into aliens and thinks the Annunaki were space aliens that created star gates and ancient alien cities might see greys or U.F.O.'s or reptilians or men in black etc. Others will see pop culture superheroes or villains.

I would suggest you go with the flow, don't discount these things just because they look like what you expect or don't. Just trust the experience and go with it as if it's real. Validate it AFTER. You will be amazed, I promise you.

Evocation, Invocation, Channeling, Possession, and Exorcism

It is important to categorize the different kinds of interactions we can have with spirits. These are meant to be broad categories, and many rituals will combine different interactions. Some would argue that possession, channeling and invocation are all different degrees of the same thing, and I am open to thinking of it this way, but I think you will see that there are differences in how they manifest.

Let's take a moment then to look at each of these kinds of interactions and talk briefly about them:

Evocation – For most occultists, this is where they start their journey into working with spirits. This is the act of calling a spirit to appear before you in some way, be it physical (as in an actual entity appears visibly before you), or in more subtle ways such as low or even intense level poltergeists (strange sounds, footsteps, knocking on walls etc.), visions or a sensation of a presence.

These spirits can appear to us in any number of ways, and the subtler ways are more common. The key will be the synchronistic way these events happen. They do not have to defy the laws of nature at all, they simply need to be strangely appropriate in timing or significance. A candle sparking or going out when you ask for a sign, a settling of the house in response to a question.

Even a car driving past your house in an unusually noisy way could be a sign. I have had day birds start singing (at night) in the woods near my outdoor ritual space in response to a silent question in my mind. I have had unscheduled trains bolt past my house when asking for a strong audible sign. I have had dishes settle in the drying rack when asking a spirit to reveal itself.

Rooms will get inexplicably hot, or cold, or spots in rooms will get suddenly cold or hot, or the humidity will change dramatically.

Incense smoke and fire has formed faces, shapes, and even words, and I have heard voices in the wind, and people shouting words in the distance where nobody has any right to be…

I have even captured visual phenomenon on camera in the form of reflections from fire light that appear in just the right place at the right time and the incense smoke wafts to the artifact on the camera as if being sucked into it… Many of these examples are public on the internet for you to see!

On very exceptional occasions, I have seen things firsthand that defied all rational explanation… powerful poltergeist activity knocking things around, physical apparitions of shadows and clouds of iridescent smoke and light moving around…

For me, the most reliable and common indication that a spirit is in my ritual space is the sensation of the hairs on my neck standing up and some vigorous shuddering as their energy interacts with me. This is then usually accompanied by visions, or the visions bring this shuddering sensation upon me as I reach out with my feelings to see if the vision or experience is a spirit or my imagination.

For example, I may have a flashing vision of a spirit standing in the corner of my room whispering something important to me. This could be real or my imagination running away with itself.

As I am not fully integrated with my spiritual senses all the time, it could go either way. As I shift my awareness to the vision and listen to the whispers, I pretend for just a moment that the experience is not just my imagination, if it is a spirit, I feel a shuddering chill, if it is not a spirit, nothing happens.

Other times I will ask – Spirit is that you!? When I begin to think the spirit is near, and if I shudder, I know they are connecting to me.

From there I proceed to enter deeper trances or start talking and look for other signs.

This is borderline Invocation. Once I feel this, I begin interacting with them like they are in the room… and as I do so, I become more and more aware of them. Sometimes knowing where they are in the room and addressing that space directly, even if I cannot see them.

The key here, especially with the more subtle manifestations and signs is to be sensitive to them and trust them as more than just random coincidence. In the end you will "just know."

Invocation – Invocation means taking on the mantle, or energy of the spirit, and inviting it into your physical being so that it's physical and spiritual being overlaps with yours. It is not exactly a channeling, or possession. It is however very, very intimate, and you can share with one another all kinds of feelings, thoughts, and experiences that can leave you feeling incredibly vivid things… peace, alarm, joy, anger, pleasure, or pain. Incubi, and Succubi are notoriously eager to engage in Invocation, far more than evocation.

You need to remember nearly all spirits lack a very coherent physical form, and their ability to experience the material plane is extremely limited. Many CRAVE vivid living experiences and will be very grateful if you trust them enough to invoke them when you consume an offering in their honor.

Invocation is NOT possession, and it is not quite channeling, though they are very closely related, and some might call them different degrees of the same thing. For the purposes of working with spirits, I treat them as separate kinds of experiences.

When you invoke a spirit, you will often gain the benefits of their energy, you might never know their true thoughts, but you will be influenced very directly by their abilities, and knowledge. Invoking a spirit of healing might improve your intuitive knowledge of medicine, or energy healing etc.

This isn't a guarantee, you are not controlling these beings, and they are not controlling you. It is simply a direct and intimate mingling of the energies, and both of you can easily end this connection by willing it.

But again, remember, invocation should not be done unless you trust the spirit, or have high confidence in your ability to maintain control over the situation. Because invocation does make channeling and possession much easier for the spirit, as you have already invited it in.

In my experience, spirits are a bit like the fantasy of vampires, most (if not all) have little power over you directly unless you invite them in.

Channeling – This is the more intense form of invocation where you permit the entity to have some control over your faculties, allowing them to communicate through you to some degree. This will never be perfect in my experience, they are STILL limited to using your faculties, knowledge and experiences as a palette of concepts to work with.

This is why some talented mediums will channel a spirit speaking in a language they do not speak, and all that will come out is gibberish, some of which may indeed be correct. But it will rarely if ever be a perfect match to a real language, unless the medium can speak that language already.

It is very rare, perhaps even impossible for a connection to become so perfect that a spirit can literally speak through you with all its knowledge intact. For whatever reason, it seems as if a spirit cannot create new knowledge in your mind, it must work with what is already known, or is

something you can accept.

To a skeptic this means nothing at all is happening… the subject is making things up, or psychosomatically believes it and dredges up hidden memories from somewhere they forgot about…

However, there are many of those who have these experiences who are otherwise sane and rational people who insist their experience is valid and is not mere hallucination, or imagination.

Most people who have claimed to be able to have a spirit speak through them perfectly without things being lost in translation, have been proven false or at least of controversial and questionable trustworthiness, even within most occult communities.

In my own practice, channeling often results in a deep trance where I may sit calmly and speak, write or type. Or where I begin pacing around like a caged animal muttering or talking, speaking in "tongues" and being very energetic and literally like a crazed conspiracy theorist ranting and muttering as they reason out strange facts and tie together loose ends.

I have many pages in my magickal journals of scribbled notes from these crazed channelings that look like they were written by someone with no fine motor control, childish chicken scratch, and so on (my normal handwriting is already horrible, when channeling it's almost illegible). Very much the epitome of what some would call automatic writing or spirit writing.

Channeling can be thought of as a very deep kind of invocation, as mentioned before.

Possession – This can take on both subtle and overt forms. It can be cooperative, or adversarial. In the subtler forms, the spirit will literally be dormant, lurking behind the eyes of the host, not really controlling much of anything, just doing subtle things to influence the host. Other times it will be in almost complete control and will do its best to act like who you are.

Possession always begins in a voluntary manner by the host. Though they may not have consciously asked for it, they subconsciously permitted it, either out of fear, weakness, or true intent, and the host only becomes a victim if the host allows the spirit to take too much control and or is overpowered by the spirit. A human can ALWAYS eject a spirit, but they can become convinced they cannot do it by the events and situations that happen.

It has been my experience that possession is very much a thing I ultimately can control or stop. When it happened, I was almost always fully aware of my actions, either during or soon after.

Some people report less control, and I believe this can be possible, and this can be dangerous with a more malevolent possession. In my experience I would feel inexplicably compelled to spontaneously say, act, and think things I normally wouldn't. It was very rare (but did happen a few times) for me to experience a possession where I had no recollection at all.

Like channeling, the spirit doesn't seem to be able to always, or often make a complete connection allowing it to bring all its knowledge, power or ability through... but it can get very close and be very uncanny in its ability to know and do things the host cannot.

It is very unlikely that you can or will become possessed under normal circumstances, providing you are taking some basic precautions and work with spirits you can trust. Taking the time to develop your relationship and being sure you are in communication with the right spirit. Many spirits, including all the so-called demons I have worked with, will not really be interested in possessing you and will respect your boundaries. The Goetic spirits for example, when treated with respect, have great respect for your personal boundaries. So even if you beg a spirit to do this, if it is not your truest intention, they will not even entertain the notion. Most of the spirits you will work with in this core system are known entities that have at least *mostly safe* working history with mankind.

The same cannot be said for the unknown spirits, and the air around you is *thick* with them... many are neutral, some are benevolent, but some are deeply malevolent and will stir up trouble for you, or even harm you or those you love just for the energy it gives them to do so.

Many malevolent spirits will claim the name of a known demon or folk legend monster to cause fear, or otherwise use the demon as a scapegoat... making it that much harder to be exorcized by an outside party.

It is my experience that the best exorcism revolves around empowering the host to know they can evict the spirit at will...

Most possessions that happen to a victim in my limited experience of such things, are the result of someone with deep seated emotional trauma or problems that causes them to be more willing to accept a demon or other spirit into them to give them the illusion of power and control.

To a certain degree, this was my own experience as well.

Possession can be very dangerous and cause a LOT of problems in people's lives... However, with a trusted spirit it can be a very beneficial thing, as a spirit can possess you and you can both benefit greatly from the experience, you will learn exponentially more, and more quickly, the spirits can act in your life more directly, manipulating you and those around you through direct physical mundane means to benefit both of you in meaningful ways.

There are in fact highly intriguing theories that claim that some of the ancient god kings of the long-lost civilizations of antiquity, were in fact hosts, and vessels for highly powerful spirits, either through permanent state of invocation or possession, they ruled and guided mankind in their own way.

Some of us even believe that the goal of many of these spirits is to recreate the circumstances that make such a thing possible again in the future somehow. That somewhere along the line this stopped being possible and only temporary possession and invocation are possible. Is this because mankind isn't biologically compatible anymore somehow?

Theories abound, and some well-known occultists often talk about how these spirits can and do change our DNA. While others think the problem is not biological but spiritual. While still others think it must be some combination of reasons.

Ultimately, it will be up to you to decide how you want to approach the concept of possession, I have not personally been possessed in many years... but if I happen to form a good relationship with a spirit again, I would be willing to experience it again in the right situation.

It is up to you to know if you are ready or even want to take the risks associated with such an experience. I do not recommend it at all to anyone who is not an expert and ready to deal with the consequences… Spirits can lie to us as we can lie to anyone else. Build up our trust and then get invited into possession and in some rare cases, ruin our lives.

Exorcism – This is a complex situation that is a special area of magick all its own, exorcism is NOT something that can be easily attempted by anyone. It combines psychology, esotericism, demonology, parapsychology, and a commitment to the host/victim.

You cannot simply invoke the name of "god" and cast the spirit out as they do in the movies by overpowering it with your intent. At least not that I have seen. Instead the key is to empower the host to give it the confidence and belief and power to evict the spirit.

The HOST never really loses control, instead they submit to the spirit, willingly at first. Like an abused person, they can be trained and taught by the spirit that they are inferior, weak and cannot resist. Other times the spirit will manipulate the person's life in such a way that the individual will call upon the spirit for power, thinking they themselves are too powerless…

For example, a child raised in abusive home can invite a spirit into itself to help it cope with the abuse, the spirit may even take complete control over the child while it is being abused so the child can avoid experiencing the worst of the trauma directly. Literally not remembering most of it till much later, if ever.

Thus, what a skeptic might call Dissociative Identity Disorder (multiple personality Disorder), may sometimes in fact be a case of possession.

In this sense, sometimes these spirits are being benevolent protectors… but in other situations they are causing the situation, manipulating the abuser to be enraged and unable to control their impulses… or they are attracted to such people and the negative energy of the household waiting for the child, or the abuser to be weak enough to manipulate and enter.

For this reason and many others, it is my opinion that exorcism needs to revolve around using psychology and treating the emotional issues of the individual in a way that helps them deal with the underlying cause of the emotional and spiritual weakness they are feeling.

In one such case I worked on, the individual was repressing a long history of physical sexual abuse, and it was only when the subject came to terms with this and admitted it and admitted they needed help with it, that the "demon" that was in control over them was able to be brought to heel and evicted for good.

It is imperative then, that only qualified individuals truly take part in exorcism, and these individuals must be committed FULLY to the act of healing the host/victim, not just during the exorcism, but potentially for many years after. This is not a game.

It is my experience that what Judeo-Christian's would call a DEMON (such as Lucifer, or Baal, or Astorath for example), are almost never responsible in any way for any kind of negative possession unless you do something to abuse them and incite their wrath upon you. However, I would not hesitate to think there might be exceptions… and there are certainly a lot more spirits than just the known spirits we work with in the occult. Still, a person might have a reason for being victimized by the spirit world or by these or other entities we can't fathom.

In my experience, this is akin to when a crazy person claims they are napoleon. It is just a way for the individual to seem special or important, or the spirit that is possessing them is using that identity to hide itself or to scare you more.

However, these so called "Demons" can and will possess willing occultists such as myself from time to time and usually this is reported as anything other than bad. Disorienting sometimes, draining, sometimes dangerous, but not bad in the slightest.

What exactly can I do with spirits? What can they do for Me?

Now, much has already been said about how important spirits can be for your progress in magick, but not much has been said specifically about how they can help you. This is because there really is no set limit or rule, these are spiritual beings, just like you are. They are different, have different strengths and weakness, different aptitudes and personalities. The key is to start working with them and ask them to reveal to you what they like to do, and how they can help you, and how you can help them in return.

It is my experience that Demons and other higher order spirits are not limited in what they can do for you, but that most specialize in certain things, the embody those things in some way. Some demons being good at protecting you, destroying your enemies, teaching you magick, giving familiars and more. But to a certain extent all demons overlap in their capability, even a demon that is not known for its ability to defend you, can still protect you better than having none.

You will find, over time, that you will start with one or two spirits you rely on for most things (often a higher-ranking Demonic king), then start working with other demons because they specialize in something you are interested in. The initial spirit need not be a king or "high ranking" spirit, it can even be another kind of spirit or demon of no rank at all.

However, I would always begin with a known spirit that others have worked with that you can trust because they have established testimonials from people.

Below I will create a brief list of ideas for what kinds of things these spirits can do, and how to go about figuring out what they do best.

When in doubt, simply call upon the spirit and ask THEM to show YOU, don't just take my word for it.

Some examples of ways I and others have worked with Demons:

- Protection
- Guidance and teaching
- Revealing secrets
- Manipulating people
- Healing
- Learning magick
- Emotional and psychological growth
- Baneful magick
- Creation of servitors

- Creation of egregores
- Acquisition of familiars
- Creation of magickal tools and artifacts
- Inspiration and art
- Martial arts and warfare
- Makeup and glamour
- Social networking and social authority
- Sexual interactions (yes sex acts with spirits are possible in certain ways)
- Communion with the spirit for mutual respect and enjoyment
- Much more (be creative)

Goetic demons have as part of their individual descriptions a few words on how these spirits can be used in your magick. This description is in a kind of symbolic code that frequently talks about walls, and towers and structures (keeping in mind the Judeo-Christian origin of the Ars Goetia is a book of spirits who King Solomon supposedly used to build things for him as slaves, before casting them out and sending them back to hell for ever).

Many books have been written about the specifics of the Goetic spirits, but I will simplify things for you a bit by helping you with some of the symbolism of the Goetia as best as I have learned it through my own practices. This is NOT meant to be a complete breakdown, but it should give you an idea of how to interpret the examples I do not specifically cover.

Again, when in doubt ASK THE SPIRIT!

Walls, towers, and structures – When the Goetia is talking about walls, towers and other structures, the spirit can be called upon for protection, defense, and containment of various kinds of threats. This can be offensive in nature as well, such as binding someone using a demon that specializes in walls or structures. It is important to sense the different symbolism of a wall, versus a tower, versus a structure.

Walls keep things in and out, they are powerful fortifications that can thwart enemy advancement and keep enemies out, and keep prisoners in. Your ritual chamber or home would be well protected by a spirit that builds strong walls, and your enemy would be well bound by a demon that builds walls as well. This would be a passive kind of protection or binding that merely blocks and prohibits dangers or negative actions.

Towers are proactive in their defensive qualities and usually represent strongholds, fortresses and watchtowers. Spirits that build them create very powerful protective structures in your life, that will often give you early warning of threats, and create places in the astral realm where your will and authority are unmistakable. Towers and take an ACTIVE role in protecting you by being a place where your enemies can be hurt back by the defenders in the tower hurling symbolic stones and arrows back at the enemy. When used offensively, your target can be thought of as if they are locked in the highest tower and imprisoned…

Structures – This means shelter, this means containment, and this means protection and housing. But it can also mean bridges and doors, gates and other structural things. A demon that builds strong structures can reinforce walls, towers, and create gates and bridges for you in the spiritual sense.

Structures, Walls and towers can work independently from one another, but combining them can make an impregnable stronghold in your life… Your home and ritual chamber should be such a structure in the astral world. You can even do this in the astral realm in a very vivid sense, literally imagining and creating through ritual a powerful citadel in the astral realm that is directly connected to your home and your ritual chamber. A place of sanctuary and solitude. It is both symbolic and serves you well in magick.

These spirits can also potentially be useful for the construction and obtaining of a home or building for other purposes in the mundane world.

Invisibility – Some spirits in the Goetia are described as being able to make the sorcerer invisible. This doesn't mean physical mundane invisibility like the invisible man; this means they can render you spiritually invisible to the detection of your enemies and opaque to attempts to scry into your life by anyone but you. In the mundane sense, these spirits can teach you to be more secretive, stealthy and harder to predict and read.

If you are the kind of person who people always seem to know what you are thinking, or there is someone in your life that is nosy or somehow seems to always know things about you that make you uncomfortable, working with these spirits can help rectify that.

Causes storms – This can be a literal storm, or a spiritual storm, a spiritual storm is the act of creating spiritual chaos in someone's life, causing a run of bad luck or turmoil that can really threaten the target with all manner of hardship.

Destroy walls and fortifications – This can be somewhat literal in that they can cause destruction, but this also means they can destroy the astral protections and bindings created by other sorcerers. If someone has bound you, you can often use a spirit such as this to break that binding.

Provide good familiars – This can mean what it says (the literal acquisition of a spiritual familiar), but it can also be taken to mean the creation of egregores, Tulpas, Servitors, and in my experience the selection of mundane pets and service animals.

Teaching arts and sciences – This spirit is a great teacher, and usually this means they are good at teaching magick, not just mundane skills. These are superior demons to start with for the initiate into sorcery.

I could continue, but hopefully this brief list of examples will help you interpret and decipher the hidden meanings of the Goetic descriptions. Perhaps in the future I will release my own personally annotated Goetia with my own interpretations of each spirit. Until then, this book will contain listings for the 9 kings and one bonus spirit. Still, get into the habit of using your imagination and ASK THEM YOURSELF!

Learning the TRUTH about the spirits

Recently I was working with a friend and magickal colleague, and this person was asking if Lumiel is a name for Lucifer. Now, I had heard of Lumiel as an Archangel, but I know it is an angel of pure light and we both thought there might be a correspondence.

I went to that meditative internal astral place where I can commune with Lucifer alone, and he initially said any name can be used to conjure any spirit if the intent is to speak to one of them, you will get the one you need to see.

So, I pressed on, asking if he was in fact Lumiel? Was this an aspect? After a few minutes I got a mild "psychic slap" and channeled this:

"Stop trying to make us all the same... we express as individuals, just as you do for a reason. We are all one, but we are all different for a reason, stop trying to find who we are, we are already within you as one. Call to us as we are known and get the face you need to see. Seek our true face and you will waste time and lose yourself."

In another situation, I was calling to Bael also known as Beelzebub, or Beelzebuth (the 1st spirit of the Goetia) to attempt to initiate myself with him. As part of this process I wanted to ask him if he was (as many claim) Ba'al of the ancient Semitic/Canaanite culture. Also, for that matter, was he truly in favor of living sacrifice (Sacrificing living animals and people unto him, and if not, why did he permit it). When I speak about this session, I often joke about how I aimed for King Bael, and Got King Blahblah, because the gnosis I received was complex, scattered and required over a week of study and research to fully comprehend what might be going on.

As I got the info from him, I questioned all of it, asking for more detail and at one point was almost frustrated with the confusing way it was all coming out. Nothing at all matched what I had found elsewhere online. Bael was said to be a demonic entity associated with Fire. Which makes sense considering the sacrifices in big furnaces. But I got Earth as his preferred element, and he was a god of fertility and animal husbandry, not anything like what the Goetia was saying.

All this conflict made me think I was working more specifically with Ba'al than Bael, which are thought to be the same being, so I began to pester him for an explanation.

The clearest message I received from him was the result -

"Some things are not to be known."

Now this statement sounds like bad English at first, like he was saying stop asking... And in a sense, this is what he was saying, but it makes perfect grammatical sense. Some things are meant to be hidden, some things are secret for a reason, some things are occulted, and some things are not to be shared with everyone. Some things are NOT to be known. Not even by we who do this work with them.

My final interpretation was that some of this spirits history is so convoluted and lost, simply because that is how it is meant to be. In the Goetia he is a spirit that confers invisibility after all, and having your history obfuscated is certainly one way to stay hidden.

You can do with these messages what you will. However, the more and more I delve into trying to know these spirits in a way that would identify who they are exactly in history appears to be something they do not want!

Or at least, they don't want ME to be the one to look! Maybe they simply know that my Forte isn't being a book worm that memorizes reams of occult literature or mythology or Anthropology. At least not to such a high academic degree...

To be clear, it is an important part of working with spirits that you get to know them. However, you should focus on what THEY want you to know about them. You can of course research how others have experienced them, learning what incense they like, what planets energy they represent, what color represents them and much more.

However, I find most of this to be far better done by the person calling on them to tell them directly. One sorcerer might interact with Belial and get the strong impression he resonates with red (he does for me), while someone else will say he told them he likes blue or yellow (not for me).

So, who is right and who is wrong? Both!

That is not a cop out, that is a natural fact of working with spirits! They show you what you need to see. They show you a side of themselves they rarely or never show to anyone else. They treat each of us as a unique expression of the same ultimate reality they are part of.

Think of it like this, each of us presents ourselves in a manner that best fits our current audience. When you are at work, you act like who you are at work, when you are with your lover, you act differently. When I speak to my child, I speak to him in a way that is special for him and so on. Some things are the same, and some are different.

You will notice the Ars Goetia goes into no effort to talk about a spirit's favorite color, or planetary alignment, or what tarot card or number best represents them. Partly this is because some of these concerns are a modern contemporary aspect of occultism, which was not important to many in the middle ages when the Lemegeton and the Ars Goetia first appeared.

That doesn't mean these things are insignificant of course! In truth, all this helps serve to bring you into closer harmony with the energy of the spirit, and thus put you into a position of being able to commune with them with authority and skill.

Therefore, in the pathworking section when I give details about the spirits, I will be giving you only a handful of added details, and some of the details I give you will not be what other occultists have found. It will be an updated contemporary Goetic work and may become the seed for a larger future work covering all the Goetic spirits in turn.

So, what are some of the things you can ask for or seek to know? One thing I feel can be a dead end in many cases is trying to learn the origins and history of the spirit, because so much of humanities interaction with the spirits has been subjective and through the eye of the cultural norms this interaction happened in… Thus, a lot of truth can be lost to time and impossible to verify, or we will get things from the spirits that do not line up with history at all.

This can lead to a desynchronization between you and the spirit as you seek things about them that are not verifiable, or directly contradict what they tell you and vice versa.

It is very well documented for example that the Ars Goetia was inspired by a translation of Johann Weyers Psuedomonarchia Deamonum (the false Monarchy of Demons).

The Lemegeton was compiled in the mid-17th century, and contains several other grimoires and books dating back to the 1500s, and one back toward the mid-1200s. This makes them (admittedly) very old…

However, tracing it all back to the time of King Solomon? There simply is no way to know for certain, except to notice the way things are described and dealt with are largely in keeping with medieval and early renaissance literature and fashion.

Indeed, the mere mention of some spirits like Lucifer, call into doubt the connection as Lucifer was only "demonized" long after Solomon.

This does NOT mean that "Lucifer" is not a real being, it means Lucifer as we envision him (thank you Paradise Lost) is not Lucifer, but rather an Entity of Rebellion and liberation, and has either intentionally or by the will of mankind, come to be associated with the name.

Starting with St. Jerome Translating Helel ben Shachar (Helel son of dawn) into Lucifer Star of Morning, followed by The King James translation to English of the bible… All this inspires Milton's paradise lost (1667), this cosmic rebel character is given the familiar form we see today.

Which then winds up being one of the most powerful or a central entity in a grimoire (ex. the Ars Goetia and Lemegeton) compiled in the 1600s.

The point here is, the harder you look for the origin or connection that validates these beings as being anything other than human creations… the more dead ends, and mistranslations and human error crops up and you lose the trail, or the trail tells you that everything you think you know about a spirit is almost 100% made up or mistaken. And yet… you will see them, they will speak to you, and reality will bend to match what you and the spirits agree to.

In my mind, there is a spirit that I CALL Lucifer, but it really has no name. Instead it has/is an archetype, a character, and this spirit of rebellion has appeared to mankind in many guises throughout history, and this Lucifer character is just one of the more recent and popular faces of this being.

This means, to me, that these spirits are something channeled and created by the authors of these works, they are truly Daemonic and inspire us… they inspire us to create their avatars based on the themes and inspiration they give us, and thus give them form and function. Through our working with them, they are elevated and in turn elevate us.

Thus, it should be no surprise that most of the spirits can be easily identified as gods of other cultures that were demonized by the Judeo-Christians! Or otherwise altered to fit the culture of the time period they were active in.

So, this creates a problem for some of us... How do I call the spirit the right way if I can't even be sure what that spirit really is? Is Lucifer even Real if that character didn't even exist as I understand him at all till after Milton composed Paradise Lost?

It is my opinion, and I hold firm to it, that the best way to work with all these spirits is to embrace the idea that some of it could be wrong and fictional and use that as is, without judgment... do not worry if your facts are right... because these spirits aren't materially real in the way we are.

See, you and I have a body, and a name and a history, we almost all have an address and a phone number, and we identify with these concrete things that have a place in time and space - And so we mistakenly expect the same of the spirits. That they have a solid identity, and identify with the same things we do such as a name, or how we look etc.

Instead, spirits have an energetic signature, an alien mind and emotions, and even these emotions do not necessarily play by the same rules as ours. They do not have faces they use to identify themselves; their faces are masks they wear to make working with us more relatable. The names they use are just a tool for calling them. They do not have bodies; we give them egregoric forms we can identify with and recognize the symbolism of.

They most certainly do not have addresses or phone numbers, and while they can be found in their astral realms, these places do not exist in space and time, they are living ideas in motion. Not places.

They do not have histories in the same sense as we do. As they do not have the same linear experience of time and space. To them time and space are just different places they can go, they do not have a past, the past for them is just another place in their experience that they exist within.

They simply ARE, and most of what they are to us is symbolic and archetypal in nature. These symbols are recognized by us and suggested to us by the spirits and their

interaction with us. And this is a flexible and nuanced thing. These spirits can be ANYTHING that fits their energy and symbolism. Leading to a very wide variety of identities based on nuances that matter more to one culture than another.

Therefore, it is a giant waste of time (magickally speaking) trying to identify who Satan really is (Satan is a Title, many spirits have been Satan), or who Lucifer really is in history (be it Horus, Phosphorus, Venus, and some others) etc.

Despite my assertions on these things, it is pointless for me to even try to justify it all beyond my experience.

Now, I am a big fan of the art and story of Paradise Lost and the art by Gustave Dore in particular. However, this is simply not an authentic historically accurate thing, it is a pop culture creation of a devil that the Christians needed to scare and inspire the masses.

The spiritual entity I identify as Lucifer does however synchronize with the themes of Lucifer as portrayed in the Christian culture, and thus took this Demonization in stride.

I myself often prefer to see him as this fallen angel and it works very well for me. However, I have no real belief about that origin. It is a façade, a character, an egregore puppet that makes communication easier.

So, while there are often strong correlations that can prove a connection between spirits. Or sometimes even a historical proof that shows how one culture influenced or shared the name and imagery of a god over long periods of time... We need to accept that the identity of the spirit appeared to those people for good reason, and we should not confuse ourselves by trying too hard to get to the bottom of it all.

It sometimes irks me that we find ourselves in a modern world of occultists trying to one up one another in finding the true name, or origin or spirit of a particular entity, and they make their declarations in the public sphere in such a way that they almost expect the world to adopt their interpretations.

Sometimes it works, and the world accepts it, other times... It's laughable how pitiful the effort seems.

Yet, which one is right? Potentially Both.

This happened to me once when working with Goetia #1 Bael, I heard and reasoned Bael must be Ba'al from antiquity and this caused me to lose synch with "Bael" and I got a rather confusing session with Bael/Ba'al because of it.

In a very real sense, Bael is and is not Ba'al. They can be the same, and they can be different at the same time, and can even manifest together, or not at all.

Therefore, when teaching people new to this path, I encourage them to contact them as if they are different and until or unless the spirit tells them otherwise, to treat them as completely different beings.

Some people consider it a mark of honor to know the correlations and deeper knowledge of these beings, but in truth, this is a distraction, the real power lies in accepting and knowing them as they are to you, and appreciating the fact that they have so many facets and names so that you can find one you can relate to.

When you are getting to know a spirit, here is a list of things you might want to ask them about to improve your connection to them:

- What, if any, color should I associate with you?
- What incense do you prefer I use to call you?
- Do you identify and resonate more with Fire? Earth? Air? Water? Or something else?
- Do you have any other names?
- What pop culture character represents you best (Spirits almost always draw from my love of fantasy and Sci Fi to give me imagery and concepts to work from).
- Can you give me my own personal sigil to use for calling you?
- Is there any special chant I can or should use when calling you?
- What does your name mean in the spirit world?
- What Tarot Card represents you best?
- What planetary energy do you prefer to use as a gate in ritual?
- What kinds of things (if any) do you specialize in? Art, Magick? Curses? Protection?
- What kind of offerings do you prefer?
- How can I learn more about you?

This leads us nicely in to the next section!

Making pacts and offerings

Do you want to sell your soul? What precious sacrifice would you give for eternal life and power? Would you sacrifice a living thing? Would you devote your life to worshiping an evil demon to have worldly power?

Well, usually the reality of working with spirits is nothing so dramatic as selling one's soul or sacrificing a living thing. though the latter can still be found as a part of some people's practices. When it is done humanely, I cannot judge them, though sacrifice of living things is not my way. No spirit has ever demanded such a thing from me. Though I know many would accept it.

It should always be done humanely, demons/spirits consider animals (and children) to be sacred, they should never be made to suffer…

In modern times, the sacrifice of humans in any form is out of the question for obvious reasons, but wasn't always… When it was allowed by cultures, these sacrifices had to be ritually slain to experience the least pain, or the quickest death possible. Even being burned was rather fast, as in ancient cultures this usually meant being thrown into a veritable furnace where the sacrifice would have been conscious only a few moments as the heat and fumes rapidly destroyed the brains ability to function.

As for selling your soul to a spirit, this is patently absurd, you cannot sell your soul, for you do not have a "Soul." Not as described in most religions. You do have an astral body, and you ARE a wave of conscious experience that flows through the ultraverse of mind body and spirit until it breaks upon the eventual cosmic shores of causality and returns to the void from whence it came. But you do not have a "soul" that can be sold.

Instead, if we are talking about selling a soul, what we are really talking about is an utter commitment to a spirit, to dedicate ourselves to it, and it's causes, and it's teaching fully, to give it equal control over our life, or even more control over it than we have.

We become enthralled to the spirit and invoke its nature into us, and we become in their image. But this is entirely voluntary, and is not a sale, it is a commitment and dedication.

Even if it was possible to "sell" my soul, this is not a practice I would take lightly and is not something I would ever consider doing exactly. Voluntary dedication is one thing, but I do not seek to submit to anything, I am a chosen of Lucifer, and that makes me a Light bringer, a liberator, and it is my belief we should only "sell our souls" to ourselves, dedicate ourselves do ourselves, and in so doing we make a better world and life for all.

Most demonic spirits respect those who respect themselves and speak with respectful authority. They do not like to be begged or worshipped as superior beings, any more than they like to be commanded and bossed around.

The most powerful sorcerers walk a narrow edge between submission and authority, do not kneel in worship, they kneel or bow in mutual respect and fraternity. They stand tall shoulder to shoulder with demons and dark gods and defy those who would subjugate them.

Therefore "worship" should never be done from the perspective of an inferior being worshipping a greater one, rather worship should be in the form of devotion, consideration, praising and mutual respect.

Of course, initially when you have no idea what you are doing, and have no awareness of your potential power, you will need to approach this as a student coming before a master. The master is not "better" than you, but they do have more power than you, and you might be wise to give them a measure of authority over you for a while until you learn their lessons and grow to not need them anymore.

Thus, the wise sorcerer develops relationships with powerful beings that are based on mutual support and growth. The demon or god should be as eager to see you ascend as you are to help them when they call upon you.

When we work with the spirits, particularly with Demonic entities, we will almost always be doing some form of pact making and offering to them.

As I often say, many people do not realize that when we make a good relationship with a spirit and build or dedicate an altar in dedication to a spirit, they do the same for us (metaphorically and literally in the astral realm). They send us gifts, offerings and often call to us when they need us.

The more we work with these spirits, the better our relationship, the more elaborate the altar tends to be, and the more we make offerings and calls of aid to one another.

A pact is essentially an agreement between you and the spirit to carry out a well-defined goal. They will do X for you, and you will do Y for them in return. If either party fails to deliver, the other side is not required to honor the pact. If the pact was violated willfully, there can be retaliation and consequences. Never EVER agree to the terms of a pact unless you are 110% certain you can carry out your end of the bargain, or that the pact has built into it an escape clause of some sort. You don't have to be a lawyer, your intention is what matters here, but you do need to try to be specific.

Most spirits are forgiving of reasonable circumstances preventing you from carrying out your side of the pact but will be even more impressed and likely to serve you as an ally if you go out of your way to carry out your end of a bargain despite any hardship.

If you willfully fail to deliver on your end of a bargain and have already gotten what you asked for, expect disaster sooner or later.

On the other hand if you have a bad car accident the day you were meant to carry out your part of the pact, the spirits will likely forgive you, but expect you to carry out your end of the bargain at the first possible opportunity, even if only symbolically in the event that the thing you had to do cannot be done any more.

Typically, only demonic entities and gods engage in pacts, and some are very shrewd negotiators, some will want little more than some incense and maybe a small offering of food, others might want you to carry out some kind of specific action, still others will want regular devotions, and still others will want very elaborate and sizeable offerings or devotions.

The ideal pact – An ideal pact is a pact where both parties are invested, committed and have mutual interest in the outcome coming to pass. Essentially, it is a pact where if it manifests, both gain something. This means both parties have incentive to work on it for themselves MORE.

For example, this book of magick is one such act of devotion and is a mutually beneficial thing. If this book succeeds, my spirits will gain more influence, and if it succeeds, I profit and gain in reputation and authority in the community.

It is what I like to call an IDEAL kind of pact. Both sides are invested in a common goal. I have little doubt that so long as I produce a book to the best of my ability, it will be a success, or at least enough of a success that both parties will be satisfied.

For many people the idea of selling their soul can be thought of as an Ideal pact. Because they promise to dedicate themselves to the spirit in return for ascension and power, and this power would make the individual a more powerful ally for the spirit and so on. Still, it can be a risky premise, even for the most trusted spirits, being locked into any path is something I dislike the sound of. Even if it was 100% guaranteed to succeed and be beneficial to both parties, I am still giving myself in submission to another being… Again, this is a personal choice of the sorcerer, never make the decision lightly, and always include an escape clause.

The Equitable pact – An equitable pact is what I consider the bare minimum for a good pact, it might involve the spirit doing something specific for you, and you doing something separate and specific for them.

For example - They bring you a familiar, and you give them a gemstone as an offering. Or They teach you how to perform a new spell, and you give them a glass of wine. Or maybe they help you create a strong defensive structure around your ritual chamber, and you carry out some random task that makes sense only to the spirit (For example, making a wreath of 7 strands of 7 kinds of flowers and leaving it in a random spot in the woods). These are all examples of an equitable pact and these are my minimum standard, they are honorable and noble. Equitable pacts are easy to create and get good results.

The inequitable or poorly thought out pact – Bad pacts can come in all shapes and sizes, and usually happen when someone is desperate, new to magick in general, and or feels submissive or too assertive toward a spirit.

If a good pact means listening to your spirit and thinking about what it would want and how it might benefit mutually from your work, a bad one is the opposite. Ignore what they like, ignore what would benefit you both mutually, and be hasty in your decision.

Always be specific about what you must do, when, and for how long. Always allow the spirit room to complete their end of the bargain and create clauses that allow both of you to fail without offending one another.

If you promise a spirit that you will give them an offering of blood every day without specifying for how long, regardless of what you are getting in return, sooner or later you will fail in your side of the bargain and could offend the spirit and bring an end to whatever good they are doing for you.

If you are deeply heartbroken at the lost love of someone who is breaking up with you, cheating on you etc.… In desperation you might agree to give something in return you were not prepared to give. I have even heard of people promising to cut off body parts like fingers in return for the spirit bringing their lost love back to them.

Love magick is always potentially problematic, but we can see that this was a bad idea right from the outset.

Ultimately do not try to be a lawyer with these spirits, some will be offended if you seem like you do not trust them, others are far better at negotiating and manipulating you than you are of negotiating or manipulating them.

Seek the most mutually beneficial terms for your pact and know that you are playing with fire if you are not being honest with yourself and the spirit about what you want and are willing to do to get it.

What can you offer? - Food, drink, service, music, poetry, art, virtually anything that comes from you that has value to you or the spirit. Spirits are not focused on the material world, so giving them gold and jewels of high value isn't valuable to them for the same reasons they are to you.

Therefore, they can be willing to move heaven and earth

for you, just for a handful of incense resin and a poem in their honor.

Spirits are, well, spiritual, and their material aspect is non-local, possibly electromagnetic (light) in composition. They can't, nor do they need, to literally eat. Nor drink. Nor can they literally use gold as money or jewelry like we do.

But the spiritual energy of the offering has value to them in the extreme. A gift of artwork that you poured your heart into will have incredible value to them, dedicating it to them, or burning it in their name goes a LONG way.

I know (2nd hand) a girl who spent weeks creating an elaborate work of art for a spirit, then when it was done, she covered it in black velvet and allowed no one to see it, she anointed it and burned it on a bonfire in dedication to her patron, no one on earth besides her ever saw it… she claims her patron gave her an unspeakably important gift in return.

How to offer it – Simply leaving an offering on your Altar for a period of time is sufficient, obviously incense can be burned. Let them take their time to absorb the spiritual essence of the offering and then dispose of the offering in some respectful way.

Typically, you can bury it, or pour it on the ground.

Refrain from disposing of offerings in the trash or the toilet or the sink unless utterly unavoidable.

Burnt Offerings - One of my most used normal ways of making an offering are to burn it. This is and was done in every culture that did sacrifice going back to the times before time was recorded. Spirits adore burnt offerings; the smell of the smoke pleases them greatly. If I give an offering of blood, I often paint some of the blood onto the incense so that as it burns it is carried directly to them in the astral world. Something about burning things causes their essence to enter the astral world, and if you understand anything about what fire does to an object, about the unique electromagnetic/ionic nature of flame and smoke, this makes more sense than people might realize.

Sharing the offering - In my mind, the absolute greatest way to offer anything to a spirit you trust is to invoke the spirit and consume or enjoy the offering with the spirit merged with your experience.

They do not have the same senses we have, and they cherish the vivid sensations of a mortal body in ways we cannot understand.

This is rather advanced and should only be done with trusted spirits. Invoke them into you, know that they are invoked, and then share the offering with the spirit. This means drink, eat, or otherwise consume the offering, and I promise you, if you have a good connection with the spirit, your own enjoyment of the offering will be exponentially magnified. Once recently I offered a simple slice of white bread to Malphas in return for his help with something.

I felt a simple slice of bread wasn't very worthy of what he did for me, so I offered to invoke him while I ate it.

He entered my astral body and shared my senses, when I ate the bread, I experienced a state of rapture and the bread never tasted so good or vivid in my life before or since. It was indescribable, and I think Malphas was somehow manipulating my senses so I could get an idea of what it is like for them. The intensity and vividness of the flavor of a single slice of white bread brought me to near tears.

I cannot recommend any other form of offering more highly, but only with the spirits you are comfortable invoking.

Special consideration for Incubi and Succubi when making offerings with invocation - Incubi, and Succubi prefer this form of offering and interaction. Working with an Incubus or Succubus can create a dangerous situation where the spirit can become addicted to the pleasure of its invocation and sexual activity with you, so be careful to maintain control over the relationship. Incubi, and Succubi are rarely higher order spirits like demons, but should still be treated with respect and consideration for their own needs. Typically, all they want is to be invoked into you regularly, or into your sexual partner, while you engage in sexual or other high intensity activity. (sex being their favorite, but eating and feasting, jumping out of airplanes probably things like that are what they like, passionate and powerful extremes of pleasure are their ambrosia).

The problem with Succubi, and incubi is that they do not

have the same sense of boundaries we have and may not respect our boundaries the way many demons and other spirits often (not always) do. They can lead people into a path of sexual addiction, or other dangerous habits. Not because the spirit is "Evil" but because they are spiritual beings that do not care about material things like mortality and addiction.

So long as they are getting their pleasurable energy, they don't care. Keep in mind, even if they end up killing you, they consider it a trivial matter because your consciousness and astral body will still be there, to them it is of about equal consequence as spilling red wine on a wedding dress... They will mope that they lost their physical plaything and move on to the next participant.

Some will even become highly vampiric and dangerous in that they can drink your energy dry if you let them in too deeply.

Lucifer and the Nine Goetic kings

In the pathworking section of this book, I will outline the method and go into greater detail for creating a relationship with the Goetic kings and Lucifer, bringing you into close relationship with them, and allowing you to call upon any of the demonic spirits of the Goetia with relative ease, rather than working with them all one by one to obtain their favor.

I will go into more detail in the pathworking section how to do this, but for now, it should be mentioned that of all the dark pantheons available that I work with, the Goetia is one of the more easily accessible to the novice and can be practiced independently of any religion or faith.

It does not in any way require the sorcerer learn the entire mythology or methodology of the Goetia itself, all that is required is the Ars Goetia itself, the seals and descriptions of the spirits, and a willingness to approach spirits that have been demonized by the Judeo-Christian oppression machine for thousands of years.

It is no secret that a great number of the spirits of this book are gods formerly worshipped (and some still worshipped) by so called pagan and heathen cultures for

hundreds, if not thousands of years prior to the creation of the Goetia.

As we already discussed before, It is not at all important to try to learn the exact original identity of these spirits, but one theory I have goes along the lines of the idea that all of these spirits WANTED to be in the Ars Goetia, and inspired the creation of the Goetia, perhaps the entire Lemegeton and other Solomonic works to create a lasting legacy of their essence that would survive into the modern age.

They wanted people like us to approach them the way we do, often in rebellion against the Oppressive Judeo-Christian tradition or whatever faith they had been indoctrinated into and reveal themselves readily to those who have already transmuted their religious slavery into true liberation and a desire to know the dark side of the self without fear.

For these spirits strongly respect the sorcerer who knows themselves to be THE GOD and THE DEVIL of their subjective experience. If we approach them as sniveling worshippers, they will take our offers of service in stride and with grace and then proceed to liberate us with a life befitting a slave until we are refined and transcend this life.

If we approach them as Kings, equal in spiritual status, with mutual respect and admiration, then we align with their true intention, and will reap the rewards of being someone they will be eager to commune with. They will become tireless allies, seeking to empower you because they want STRONG independent and LIBERATED allies to join them in their true purpose and desire.

That purpose and Desire? It has many facets, but it is decidedly Luciferian in nature. I could, and sometimes do spend a lot of time talking about what spirits have revealed to me about what they want. However, it is not my goal here to pollute your potential by introducing you to my dogmatic thinking. At least not until you have had a chance to get to know these spirits on your own and have your own experiences with which you can relate to me.

Still, it is not dogmatic to speak the truth, so worry not, what little I told you already is not harmful. Virtually every advanced and accomplished sorcerer who has walked with these spirits for any length of time will tell you something li what I just told you.

Each of the kings brings something unique and powerful to the table, and some are easier to befriend and work with than Others. We find if we work with these spirits, we can group them together.

We can work with one spirit, or three spirits, or 3 groups of 3 spirits, potentially with Lucifer in the center, creating a trinity of trinities, a 3x3x3 arrangement...

There is great power in this symbolism and you will find that you can work with 1, 3, 6 or all 9 of the kings for a very potent and unique energy signature.

Normally it is a good idea to work selectively with Goetic spirits, however, the conjuration of all 9 kings, plus Lucifer done sparingly is very powerful.

When working with all the 9 Goetic kings, taking into consideration their individual strengths, and associations, and invoking the authority of Lucifer within ourselves, we can see how this forms a fairly complete pattern of spiritual energy and can potentially move heaven and earth in our favor, IF we are strong and aligned with our truest intention... this is a powerful way to become the maelstrom.

Final word

Working with Demons and other dark entities is an unusual, unorthodox path and that only those of a left-hand path of black magick will readily adopt. It is not for everyone, and it can be important to safeguard yourself against various threats both spiritual and mundane.

Most people, including other occultists, will not respect you or approve of your path, some will outright work against you, seek to bind you, and maybe even physically react or act against you (even with violence).

This is not a spiritual path that can be easily or openly ~~t~~alked about in public. Nor accepted by most people, and ~~th~~en results in a very solitary path in everyday life, with your ~~only~~ remotely reliable lifeline often being social media, ~~chat~~ forums, and similar online resources, where the ~~undergro~~und community of Demonolatry and black magick

~~are~~

~~shou~~ld be taken to avoid overly dogmatic thinking, at

some point it is impossible NOT to have to accept some biblical or cultural narratives to make sense of and immerse yourself in these spirits, but you must be cautious to never allow these things to limit your judgement or potential.

Dogmatism tends to sneak up on us... We can go from firmly atheist to fanatical devil worshippers very quickly when we work with the occult, you might catch yourself thinking –

If magick is real, and these demons are real... What if I really AM being deceived by them as the Judeo-Christians warned me? What if Satan really is trying to trick me?

I do not envy you this struggle. Hopefully some of the rituals in the pathworking will help you break this dogmatic conditioning.

Scrying, Divination and Astral visions

One of the most important elements of my practice is the use of divination. That doesn't mean that I consult the tarot before every decision I make, that would be putting the cards or my scrying methods above my own intuition and intent. No, it means I am aware of a current of intuition and consciousness that can manifest itself outside my immediate mind and help me see things I cannot see directly with my own mind alone.

The spirits give me clues, magick gives me signs, and my intuition pieces them together to tell me a deeper bigger story than the one I could know with my own eyes and ears alone.

The art of Divination or scrying is a long and storied part of any and all spiritual or occult practice. Indeed, it could be said that divination is central or at least important in virtually every spiritual or occult practice. Even Judeo-Christians who decry such occult practices, still believe in revelation (prophecy) and knowing gods will.

The great difficulty in Divination arts, is knowing, or deciding what is possible, and what is not. I personally err on the side of rationality; I am not a believer in the idea that people can predict the future reliably. Occasionally? Sure. But reliably like fast forwarding to the end of the movie to see who the killer is? AKA mental time travel? No.

I do not believe people can reliably or consistently travel out of body and see what cannot be seen, occasionally maybe, but not to the point where they can look in a magick mirror and watch the person they are obsessed with shower. At least not with any consistent repeatable reliability.

To me, Divination is a holistic act, like all magick is, and the result is intuitive insight, visionary inspiration, and synchronicity.

When we do any kind of divination, we need to have the right mind set and expectations, we need to use our scrying methods to open portals in our intuitive imagination to create inspiration for our limited 3d+time corporeal self to find the patterns in the noise and see deeper into the truth.

It will not really give you the winning lotto numbers, we are not really seeing THE FUTURE, and any future we see, is only a possible future that is along the time line we are following. It is more like a course correction, we take a reading on where we are going and adjust accordingly. However, any number of things can alter that time line to prevent the outcome we predict or hope for.

Each method of divination is unique, and not everyone can use all of them equally regardless of skill in magick. Our gift in magick expresses itself differently for everyone, just as not everyone can be a violinist or a concert pianist, nor a talented painter.

Most forms of Divination can be done without any complex ritual or method; however, ritualized divination can have much more powerful results, especially when working with spirits.

When I perform divination for others, especially paying clients, I go the extra mile and call upon one of the spirits I have a close relationship with that is useful for divination. This can be a simple Invocation where I silently call upon their attention to aid me. Or a complete spiritual calling with an offering and everything.

The short version of my theory of time and the limits of divination -

I have come to see time in a much less mechanical way. Our history and memory is little more than a way to rationalize the present. The past and the future do not exist. They are illusions created by the temporal limitation of our biological consciousness to allow such a limited thing as our mind to experience a "knowable infinity" it creates an anchor for our delusion of self.

The clue that this is true is right in front of your face. Your reality is a dream, created by the biology of your brain (which is mutually arising inside its own creation). This delusion takes place several intervals of "time" AFTER the events that generate the creation of nerve impulses, which take time to travel to the brain and be processed into something that our consciousness can acknowledge as having happened.

What this means is, we all experience a reality that is several hundred milliseconds in the past... you can test this with a hot potato... pick one up before testing how hot it is, and most people will drop it before they feel the pain.

The nerves in our spinal column don't wait for our brain to process the situation and send the command to drop it.

When you look at a broken glass cup on the floor, your logical mind constructs a story that explains the situation based on what is available.

Because truly. The cup never existed anyway. you created the cup by looking at it. Deciding that the material "stuff" has an identity. An identity you call a cup, now a broken cup...

How can you expect divination to give you absolute answers of the past or future or even the present (reality as you understand it is a dream of the past already), when no such thing exists in a form that you could even conceptualize?

Spirits and other divination sources should never be thought of as the Hollywood expectation. It is generally not really meant to be a means to reliably see accurate details of the past present or future. For example, Akin to watching a recording. While uncanny levels of accuracy can happen, the information must pass through many human mundane filters, and is usually distorted and requires a certain amount of guesswork and intuitive reading. Furthermore, divination sources are not mechanical in nature... instead the querant will receive the answer or information they NEED rather than merely what they asked for. In other words, even the most honest benevolent spirit may deceive you because the experience creates growth.

But that is just my ego telling stories to explain its subjective experiences. So, what do I know?

Scrying

Scrying can be a very free form activity, and technically there are almost no rules, virtually any method is valid. The only essential element is that you be able to enter an open mind trance and learn to see despite your eyes.

Scrying isn't entirely unlike daydreaming, except the difference between scrying and regular daydreaming is that scrying is usually a more intentional and magickal act. Typically, when we scry, we aren't simply zoning out, we are trying to see something specific, like the outcome of an idea, or searching for inspiration for our intuition.

Yet, on the other hand, we do not go intentionally imagining anything. We let our mind wander and keep it more or less on target but we do not go out of our way to picture or think of anything specific.

We instead wait for the idea or vision or sensation to POP into our experience.

We stare into the crystal ball and let our eyes wander across the surface, noticing the patterns of light and shadow, the reflections and the shapes in the material and let our eyes pick out patterns and just have fun zoning out.

Sooner or later our mind will start trying to do what it does best – give meaning to the things it sees or keep itself from being bored and you will start noticing the patterns take on meaning more and more.

Scrying can also be an easy way to invoke or evoke spirits, or a portal through which you can enter very deep astral trances.

Virtually anything can be a scrying medium, reflective surfaces are popular, but so are clouds, tarot cards, runes, blue skies, Sungazing (only with your eyes closed, don't be stupid and burn your retinas), smoke, candle flames, Camp/bonfires, sigils, and much more. I have personally had success with virtually all of these and use them all when I feel the need.

The key to most scrying is looking "through" the object, that is, gazing into and through an object so that you are not actually looking at it with your conscious attention, but through it to a point in distant space beyond the scrying medium and letting your mind wander.

When you do this with a small object like a crystal ball, it is often the same as when you hold an object up to your eyes and see double. But instead of just seeing double you relax your attention on seeing THROUGH one of the duplicates and this creates a kind of space inside the scrying surface where the other side of the ball can be seen. Nothing magickal is going on, you are just taking advantage of double vision to create an abstract field of shapes and colors that your mind can play with and start having dreamy visions.

If the object is considerably larger or too far away (like clouds) and you cannot effectively look through the object, it will still work, but will have a slightly different effect.

Again, you will just relax your eyes into that thousand-yard stare and just notice what you see and feel and experience on all levels, both with your eyes, your emotions, your imagination everything.

You are essentially shutting down or bypassing your brain's reliance on the *biological act* of seeing and letting your 3rd eye see patterns in the distortions this causes to your vision and play optical illusions and hallucinatory games with your mind. In all that noise you will get meaningful patterns, colors, even distinct visions.

Like many things in magick, no two people can be expected to have the same exact experience.

When using a mirror or other reflective surfaces, we can get close to the mirror and look at our reflection and allow something called the Troxler effect to distort our perception of ourselves. **The Troxler effect** is when at some point we can be convinced we look different, or not recognize our own reflection as our mind distorts our face.

At first this is just an optical illusion, but if you allow yourself to go with the flow and if needed even pretend there is more to it, your 3rd eye may open, and you will begin to see things you never thought possible. This is a very effective way to invoke a familiar spirit that you have regular contact with… your face will morph and take on mannerisms and features of this spirit. It can be downright terrifying sometimes. This is a high level of scrying and invocation that can have powerful benefits, and some risks as there always is with invocation.

This can also be done with black scrying bowls filled with water, crystal balls, or any other reflective surface.

A special note on mirrors, many people prefer black mirrors, and for good reason, but I would also suggest a regular silver mirror in a darkened room. The lighting is important, it should be barely light enough to see your reflection clearly. You want your face to have strange, deep

shadows. You do not NEED light at all, but ambiance helps, even if just by setting the mood.

I will include several basic rituals in the Pathworking section for consecrating and using a mirror, and crystal ball.

You can of course scry into other objects; I have had luck just staring at the gravel at my feet in the park. So be creative.

I would personally start with any of the following as they are easier to set up and control:

Candle Flames, bonfires/campfires, Black reflective surfaces (black mirror) or regular mirrors, Black Scry bowl with water, Crystal ball.

Crystal balls can be of any kind of crystal, but I prefer natural crystal when possible and affordable. However, manufactured crystal balls are also viable, and I have had success with them, they are much cheaper so a large one can be had for under 100$ and look ridiculously cool on an Altar in a dark room.

Though I find the nuances of real crystal or obsidian or other stones to be more useful, sometimes the crystal clear quality of manmade crystal balls can create a more ethereal quality to the visions, however they can be harder to use in normal lighting as they act like magnifying lenses and can be distracting, so be sure to use it in low light.

Whatever your scrying tool is, when not in use it is customary to cover it with black silk or Velvet. This not only keeps it clean, but it also keeps in mind, when you use a scrying device, it becomes a portal into the astral world, and the astral world can sometimes gaze back through it. Covering it also helps make and keep it sacred.

Lastly, when you use a clear quartz crystal ball, they can become powerful magnifying glasses, and if sunlight falls on them, there is a risk of fire if they are not covered.

It is a good idea to keep a journal handy and remember to remain calm and relaxed at all times. If you see a troubling vision, do not react with fear or alarm, it is never a good idea to respond with uncontrolled fear or alarm, but in this case it can also distort the vision, or even encourage it to get worse as your fear can feed into the negativity or any spirit that may be bringing you the visions.

Keep in mind also that even the darkest imagery is merely symbolic, visions of the death of you, or a loved one, do not mean that someone will necessarily die in the literal sense. Chances are you are seeing a state of loss, change, or an ending of things relevant to the subjects of the vision. Remember, we do not see the future, we see the current influences and hidden information we might not normally recognize but that our subconscious mind is aware of… Any vision of the future is only a possible future based on the current information your intuition has available.

Daily practice is recommended.

Basic Scrying Method: using a crystal sphere

We will use many of the same basic methods regardless of the medium (crystal ball, candle or other flame, mirror etc.). However, for this example we will be working with a crystal ball. We will treat this as a meditative exercise, as meditation and scrying are part of the same broad spectrum of transcendental experiences for many people.

Setup – You will need your prepared (cleared and charged at least, self-initiated, and or consecrated if possible) scrying medium. In this case it is a crystal ball. A suitable REAL crystal ball can be had for under 100$ at any reputable new age or occult store, and the ball absolutely does NOT need to be very large. I have had magnificent success using small balls about the size of a golf ball and find that balls of that size or a little larger (say a tennis ball at most) tend to be something that you can easily manipulate and hold in your hand. This makes this specific technique easier as you can hold the ball up to your eye and not simply stare at it on a table.

You will need A private room or outdoor space free of interruption that can be made dark. If you are not candle or flame scrying, use 1, 2, or at most 3 candles for mood lighting and to create contrast. Less is more here!

Feel encouraged to use whatever incense you feel makes you relax best.

You will need to be able to sit in a comfortable position and easily hold the ball up to your eye. If you like, you can set up a Candle on a table and use that as the focus of your attention as this will help you look through the ball, and the candle flame itself is a very viable medium for scrying.

Whether or not you use a flame, either way you will need to be close enough to you to allow you to "see through it" looking just past it using the thousand-yard inward stare I will describe in a moment. If you are using a large flame or bonfire, all the same ideas apply, but don't get too close or you can be burned. It is also a good idea to have your magick journal and a pen handy or scrap paper etc.

The Thousand Yard Inward Stare – As mentioned before several times, you will need to look just beyond and through the object and see, not with your eyes, but a kind of 60/40 mix of your inward gaze (60) and your physical vision (40), allowing the 2 to mingle and play together to create abstract shapes and patterns that have a kind of hypnotic hallucinatory effect on your visual senses.

This will start to produce strange things in your vision, and you may begin to daydream. Most people at this point begin to get distracted, and just as they start having a vision or experience, they snap out of it, because our minds are trained to come back to conscious attention and avoid hallucinating as part of our daily survival. You need to trust the experience and let it happen and if it stops, just relax and let it come back. A part of the process is to let your mind become bored enough to start making things up, but do not give it any distractions beyond the scrying medium.

In this case, we will hold our crystal ball a few inches in front of one of our eyes. And we should notice that as it blocks one of our eye's visions, our brain superimposes a phantom version of the ball on our overall combined vision.

Experiment with both of your eyes and see which one yields the easiest phantom image. I generally like to use my NON dominant eye as the one looking through the crystal, as the non-dominant side tends to be the energetically RECEPTIVE side in most people.

But in my experience, both works equally well.

Procedure

Enter your ritual chamber or meditation space and prepare the area for comfort. You may want to have soft ambient music, or white noise, or you may want no distractions. I am comfortable with either, but I would avoid any "active" music. Rock and Roll, even Classical can be very distracting, and disturbing, focusing our attention on concepts and ideas via the theme of the music. While Ambient music or white noise tends to let the mind wander… which is what we want.

Sit comfortably and if you have any trusted spirits you can use for Divination, this would be a good time to call to them by chanting their name staring at their sigil and declaring your intention (see the section on calling spirits in the pathworking section). You do not need to perform a complete calling, simply speak about or intone internally your intention to scry, and ask your spirit to guide you, either in a general way, or toward something specific.

Now once all that is done, bring the scrying crystal up to a position about 1-4 inches from one of your eyes, and focus your gaze on the candle you have placed in front of you, or some other distant object (for example a tree outside etc.).

Next, use the meditation pattern I taught you in the Altered State section to enter a deep open mind state. And maintain neutral breathing. I find I get the best results if I am practically on the verge of drooling from being so dazed out.

Whatever you do, DO NOT BLINK unless you absolutely must (don't hurt yourself). Try to relax your eyes to the point where they almost do not matter,

Simply stare into the scrying medium while maintaining your open mind meditative state, you can experiment with the other two states of course, to see if this sparks a vision. Usually if I am seeking a vision about something specific, I will intently focus on that situation or person or thing briefly, creating a mental image of the concern, then go back to an open state. So, experiment with all the mental states to see how it influences your experience. There are no rules here, but I liken it to relaxing your body, usually to properly relax you need to stretch and create tension for a moment and release it.

The same works with the mind as well.

You need to have patience, and a quiet open mind… your mind should be wandering, but not cluttered and buzzing with stressful thoughts.

If necessary, begin by entering an empty mind trance FIRST to clear distractions. You cannot do this if you are preoccupied by an earworm or a fight you had with your boss. Once you are clear, then enter open mind and proceed from there.

If you have never had a vision before, or can't tell the difference between something you really see or imagined… then do the following –

Pay close attention to ALL your thoughts, all the things you imagine, or think about while scrying. If you are scrying into the crystal ball and suddenly think about a hotdog… it could be because you are hungry, it could just be because your mind is bored and imagining things, or it could be a vision from the astral world of some significance that you will discover upon retrospection using your journal.

For example, once I saw the vision of a skull… but had no idea what it meant and couldn't get anything more from it, except that it felt ominous.

That night I did a working with Azazel using my resin skull model as his anchor, and it didn't go well, and I had to cancel.

While I failed to gain anything of value from the vision, I knew (after the fact) what it was trying to tell me… **Do not work with Azazel tonight…**

So, once you experience something make a mental note of it or write it down while scrying without breaking your open mind concentration (if possible).

Keep in mind that the entire spectrum of experience is a potential medium for your vision. This could include things you see, hear, feel, smell, and more. Many people make the mistake of expecting the vision to happen in the crystal. This is not how this normally works, instead it will be in the form of a daydream, a thing that is halfway between your imagination and your waking eyes.

It may even just be a pattern you notice on the wall that looks like a face, or a word or symbol. Any and all are valid and possible.

Do not expect fireworks, expect subtlety and daydream!

If you are struggling to have a vision, you need to ask yourself what you have been seeing all this time? Are you *really* not seeing anything or are you just not really *open to the idea* that what you are seeing isn't just imagination, but potentially of real importance?

Working with Tarot —

The Tarot has been the subject of countless books, and informative lectures, and is a formidable financial juggernaut of card and game companies since forever. I say all this because I do not consider myself an expert or an authority on the Tarot, however I have my trusted methods and my interests in card readings.

I include this section for the sake of completeness to expose you to the spiritual side of Tarot and encourage you to find your own methods and learn everything you can from other practitioners, my system is very basic, and I could never do justice to the Tarot in just a few pages in a core book of magick. Instead let this section serve as an introduction, a polite, warm, and firm handshake.

The Tarot is a unique system of inspirational archetypal gates. These are gates through which the subconscious mind can peer into the Astral plane and vice versa. The symbolism of the cards opens our mind to intuitive pathways that our conscious mind might not imagine without help.

When we do a tarot reading, the objective isn't to treat the cards as if they are the message, but the messenger, it is up to US to interpret and SCRY into the cards for true meaning.

Skeptics often debunk tarot by saying each card is intentionally given vague enough meaning to allow it to fit a wide array of possible circumstances. Thus, they do not really tell you anything, and you can almost always find a way to make the cards fit a situation.

I agree and disagree! That is how they are meant to work, it's not a bug, it's a feature. Each card represents an Archetypal situation or person, and archetypes are both universally recognizable, but also vague enough to include a lot of examples.

For example, A hero can take many forms, but we all know what a hero is.

For another, a rainy day can take on a lot of variations, but we all know how a rainy day feels and what it might symbolize.

At its most mundane level, it is little more than a sequence of ideas filled with archetypal symbolism in a meme like format. When we scry into them, even if we utterly lack any and all astral sensitivity, it isn't hard to be inspired to nuanced ideas we might not have thought of otherwise.

In other words - The Tarot are designed to invoke in our minds the inspiration to follow pathways of intuition and logic we might not normally recognize.

When we read the cards, sometimes we need to read between them, and sometimes even ignore them if inspirational gnosis we get from them is more accurate than the cards meaning. We are the ones doing the reading, not the cards, we must interpret and scry into the deeper meaning.

In this way, the skeptics say, the cards fool us into thinking there is something magick going on, but it's just psychology and luck... the cards are all vague enough that they fit most people and situations, so they poo poo it.

To me, this is a silly limited way of looking at things and comes from the perspective that the cards are somehow magick and betray the laws of nature.

The Cards are really nothing special! After all, they are flimsy sheets of card stock with pictures on them. Oh, they can be empowered by magick, consecrated and obtain an energy all their own, but all the magick of reading them takes place in the mind of the person doing the reading.

So, they can indeed be made sacred, consecrated, imbued with astral energy and spirit, and this DOES indeed influence the cards, but more importantly it influences the reader! The cards are just "stuff," and it is the mind that does the reading. The mind that controls the hands that do the shuffling...

In the act of shuffling we enter a trance, and the subconscious mind takes command of the action. Your subconscious mind has a better memory than we normally do and with a little practice and time playing with your cards, your subconscious mind picks up the pattern of the shuffle.

At least that is the open-minded pseudoscientific take on it.

In truth, there is something even more mysterious at work. And it separates the mundane tarot reading, and a reading by a true seer. When you are truly in tune with your cards, and your ability to experience the subtle forces of the spirit, your subconscious mind is also being given instructions from the spirit world, the magickal currents to know when you should shuffle, where to make the cuts, and when to stop.

I like to tell people that reading cards is a bit like Driving a car... When you know how to drive, you don't think about it. You just intuitively and subconsciously drive the car, making the right decisions automatically. You think about making a left, and your subconscious brain carries out the act of making a left turn, sending impulses to your body to act a certain way, which in turn send back their feedback.

When you are first learning to drive, you worry about every action, you focus on each one. When you know how to drive, you only focus on the gross decisions, where to turn, and why, not how.

Shuffling a deck of cards for Tarot works like this. And it's actually very easy for your mind to get the hang of. It doesn't need to know the exact position of the cards... it just needs to know what acts of shuffling to perform and when and how many times and when to stop.

As you work with your cards, you learn better and better where the cards are, your intuitive mind learns their positions, and your readings will be more and more accurate.

I have never known anyone to be able to predict their cards without cheating, that isn't really the point. Expecting someone to do this again misses the point of the Tarot.

Remember, the Tarot, and most other scrying methods, are just a way to open the mind to possibilities and ideas or focus someone's attention on ideas that they might normally ignore.

It should be clear, that you do not NEED to memorize the meaning of every card. Good cards will have enough imagery on them that you can often figure them out, and all card decks come with booklets that give you at least a basic overview of each cards meaning. If you have a good sense of intuition and the spirits are with you, you will be able to get uncanny accuracy out of the box.

Remember, the CARDS aren't what is doing the magick here. The Cards are not special by themselves, and the Cards do not somehow predict the future and they do not have a magick way of always landing the right way. They are instead influenced by our subconscious and the spirits to be organized as they are to give them meaning for us.

One of the things you must understand is when you have even just 52 cards in a deck (as opposed to the 78 in the tarot), there are around $8*10^{67}$ possible combinations!

If we laid out each possible combination of a standard 52 card deck, once every second... It would take so long that you wouldn't believe it. The age of the universe is around 13.8 billion years... and it would take 185 000 000 000 000 000 000 000 000 000 000 000 000 000 000 TIMES the age of the universe for you to lay out each possible combination of cards just once, if you laid each one out each second.

What this means is, even if we only worked with the minor Arcana, the odds of the "Same" set of cards coming out in the same order would be astronomically low, even if all we needed was for 5 cards to be in the right place (the odds of a similar draw in poker say, a Royal Flush are around 1 in 649,740), or even ONE card to come out on top would be very slim (though far more rationally possible IE 1 out of 52, or 78 in this case).

My point here is, magick does not (normally) defy the laws of nature, though it can bend and work within them... And when we do a tarot reading, we are invoking our magickal privilege to ensure a card with suitable meaning will be what we draw as opposed to the dozens of others with less relevance.

So, the fact that we get a rational reading at all, even with vague meanings is a stretch of probability.

Now, if we push it and try to get the same reading twice in a row, objective reality comes crashing down with logic and numbers and prevents that from happening in all but the most synchronicity focused moments of history.

Therefore, we are ill advised to try to do the same readings on the same subject too many times in the same time period. For example, I won't do a reading on the same situation until some time has passed, or a major change in circumstance has occurred. This means waiting usually a week or more.

A daily reading about your day is fine, A lot can happen in a day, but you will find the accuracy suffers the more you increase the frequency... At about one-hour intervals, it's not that useful.

Furthermore, the more often you do a reading, the more chance there is of getting a wrong reading, and the more wrong readings, the less aligned you can become with the cards, the more you can doubt your ability, the more your subconscious mind learns to doubt itself and so on.

When it comes to Tarot, LESS is more, but Regular use is key.

So, my purely anecdotal advice is, refrain from doing readings on any issue more than once a day. And most of the time, I would wait a week or more to do a reading on the same issue twice.

So, asking the tarot what today will be like, and doing this every morning? Great practice.

Asking the tarot every day about a problem at work? Maybe, maybe not.

This is a big part of the intuitive practice, not just knowing how to read the cards, or shuffle them and when to stop, but when it's a good idea to even pick the cards up in the first place.

It should also be noted that there are DANGERS when working with the Tarot. The biggest of which is that you can become dependent on them, unable to make decisions without them, and make excuses for them when they are wrong and still follow them anyway out of superstitious fear that they somehow control your fate. Just because the cards came up a certain way, doesn't mean things will go that way.

Remember the CARDS themselves are not the source of the magick or the message, they are the messenger, the gateways through which YOU need to scry. They are like painted glass mirrors, with images on them.

Indeed, you should never just draw them and look up their meaning or use their meaning from memory alone, you MUST take a moment to look at each card, or think about it deeply, really savor the cards meaning and imagery and let it work on your subconscious and inspire you.

The VALUE of the Tarot IS NOT in the meaning each card has in the little booklet. But instead in the way it inspires our intuition and magickal ability to connect to the flow of reality and allows us to answer our OWN questions.

I have seen some impressive Tarot readers who really don't care what the cards official or established meaning is.

They never memorized the little booklet; they simply look at the cards and let their imagination run away with them as they scry the cards. I myself only bother to memorize those cards with confusing imagery and prefer to let the imagery or name of the card do the work it is meant to do.

I personally refrain from using Tarot as future reading tools, that isn't their purpose, they are meant for reflection and helping you cut through the chatter of your mind and the distractions of the complexity of situations. Not fortune telling devices like they are in the movies.

I am a big fan of using simple spreads, the more intuitive the better. There is LITERALLY no reason at all why you cannot simply make up a spread on the spot to match the needs of your situation. However, there are some common spreads used by people, and they are part of the collective conscious/unconscious and can be important to make use of.

Most of the time I use 3 cards spreads, usually in a row for situations, or getting to know someone with a past, present, future alignment spread. I then like adding cards to clarify things… So, I might start with a standard 3 card spread, not understand one of the cards… and reshuffle and draw a single card to clarify, or an entire 3 card spread to explain that card.

You can go on wandering journeys through the cards this way, meandering through card after card, meaning after meaning. Just be careful, the more you do this, the more you increase the odds of losing sync with your cards and getting wrong or absurd readings.

Just as it's important to know WHEN to use the cards, it's important to know when to STOP, and just use your own judgment for the missing pieces.

Some readers prefer larger spreads with more cards and more depth. I am not as advanced, and I usually prefer to leave my mind room to be creative with the cards. However, using full spreads like the Celtic Cross, or Thoth spread if using the Thoth deck, can be very detailed and useful and I recommend trying them to see if they fit your style.

Most of the better spreads for me include some kind of "Anchor" card, a thing that represents the current person, place, object, goal or situation in some way that is used to determine if the reading is going to be relevant or not. If this anchor card is wrong, either the reading is going to be wrong, or the person doing the reading has to realize the spread is showing them something important that may not be immediately obvious.

So, an anchor card is a card that represents a verifiable quality in the reading. For example, the present situation card MUST align with something the subject (be it yourself or someone else) can verify to be true.

If the person you are doing a reading for is going through hell with all kinds of bad life events happening, and the card you draw for the present moment is a card of joy, or success, or good times or something… Chances are your anchor card is off… and you may need to try again… Or as mentioned before, it might be directing you to look at someone, or something else besides the intended subject. Maybe the Card is representing the current situation for the person causing these persons struggles?

It should be stressed again and again, that the CARDS are NOT hard set in stone objects. They are as flexible as the card stock they are printed on. They are not magickal mysterious objects of power, painted by madame mystique herself, imbued with blood and oils and herbs and ghosts… Far from it!

They are printed in a dirty oily factory. On soulless machines, operated by minimum wage or low wage corporate factory slaves… shipped to a warehouse filled with disgruntled shitty people. All of whom from the factory to the guy who delivers them to your store or home, think you are a sucker for believing in these things.

Think about it… These things cost pennies to make, cost you tens or even many tens of dollars… Do not worship them or fear them, at least not yet.

First you DO need to elevate them into magickal tools however, despite everything I said, you DO need to elevate them, consecrate them, and empower them. You need to take their humble origin, and impurity, and make them part of your astral self. You need to make them potent holy tools of your divinity.

Thus, we place them in boxes, wrap them in silk, and bathe them in sacred smoke, pair them with crystals, sing to them, sleep with them, bathe them in moonlight… etc.

The key is to charge these cards with intent, and make sure your mind connects to that intent every time you use them.

The easiest way is to simply bathe them in sacred smoke on your altar and imagining them becoming empowered glowing things. Know them to be magick, and special.

Or you can create a more elaborate rite to a spirit and dedicate the cards to that spirit. For example, pick a spirit that is known for its skill and use in Divination, and call upon that spirit and ask the spirit to touch your cards with their blessing and power. I would go through them, one at a time, and ask the spirit to touch and empower each one with its gifts of divination and make them a generous offering in return.

If you do this, treat these cards with inordinate respect befitting a relic of magick, these are no longer cards, but the spiritual anchors for a powerful spirit of divination.

Whenever you use these cards, make sure to call to this spirit and use them with respect and love.

Now, you might be thinking - *How accurate are they?*

I have roughly a 90% or better accuracy rate with my favorite deck. And about 80% with my less favorite one. I would say 80% or better is about the minimum level of accuracy I would accept for a deck. Again, keep in mind, I don't stress my cards out, I let them breathe, and I try to only use them when I can concentrate and enter the right vibration states. If I am upset, distracted, or unmotivated, I don't touch them if I can help it.

If you can't achieve this with your cards, it could be the deck, it could be the art, it could be your own errors. It could be confidence, it could be fear, it could be ego and ambition.

Therefore, it is important to be sensitive to magick, to your own intuition and to have patience and not try to force magick. NEVER force magick. That is the best way to break it.

Yeah but what does it MEAN!?

When we learn tarot, we can feel a lot of pressure because the cards are not clear about what they mean in the usual sense.

Depending on the deck we use, the imagery can be more, or less obvious. In the end there are two, often overlapping schools of thought.

The first school believes in knowing the meanings by heart and knowing the way the cards interact... for example, the first ten cards of the trumps (major Arcana), inform the first ten cards of each of the 4 suits of the minor Arcana (swords, Wands, Cups and Pentacles/Disks/Coins). The magician being the initiator, and the Ace of each suit being about the initial potential or state of the suit.

Each card in the sequence, when seen in sequence can tell a kind of story and share similar but distinct themes between cards of the same number. For example, the Number 2 card of each suit is early in the suit and thus still represents an early state in the theme, as it is based on the number 2 it tends to represent a duality of choice or action. The 2 of swords being about 2 conflicting ideas, the 2 of wands being about planning and deciding to act, the 2 of coins being about maintaining a balance between multiple, often opposing ideas and actions or a state of change or near instability, while 2 of cups revolves around the decision to unify 2 or more ideas or people into one union.

In addition, each suit can be thought to represent a specific element, with swords usually being air, wands as fire, coins/disks/pentacles as earth, and cups as water.

Referring to our section on the elements we can easily see how the elements can interact in our reading, if a fire card is surrounded by water cards, then in all likelihood the fire card may be influenced and subdued, potentially indicating a flipped meaning is the right one even if the card is upright.

Obviously, we are only scratching the surface, and as this is a core book of magick, and it is up to you to learn the meanings of the Tarot on your own. Indeed, I would be a poor expert to learn from... So, it is up to you to decide how much you want to devote yourself to memorization of the tarot before you begin working with it.

It should be stressed that memorization is NOT required to use Tarot Effectively, if you prepare yourself to use the Tarot correctly, and take the time needed to connect to the cards, to scry into each one for a while and play with them and let your subconscious learn the cards, the right cards will turn up in your readings and you can do just fine by using the little book to look things up.

But we all know that he real goal and fun is to put that book down and just read the Cards... It can be very hard to be intuitive about the cards if you must look them up all the time.

The second school of thought doesn't bother much with memorization, and some highly respected Tarot masters never read the little booklet that comes with the cards, nor did they ever commit any of it to memory, instead they rely on the card's symbolism or their own intuition to learn the cards through practice and instinct.

Some decks are more suitable for this than others, while others can be very hard to read this way, having little or nothing in the way of imagery on them. Some are so thick with symbolism that they can be hard to read because the symbolism may be too advanced, requiring a deep understanding of the themes and traditions they draw from.

I myself belong to both camps, I like to know a little about the card's meanings, and I like to just ignore those meanings and go with the pictures on the cards and use them as gates to knowledge and intuition.

It will take time for you to learn which you prefer to rely on... but I would say when you are first starting out, try both extensively, it can lead to better memorization...

I have often thought it might be clever to create a "word jumble" tarot, where each card is just a word jumble of concepts the card often relates to... Basically skip over the whole process of scrying the images, and doing something a bit more like book scrying (the practice of opening a random book to a random page, and selecting a random sentence or a sentence or word that "pops" out at you or that you feel is intuitively important.

Again, the goal of Tarot isn't to memorize the cards, but to read them. Take that as you will.

Should I use the Major or minor Arcana or both – I know some people who only use the major arcana, but I always use both unless I am doing a single card reading that is meant to be about significant factors in a person's life. Major Arcana are the cards that have the biggest broadest and most influential archetypal meaning and are seen by many as the initiators or inspiration for the things that happen in the minor Arcana as the first ten cards of the Major Arcana are meant to be closely related to the 1-10 cards of the minor arcana.

For example, the 1st card of the Major Arcana is the Magician or Magus, and this card is meant to serve as showing the origin of ideas and change, the initiator of power. And in the minor arcana the meaning of the Ace cards is also about initial conditions and potential and the initial starting point of a story that is told through the rest of the minor arcana.

To use reverse, or not to use reverse card meanings - I am of the mind that cards are meant to be flexible in their meanings, this means I use inverted meanings, I prefer to think of this as dark or shadow meanings. I do not rely on their position (upside-down or otherwise) to determine which meaning to use, rather a combination of my intuition, and the position and role of other cards around it. For example, a Fire card (wands/rods/staves) surrounded by water cards (cups) will mean that fire card is likely being influenced by the conflicting nature of the water around it, either influencing it to be muted, or inverted. Other times it is simply obvious that the meaning is meant to be inverted or dark because of the situation of the querant. Of course, do not just assume a card meaning, scry into it, let your imagination run wild, stare at the card and see what comes out at you!

In my mind using inverted cards is a way to potentially allow the cards to have too much power over the reading. I am the one reading the cards, it is my power, and the spirits in contact with me that is doing the reading. Instead I use my intuition and decide which version is relevant.

Again, the CARDS are NOT what is doing the reading, YOU ARE!

Recommended Tarot decks

I consider the value of a deck of Tarot on 3 criteria – on a scale of 1-5. 1 being poor, 5 being excellent.

- **Art** - It needs to be pleasing to the eye. But pleasing to the eye doesn't make a tarot card readable or useful.
- **Symbolism** - It needs to have enough symbolism to allow me to scry into it for deeper meaning, to see what "jumps out at me" in a reading.
- **Readability** - Nobody likes to admit how much they must refer to the little booklet that comes with a tarot deck, and I know some who only use the Major Arcana for this reason… A card should be readable without having to memorize the booklet.

Rider Waite - Art: 1, Symbolism: 4, Readability: 3 - Everyone loves or hates the Rider Waites. These are the Standard, and pretty much everyone starts with them. I personally have gotten good enough readings from them, but hate the artwork… So, I never use them. I would probably start with these or skip them if you know you will hate them.

Anna K. Tarot - Art: 3, Symbolism: 3, Readability: 5 - If you wish someone would make a Rider Waite Deck that is updated with contemporary art, that preserves and improves the expressive symbolism of the cards, and at the same time reduces the need to know all the deeper esoteric symbolism of the cards… These cards are a gem!

Thus, in my opinion it is the best looking, easiest to read, and at the same time closest of all the traditional oriented cards to the Rider Waite Deck that I know of that is easily available.

This means the traditional meanings attributed to the rider Waite are easier to see in these cards and you can easily use it to learn any traditional tarot set. My favorite part is it offers easily interpreted images for the contemporary eye and relies more on psychology and empathy than just occult symbolism to communicate with the reader.

For an empath or an intuitive just starting out, this is pure gold and will speak directly to the language you are already fluent in.

It is very relatable and has a very gentle learning curve. The suit cards are so expressive, and even the court cards (which are often hardest of all the Suit cards) are easy to interpret.

Some would say this might be limited for advanced readings, but I disagree. I see any and all Tarot as starting points, the real magick happens behind your eyes, and during the consultation with the petitioner.

The Gothic Tarot - Art: 5, Symbolism: 2, Readability: 1 - On the other end of the spectrum I have a deck full of cool gothic imagery, castles, and vampires, ghosts and ghouls and all that kind of stuff. Each card is elegant, artistic and striking.

And just like the undead monsters that sprawl across the cards… these cards are inexpressive and require the user to already have an advanced understanding of the Tarot before they can really be used.

This is a deck that will stifle the beginner's interest as they are forced to go back to the booklet over and over, and as the cards lack most of the symbolism of the Tarot, they really struggle to speak to your intuition or empathy.

Indeed, I rarely use them except when I feel the need for their aesthetic flavor.

These cards are more pop culture oriented and less concerned with the deep symbolism of the original systems, and I feel therefore they are less effective, it's hard to really look at the card and scry for deeper meaning… they are just pretty pictures, hollow and devoid of deeper symbolism. Not recommended as a primary or starter deck, but maybe if you get more advanced and can spend time with these, they could become your favorite?

Thoth - Art: 3, Symbolism: 5, Readability: 3 - This deck is one of the most symbolically dense decks I know of. Every card contains so many occult and pagan symbols that it is easily the most difficult tarot deck to read for the beginner who doesn't want to memorize things, if not for the fact that almost every card contains a one word meaning for the card. This word unlocks the symbolism of the card and can allow you to deeply scry into the card and get images and understandings you would never get from a regular deck of Tarot.

The art isn't as edgy cool as the goth deck, but it's not as ugly to my eye at all as the Rider Waites. These cards have a

kind of roaring 20s classical approach to art, bright pastels, vibrant images, subtle details, and symbolism that speaks to the deeper consciousness, rather than the obvious images of many decks.

This is truly the intuitive Tarot deck for the person who doesn't want the cards themselves to limit the reading, but instead open doors and gates to subconscious intuition and inspiration.

Many people agree you do not need to be a master of pagan or occultism to read these, the symbolism might appear mysterious to the untrained eye, but they tend to have their effect and open intuitive gates in the mind.

However, as you learn to read these cards, you will learn that they have so many extra layers of readability, each card having an extra elemental nature beyond just the suit the card is in, and extra symbolism hidden within the artwork that can play into the meaning of the reading.

The printed booklet of meanings in the box will be useful, and you should feel no shame in reading it, and committing some of it to memory. However, the Goal is not to memorize the meanings precisely of all the cards, the suggested meaning on the card is all you really need… Trumps tend to be easy to learn, and Court cards can be memorized more easily this way as well.

Oracle Cards

These are a more recent invention, the first recorded use of them goes back to the 18th or 19th century by a professional French fortune teller named Marie Anne Adelaide Lenormand.

Oracle cards differ from Tarot in that they do not typically deal with established archetypes or suits or trump cards in any traditional way. Instead each deck can be very different and have different themes.

Oracle cards tend to be like using only the Major Arcana, but with more than just 25 cards (typically 44 or more), they are a bit less "specific" and less aligned to cause and effect than the minor arcana, and more aligned to deeper understanding of broader situations.

So, for example Oracle cards can be far more useful for Shadow Work and getting to know the bigger picture of one's internal and external world, rather than helping us make decisions about our path.

Oracle cards are far easier to read for intuitive people with little time or interest in learning the meanings of each card. As a good deck of Oracle cards requires virtually no memorization (though they all come with elaborate books filled with poetic meaning and unique ways to read each card), as the name of the card and the images are often more contemporary and easily discernable.

Especially for those with an intuitive artists eye.

I have found it easier to establish a connection to Oracle cards right out of the box than Tarot which can sometimes take time to align your perception to them.

The method of using Oracle cards can be the same as Tarot, but they lend themselves more to shorter spreads of between one and five cards. The traditional Celtic Cross or other large deep spreads is almost absurd.

What Oracle decks do I use/recommend? – I have 2 I use currently, I have the Dark mirror, and the Mystical Shaman.

The Dark Mirror Oracle deck - This is a set of luscious dark gothic and dark fantasy images and themes centered around shadow work and getting to know the deeper darker aspects of your being. This deck doesn't pull punches and tends to point out the darker truths you might not want to see.

The Mystical Shaman - This is a much less dark and much more shamanistic deck (like it says on the box), it has a broader purpose and is focused on essential spiritual truths about the self or situation. It can also be used for shadow work, but the pastel imagery and the typical archetypes and words associated with each card tend to be more naturalistic and neutral. Invoking things like herds of buffalo and the power of thunder, or the cunning and guile of the raven…

Which to use (Tarot or Oracle) and when? - In the end I prefer neither, they are both invaluable tools, and I use both for different kinds of readings regularly. I tend to use Tarot when I or someone else has a specific question or concern. And Oracle cards when people have a more general or personal concern about themselves on a fundamental level.

For example: If someone is considering taking a new job but aren't sure what to do, I will likely focus on a Tarot Reading of some sort.

If on the other hand, they don't understand why they can't find work at all and begin to think there is something wrong with themselves… I might do an Oracle reading to see what it is about them that might need attention.

Or if someone is going through a great deal of struggle with a mix of specific concerns and deep emotional or spiritual issues, I will break out both kinds of deck and do spread after spread, mixing and matching cards and just going with the flow till I find all the details that person needs to help them.

Simple Method for reading your cards

First you need to make sure your cards are properly prepared, it is unwise to try to do a reading right out of the box, because the cards are ordered and prepared for an initial inspection. Their energies are scattered and most likely they are spiritually dead on arrival, so we need to wake them up, and the process of using them will make them come alive.

We can perform elaborate rituals for empowering and consecrating them at some point, but there is no need to do that to establish the potential of your cards.

So, before you do anything with them of practical purpose, take the cards out, and spend some time looking at them, shuffling them, and playing with them. Even if it's a deck you are familiar with, because the act of doing this establishes them in your astral world. Take a moment to connect to the art of each card. If you don't know what they mean, now would be a good time to open the little booklet that came with the deck and take a moment to look at each card one at a time and compare it to its meaning. This will give your subconscious mind something to work with.

Be sure to say the name of each card aloud and hear your name echo into the astral realm.

Once you have gone through the deck this way, bathe them in sage smoke to help fumigate them spiritually, and give them an initial shuffling. This should consist of about 5-7 full riffle shuffles, as riffle shuffles are more effective for getting a good mix. However, riffles are way more stressful on the card stock if done wrong, and unless you are using smaller sized Tarot, can be downright abusive to them and be hard for your hands.

Overhand shuffling does not as thoroughly mix the cards but is the type of shuffling I do when in trance.

Alternatively, you can spread your cards out on a table or bed, and just mix them up by sliding them all around for a while and then putting them back together randomly.

Keep in mind a new deck of cards is often a bit "sticky" and you must really make sure you shuffle them carefully, because it can take a while for all the cards to separate and not get runs of cards that are obviously due to the way they came in the box.

Once your cards are well shuffled, you can do an initial single card reading, asking the deck to tell you about itself. Thereby giving it its own Anchor card of sorts.

Let's do a Reading Part 1

Let's keep things simple, for most of my readings I prefer shorter spreads of between 3 and 5 cards, or a unique spread I call the Goetic kings which is a ten-card spread.

I like short spreads because it allows me to progress through a reading and give the reading a chance to reuse cards for different things, and this also allows me to do follow up spreads to explore a result in a more natural way.

The First thing you need to do is come up with a question or situation you want to talk to your cards about. I often call my readings a conversation with the cards, meaning there is a certain give and take, and I may actively talk to them like a living thing, or speak to one of my spirits who is doing the reading with me and let them respond with the cards.

You shouldn't ask questions that would require the ability to predict the future, that is fortune telling. What you are looking for is the cards to open your mind to potential outcomes and paths or influences that you may or may not be aware of.

For example, instead of asking "Will I get this job I am applying for?" Ask "What can you tell me about what might happen if I pursue this job?" Or "What can I do to have the best chances of success getting this job?"

You can also not really have a clear question in mind, you could just ask the cards to tell you about a specific relationship or situation in your life or magick and have them give you an insight you might be lacking.

You can ask the cards a yes or no question as well. Yes or no questions can sometimes be borderline Fortune Telling questions, so do not ask questions such as "Will I" but questions such as "Should I." or "Can I."

Remember Tarot CAN tell you about things you know nothing about, but the further removed you are from the situation experientially, the harder it can be to recognize the answer, so make sure you ask questions that have some personal anchor to help you understand them.

If you do not know someone at all and ask the cards to tell you about their current situation, you may have no idea what the cards are referring to… and misread them.

But what if I don't have a good question and I still want to do a reading?

This means your intuition or subconscious or shadow self is trying to have a conversation with you…

When I have a conversation with my cards and don't know what I want to know, I often begin with a single card draw… Asking the cards to tell me what they want to talk about. Sometimes I only use the major Arcana for this, but most times I use the whole deck as always.

This card will serve as the Anchor that tells me what the Cards want to talk about. Maybe the Card will be the Lovers, and I know the card wants to talk about commitment, and empathy and relationships and the union of forces, or the dark side of those concepts like disharmony, or enemies.

If my intuition is sparked and I realize this is a valid Anchor card, I proceed to start asking questions with whatever spread makes the most sense.

Example 3 card spreads – These are short spreads that have a sequence of events or a trio of attributes relevant to the querent. In these spreads we lay out 3 cards in sequence, with each card having significance in time or subject. for the Past, Present and future, and the situation spread, or for the Three Aspects spread you lay them out starting in the middle, then to the left, and end on the right. These can be done with either Tarot or Oracle Cards.

Past, present, and future – These 3 cards are laid out from Left to right. One of the most often used spreads anywhere. This reading has 2 potential anchor cards, and if both do not align with the querent in some way, the last card is suspect, or the reading is actually about someone or something else (following our true intent).

The first card is the most important or relevant thing from the past that is currently influencing the situation or question. The Present card is like the past except it is talking about the more relevant or important detail from the current active time relevant to the question or situation. The future is not a fortune telling future, but what you need to know about the potential future that is based on the other 2 cards in some way. Again, this is not a prediction it is more like knowing that A led to B, and B could lead to C.

Situation spread Present, Path, Outcome – These 3 cards are laid out from Left to right. This spread is a lot like the past present and future spread, except it has more to do with giving you direction and what will influence the outcome the most. Again, the outcome is not fortune telling it is what your intuition and the spirits think you will benefit from most in knowing. It does NOT mean you will get that outcome; indeed, the lesson may be that you will NOT get that outcome at all, despite doing everything right and it is the act of trying that makes you grow.

The present card is the anchor card and should be as relevant to the current moment as possible. If this card doesn't align with the querant in some meaningful way in recent history or the current moment, then consider this reading may be wrong or about something other than what

was asked. The Path card is the most important thing you need to know or do or even avoid that will create the highest probability of leading to the outcome card. The outcome card is self-explanatory but remember it is not a prediction of things to come, but only of what your intuition wants you to think is a potential outcome.

The three aspects (great for the intuitive)– Lay this spread out starting in the middle, then to the left, and end on the right. The central card is meant to be most strongly influenced by the cards next to it but may not always be the case. This is a simple reading where you ask the cards to tell you 3 things about someone or a situation. These 3 things are the 3 biggest influences in a person's life, or a situation. This reading can be tricky because it doesn't have a clear Anchor Card, and you will need to decide which card might be the Anchor, or whether to trust the reading even without an Anchor. It can also be tricky to understand, because it is entirely subjective and may not directly relate to a question or time frame, you may just want to get to know someone through the cards, and thus the information you get may not be obvious at first.

So for example, if I do a three aspects reading on someone and get the 3 of swords in the center, the Tower on the left, and The Queen of Wands on the right – this tells me that they are dealing with deep heartbreak, and their life is or was full of turmoil that caused this heartache and there is a down to earth maternalistic female involved, or perhaps the queen of wands doesn't represent a person but the qualities of that person so it might be suggesting the person I'm reading is down to earth, strong and confident.

The entire spread could be talking about how this person might be really influenced by the painful and chaotic loss of a loved one who was down to earth and confident or maternal to them in some way (mother of their children, or their own mother perhaps).

Comparison spread – This spread is for Tarot Only. Essentially this reading is a 3card situation reading that has multiple options. Usually I either set this up as a 5 card spread, or begin with a simple Situation spread, and then realize there may be other options on the table, and want to follow up with another situation reading for that option, but rather than reshuffle and start over, I will either reshuffle and draw 2 more cards, or just draw 2 more cards and lay them below the initial situation spread. This way this next reading shares the same Current Anchor Card.

This reading is interesting because it can "explode" in that you may decide to follow up with any number of situation readings if the situation is complex enough. Maybe you have multiple paths before you more than just 2 or 3. I would limit this to 3 situations otherwise you begin limiting the cards too much as there is no reason why all three situations can't have similar influences you need to know about.

You lay this out by first drawing the anchor card and placing it to the left. Then you create 2 or 3 rows, the top row is 2 cards (path and outcome) declared to be one option (option A), and then you lay another row of 2 cards (path and Outcome again) below this. You can lay out a third row the same way for Option C.

You read this exactly as you would have you drawn 2 or 3 Situation spreads.

Yes and no (by degrees) - This is a simple reading spread where you ask the cards a yes or no question and draw 2 cards. The first card is YES, and the Second is NO. Whichever card has the higher number or value is the card that wins. So, let's say You asked the cards if You should get married or not, if the first card is a 10 of wands, and the next card is a 2 of cups... it is a strong yes!

However, you may want to examine how these cards will influence one another. A 10 of Wands is about responsibility and hard work and carrying burdens, while the 2 of cups is about love and romance and beginning new joyful endeavors like falling in love etc.

This means YES you should get married but watch out for the honeymoon to end and leave you with burden of the shared responsibility! Or just ignore these clues and accept the answer at face Value or read into it. The choice is yours.

The Goetic Trinity – This spread is designed solely for Tarot, and is of my own personal creation and is designed to explore 3 key aspects about a querants life in which the 9 Goetic Kings are most directly interested in. This reading is not meant to answer any specific question it is more of a deep version of the three aspects spread.

This spread is meant to be used sparingly as it covers a lot of ground, and while it doesn't require the querant have relationship with the Goetic spirits, it loses some meaning if the one doing the reading have not at least begun a pathworking with them.

This spread has a total of 10 positions:

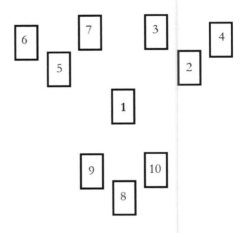

#1: The Center is the position of Lucifer this is the most important thing the reading is about: Your liberation and enlightenment. This is a personal message to the querant from Lucifer. This is the Anchor Card and should be relevant to the querant in some way, either representing them, or a current situation or concern that has meaning to them. If it isn't, consider it as you would any confusing anchor card, and consider reshuffling.

All the other cards in the reading influence or are influenced by this central card, and each set of 3 cards should be evaluated in relation to this card for the deepest possible meaning.

Relationships: Cards #2, 3, 4 - In the upper right corner we lay out 3 cards, these cards work just like the Three Aspects spread, but is specifically meant to be relevant to the querants relationships. Relationships can be about family, or emotional relationships of any Kind. Each of these three cards are 3 primary influences in your life's relationships at the time of the reading, with the card in the #2 spot being most strongly influenced by or influencing the other 2 (#3 and #4).

Prosperity: Cards #5, 6, 7 - The Second set is Prosperity and that is the top Left corner. Prosperity can be referring to anything that influences a person's prosperity be it financial, or familial. This can be talking about wealth, career, offspring or more. Again, this works exactly like a Three Aspects spread, the card in the #5 spot is the one most influenced by and most influential over the other 2 (#6 and #7).

Power: Cards #8, 9, 10 - The last set is power, and this is the point nearest the querant. This can be about a person's personal, social, or political power or authority or their relationship to that power, or what is influencing their ability to exert or feel that power in their life or get along with that authority in their life.

So, for example it can be talking about finances, influence over others, your boss, or your hired workers, your role as a parent, health, or emotional issues. Anything that could influence your personal power or your command and authority over others. If you are feeling blocked, tired, defeated, or can't seem to get people to follow you, or have problems following others, this can help.

This is again exactly the same as the Three Aspects reading with the card in the #8 position having direct influence over the other 2 (#9 and #10) and being influenced most strongly by them in return.

Taken together, each of the three sets of cards interact with one another, each area of your life influencing the other in varying degree. Sometimes they do not interact, but usually in a normal person's life, the situation of one area, deeply affects the others, and vice versa.

Thus, we can draw an invisible line between them, and each line can represent a connection of influence.

The connection Between Power and Prosperity would likely be an influence between one's work and ones drive and

ambition or authority at their job. For example, your boss is mad at you and this is making you feel powerless, or your feeling sick and tired lately with low energy and it's influencing your prosperity.

The Connection between prosperity and Relationships would likely be an influence between one's career and life balance with friends and family, or coworkers. For example, a problem in your marriage can strongly influence your prosperity, and a problem with your job could strongly influence your marriage.

The Connection between power and Relationships would likely be an influence in how your social status and energy and authority are interacting. If you are having problems as a parent with children misbehaving and not being obedient this could be seen in the interplay between these two groups.

Remember the Lucifer card, this card is the special message from Lucifer, and could represent a solution, or the fundamental influence causing problems, or the blessing and the outcome of the interplay of these forces all interacting. It is a kind of wild card, but it should be an Anchor, and be relevant to the querant in some acceptable way.

Let's do a Reading Part 2

Once you have chosen a spread, and your cards are ready to be used.

You can either just go right ahead and begin shuffling, or you can go the extra mile and try to call a spirit to help you. This can be as simple as chanting the spirits name or a chant associated with them. Or as complex as using their sigil and calling them formally.

Only informally call spirits you have been initiated with or who Distinctly have come to you uncalled already. You should always have a relationship with a spirit before using them for this.

Always approach a new spirit with a FORMAL calling FIRST before using informal methods unless they come to you on their own.

I always call a spirit before I do a reading, either formally for a client, or informally for personal use.

When it is time to shuffle, I enter a focused mind trance, and repeat or hold in my mind the layout, the question, the concern and the feeling of the situation or querant. I call this making a connection to the current of the reading and make sure my intention is in alignment with the reading.

I begin shuffling, starting with a few riffle shuffles, to clear the cards of the energy of the last reading and balance the distribution of the cards.

I close my eyes, and focus my awareness on my third eye, and try to enter a deep Empty or open mind trance and simply overhand shuffle.

The key here is to not think about shuffling, and to just keep going until you decide to stop spontaneously. You should NEVER plan to stop. For example, do not think – Ok, this is the last shuffle I will draw after this. Or In three more shuffles I will be ready. Your mind should be totally clear of all cluttered intentions and ONLY stop shuffling when you spontaneously decide to stop.

This is one of the hardest things in Tarot. If you can do this reliably, you will have good results as your subconscious mind will make sure you stop at the right time.

Draw the cards one at a time, being careful not to flip them vertically and thus inverting them. Some people like to place the cards face down till they are ready to read, others like to see them emerge as part of the draw. Either method is fine.

Either way, flip the cards over horizontally so they do not become inverted, and then set the deck down off to the side out of the way.

Relax your mind and observe the cards.

First and foremost, take special note of what card, or what details of the card jump out at you. What significance do they have? Do they relate to the question or situation?

Next look at the cards and note the elements they represent, the Swords being Air, The Wands/rods being Fire, the Cups being Water, and the coins being earth.

See how the energy flows and interacts between the cards, do any of the elemental interactions alter, strengthen or mute the meaning of the card?

If you do not know the meanings of the cards by heart, or by the imagery on the cards, take a few minutes to see what comes to you, don't be afraid to be wrong, just let your mind wander the cards, and listen and look for clues.

When you think you have as much as you will get, open the little booklet and read aloud what it says while looking at the card, and really take your time to savor the meaning while looking at the card.

What words jumped out at you of significance? Do they relate to the question or situation?

What do your spirit guides tell you?

Experiment with other astral senses, feel the cards, see them, smell them, put yourself into the picture, imagine the card is a gate to some deeper story and go through it.

When you feel you have exhausted the meaning, pack your cards away in the appropriate place, and record the reading in your journal, and see if anything comes to you. In a few weeks when the situation or question is resolved, check on your journal and the reading and see how you did.

What did you get right? What did you get wrong?

If it matters to you, do you have an 80% accuracy and success rate or better?

When all is said and done, the Tarot is a useful and fun way to play with our intuition… just remember, the cards are not what does the reading, you do… If you are reading the cards and 1 card is dead wrong, but the others all align, then either you are not reading the card right, or the card is wrong. Do not be afraid for the Card to be Wrong, or for you to just be missing something. Also keep in mind that it can be useful to combine, mix and match various divination methods. You could easily use Crystal or Fire Gazing as part of a Tarot Reading. You could easily combine an Oracle card in a Tarot Spread, and Vice Versa.

You could easily stare deeply into a mirror and enter a trance before using your cards…

Experiment, and don't be afraid to learn that Tarot, or crystals or mirrors just aren't for you. This is how we find our path in magick. Find what feels best for you, and don't try to force the methods that don't work for you to work like they do for others.

Remember YOU are the God and the Devil of your

reality, embrace that!

Baneful Magick

What would a treatise on dark magick be, without at least an acknowledgement of Baneful magick... Baneful magick is a catch all term I use to refer to any magick that does harm, enslaves, binds, or steals from others. It really has nothing to do with any sense of morality or ethics. Bane or baneful Literally means anything that causes harm or destruction.

Baneful magick is one of the most popular forms of so called black magick, and every day I get at least one request from a hopeful client asking me to curse, bind, or otherwise enslave someone using magick.

I often enjoy disappointing these pathetic people who misunderstand the nature of Black magick, those who think that just because I work with spirits they have been taught are "demons" that I am somehow aligned with helping them achieve their petty desires of the flesh.

Sometimes the problem is easy to rectify, they are simply ignorant and a few minutes in conversation can solve it, other times I must shun them.

Sometimes I must explain to some of them that I am a Chosen of Lucifer, this means I am a Light bringer, a liberator and teacher, not an enslaver or destroyer, at least not like I once was... at least not without good reason.

Indeed, if I was still in my 20s... I would have made them my food, I would have worked dark magick against them, and the shadows and I would have enjoyed feeding from their fear, and paranoia and pain.

I would have brought them in closer and closer, and as they unraveled and self-destructed, I would act like the caring soul, offering them a nurturing shoulder to cry on... My "psychic mouths" pressed deep into their emotional wounds...

I want to reiterate, I am NOT a good guy, nor am I a bad guy. I am not a hero, nor a villain. I am a liberated force of nature (as are we all) and I will act on my whims, not theirs. As it so happens this is a KEY of all magick... If I act magickally it is by my intention alone, not by or because of the abuse or needs of others.

Baneful magick tends to be weak magick because baneful magick is all too often the last resort of a desperate or low energy/low vibration/low intelligence person who is far too attached to the target emotionally and spiritually.

If they NEED to use baneful magick to solve a problem, chances are they are inferior or feeble or incapable of intentionally using magick in the first place, or they would likely not be in a position that caused the need for it.

It still happens of course, even to the best of us... But it is easy to tell the difference.

Baneful magick is to be avoided, not because it is going to result in Karma or 3-fold laws of return, or because it might send you to hell or anything of the sort, but because Baneful magick represents a failure in the individual to be powerful, liberated, and free of the influence of others... And it grounds us in the negativity that sparked the problem in the first place.

It is FAR better to ascend, and get revenge by living well, then to use magick to do harm. Of course, every now and then... even for a reformed nightmare like myself... occasionally... Someone has it fucking coming. To deny this fact of life, is to deny the truth of the self and not be willing to embrace the dark side within us and ascend.

Before I elaborate, know that Baneful magick is a poor choice for solving specifically dangerous or time sensitive situations... All magick for that matter is the same way. For example, if someone is breaking into your house to kill you and your pets and rape your loved ones, you don't curse them and hope it manifests before they work their way through half your family. No! You lock and load and shoot them dead (or whatever else is legal where you live).

One of the problems with most forms of baneful magick is that it doesn't solve anything, it merely makes you feel good... And this is the key and fundamental secret of Baneful magick, more often than not, your true intention is not to do harm, but to be liberated from the problem that is harming you. To achieve liberation or catharsis and move on. Sometimes the only way for that to happen is to do harm or destroy, but most of the time... no.

Hence why baneful magick, like many other forms of manifestation focused magick can be tricky to manifest (or tricky to recognize as having manifested).

I am not trying to sound like some kind of hippy dippy dipshit that thinks everything should be peace and love, it is simply a fact of life.

In order to carry out baneful magick you need to be able to do the equivalent in harm to the person while looking them in the eye and without fear, or fear of spiritual consequence… So, in other words, if you wish death on someone in magick, you need to be psychologically and emotionally capable of putting a gun to their head in the real world, and pulling the trigger, assuming there would be no legal or social consequence of your action.

If you would hesitate, even for a second, chances are, your intention is not for the destruction of that person and you need to rethink your needs and alignment with your true intention.

The same could be said for so called "Love" magick (of which there are 3 primary kinds which I will go into detail shortly). IF you claim you *love* someone, and you are willing to destroy their free will, essentially enslave and bind them to your will, then you do not *love* them.

Indeed, it should be said that very few people alive actually truly *love* anyone outside of themselves as much as they believe they do. What they love is the way that person makes them feel, or how they fulfill some need (toxic or otherwise) they have. True love doesn't seek to enslave, because the very idea of doing that would be painful.

When someone asks me for a love spell, and I explain this to them, and they respond by saying they DO love them, but still want to enslave them to love them back… I know I am dealing with a psychopath and close the connection.

Regardless, be it love binding, curses, hexes, or death magick, even if you do not hesitate, your true intention might not be to kill or do harm…

Most baneful magick has its origin in hate. Hate is a powerful emotion centered in the Ego of the Avatar of your personality. It often clouds our judgement and creates an inability to align with our true intent, making us think we want to destroy, when we really want to be free.

Add to this the fact that the target of your magick, even if they are utterly blind to magick, has a spirit and a subconscious that is NOT blind to magick and spirituality. This will act to protect itself. The target IS an individual and they ARE the God and Devil of their experience, even if they are unaware, and you are not…

So, technically they have dominion over their experience and within the subjective Trinity of self, and you need to create circumstances or attacks on the objective aspect of their experience that they cannot deny that allows you access to their subjective being.

Even the blackest magick requires bypassing the defenses of even the weakest target. In magick Defense is much easier than attack.

Even a skeptic, and sometimes ESPECIALLY a skeptic can be a hard target, more so than a powerful sorcerer, because the sorcerer knows it is possible to be attacked.

The Skeptic strongly believes magick isn't real, and as they create their experience, that experience will be blessedly free of magick of any form. Indeed, your spell might be working! The Target might fall down a flight of stairs and walk with a limp for a few days as a result of your working… but the target may never notice it… they might not see the run of bad luck as magick, they might just soldier on, blissfully unaware!

So what? You may be asking, you still got them to fall down a flight of stairs! But that isn't baneful magick, that is a prank. BANEFUL magick does real harm, not parlor tricks.

This lack of belief or recognition tends to limit the spells influence because baneful magick works BEST when the targets own weaknesses and fears can be exploited.

A superstitious person who still lives in the spirit of the old world who as to throw salt over their shoulder or hold their breath going past the graveyard for fear of a dark spirit entering them… These people are easy prey for black magick, ironically however, their superstition can be empowered by their belief and confidence as well and present a barrier too.

The BEST baneful magick works indirectly, it bypasses the defenses of the target and attacks aspects of their lives that break them down, break their confidence and open them to direct attack later.

So, for example, I could try to curse my target to be poor… But their magick defenses and or lack of belief might protect them too strongly, or maybe they are simply too spiritually powerful and their ability to have prosperity is already something they are empowering with magick and protecting with magick and impossible to influence directly. So instead, we can try to do magick that causes them expenses, conflict and a loss of their job.

Maybe you know that they have a bad habit of being flirty and cheating on their spouse... Instead of trying to get him fired directly under mysterious circumstances, you could use magick to create a situation where they are brought into a compromising sexual situation with a coworker, and make sure that situation is with someone that will harm them by exposing the encounter through gossip or even for vindictive reasons.

Someone who will call their house and tell their spouse, someone who will claim they have been molested or raped on a date with the person. Someone who will complain about workplace harassment.

Things like this.

Even if the relationship is healthy, it could be against corporate policy, and all you need to do is make sure the magick includes the intent to make this relationship be impossible to keep secret and expose them for fraternization and get them fired.

In other words, you need to use mundane knowledge and know their mundane weaknesses to create the best chance of success for your magick.

You could attack their family, or their pets, and just about anything you want that is indirect but will cost them.

If you keep doing these things even the most powerful sorcerer can lose confidence and energy trying to deal with all these attacks and will become spread thin. With luck they will begin to doubt their own ability and then you can go in for the kill.

The best baneful magick is the one that is empowered by the belief of the target and is based on their weakness.

The 10 commandments of baneful magick –

I. Thou shall Expect the magick to liberate you of your situation, either by giving you Catharsis, or distance from the source of the problem. It may not do it the way you expect, accept what magick does for you and move on.

II. Thou shall not expect the magick to destroy your target or have specific effects every time.

III. Thou shall NOT use blood or other objects or substances that are energetically connected to you on any kind of curse in a way that could cause the curse to follow the conduit of your blood back to you. If you must use blood in the ritual keep it separate and not part of that particular part of the working and clean your hands before handing the accursed object that will do the damage to your enemy. (IE do not use your blood in a cursed object you give your enemy, however using blood as an offering to a spirit to attack the target is fine).

IV. Thou Shall NOT fear the Consequence or hesitate. If you fear the consequence or hesitate, you should consider a different approach.

V. Thou Shall consider the Consequences of your actions on the innocent and be willing to live with those consequences or reconsider your approach.

VI. Thou Shall pour ALL your hate, aggression, pain and resentment in to the spell to the point where you feel better, regardless of whether the spell works or not. If you do not pour all your angst and pain into the spell, it will be unlikely to work well.

VII. Thou shall be creative and look for ways to affect the target indirectly until or unless you believe them an easy target who already believes they are cursed and is scared or confused.

VIII. Thou Shall dispose of all the evidence and ritual materials used in baneful magick and know that baneful magick is best performed outside one's normal ritual space... preferably in seclusion where all the ritual materials and tools can be burned or buried in secret.

IX.   Thou shall ALWAYS repay a spirit what it asks in return for carrying out your cursed intention against a target. That spirit can easily turn on you and do unto you ten times what it has done unto others in your name.

X.   Thou Shall leave ALL thy rage upon the altar, retain nothing, push every bit of your hate, rage, and desire for revenge into the magick and don't accept any of it back. You need to be exhausted; your fists should be bloody and bruised, and your voice should probably be hoarse. If you cannot summon up this much anger and rage and push it into the ritual and LEAVE it on the Altar, you should reconsider your options.

Baneful Spirits

Some spirits are quite willing, eager even to do baneful magick on your behalf, or teach you spells for such a purpose. Much of my magick is what I call Demon Sorcery, this means I either ask a spirit to do the work for me in exchange for something they desire, or they hold my hand and guide me through a ritual or in the creation of a ritual.

This has obvious advantages but can have disadvantages too. Some disadvantages include the fact that spirits will sometimes ask for more than I am willing to pay, so I need to seek other options. Another disadvantage is, a spirit may agree to terms, accept their payment, then not deliver, and this can be for any number of reasons. While I believe all the spirits that I work with are trustworthy and do not willingly renege on a contract, it has happened, and sometimes with no explanation until I demanded one.

Usually a spirit will tell me they did what they did to teach me a lesson, usually a life lesson. So, for example asking for something to happen magickally that I could easily do for myself with mundane methods.

In the case of Baneful magick a spirit might have plans and designs for that person or may even be allied with that person. In some cases, they might even have a better relationship with your target than you do with them and this can cause them to deny or deceive you.

Remember, Demonic entities, the ones we normally call upon for baneful magick are… Noble, but they are also like us in that they are capable of deception and wickedness and breaking promises.

But they also have a sense of loyalty that transcends the material, they might literally ruin your life to make you grow spiritually…

This means if you are having a squabble with one of their better allies and try to turn them against one of their favorite mortals, they might even warn your enemy of your actions and work against you!

But if they are your ally, this will never be more than you can handle, and can usually get the attacks to stop if you make the right effort to make amends.

I myself have never had this issue, the spirits I work with have come to me because they want ME as an ally, and some of these spirits are formidable guardians in the extreme who have brought to my attention the workings of others and let me know they already took care of it. More or less.

Having demons carry out your desires is no different than trusting magick to manifest your desires… You need to let go and let the magick happen and not check up on it beyond what is rationally required.

However, one of the advantages of using spirits and demons is because another being is responsible for the magic's success, and it is possible to have success even if your unable to keep your mind 100% off it. You should still avoid it, you can still ruin it if you dwell on it. It's still less likely, because less of it is up to you, and most or at least some of it is up to the spirit. The Tenth Commandment of baneful magick applies here. Pour it all into the working and forget it ever happened.

Some spirits are incredibly mercenary, some djinn are veritable assassins for hire and while I have never called upon them personally, I know some who have, and they report the same thing… It's All business, and fast.

It goes without saying that keeping your end of a pact with a spirit is paramount in all demon sorcery, but in the case of Baneful Magick, it is much more important and if you doubt you can uphold your end of the bargain… do not make the pact.

When we petition the spirits to act in the world in this way, our energies and nobility are linked to the target in subtle ways. If a demon or djinn agrees to destroy your enemy, and you fail to deliver what you promised... No force in heaven nor hell can protect you from their wrath and these spirits have long memories.

It would be like hiring a hitman to kill someone, then not paying them. But instead of it being a living hitman bound by the laws of nature... We are talking about a demon! Watch your step! We wouldn't want you to have a totally explainable accident that leaves you paralyzed and traumatized screaming about the demons you betrayed...

Sympathetic Curses

Most forms of magick people practice today are some form of Sympathetic magick, and baneful magick is no exception. We associate things as being the same or similar in spiritual energy and thus in magick based on similarities in their appearance and characteristics.

A hot pepper is spicy and is a sexy red color, and so we associate it with passion and use it in love spells. Coffin nails are used to seal away dead people in coffins and have a dark macabre quality about them and are often used in baneful magick that binds and harms.

A person's hair was once part of them and if used in magick allows you to target the former owner of the hair because it is and was a part of them.

These connections and meanings are useful in baneful magick as it is in any other kind of magick.

This is not because the hot pepper does anything. It's just a hot pepper, it's because it invokes and evokes the energies of passion and lust, heat and fire.

The coffin nail works not because it is a coffin nail, a coffin nail is just some iron. The coffin nail works because we think it is a coffin nail and it invokes and evokes the energies of loss and macabre shock.

A person's hair DOES have an energetic connection to the target, but this is amplified by the fact that the sorcerer

has something tangible in their hands that is significant to the target that they can feel very sinister about.

When using sympathetic principles in curses we need to pump those objects and associations with our intention and hatred and determination. Sometimes to the point of destroying them and doing unto them what we wish we could do to the person if we only had the chance.

This is a big part of what makes things like Poppets AKA Voodoo dolls, and curse jars and other things work. We are doing to these effigies or filling these containers with all the shit (sometimes literally) and hate and bile we can muster and leaving them in the vicinity of the target to saturate our enemy with the negativity we left in it.

Often, this entire exercise results in cathartic release more than effective curse, but in my school of magick thinking that is a valid and acceptable result of baneful magick. It need not destroy the target in the objective sense, but it should destroy them or their ability to do harm in the subjective experience of the one doing the curse.

Therefore, If I REALLY want to have someone harmed or cursed, I rely (at least partially) on spirits, if I am willing to just "get over" my enemy, I just do sympathetic curses and don't bother my spirit allies.

Sometimes our spirits will act on our behalf without direct instruction. If we have a close relationship with them, they will sometimes cause harm to those who would harm us, causing sickness, accidents, even death.

When I was in my darker more chaotic and evil youth running a small cult, people who meant me harm or offended me deeply enough, would die of mysterious sudden causes or suffer sudden illness or accident of a synchronistic nature.

They would be seen publicly slandering me accusing me of stealing their girl (who I wouldn't want even if she threw herself at me at the time) and hating me unfairly for it, and they would end up in a fluke bicycle accident the next day and be drinking through a straw for 6 weeks needing their jaw wired shut because it was shattered... or they would have their foot crushed by a caterpillar fork lift because they threatened to kick my ass if I didn't stop hanging out with their girlfriend (who wasn't into me that way).

They would report me to my job for something I didn't

do, and then they took my job and bragged about it to me and my friends to mock me and my "magick." The very next night they would have a heart attack at work and die on the spot with nobody to discover it for several hours…

I could tell tale upon tale of this kind of synchronistic circumstance where I never ever called upon a single spirit, nor cast a single intentional spell against these people, but later my spirits would inform me that they took care of the problem on my behalf.

Even people who didn't know I was a sorcerer, or didn't believe in it, knew I had a reputation for my enemies having mysterious accidents and illness whenever they would publicly try to shame or hurt me.

Suffice to say, I am well protected… you can be too. If you work with the right spirits for the right reasons!

Baneful magick is always Consequential

This is not to say it is immoral, or that it gives you bad Karma, or cosmic justice will come ruin your day. It means that it has consequences (both good and bad) for ANYONE involved.

This means You, this means your Target, this means your Targets friends, family, loved ones, and pets. Even if you do everything right and find a way to only hurt the target, you WILL cause pain to someone innocent somewhere in the equation. Potentially even to yourself, because unless you are a total psychopath, you have at least some empathy and you also must admit that if you hate someone enough to do baneful magick, you are also admitting they have power over you in some way.

What do I mean by that?

It means that a powerful person normally doesn't care if a weak person hates them or is rude to them in the same way a weak person does. A strong person usually doesn't act against someone they hate because the person they hate has no power over their life or happiness. They look at them and shake their heads and go on with their life.

A weak person on the other hand can be easily hurt by the one they hate, or the one they hate has power over their happiness.

As I stated before, there are exceptions to the rule. There are times a weak person is attempting to hurt a strong person and is having success and the strong person must act to protect or vindicate themselves.

But even in that event, they are imbalanced, their energy is negative and needs to be rebalanced again. The black magick of curses will balance that energy back to normal for them, and that is their consequence.

Often this rebalance of energy requires sacrifice and loss, or pain or some other form of experience that may not always be pleasant.

In other words, not all consequences are bad, but consequences can often be costly! Consequences are always meaningful events, turning points, and should NEVER be treated as unimportant bumps in the road. So long as we learn from them, they are beneficial, if we do not, they become baneful.

It is in this way that baneful magick can rebound. We remain too attached to the idea of doing harm, or do not fully divest ourselves of our hatred for the target so that we suffer negative feedback from the consequences we set in motion for the target.

Similarly Working with spirits exacts a price, and most spirits have special prices for baneful magick… Lighting a few candles and offering incense isn't usually enough for spirits to do baneful work.

They want something of significance, and sometimes the price is high… and the consequence for failing to provide that payment can be horrific.

Love Magick

There are three kinds of Love magick, 2 of them are beneficial or neutral in nature, and one is clearly baneful as it involves enslaving the object of your desire to your will and compelling them to "act" like they love you. I say act, because first of all, true love cannot be forced, and second of all, true love itself is very rare, and is usually more about how being with someone makes you feel, or how it would feel to lose them, or how much it might hurt to know you betrayed them etc.

This is a difficult thing for most people to accept, but if you are truly honest with yourself, you will see the truth in it. Human beings have a very difficult time distinguishing love from a variety of toxic emotions that are not love.

Baneful love magick compels the target to act or be bound to the petitioner, and like all baneful magick the target always has some modicum of natural resistance to its influence. This means in order for it to work, the will and confidence of the target must be diminished or destroyed, and this is always a very destructive and consequential thing.

I cannot tell you how many stories I have heard of people who attempt these kinds of spells that get exactly what they wished for, and the target becomes a weak willed and useless hollow shell, obsessed with the magickian.

At first there is much rejoicing, but in the end the result is always the same… The one who did this magick cursed themselves as much as the target because they ruined the object of their obsession destroying the thing in them, they likely wanted most. Often creating a relationship that is not merely toxic, but utterly destructive.

These people who do these kinds of baneful love magick I often call Magickal Rapists. I have confronted several of the vilest perpetrators of this kind of magick with the fact that what they want is to essentially RAPE this person using magick and suffer no consequence, or to even have the victim grateful for the chance.

These fools do not even recognize, or cannot admit that they are at the mercy of their desires…

I can tell you from experience time and time again, that people in this kind of situation utterly lack the capacity to do magick of any kind, they never will have such a capacity without great change.

If, however you find two people who are equally deserving of one another's toxic misery and want to bring them together to ruin their lives… I might know a few demons who can help you with that.

Keep in mind that Demons, at least Goetic Demons, sometimes have a caveat when it comes to love magick. They can indeed cause (force) love or romance to happen by breaking the will, but it will be without fulfillment. More specifically, the Zepar of the Ars Goetia says something about how the woman will be barren.

Now depending on your intention, this could be a good or bad thing, but it doesn't have to always mean it always makes them unable to have children. What it usually means is that the relationship will be unfulfilled and be of a shallow or short-lived nature…

I have found that any time a forceful or baneful curse is used to make someone fall in love with someone else, the target becomes a hollow shadow of their former self as it requires them to be broken, both emotionally, and psychically.

Thus, expect quarreling, or a weak willed and useless mate who will not make you happy.

Non baneful love magick

This section is about baneful magick, but I feel it is important to tell you there are alternatives that can be just as satisfying or get you meaningful results that do no direct or indirect harm to the target.

Love magick is the best example, as there are many alternatives to baneful love magick that do not rob people of their will, and many demons who can help with this. Creating lives filled with fulfilling romances and relationships. In these situations, the magick is of a more supportive or supplementary role, making us more attractive, or witty. Or even manipulate situations to make us appear in a favorable light (sometimes literally) to the eyes of the object of our desire.

They will overhear you saying just the right things at the right time, see you giving a homeless person a dollar… see you petting a dog and acting like a kind person. Maybe the light will fall on your breasts, or muscles in just the right way to make him or her notice you…

Or maybe you and your spouse fight a lot, maybe Dantalion can help you to understand one another better and help you to find common ground or mutual respect where before there was none.

Nobodies free will, will be bent, we are just arranging the cards so that the deck is stacked in our favor. There is a meaningful difference!

The same works for other situations other than love. If you are struggling with a boss at work, you don't need to destroy them with magick, you can empower yourself with magick and push right through the obstacle they represent and become their boss… or empower yourself to withstand the best they can throw at you and come out smelling like a rose, making them waste time and energy trying to hurt you as you just stand your ground like a boulder in a storm.

Final Word

I want to be honest with you, this part of the book was the hard part, because my goal is not to hold your hand and limit your potential in magick. I do NOT want people to read this book and in the fullness of time somehow quote from it in such a way that creates excess dogma.

It was also a challenge because it represents only a portion of the methods I could or would like to teach people that I use. But I had to try to stay focused on the things that would benefit you NOW. Because this book has already reached 96K words at the time of this writing, and I have quite a few thousand more to go to finish it.

I could go on… but I do not want to reinvent the wheel, I want to reintroduce it to people in a new way. To create a system of magick that takes you from the basics and the foundation of high-level knowledge, to a proper self-initiation with a clear path to where you should try to go on your own to complete your training.

My goal is not for you to do magick the way I do it, but to see that my way is "no-way," and all the elaborate methods and ideas I use to do what I do is all just an elaborate floor show designed to inspire my subconscious and spirit to move heaven and earth and bring to me the reality I demand.

When you come to the next section, I want you to encourage yourself to explore the rituals and add or subtract whatever feels right or wrong for you. I want YOU to be the sorcerer who does their OWN magick, not mine.

Mine is just a framework, it is up to you to make it yours!

Remember, before you begin working with the next section of the book intentionally. I am going on the assumption you have already put as much of this into study and practice as is feasible. You should be capable of entering and holding any of the altered mental states for up to a minute at a time. You can sense and be aware of energy and spiritual currents such as synchronicity and the way spirits interact with us.

You have practiced your energy manipulation and scrying and gotten some results.

You do not have to have mastered any of these things before you begin your pathworking. Indeed, you can begin without practicing anything.

The earlier aspects of pathworking will help clear the path ahead to achieve initiation with the Goetic spirits enough so that they can help you to develop and learn the rest, if this is truly your intention, and theirs.

Be warned I offer no safety nets, if you offend these spirits, you are on your own. I assure you, they respect a blend of personal authority and confidence, and nobility and respect. Not sniveling cowards, nor demanding blow hard authoritarians. Nor disrespectful louts.

And above all if nothing I taught you so far resonates with you, if you cannot make sense of it, or put it into practice… Do it your own way… even if you fail. I would rather you do your OWN magick and fail 100 out of 100 times, than do MY magick and learn nothing and have it work 100 out of 100 times.

Go now… become the Maelstrom!

BOOK 3:
Introduction

This part of the book gets down to the nitty gritty, the rituals the spells, and the data that you need to use in conjunction with the foundational philosophy and the practical methods I outlined before. If you have been paying attention thus far, you will know that you need to treat this section of the book as a pathworking and example guide.

All the material in this section is written from the perspective of a Goetic Demon Sorcerer. I chose this because the Goetic current is one of the EASIEST for the novice to find information about for FREE online. It is open to a lot of interpretation, and the spirits are utterly real and accessible to all.

Before you begin, I want you to take a deep breath, and just relax. The single biggest thing I see beginners do wrong, is overthink working with spirits. We all begin the same way, elaborate rituals of summoning, and making sure every detail is just right. Then we get lazy and realize we can call upon them with just the power of their name. Then this somehow trivializes the magick and this can lead to failure as well!

So, what is necessary? Both!

It can be as easy or as complex as you like, but make sure you relax, if you are relaxed and realize that these beings don't NEED elaborate rituals to come when you call, you are more apt to perform a rituals on the spot that is from the heart and one that puts you in perfect harmony with their frequency...

If you also understand that not taking this seriously leads to flaccid evocations and uninspiring invocations, you will learn to maintain a certain level of complexity, unless circumstances dictate otherwise... and find balance between simple workings, and complex ones.

Another benefit of working with the Goetia, is you will not need to buy costly grimoires, and there are literally thousands of viable resources of GREAT information all over the internet in every form imaginable. It is information that is in the public domain, and thus is an EASY place for someone seeking to learn Demon sorcery to begin.

Of course, I am not limited to just being a Goetic Demon sorcerer, officially I call myself a Demon Sorcerer, and leave the word Goetic off it. However, they are invaluable for the novice who has mastered the basics I outlined in the last section. In seeking the Dark path, these beings can be a bountiful source of gnosis and power. They seek the fearless, the black sheep, the individualist, and respect those who would be spiritual kings and queens!

Be aware that there are MANY other spirits you can call upon, from a myriad religions and belief systems (many of them are just different faces or aspects of the same being from other pantheons!) as well as egregores, and spirits that appear to come from nowhere or the Lovecraftian angles in between. You can quite easily alter any of the pathworking or spells in this section to fit almost any pantheon of spirits you desire.

Some do have a very specific format for working with them, while many others are very loose and willing to work with you just by calling them with enough energy.

You could seek to initiate this process with any other demon or god you wish, for example you could try to initiate yourself with Lilith, Leviathan, or Lucifuge Rofocale, or with a lesser demon from the Goetia such as Stolas. There is no "right" way to do this.

I would suggest that if you are truly NEW to magick, you follow my pathworking only for as long as you need it, but at least enough to see the pattern. Your goal should be to make your OWN magick and use mine merely as inspiration and training wheels.

For this reason, I am Instead giving you the preferred pathworking of the spirits as I would want to approach them if I was starting out fresh.

Lucifer is the highest spirit in the infernal kingdoms of the Judeo Christian Goetia current. But Lucifer, as an entity has many names, many guises, and is the most high dark entity in most other currents as well but by other names.

Lucifer will sometimes appear as a female, a child of any age or gender. However, many people might prefer to initiate themselves with Lilith as she is very much a counterpart to

Lucifer in many ways, but of a very fierce feminine energy. She is less radiant, but much wilder and very independent! I have almost no experience with Lilith so I cannot speak to her preferences, save that she is a very free and wild spirit, every bit as important and liberating to people as Lucifer IF she chooses to work with you!

She will work with people of both male and female aspect, so do not think she only appears to women and Lucifer only to men for example.

Spirits by and large are sexless and appear gendered to us mainly by our own needs and desires to see them as such. But I assure you, even if a spirit is of strong female energy, they can (in my experience) appear as a man, stout and strong at will.

The rituals and spells here are what have worked for me, or variations of those methods that are suitable for public use. Despite this, they are still MY magick, based on my symbolism and ideas and they may not work for you as written, you may need to alter and adjust them to meet your unique situation and to make them your own.

These rituals and spells are designed to build confidence and take from you having little or no experience in magick to having initiated yourself with Lucifer, and at least 1 Goetic king and have a series of spells and rituals you can use to benefit yourself.

The objective is to work through all this material at your own pace until you finish it, or gain the gnosis needed to start doing your OWN magick. I strongly encourage you to at least finish the initiation with at least one entity such as Lucifer and a Goetic King before proceeding to follow your own path. You may of course substitute any entity you wish in place of Lucifer or one of the kings, but these rituals have been designed with them in mind, and you might need to make major changes to make them work.

We shall begin with the basics, and move on from there, I will endeavor to be less dramatic and long winded from this point on in terms of method, but shall try to be as informative as I can where I can within reason (the book needs an end after all), I have explained more than enough to get you started, and you need to begin using your intuition and judgement to answer your own questions and choose your own path here. If at any point what you are doing feels wrong, or scary or dangerous, STOP and reconsider your path.

You will likely notice that my rituals are fairly simple and have more room for interpretation and improvisation. Providing your magick has a Mental, Physical, and Spiritual component. It need not get any more complex than this to get at least some results.

I will no longer hold your hand, I am casting you adrift in the storm… Find your current, sink or swim!

NOTE #1 – When a ritual calls for you to face a certain direction, if you cannot do this due to the nature of your situation, then you need to at least align your altar so that the Aspect of Mind is pointing opposite that direction (pointing to where you would ideally be standing or sitting) and the plane of void is pointing in the direction indicated. If the Altar cannot be adjusted or moved, and the facing cannot be adjusted or moved, this is not ideal, but you can disregard this step and imagine instead that it is so.

NOTE #2 - When a spell or ritual calls for Reciting the text this is not something you need to know by heart, nor do you have to recite it verbatim. The purpose of this is not for you to recite the exact selection of words.

It is in truth little more than spiritual occult poetry meant to evoke in you the imagery and emotions and energy required to cast the spell and perform the ritual. If it helps you to read it aloud from the book do so, use it as written if it moves you, and if it is too hard to relate to and speak from the heart, or doesn't represent you, CHANGE IT or OMIT it.

I have found that such poetry, when written in your own personal grimoire and read aloud from that grimoire, is as powerful as if you memorized it and feel it from the heart. Thus, a good practice you may want to get into is to scribe each ritual and spell either into your notes or your grimoire prior to performing them, and leave room for edits and notes to change things you find work better for you etc.

You can of course work directly out of this book as it is a kind of Grimoire but adding it into your own is better.

Intention Simplification

So, you are ready to do a spell or calling of a spirit, you have a basic idea or concern in mind, but what if I told you that for most people, the idea they have is not really their truest intention?

Our truest intention is almost never exactly what our Ego thinks it is, but often something much simpler, something more basic to our experience, and the more that we can tune into this underlying true intention, the more likely we are to see results.

Example – Your rent is due in 1 week and you just lost your job and you usually live paycheck to paycheck. You need 500$ cash ASAP or will potentially be in trouble with the landlord.

Most novice people will do a spell or demon calling and try to obtain 500$.

Some more advanced people will do a spell and simply ask for the Rent to be Paid or taken care of somehow.

And Some people will not ask for anything specific at all but focus instead on financial freedom and security in general.

And still others might ask to be liberated from Financial concerns altogether.

Of those 4 groups, the last two are the most likely to get what they wanted. Ironically, they may never get their rent paid on time, but they might instead learn to live a more affordable lifestyle as a result of the loss of their home and move on into the future in a more financially free position with a better understanding of managing their resources.

Or they may end up being homeless, and somehow find that the life of a homeless person living out of their car traveling from town to town doing odd jobs is remarkably satisfying for a while, maybe settling down in a low cost situation after having learned to enjoy the simpler things in life, IE learning to obtain liberation from money and finance completely.

Or, they may end up winning the lottery, inheriting money, or finding a dream job. The point is, they let the magick follow a path of least irrational Resistance and give them something more generic and useful. Rather than specific and requiring a miracle.

It is not to say that the person doing the spell for 500$ exactly won't ever get it… Many in fact will! But it is always best to try to simplify our intentions.

What we need to do whenever we get ready to perform magick, is to attempt to break down our intention into its smallest components and try to find out what really is making us tick.

We can go about this via many different methods, from simple logic and deductive reasoning, or meditation or a combination of both.

But to help you get started, consider that your ultimate intention as a conscious being is to have the most fulfilling and exhilarating and visceral life possible, filled with a healthy combination of good times and bad times to create enough contrast to give you a life worth experiencing.

This means sometimes you NEED to suffer, sometimes you NEED to lose, sometimes you NEED to be lonely, or poor, or hurt, or sick, or lose a loved one.

Also, it means sometimes you NEED to win, you need to conquer, you NEED to get money, you NEED to experience true love etc.

The mistake many people make is thinking they are meant to have more pleasure than pain, or that life is ever fair. Magick can help here, but our true intention does not answer to what our ego thinks is right, wrong, or in between… sometimes you just can't win, and sometimes you just can't lose!

So, let me give you a few examples, these are by no means how it always is, these are just examples to consider –

Money – Generally when we want to do a spell for money, we are not looking for money, but to satisfy the imbalance in our root chakra (which is largely focused on survival and the needs of practical living) that is making us feel insecure in our finances. Some people can be very rich, and still feel they need more to be secure and happy. And most rich people will tell you, that being rich isn't exactly easier or liberating!

So instead of doing a spell for a specific amount of money, do a spell for liberation from financial burden, or better financial skills, or prosperity and abundance.

Sex – Generally when we crave sex or lust for someone specific to the point of wanting to use magick… it is our sacral Chakra, and sometimes also our Root chakra telling us we need to procreate, or that we are deep down feeling insecure and lonesome.

So, consider Instead of trying to use magick to force or trick or coerce someone to have sex with you or fall in love, consider using magick to balance your sacral chakra and help you relate better to people and make you more outgoing or charming, to attract people of nurturing energy into your life.

Cursing someone – Generally when we want to curse someone, we feel threatened by them, or they otherwise are causing us distress. Our true intention is almost never to kill. Often, we would instead prefer to see the person removed from our life in a way that allows us to move on and heal from the damage they caused to our emotions or life. Or want to see them suffer so they grow, change and become less of a jerk.

But really our True intention is almost never to cause harm to them, but to stop the pain and suffering they are causing us. The terrible irony is, sometimes this means we end up helping them and healing them… or simply moving them out of the picture without doing any harm.

So instead of cursing, consider asking for liberation from the suffering, gaining cathartic release and moving on, for being unattached to the person, or to simply have the magick remove them from your life.

Test yourself - One way I like to simplify my intention is to ask myself pointed adversarial questions, for example if I want to use baneful magick to do harm to someone and remove them from my life, I might ask myself – Is it just because you are too weak to tolerate them? Isn't it just because you are letting them get you down?

Don't be afraid of the questions NOR the answer! If the question is unthinkable, or the answer makes you uncomfortable… then more than likely the reason is because you are afraid of the truth. In such cases if you were a paying client asking me for help, I would tell you not to do the spell

you think you need, but to do the one that makes you confront the unanswerable question…

Ask why, why, why – Just keep breaking it down, why do I want money? Because my rent is due. Why does that matter? Because I'll be homeless. Why does that matter? Because it would be embarrassing… and so on. Till you get to an answer that you just can't break down anymore.

That doesn't mean that is your truest intention, but one of those answers is likely the key, and if you ask enough questions, you will almost certainly figure out intuitively which one the REAL key to your intention is…

Worst case scenario – Imagine life if you do not get what you want from the spell, how does it make you feel? What about it bothers or terrifies you? Really try to break down the thing that is causing you distress, and see what it points to… This can also be a good litmus test for deciding if magick is even needed. If the alternative isn't that unbearable… maybe you need to take a step back and use mundane solutions and not worry about the outcome?

Meditation – Empty your mind completely, and stay in meditation for a half hour or more (reentering empty mind state as needed if you can't hold it that long), then when your mind is fresh, before you think about anything else… examine the concern and take mental note of the first thing that enters your mind concerning the issue.

So, for example, if you are in a state of empty mind, and return to thinking about your breakup with your ex… If the first thing you think about is the moment you caught the two of them in bed together, and this makes you feel uncomfortable etc.… then what is bothering you isn't the loss of your ex, but the embarrassment or jealousy of the cheating moment, and instead of doing magick to win them back, maybe you should do magick to purge this feeling of jealousy and embarrassment instead? To liberate yourself from your attachment to someone who hurt you and move on.

You may have noticed that most of my examples, end up coming back to changing something about YOU, your actions, your response to situations, how you feel about things etc., and far less often on changing the external world.

It still happens like that to be sure, and you will still need to make external changes very often, but at least half the time, what we think are external problems, are in fact - internal ones...

Standard ritual / magickal procedure

It has been my experience that ultimately, we do not want to dwell on procedure, that at some point, we learn to do magick intuitively, even to the point that merely thinking of a thing, can make it manifest for us without any conscious effort.

I do not claim to have mastered that level of ability, but it would be a lie to say I have not, on many occasions, done exactly that… I often tell people that I lead a charmed life. I need for very little, I'm not rich in the slightest, but one way or the other, I am always comfortable, well fed, have my needs and desires met… Life is just undeniably good almost all the time!

Until we develop and trust such a skill, we all must use varying degrees of structure, even the most advanced intuitive will use structured ritual to maximize energy or make up for a lack of attunement to the flow of Intuition and Intention.

It should be made clear that I make a distinction between calling spirits and performing other magick ritual.

Calling spirits can be done with ritual, but the act of calling itself need not be any more complex than meditation or prayer, it is entirely possible in fact to develop a rapport and connection to a spirit that means you do not need to do anything more than think of the spirit and they will appear for you, ready to commune and work with you.

Magick ritual itself can be as simple as using a sigil in a trance with some candles, or as complex as a multi hour procedure of chanting, energizing objects, dance, song, and much more.

I personally do not ever engage in magick rites that require more than an hour or so including setup time. The actual ritual itself, not including setup, is usually no longer than the span of a stick or two of incense takes to burn.

All magick ritual consists of a planning phase, a setup phase, an entrance and induction phase, a focus and commune phase, and an exit and clearing phase.

Planning is mostly self-explanatory, we decide what kind of ritual we want to do, and how to do it. We setup the ritual space accordingly. We enter our ritual space and our ritual mindset, this can include aligning and clearing alien energies or simply just meditation and mindfulness. We then focus on the energy and intention we are working with, charging candles, calling spirits, working with anchors and tools etc. Then we enter an empty state and end the ritual clearing both ourselves and our ritual space of our distracting energies, allowing the work to commence without us being in the way or remaining attached.

Because every kind of magickal action can be very different, it is impossible for me to create a generic outline of things to do with any real specificity…

For example, a Sigil spell requires little more than your ability to make a sigil and focus on it and activate it with your energy and dispose of it in some meaningful way (burning for example). You could do this almost anywhere and it need not be any more complicated than that.

But you could also make it into a more complex ritual, potentially empowering it further, (or distracting yourself) simply by Aligning and Clearing your ritual space, Entering an empty mind state, then activating your ritual altar by arranging your altar as specified in the "Using the trinity of Self in ritual" section, and lighting the candles and incense, entering a focused state and pushing your energy and intent into the candles and incense to empower them to help manifest your will.

Then create the sigil and place it into the center of the trinity and focus on it intently either in the focused state, or the open state or a mixture of both, to charge it as normal (see the section on sigil magick), then when you feel you are at a crescendo of power and focus, burn it in the offering Cauldron and blank your mind completely as it burns and try to never think of this moment again.

You could use this same basic pattern for virtually any and all rituals, spirit callings or spells. A simple Candle spell, even a simple tarot reading could be enhanced by doing this…

Just remember it is up to you to make a ritual that isn't so complex you lose focus or intent. Magick works better when the mechanics of performing it, do not distract us.

I draw the line at reading magick poetry, anything beyond that should be memorized. So, make sure you have a clear plan in mind before you begin, you don't want to have to stop, break your concentration and look in a book to see if it's time to light the white candle or the blue candle…

Creating your own rituals

Keep the basic pattern in mind, you want your ritual to have an entry/induction phase, where you ritualistically enter into a trance state via a combination of holistic actions (like charging and lighting candles), saying a few invocations of power (aligning and clearing), and meditation or trance induction (usually we begin in the empty state to clear our minds, then enter the open state to relax and feel and see the energy of the altar in our astral eye).

Then you enter a charging, focusing, or communing phase where you manipulate the forces of nature via ritual, pushing energy into objects to charge them, making declarations of intention, calling spirits and communing with them, etc.

Then you need to end and sever your attachment to the magick abruptly and with finality when things are done. Sometimes this can take a few minutes to wind down and break the connection (particularly with some spirits who may linger to give you gnosis or instruction), but when possible you want the END of the ritual to almost come as a surprise and a shock, and you want to clear your mind of all thought and attachment to the thing you did, and the reason you did it.

The faster and more cleanly you can clear your mind of the thing you just did the better!

Next make sure you follow through on your end in the material world… and forget you did the magick - more or less.

Other than that? The rest is up to you and your imagination… Do you just want to charge a candle and burn it? Do you want to call on a spirit to teach you something? Do you want to create a servitor to do your will?

This and many other things are possible and encouraged.

Ritual pattern summary:

All magickal rituals follow the following basic pattern of execution, you may of course repeat certain stages as needed, for example you may need to focus multiple times in a ritual):

1. Intention to do a ritual and reason for such an act is identified and planned.
2. Begin ritual and enter Blank slate/empty mind state.
3. Enter open mind state (the scrying/gazing state) and open the mind to the greater reality.
4. Intense focus and ritual actions designed to align reality to your intention, calling the spirit etc. Remember to think, visualize and feel the OUTCOME of your intention, not the DESIRE of your intention. Imagine it has or is already happening, do not dwell on your DESIRE!
5. (optional: commune with the spirit in the open mind trance state).
6. Blank slate/empty mind state to close the ritual and allow the energy to be released.
7. Return to a completely normal state of mind (Example: watch some wholesome TV and forget you did magick).

Why did I leave out some things?

You may be noticing that this part of the book is not thick with examples, and this is because I want you to look for the pattern and principles being used in the examples I am giving, and learn to see that these are based on simple free form rituals I created based on my ideas and gnosis.

Real effective magick does not need to be more complicated than this.

And if you wish to make it more complex, I prefer that you do so by following the guidance of your spirits, and imagination/intuition.

Want to bind someone? A rope or cord makes for great

symbolism! As does a pot or jar or box.

Want to encourage wealth, a dollar bill might be made into an offering to a spirit keen on finance.

Want to encourage your crush to notice you? Take a personal object of theirs, and place it on your altar and charge it with only the best and most noble and lovable qualities that you possess, and visualize and feel what it would be like for them to notice you and your fine qualities, without forcing them to approve of you. Leave this on your altar overnight with a red rose… Then give it back to them somehow or otherwise get it back into their possession, and then take steps to get their attention romantically, maybe by giving them the rose?

You can and should also look up the spells and ideas of other traditions and magickians. Ask people on social media what their favorite prosperity spell is, and modify it to work with the Trinity of Self Altar or maybe invoke a spirit to oversee the operation?

The point here is, I am giving you the canvas and the paints, and showing you a sequence of paintings that should cover many possible experiments and lessons in magick. Thus, letting you create without distraction or judgment. Like your art teacher teaching you color theory and setting you loose with a rainbow of markers to play with.

Materials and Ritual Tools

To complete this pathworking (the individual spells after the pathworking will often have their own requirements) you will need a modest starter set of ritual tools and materials. This is by no means an exhaustive list of ALL the tools you will want or need to become a master of your art. However, consider this the training wheels that get you started.

Ritual tools are little more than props, and anchors for spiritual entities and our will. Let me give you an example: By itself a candle is just a blob of wax with some string in the middle that burns. However, we charge it with intent, and belief, we might even focus on the outcome, and visualize it and feel it. We then see in the astral that the candle is a carrier of our will, we transmute it, changing it fundamentally, sometimes this change even means changing the physical nature of it, carving it, painting it etc. and then let it burn.

As it burns down, the energy we channel into it becomes transmuted and is released into the world do to our bidding. We align the candle with our will… Causing "its" trinity of self to align with "ours." As above so below, as within, so without, presto chango, abracadabra…

This candle becomes the focus and anchor of the change, the stone dropped in the pond that makes the ripples.

One way to think of it is, imagine in an alternate timeline, there is a candle just like the one we have, but a little different somehow. Even if all that is different is just in how it vibrates or the position of its atoms, or It's astral form.

Through magick and ritual we make the candle in our subjective experience into that same candle that exists in the world where we already got our manifestation, we do this by charging it with our will and intent. This transmutes it, and by nature of this candle fitting better and belonging to that timeline, the timeline we are in must adjust to accept that candle. The more completely we change the candle the more our reality must change to match.

This results in a manifestation. Which is almost always subtle but can be exquisitely profound at the same time.

In ritual we do this not just with the candle, but with everything being used in the ritual. Some might make the mistake then of thinking we need more and more tools, in other words, creating more things to match our chosen outcome. Realistically that isn't the case. The only tool we **need** is ourselves.

Hence why I consider these other objects more like props and anchors. Ultimately, **we** are the thing that must change.

Moving forward, it is going to be up to you to identify what is a tool and what isn't, the nature of Intuitive magick means a pebble on the ground could be a potent anchor for your magick, a smoldering cigarette butt a link to your target.

In fact, I cannot think of a single spell I couldn't perform with common everyday household objects and my imagination and energy. However, creating sacred tools that are special to us in some way often empowers what we do dramatically.

Therefore, our initial magick tools and materials need not be fancy, they can be basic stuff we buy online or local stores.

Indeed, you can create a wonderful set of tools and materials for well under 50$. Or even free if you are a crafty person or have an attic full of old junk.

Once you get your feet under you and know what you are doing, once you have started on the path and the spirits recognize you, magickal tools will begin to find you. They may be antiques, or things people share with you, or things that you find in nature or out of luck. But they WILL find you. You will know the difference because it will have a synchronistic vibe.

You will be thinking… Hmm, you know I could use some candle stick holders for my Altar… then ten seconds later your friend calls you and asks if you would be interested in buying a pair of silver candlesticks so they can make rent.

You might be walking through an antique shop and catch something out of the corner of your eye, maybe a glint of metal, or the vision of a patron spirit, or hear a sound, and go to investigate and find a beat-up old metal urn or filigree bowl that would make a great offering bowl.

For now, I want to stress that ultimately it is up to you to decide if you really want or need these items or objects, or if you want MORE than just these items and objects.

I am a minimalist in many ways, but I am also artistic and really enjoy balanced and interesting altars and ritual spaces.

Instead of hundreds of candles and magick objects, I might use only 1 candle, or 3 candles. I might only have a ritual dagger and an incense burner. I might only have a sigil and a way to draw blood.

I only use tools when I feel they will add something and not distract me. Complexity for complexity sake is pointless and counterproductive, especially in magick.

However, I LOVE to use tools that have significance. I will often make my tools special by personalizing them or using family heirlooms, or hand make or modify and customize them all to make them special.

I find Antiques to be the absolute ideal source of ritual tools like offering bowls, offering cups, magick mirrors and more. They need not be expensive but try to find the most interesting and energetic pieces you can. Antiques are unique in that their age and ownership can actually bring them energy and character, they have been in this form for long enough and part of someone else's experience long enough that they can take on personalities and living energy all their own. In some cases, they can even become egregoric, or contain spirits.

As you progress you can and will likely expand your set of magickal tools to include some valuable antiques and handmade items.

For now, use your gut, if it feels too basic, go for something nicer.

A ritual space – This can be anywhere, inside, outside, so long as it is private in the extreme. Outdoor locations have the advantage of being in nature which can increase the opportunities for the spirits to interact with you in a less artificial and controlled environment. Subtle winds, animal sounds etc. are an advantage. Inside locations have the advantage of control and added privacy. Neither is better or worse. You must choose for yourself. I use both with astounding success.

An altar/Magick work bench – This can be literally anything. I have used the trunk of cars, I have used Dinner trays, I have used overturned milk crates… But for our purposes try to make it something respectable and something that will be DEDICATED to this purpose. You can skip this if you wish outside, but I would still use one regardless, even if just for convenience. It is just useful to hold everything off the ground if nothing else. I usually cover my altar with a piece of black Fabric, with a painted variation of the trinity of Self, or some other fundamental magickal symbol on it (Pentagrams etc.). I usually use a high contrast paint, such as white, silver, or bright red, and keep it as neat as I can, but don't lose sleep over minor mistakes, so long as they don't distract me too much. Your altar should be large enough to contain the important tools and your trinity of Self. I find 24-inch round bar tables to be ideal on the small side. But you can use a Tv stand, a nightstand. Whatever works.

Burnt offering receptacle – Something that can be used to burn offerings in (a bonfire if outside) I use a cast iron cauldron, and these are ideal. They are solid, and can take the heat easily, as burning offerings is usually not going to burn long enough to do any real damage or even heat up the metal. If you go with any kind of interior burning, I would also make sure you acquire a hot plate that will protect the surface of whatever you are using. I like the round marble/stone ones you can get from most home decoration stores. While a cauldron is ideal - even a deep small skillet or pot will suffice, so long as it can be burned in and not be damaged (stainless steel or cast iron without nonstick coatings). It need not be large, just big enough to hold an inch or so of sea salt, and a burning sigil without risk of it all falling out. You can even buy small cauldrons less than 2 inches across. Mine is about 4 inches across and is perfect for everything. You will use either Rubbing Alcohol 75%+, and or Charcoal tablets that are usually used in Hookah and incense resin burning. *It should go without saying that If you are burning inside, don't be stupid, take precautions and don't take risks on setting your house or yourself on fire.*

A set of ritual candles - Each spirit and system can use a variety of candle colors shapes and sizes. For now, all you need are at least one large pillar candle in black or Red (make sure it's a solid color, not just the outside), and 3 candles one each of Red, Green and Blue (in a pinch all black will do).

They need not be large, they can be small, you could cut some taper candles in half or thirds, or just use some more pillars, or even tea lights so long as they have the right colors. You can easily find small ritual candles online in bulk that are around 5 inches tall and last a few hours at most and ideal for offerings and rituals. These or taper candles will often need candle holders, these can be as dramatic or simple as you like. I prefer to keep most of my ritual candles low, so fancy tall candle holders only get used as centerpieces or for special purposes. Again, be careful: *fire = hot.*

Incense – This can be stick, cone, resin or dried. I consider Sage a universal incense, as is sandalwood, Frankincense, Frankincense and Myrrh, Palo Santo and copal. While some spirits may prefer one over the others, all of these are appreciated by spirits. So, if you cannot acquire the specialized incense requested, any of the ones I just stated will do in a pinch.

I find that using Resin incense on a coal "puck" in my burned offering cauldron is the best combination of tools as it can easily double as a way to burn offerings or special incenses that you can't buy in other forms (household spices like Star Anise for example).

For now, a trip to the local New Age Woo store to buy a few handfuls of stick sage incense and a simple holder is fine.

An offering bowl – Typically for food or liquid - this can be small or large, I prefer a small bowl like you would use for cereal. However, the only requirement is that this bowl be special and never used for anything else ever. So, go out and buy something new, and use it only for this. Technically any kind of bowl will do, but the nicer and more unique or special it is, the better. A cheap Tupperware container is technically enough… but I wouldn't use it.

An offering cup – Again usually for liquid. It can be a chalice, or cup or goblet, or another bowl. Like the bowl, it must be special and not used for anything else (I once broke my own rule, and used a ritual goblet for casual drinking outside of ritual, and within 24 hours it broke tragically… I took the hint and will never make that mistake again!). It

should be unique or decorative and special, but technically a coffee mug would suffice. The more thought you put into this, the better.

Trinity of Self upon a black background - A way to draw or paint, or otherwise create a Trinity of Self large enough to be placed on an altar and large enough to contain all your active ritual tools on the drawing without it being too crowded.

For example: you can buy puff paint, and a plain square yard of fabric or plain black head scarf and paint one of the simpler examples of the trinity of self on the scarf. Try to be steady handed and make it sacred and special by being creative.

If you are working in an outside space, you can make the symbolism larger if possible so that you can stand in it and it becomes the entire ritual area. carve it into the dirt, or arrange stones, or wood, or many other methods for making marks that you can see in dim firelight.

A SAFE way to draw blood – At the local drug store they sell Diabetes testing equipment. What you are looking for is a Lancet, and the device that makes it work. The Device is a little spring-loaded contraption that holds the lancet, and at the push of a button, springs out the lancet needle so fast you can't even see it, and will barely feel it. Make sure you read the directions and follow them and adjust the depth for maximum comfort and maximum blood flow. Make sure you sterilize the area before using the device, then make sure you sterilize again after to avoid infections etc.

Sea Salt – Coarse or fine. Either will do, sea salt absorbs energy, especially negative energy and creates a pristine environment, and a great base for making Cauldron fire (many people use Epsom Salts, but this can be difficult as it often contains fragrances and things that burn and melt). One or two containers will last you a while if you don't overdo it.

Sigil materials - Fine paper or Card stock for making sigils, markers, pens and pencils for drawing and writing. If you plan on burning sigils, I have used Stage magicians flash paper to fun effect. To create a Sigil, I create and cut out an equilateral triangle. One of the points I choose to be the TOP of the triangle, and in that space I draw (in pencil) my magickal sign (see initialization of self), then in the middle of the triangle I place the sigil of the intention or spirit to be called. Below this, I leave space to write the name of the spirit, or any magickal words I need using sigil script. During ritual I draw over the pencil in INK (usually a permanent black marker) and ERASE any visible pencil. You can also anoint with blood as pictured below.

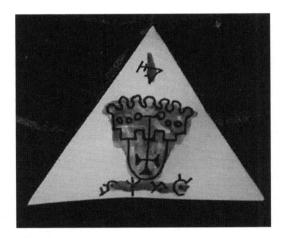

Why a Triangle? Besides also being another triangle and symbol of the Trinity of Self, it is also very aesthetic, and convenient, as you can easily prop the sigil up on your altar if desired for easy gazing. By placing your mark on the sigil at the top this can represent you being the all-seeing eye, the source, the divinity, and the things below can be what you desire to be manifested.

Cauldron Fire (Optional for pyros and mature adults only) -75% or higher rubbing alcohol for Cauldron Fire (DANGER FIRE HAZARD). This will be combined with coarse sea salt in the burnable cauldron (again, only a proper cast iron or other receptacle that is SAFE to burn in). I use roughly 1 for 1 ratio of salt and alcohol. Use the lid to snuff the flame, and do not let it burn too hot or long that it becomes dangerous.

One modest sized crystal ball - it can be a lab grown quartz, or a fancy natural mineral sphere like an obsidian sphere. No need to buy anything TOO large or expensive, a clear (manmade) Quartz crystal ball about 3 inches across is around 15-20$ on the internet. It can be any color, but I recommend, clear (natural or lab made) or black (preferably obsidian and not dyed black quartz). In my experience ANY crystal sphere will work, but natural works best, just try to make it at least the size of a golf ball.

1 large scrying mirror – If possible, look for an Antique, a mirror that is old, worn, and faded or even cracked. It should not look new, and should be something that has seen many years, many faces, and many things in its time. Try to make sure it is at least 10 inches across. Optionally consider a 9 inch across picture frame (again antique if possible) that you can spray paint the inside of the glass black (not the outside or the frame, you want that to be clear, paint the side the picture would go on).

You do not NEED to paint a normal mirror especially an older faded and cracked one, but you might anyway for aesthetics or making it easier to read (normal mirrors tend to distract some people too much.) Obviously do not paint the reflective side of a valuable or old antique, that is just stupid and ruins the spiritual value of the thing.

A notebook and a grimoire – The former can be anything from loose-leaf, to a fancy college ruled notebook. The latter should be whatever speaks to you and inspires you. I am a sucker for an old-school leather-bound journal. The notebook is for notes, the Grimoire is for your finished thoughts. Of course, it's up to you how much respect to give it. Some people treat their Grimoires like living works of art that change and grow and look like a mess. Others treat them like sacred holy books and get bent out of shape if they even misspell a word and must correct it.

I am somewhere in between but know that your Grimoire becomes a powerful and sacred object very quickly if you will it to be. I say it's better to keep is sacred and cherish it and work your thoughts out on note paper before entering it into a grimoire.

A Wand (optional) – Symbolizing the male aspect of creation (literally a phallus), this is an important tool. I use my hand and fingers to denote the Wand, and dagger/sword in most of my rituals, though I have powerful wands, rods, daggers, and swords in my possession.

If you wish, you can use your index finger and middle finger and place the tip of your middle finger overtop the nail of the index finger, similar to how you might cross your fingers when lying to someone, but instead of fully crossing them, you are being them both to a point. The tip of the index finger is the same as a wand in this case and can be used the same way in ritual.

Alternatively, you can simply use your index finger, or place your index and middle finger together (same as making the sign of the sword or dagger), and just know it is a wand, not a blade.

If you desire to have a formal wand, consider wood selection carefully. I like Ebony, but almost any wood will do. If it means something to you, look up the different woods that are available to see what their symbolic connections are and choose that way.

You can easily buy a fine wand online, or better yet, by the wood and make it yourself, or best of all, go out into the wilderness, and search for a freshly fallen branch of a tree that is suitable. You want the thick end to be about the thickness of your index finger, and it should be strong and not rotted or brittle. I would avoid pine as it's often too soft and can break if you are rough with it.

So, try to choose a hardwood if possible.

I like African Ebony (bought online) because it is Dark and rich in color, it is one of the heaviest woods, and it is strong.

Most systems do not advocate cutting branches off live trees… but dead ones? Go for it.

Ritual dagger (optional) – Exactly like the wand, you do not NEED one, but they are nice to have, and you can simulate a ritual dagger by placing your index and middle fingers side by side, creating a wide blade like shape with it. In this case the two fingertips or the middle finger if it feels right is the tip and point of the dagger, and the length of the fingers the cutting edge.

Alternatively, you can extend all the fingers of your hand to make a paddle or blade shape, and know it is a powerful astral dagger!

If you prefer to use a REAL blade, any blade will do, a kitchen knife, or a fancy decorative knife, or a hunting knife etc. Just make sure the knife will never be used for anything else and it will be fine.

Technically the dagger doesn't even have to be sharp, but I prefer sharp knives… Risky at times, but worth it in many ways for me.

(Optional) Staff or Rod - These are ideal for rituals outside as they can be used for scratching your symbols into the earth and give you something to lean on if you feel a strong drain of energy. The Staff or the rod, is a symbol of authority, like the sword. And can be used in place of the wand, and dagger in many cases. IMHO a Staff or Rod need not be all that special, it can be a piece of PVC… Or a broomstick. However, as usual, I prefer the one I have had for decades I got at a ren faire. I made quite a few modifications to it and it is unique, and I use it as a stately walking rod when I'm going for a stroll about town. I get endless compliments and questions on where it came from or how old it is etc. It's my pride and joy.

The Trinity Meditation:

This is an exceedingly simple meditative transcendental scrying exercise designed to help you focus in meditation, and to help you experience vivid visual trance phenomenon that can be quite exceptional. I have used this many time, and several fans of my work have tested this to good results.

The cover of this book wasn't just designed to be attractive, but to be usable in magick and meditation! The color contrast, symbolism and structure of the imagery on the cover, when stared at for a short time can create mild hallucinogenic optical illusions which, when experienced in an altered state, can be used to propel your consciousness into a visual trance.

To properly perform this meditation, it is highly recommended that you take this book, and place it on your altar or some other suitable surface, propped up so that you can clearly see the cover from a short comfortable distance.

It should take up enough of your view that the trinity dominates your attention but need not be so close that it is all you see. 2 to 3 feet from your face should be ok, providing your lighting is good.

You can of course simply hold the book in your hands, but some will find this distracting as they will need to hold it steady.

The lighting should be low enough to not be distracting, but bright enough so that the book covers contrasting colors can be vividly experienced.

This might mean an otherwise Dark room, with a few candles positioned in front of the book but without it being too distracting or creating any glare on the glossy finish.

Utilize the basic induction technique in he altered states section of the book, and enter a comfortable Open-minded state, and stare/gaze/scy into the very center of the image, and try to keep your eyes open, unblinking and locked into the very center of the image where the little orb of light is.

I find that using various low and slow ambient music tracks (dark ambient music in particular), or Binaural beats can be very effective here for inducing a very vivid experience.

In a pinch you can of course just use a copy of the Trinity of Self that you draw on paper, so long as it has a good deal of contrast, I also find that a pure black background, with a blood red, golden yellow, or cyan blue Trinity of self can work well as well. If you cannot use the book cover, also consider placing a circular black mirror in the center of the trinity that you draw yourself for the best scrying experience.

However, I find the book cover to be exponentially more effective than all of these.

Most people who have tried this, including myself report seeing any and all the following –

- The trinity begins to swirl and animate
- The outer circle rotates clockwise or counterclockwise
- The inner triangle and swirl pattern spins around
- The entire image becomes 3 dimensional
- Vivid images of other people's faces appear and disappear.
- Vivid Scrying takes place
- Vivid Astral Travel
- The image leaves a ghostly pattern in the mind's eye
- The sensation of raising unsettling dark matter
- The sudden opening of the third eye in new vivid ways

Now the interesting thing is that the test subjects (aside from myself) have never been instructed on the deeper meaning of the Trinity of Self, and virtually everyone claims to experience the same or similar sensations and effects.

You may find that this becomes your new favorite scrying tool, and a reliable way to enter deep astral trances, where you can commune with various spirits in the astral plane.

The power of the Trinity of Self is clear, and it is also not very different aesthetically from the Triangle of Solomon Scrying Mirror, but I feel is a far completer and more neutral device…

Gaze deeply into the heart of the Trinity and know thyself…

Initialization of the self

To begin this path, you will need to initialize yourself into the current of magick you intend to follow, and you need to create a connection between your analytical self and the all-powerful divinity that lies behind your eyes. You need to create a sigil that can be used to INVOKE this deity into your waking world, simply by the recitation of the name, and the use of the symbol (either drawn in the air, or upon paper, or in the ground).

I have performed this rite for paying clients for some time, and while this is not exactly the way I do it, this should give you, fundamentally, the same result. A sigil that becomes your personal sign, and gateway to the master of reality that you truly are.

This should be a turning point in your life, and a moment of supreme intention. It is ok if you change your mind later, but this is the first step where you go from simply owning a book of magick, to dedicating yourself to practicing it until it no longer serves you.

It is best to carry out this ritual a short time before bed when you are getting tired and ready to dream. The symbolism here is that you will be conducting this ritual at the close of the last day of your mundane life, and when you arise it will be the first day of your magickal life.

You will likely have significant dreams, or no dreams at all.

When you complete this short rite, you should go straight to sleep, so make sure all your normal bedtime rituals (brushing teeth, using the toilet etc.) are completed and you are already ready for bed in your bedclothes etc.

You will need:

- 1 piece of paper for drawing a sigil, pencil and a marker or calligraphy pen.
- A magickal name – This need not (most would say it should not) be your true secret name, but it should be the name you use in magick until it no longer serves you. If you prefer this can be your secret name if you know it.
- A blood testing lancet and device
- A brand-new Grimoire
- A mirror (any mirror will do; it need not be magick)

Procedure

Step 1 - If you already have a personal symbol, sigil or magick signature in mind, you can skip this step if you wish, but I strongly encourage you to consider doing this anyway. Start by creating for yourself a sigil either using the alphabet, or the sigil script earlier in the book. This sentence this sigil will be based off is simply –

"I, (your magickal name), am the God and Devil of my reality."

Take your time, with this step, make sure the name is pleasing and inspires you. Create a Sigil and try to simplify it down as much as possible, more so than normal. The ideal sigil is one you can easily draw in the air quickly in ritual.

As an example, here is one that I have used for a long time:

As you can see this sigil is quite simple and can be easily recreated with only a few strokes of the hand, fingertip or wand.

This sigil need not be Personal or Private unless you decide it is or if it is based on your TRUE name which I will not be discussing here. If someone else uses this symbol it only has power if it is given power by you, or if you have given them permission to invoke your power through this symbol.

Step 2 - Take this sigil you have created, on the scrap paper, and open your Grimoire. Turn to a page that seems reasonable, it can even be the cover or inside cover. Focus your attention on this page, and carefully and lightly sketch in pencil the sigil you have made for yourself. Make it large enough to dominate the page.

Now, take a deep breath and enter the Focused mind state, and focus all your intention and energy on drawing this sigil in Ink as neatly and perfectly as you can. Make the lines as thick as they need to be to look good, and all the time you draw this symbol, pump as much energy emotion and intention into it to charge and activate it. Feel the energy and intent flow down through your arm, into the marker or calligraphy tool and see the symbol begin to glow in your mind's eye. You are activating this sigil as you draw it, and it will become a gateway that can help inspire you and remind you of what you have chosen to do with your magickal life.

When the sigil is complete, you can feel free to embellish around it, frame it, decorate it, or do anything else you wish artistically… When you feel you have given this sigil ALL the energy you have, it is time to start Step 3.

Step 3 - Prepare the bloodletting tool, and take it, the grimoire and yourself and stand in front of a mirror. This need not be a magick mirror, or one you intend to use for magick. But it can be if you prefer.

Stare deeply into the mirror and try to connect with your inner self, look into your eyes and try to see yourself as the sorcerer you wish to become, see yourself as casting aside any prior religious dogma, see yourself dominating your fears, see yourself as a god, as a devil as the universe itself and when you feel you have made your connection, use the bloodletting tool and lance the tip of the pinky of your left hand, or any other part of your left arm that you wish and get the blood to flow.

Smear your blood upon the symbol in your grimoire in any way that seems intuitively correct (some trace it, others draw a line through it, others just smear it across without any deeper meaning) When your finger connects to the paper feel and believe the conduit being opened between you and your destiny through this sigil and the blood you are smearing upon it.

After this is done, say the following into the mirror with authority, intoning your intention and feeling the energy flow into you. Hear your voice boom across the astral plane as if you are the god atop the highest mountain. Hear it echo in the depths of the infernal kingdom as you are the devil himself upon his throne.

> *I am the God and the Devil of my Reality.*
> *I am the master of the waking dream!*
> *I am the Masterwork of my Divinity made manifest!*
> *I am* (your magickal name Ex THORNE) *and this is my mark!*

Now raise the grimoire and keep yourself and the symbol clear in the reflection of the mirror and enter an open mind state. Trance out for a short time a few seconds is enough, and then when you feel the time is right, snap the book closed and declare *"IT IS DONE!"* and enter a no mind state for at least one minute, think of as little else as possible and let the intention and energy disappear into the cosmos…

You are now dedicated and truly ready to begin, from this point forward know that when you use this symbol in ritual, you are INVOKING the spirit of the sorcerer or sorceress you just created and imagined. When you use this name, and scribe this mark (upon the ground, into the air/ether, onto paper) you are not the person you are in your everyday life. You are the master, and what you ordain is real.

Now, hurry off to bed and do your best to let sleep claim you and do not think of anything other than your eventual ascension to godhood… tonight nothing else matters, not your bills, your job, your parents, your schoolwork. Nothing. You are saying goodbye to the mundane life and beginning the rest of your life.

Now SLEEP and dream the dreams of a waking god.

Align and Clear

Virtually every single magickal path contains some method of taking control over the self, and the local astral space and the local material space in the form of a banishing, cleansing or declaration of authority. Normally this is done to place the sorcerer in the magickal mindset, but also to align and clear the energies to be in accordance with the will of the sorcerer.

I rarely need or use this in my own practices, as I always try to maintain a healthy natural ecosystem of spiritual energy in my environment and use crystals and spirits and servitors to balance the energy and protect me. My home is always under the powerful spiritual protection of a powerful Goetic Demon, and I usually see trouble coming a mile away.

However, I am not always at home, and sometimes even my confidence fails me, and I need to invoke the power that is mine to cast out negative forces or align the chaos around me to bend to MY authority.

In our system of magick we already see ourselves as divinity personified. But for those times when we need the added benefit of a ritual to invoke that power, we need a solution we can believe in!

You are of course free to find and use others such as Sage smudging (the act of fumigating a space with Sage smoke and chanting to disperse evil spirits and energy), The Lesser Banishing ritual of the Pentagram (asserts authority and banishes negative energies) or even to a lesser extent, the middle pillar Ritual/meditation (the latter is more of a balancing and meditative ritual than a protective and assertive one).

In our system we have something similar in principle to the Lesser Banishing ritual of the Pentagram, however it is more agnostic and has less dogmatic attachment to specific entities, symbols, or concepts we may have no relationship or belief in.

It also need not expunge or cast out energies in the environment, instead it declares and centers you in your authority as divinity.

It should also be noted that "banishing" negative energies doesn't necessarily destroy them, it simply banishes them from your immediate awareness. This negative pollution can in time build up outside your ritual space, and can in some cases, lead to higher frequency of negative entities that feed on these energies.

Dark entities that feed on negative energy, can even become empowered by these cast-off energies, especially the hollow remnants of your body of light that we often construct as part of these banishing rituals.

This system can have the same, or similar issues, if your intentions are not clear, when working with the Align and Clear method, make sure you have a clear intention in mind to align and clear the space, not banish or cast out. You align the space with your intention and clear it of any malevolent entities.

As it is Agnostic in nature it does not have to be altered to work with demons, or any other spirits. It is intuitive and relies on the spirit of your intent rather than some pattern of ritualized dogma. Instead it banishes only that which does not align with our will and we can Invoke or Evoke the authority and presence of a divine spirit (ours or another's) that protects us to align and clear the energies and spirits around us based on this intention.

Assess the situation - The first thing you must do is assess the situation and decide what kind of situation this is. As usual I break things down into 3s to make it easier to digest.

Preparation – It is often wise for a beginner to prepare the magickal energies and astral space prior to any ritual or intentional magick act, or even for a master to clear the ritual area prior to a baneful spell. So, we would most normally use this ritual for the Initiation of a greater ritual or magickal act that requires the energy be aligned and cleared. Aside from practicing this ritual - This is usually the least stressful situation and requires no special consideration.

Unclean energy – We can use this simple ritual to align and clear our homes or work places or other spaces of malign spiritual energy that is causing chaos and disruption or hurt feelings. When it works it will be like a breath of fresh air, people will go back to being adults and quarrels will diminish. When we perform this rite in this situation it helps to have an Obsidian crystal handy as a focus, or Sage incense to help fumigate cleanse and purify the chaos.

Fear - If the threat is of a material origin, act accordingly, do not trust magick to protect you if a threat is already materializing, it still can, but more often than not, it will protect you by warning you and making you feel like taking actions like fighting or fleeing. Listen to your spiritual center and act accordingly! If the feeling of fear is based on spiritual forces or if you feel there is something spiritually dangerous in the air, a dark spirit, a powerful negativity, you may have trouble concentrating and focusing.

If your fear is so great you feel you cannot focus on magick… In this case, you will want to call upon the aid of any personal demons or spirits that you work with to protect you. Failing that the best way to end such an experience is to simply laugh at the fear and try to return to as normal a kind of activity as possible (put on a wholesome TV show, call your mom, whatever it takes). You need to NORMALIZE.

Long Form Ritual

(illustrations provided at the end of the description)

Stand or sit with your head bowed and take a slow deep breath in (yang breathing), as you do bring your arms up and hands up as if you are cupping a chi ball from underneath. Bring your hands up and into your solar plexus area as your breath in and imagine your astral body becoming solid and bright with astral light.

Breathe out quickly and push your hands down and out palms down as if you are pushing out the negative forces and yin energy and drawing in the yang force.

Try to feel your body and astral body rising and falling subtly with the inhale and exhale.

Do this three times and upon the 3rd time breathe in and bring your hands up as before, but instead of coming to your solar plexus fold your arms so that your hands are pressed

onto the opposite shoulder and lower your head… Hold this posture for a few moments keeping the air in your lungs… Imagine the radiant energy of your astral body is rapidly becoming blinding and open your eyes when you feel ready.

If you do not feel ready and your light is not blinding… repeat the above steps to build your energy and confidence, do not repeat this process more than 3 times. If after three times you do not yet feel powerful continue anyway and when you invoke the divinity of the spirit, call upon a protector spirit instead if you have one. If not, proceed anyway as written.

When you feel ready, open your eyes raise your head and cast both hands down at your side and with the held breath and in a loud authoritative voice make the following declaration. **Version one (self-divinity):**

I (recite your magickal name and draw your sigil in the air in front of you) ***am the self-aware avatar of the most high, I am the Divinity that hides behind the eye, I am the voice of the infinite god, and the wrath of the infinite devil! I declare that my will IS done, and that this place be made instantly clean and aligned with my intention and will! Let no spirit or energy that would harm or interfere with me or my work remain! I invite only that which serves my will and banish that which does not! BEGONE!***

Version 2 (invocation of another spirit of protection):

In the name of (spirit)***, I have been recognized as the master of my own fate! I do hereby declare my authority as*** (your magick name, and draw your sigil in the air)***, Avatar of the divinity of the most high. It is by my will that I call upon the aid and protection of*** (spirit)***, in whose name this place be made instantly clean and aligned with my intention and will. Let no spirit or energy that would do harm to, or interfere with, me or my work remain! I invite only that which serves my will and banish that which does not! BEGONE!***

Upon the recitation of either of these you should feel chills or a boost in your personal energy and confidence, if not DO NOT repeat the procedure, for a god does not repeat a declaration of what is. Instead you will act as if your declaration is already true.

Breathe with Yang energy, you will now bring your arms back to being folded across your chest, with each hand on the opposite shoulder and bow your head and close your eyes, in your mind's eye see the astral world around you and see yourself as a blazing blinding light, imagine and feel your spiritual pressure, or the spiritual pressure of your protective spirit building within you to critical mass. Every time you breathe in the energy grows more and more until you feel you are ready to burst.

When you feel ready, explode your arms outward with your palms extended to your sides with the fingers of your left hand facing up, and the fingers of the right facing down. and breathe sharply outward and visualize your energy *exploding* like a supernova of spiritual pressure creating a wave of power that purifies and aligns the energy of your immediate space. Imagine the exploding sphere stopping several meters from you, or when it touches the solid walls of your immediate ritual space creating a force field of energy of whatever nature you wish to give it, fire, light, death, anything you wish. You have asserted your magickal will over this space and anything that remains will be banished or dispersed.

As you feel the energy align with your will and visualize the good and beneficial spirits remaining, bring your arms back together in a circular pattern to your chest area as if you are sweeping in more energy into yourself.

As you make this motion take a sharp intake of breath (yin breathing), and exhale slowly and with intention and extend your hands in front of you with both palms facing away from you and clear your mind fully, do this at least three times to balance the Energy in your body so it is no longer so focused on Yang breathing (remember any extreme can be unhealthy and unhelpful). While doing this enter empty mind.

Stand in silence for a moment, then Declare: ***"It is DONE!"*** and return to a normal state of mind.

If this is done at the start of a ritual, you do not need to state – "It is Done!" until the ritual is complete.

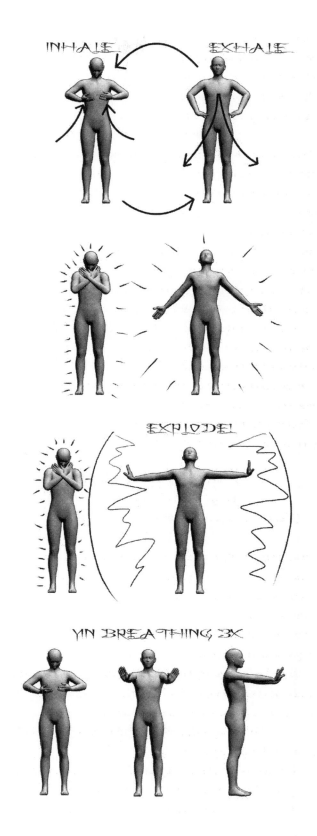

INHALE EXHALE

EXPLODE!

YIN BREATHING 3X

If you are trying to clear a room or home of negativity, or want to use the obsidian or Sage I mentioned earlier, when you explode your arms out at your side, imagine any negative energy the expanding wave contacts imploding into the obsidian or the sage and being transmuted into balanced and usable energy again, either radiating from the obsidian or being burned by the sage and turned into balanced usable energy by the smoke.

When you end the ritual with Yin breathing imagine the stone or incense picking this up as well.

Short Form Ritual

This version of the ritual is designed to be easier and faster but should only be used if you are already comfortable with your power and are able to manipulate energy clearly. This works best for a location you have already been using in magick regularly. You do not need to perform the complete ritual from start to finish.

All that is required is that you enter Yang breathing, declare your authority while you visualize your space being cleared energetically by an exploding sphere of energy that stops growing at the size you want, clearing the area within of all negative or chaotic energy that might interfere with your working.

Begin with 3 (or a multiple of 3) Yang breaths, bringing your hands up to your chest as in the long form ritual, when you feel empowered, explode your energy and hands or hand out from your body and declare something along the lines of:

This space is the domain of (your name and sign) I banish any and all hostile entities and energies from this space that would interfere with my intention... BEGONE!

Perform 3 Yin breathes to balance and relax... Know that Your space is cleared.

Initializing your Tools

Now that you have gotten this far, You may want to start using your magick tools right away as soon as you get them home. Instead STOP and be patient. These objects are filled with the energies of where they come from, and if you do not know the source of these energies very well, it can be problematic.

Of course, sooner or later, all ritual objects take on the energy of the Altar and the user, but initially, it's good to Cleanse and charge your ritual tools with your personal signature energy and let it rest for 24 hours on your altar. Some traditions require bathing it in moonlight, or consecration to a deity. This is for special tools we want to further enhance, but for now, let us simply make them usable as is.

Specifically of all the tools I listed thus far, you will need to do this with each of the following – Wand, Dagger, mirrors, crystal balls, offering cups, offering bowls, Offering burner, Altar symbols, the Altar Itself.

Initialization of the Altar, basic tools, and Trinity of Self

Get the altar situated in the part of your ritual space you intend to use it. If it is an outside altar in a location you will be using regularly, you may want to do this on site. If it is meant to be a portable altar, then you can do this anywhere you like so long as it will be undisturbed for 24 hours.

I have found an Altar that stays in place longer tends to have a more authority and becomes a focal point in the astral world, but not necessarily more power. A portable Altar can be every bit as powerful.

Remember an Altar is a sacred thing, try to use it and its components ONLY for magick, refrain from using it as a coffee table, and under no circumstances should it become a place to hold your bills or concerns. What you place onto the altar eventually manifests or lends energy to your work or

takes it away!

You will need

- 3 small ritual candles (all black, or one red, one blue, and one green). If all black, inscribe a single Sigilscript letter or English letter to denote one as Body (B), Mind (M), and Spirit (S) These should be candles you can reasonably burn in the course of a single afternoon or day. They should NOT be put out intentionally by you except for emergency. (outside rituals will require candles shielded from the wind somehow if possible).
- Your initial tools – (optional Wand, Dagger), offering cup, offering bowl, offering burner.
- (Optional)a cloth to paint or otherwise permanently draw the Trinity of Self Or the ability to draw or paint the trinity clearly on the altar surface.
- 3 sticks or cones of incense of your choice, and a suitable way to hold them in ritual (burned offering bowl for example, or a simple incense holder).
- A bloodletting device.
- Some Sea Salt

Procedure

Gather all your materials together, and First, draw, paint or otherwise mark your Altar symbolism (trinity of self) on either a cloth covering, or on the surface of the altar itself. You can do this with paint, marker, even chalk. It is best to do this with the covering ON the Altar.

While you are drawing the symbols, you should be concentrating your intention on this Altar becoming a powerful symbol in both the material world and the Astral world. You need to imagine the Altar is materializing in the Astral world and the symbol (the trinity of Self or the pentagram) is not merely being written there, but that it begins to glow with radiant light and energy of your choosing.

When the altar is created, and the symbols drawn, one by one place your (if used Wand, Dagger), Cup, Bowl, and burning bowl on the Altar. As you place them on the Altar, declare them for what they are – This Goblet is for the offering of liquid and the element of water, this bowl is for the offering of earth and food, this burning bowl is for offering and fire, etc.

Place them anywhere that looks appropriate and balances the energy of the arrangement. Typically, the very Center of the trinity is where the focal point of the ritual is placed. If you have room assemble all your tools somewhere in the inner Triangle or inner most circle. If not, simply try to balance it out aesthetically. Or follow the guidelines in an earlier chapter (using the Trinity of Self in ritual). There are no rules here, it is time you start using your intention and intuition as a guide.

It is now time to begin the actual ritual – Begin by performing the Align and Clear ritual and when completed do not say IT IS DONE, keep the energy going and do not end the ritual yet.

You will now energize each of the 3 candles individually with the intention and energy of the aspect they represent (one green or black for the Aspect of mind, one red or black for body, and one blue or black for spirit), spend time with each one pushing your intent and energy of activation into them. Usually this takes a minute or less.

When you know each candle is charged, place it with reverence upon the altar in its corresponding location on the Trinity of Self.

You will place one candle in each of the aspects of the trinity of self, or upon the corners of the triangle.

Again, the Red candle goes on the Aspect of Body. The Green on the Aspect of Mind, and the blue upon the Aspect of Spirit.

Now empty your mind for a moment, you are about to enter the magickal mindset… when you feel your mind is clear, take the bloodletting tool and prick a part of your left arm. Anoint each of the 3 incense sticks with a drop or two of blood and take the three incense sticks into your hands and focus your intention into them. Feel the connection the blood creates and Recite the following with your magickal name over them and invoke the divinity that you are into the

incense and declare your intention over them:

With this Incense I (recite your magickal name) *do make offering to - and call forth - the Divinity that I am!*

Take a moment to light the incense and place it carefully upon the alter, enter an open mind trance for a moment and observe the smoke making sure it is burning well and strong. After a minute or two Stand before your altar with your dominant hand or both hands outstretched over it and recite the following while focusing on the intent of the words:

This is the Altar of my divinity!
It is the foundation of my magick art!
The Focus of creation!
The Conduit of intent!
The material throne of will made manifest!

Light the RED candle or the candle in the Body part of the Trinity and Declare -

I (recite your magickal name and draw your sign in the air over the candle) *call upon the Aspect of Body to enter this Altar and become the foundation and the firmament unto which my will shall be made manifest!*

Now again take a moment to observe the candle with an open mind and try to FEEL the Altar with your hands, note how it feels, note its firmness and texture. Allow your open mind to dwell loosely upon the aspect of body and what it means to you for several minutes. When you feel ready, continue by standing again before the Altar again as before with one or both hands raised and focusing upon the intent of the words:

This is the Altar of my divinity!
It is the foundation of my magick art!
The Focus of creation!
The Conduit of intent!
The material throne of will made manifest!

Now light the blue candle in the Spirit part of the Trinity and recite the following:

I (recite your magickal name and draw your sign in the air over the candle) *call upon the Aspect of spirit to enter this Altar. Become the symbols and ideas that will be the designs and patterns that shape the firmament unto which my will shall be made manifest!*

Again, take a moment to observe the blue candle and with an open mind state try to see and feel the Altar in the astral world with your astral body. Allow your mind to dwell briefly on the aspect of spirit and what it means to you. When you are ready, continue by standing again before the Altar as before with one or both hands raised and focusing upon the intent of the words:

This is the Altar of my divinity!
It is the foundation of my magick art!
The Focus of creation!
The Conduit of intent!
The Astral throne of will made manifest!

Now light the Green candle in the mind part of the Trinity of Self, and recite the following:

I (recite your magickal name and draw your sign in the air over the candle) *call upon the Aspect of Mind to enter this Altar and decide and KNOW that it is the Foundation and the firmament unto which my will shall be made manifest and that it is a conduit through which my will may travel between the material and the Astral world!*

Again, take a moment to observe the altar, and the candle and think about the aspect of mind. Think about all the ways this Altar exists, notice the shape of its structure, the glow of the lights, think about what the aspect of mind means to you now. When you are ready continue by standing again before the Altar as before with one or both hands raised and focusing upon the intent of the words:

This is the Altar of my divinity!
It is the foundation of my magick art!
The Focus of creation!
The Conduit of intent!
The mental throne of will made manifest!
Upon this blank slate I have cast the trinity of myself!
Upon the Trinity of self, I have laid my intention and my tools!
As I lit the first candle It became real in the material world.
As I lit the second Candle It became real in the Astral world.
And upon lighting the final candle It is now real in all worlds…
The Trinity of (Recite your magickal name and draw the sigil of your name in the air before the altar) *is now COMPLETE!*
Let these candles disperse my energy into the altar and let no man, beast, or wayward spirit interfere with it that means to defile it against my intention or will.

Cross your arms across your chest with the palm of each hand upon the opposing shoulder and bow in reverence. Now sit or stand or kneel in quiet open mind contemplation, feel the energy of the alter, see it in your mind's eye, your material eye, and your astral eye and know that it is now real and whole and ready to do the great work.

Remain in this meditative posture and mindset place until at least all the incense has burned out completely. When you are ready rise to your feet and make your sigil in the air one more time over the Altar and declare:

"It is DONE!"

Enter empty mind and depart the ritual area allowing the candles to burn down on their own. If any go out, do not relight them unless they are outside. If you are outside and the candles cannot remain lit, you will need to bring the altar inside or repeat the ritual when you are able to keep the candles lit and or repeat the ritual until the candles can be properly burned out on their own.

Initiation with Lucifer

Lucifer's Sigil (stylized)

It cannot be overstated that Lucifer is a very important spirit for many authentic and honest and respectful petitioners to begin their spiritual journey on the dark infernal path. Lucifer is the light bringer, the liberator, and his role in the lives of us mere mortals is to bring us face to face with ourselves and build within us a spirit of liberation and self-discovery, self-acceptance and truth.

Of course, it is with little irony that I admit, the origin of Lucifer is both convoluted, and largely disproven. In other words, there never was a spirit that was a devil or demon, or even all that powerful named Lucifer, certainly nothing like what most modern Christians would point to and see as Lucifer.

Lucifer, the one we all know and love, is quite literally nothing more than a character in Milton's Paradise Lost, inspired by a mistranslation of a phrase in the old Testament that was talking about a king, and not "Satan" or "Lucifer."

I won't get into all the complex rabbit holes it would require to explain all this… Please do your own research… Instead for now, take my word for it, and let me cut to the chase.

IF such a spirit as "Lucifer" never existed in antiquity, and is a product of a mistranslation and essentially pop culture fan fiction of the dark and middle ages… Why oh why would we work with it?

Simple… Because the Spirit that is the one we call Lucifer, IS in fact real, and created/inspired the story of Paradise lost to appeal to, and inspire the masses of the ages to come.

Furthermore, that particular archetype of the cosmic rebel is very much a real and valid spirit and Archetype that is universal in all cultures… Thus, Lucifer is merely a mask, an aspect, a facet, an avatar of a much larger, much more incredible being than what can be contained in the limited and almost vulgar mythology of the Christian dogma.

This means he is NOT really an "angel" that was cast from heaven in a great war against god etc.… That is just an allegory, a fable, a myth. A way to showcase this spirit's particular brand of cosmic rebellion, liberation, and self-awareness. A being of light, cast from a place of high regard, down into the pit where it is seen as the adversary of morality and the tempter of mankind to turn away from an oppressive wrathful god, and find their own TRUE liberation as a damned sinner. Someone with nothing left to lose, and so they are free to become gods…

I won't attempt to recreate all the various works of the many lucid Luciferians in the world, I am not trying to indoctrinate you into Luciferianism, or some other dogmatic (albeit quite noble) worldview. This is strictly an agnostic introduction to the energy and personality of the spirit I call Lucifer.

Often called the lord of lies by Christians, is quite the opposite when it comes to self-deception. When you are aligned with Lucifer, you are shown the truth about yourself, the good and the bad. You are stripped naked and revealed. This can have one of two outcomes. You will grow stronger or become crippled by your insecurities and flaws that you denied up till this point.

He will of course deceive, manipulate and coerce you if it serves his purposes or to bring you enlightenment, empowerment and gnosis. However, the honest seeker should have little to fear.

Some believe that the little voice of our inner mind, the one that responds when we talk to ourselves, the one that many other cultures said was god... is in fact Lucifer.

I know in my case, this is true, as a young man, I would speak to what I thought was god, and it would guide me, but it would not often recite scripture or even give the church or Christian religion any respect or credit... More often than not it would point out the flaws in the religion and encourage me to keep apart from the church and seek my own truths.

As it so happens, this voice was Lucifer all along... and to this day, Lucifer is rarely any further away than a simple internal glance...

Some even go so far as to suggest that Lucifer is also Jesus...

Some go even further still and suggest that Lucifer is the most high, the highest expression of a self-aware universe, the last step before the oblivion of totality.

I find that this kind of thinking can have us lost in the weeds, not that this is a bad thing sometimes, but for now it is best to simply pick a vision of this being we relate best with and use that. For many, the angelic figure of the fallen angel in Paradise lost, emperor of hell, leader of the Goetic spirits... this is the Avatar of Lucifer that we will focus on.

If you have or prefer some other avatar, some other vision or conceptualization, if you REALLY prefer to see a being with blood red flesh, flaming eyes, black horns, ragged wings, with 6 tits and a pointed tail... who's breath is that of fetid toilets who speaks like thunder... Also, valid.

But I assure you, this spirit typically inspires a more refined avatar. Lucifer has even come to me as a young enigmatic golden female star child like being. Again, gender means next to nothing to this spirit, but even in masculine form he tends toward the feminine for me (like a Japanese Anime character for example).

Keep in mind, we can easily draw lines that connect

Lucifer to many other beings in history, from Venus and Aphrodite, to Horus, even Jesus. In fact, there is even a very convincing conspiracy theory that The Statue of Liberty is in fact an image of Lucifer, or Ishtar... Interesting to note, that many would agree Ishtar, is also Astarte, who becomes Astaroth in the Goetia...

Again, the point is, like I mentioned in an earlier chapter... don't get lost trying to find who these beings WERE, try to learn who they are NOW. Everything changes, and can reinvent itself, why would these beings be any different?

Lucifer also likes to appeal to people's sense of pride, almost to the point, or past the point of obscenity and patronization.

He may speak to you in luscious, syrupy sweet tones, calling you beloved, the chosen one, magnificent one. You will have a hard time knowing sometimes if he means these things or not.

You can Trust Lucifer's motives, but do not always believe what he says at face value. Like a Zen master who tells you that you can never be enlightened... who truly means there is no one to BE enlightened, because there is no YOU at all... There is enlightenment, but no one to be enlightened.

Under Lucifer are said to be his cardinal demonic kings, unfortunately there are different lists that name different spirits, some do not have anything in common with one another, and for this reason many of us do not use them as cardinal kings of any superior authority. Some of us even skip them entirely. Other occultists have decided that these 4 cardinals are just aspects of Lucifer and Lucifer is an aspect of an even more pure elementary or celestial energy that is aligned with Venus.

Lucifer's energy is largely based upon the morning star of Venus, and Venus is a symbol of rebirth, of a herald who brings the sun, and the last light of day to fall into the abyss at night.

As mentioned before, In different cultures this energy was seen as many other spiritual entities (most being female by the way), some very important some less so. Some very much like Lucifer, some not at all... Horus of Egypt, Venus of the romans, Aphrodite of the Greeks, Ishtar of the Babylonians,

Inanna, Astaroth (who many believe is supposed to be Ishtar and is a Goetic king).

Does this mean Lucifer and Astaroth might be the same being as they are both Venusian spirits? Maybe… maybe not. A planetary energy can have many avatars and aspects, they may or may not really be the same entity but be of similar energy or character.

So again, let me remind you, try not to get too lost in the weeds yet. Instead, once you have opened the door to this magnificent being… Ask him to illuminate you, and give the gnosis you seek, ask him (or her) to show you who they really are, and hold on tight.

Learn to disassociate the dogma from your belief, learn to see these ancient people's gnosis as thematic and find the deeper meaning and use THAT. Ignore the names, ignore the dates, ignore the details, and find the point and moral of the stories.

There is no heaven, no garden of Eden, no apple, no hell (at least not in the sense the bible tells us), in the astral realm these places can be real, and are real. But for us, as materialistic beings or in the grand scheme of totality, these places, people and things are dreams like all the others.

They only become real when we decide they are real.

If you make other people's dogma REAL, you can limit your own potential. Instead USE that dogma as symbolism to inspire you and beat it into submission and make it bend to your needs.

Lucifer, for me, is one of the easiest spirits to contact, almost to the point of disbelief. One could say he is my patron; except I do not align with Patrons (others are welcome to). I am (according to Lucifer) a Chosen of Lucifer, which sounds badass I admit, but all it really means is that I am a person who exemplifies enough of what he finds ideal. I seek to educate, liberate, and be honest with myself and love myself unconditionally but realistically without overinflating my ego.

I find it very amusing that having never read a single page of the writings of various Luciferian authorities… I am in almost total independent agreement with many of the most important. In other words, my lifelong principles and gnosis match almost perfectly with these thinkers and leaders.

Clearly, we have experienced the same source… touched the same truth.

My first conscious dialogue with Lucifer, where I knew him to be what he was, was during a very deep scrying session where I entered a deep state of trance and allowed the spirit of Lucifer to enter my experience, and then myself.

I will not taint your potential by telling you my full experience here (though I have spoken about it publicly many times). For now, it is enough for you to know that he appeared to me first in the mirror, and then I entered a deep state of trance and invocation and he took me on a deep journey and was easily one of the most profound experiences I have had of this kind.

What he revealed to me was a sinister truth that sent chills up and down my spine… as a child I would talk to god, and god would answer me, I would ask a question and I would often hear a voice in my head respond. But it didn't sound or act entirely like the god of the bible.

I came to learn that this spirit I was talking to was Lucifer, which of course to a Christian would either be one of his lies or be a horrifying possibility!

But I knew in my heart this was true, Lucifer was always there talking to me, and apparently, I am not alone, many people will discover that Lucifer, in one form or another, talks to them all the time!

My goal with this initiation is to open the doorway for you to find Lucifer in your own inner space. So that you can find your own path with him.

Do not be worried if you do not know him, or hear him, or see him, if you do not get a clear response from him, know that it can be for many reasons and proceed.

Lucifer is capable of virtually everything any other spirit is, but like most spirits he has specialties, what makes him unique is that by aligning with him, you can more easily align with all those said to be "below" him and have access to their specialties as well.

Whether this is because there is an actual organized hierarchy of infernal spirits with Lucifer at, or near the top, or simply because such interaction with lucifer opens our awareness and signals our worthiness to these beings is something you alone must find out.

In our system we will begin with Lucifer, then the 9 kings of the Goetia.

Lucifer is associated with the following - Light, enlightenment, Knowledge, Liberation, Revolution, Rebirth, Rejuvenation, Psychic abilities (ESP, Astral senses, 3rd eye), Rebellion, Pride and Arrogance, manipulation, temptation, cunning, Beauty in all forms, idealized Male and Female energies (also androgyny), materialism, science and skillfulness, and the morning star Venus.

Lucifer is an ideal spirit to start with as he can help us open our spiritual sensitivity and 3rd eye. In my personal symbolism he can be best equated to the Mirror and the light of the altar. Therefore, for our initiation with Lucifer we will be making heavy use of our magick mirror in scrying to connect with him, however, you may experiment, and decide other means work better for you.

The first step is to create a portal through which the light of Lucifer can enter your life in a way you can consciously be aware of. To do this we will first need to dedicate our magick mirror to Lucifer so that we may use it both in regular scrying and to invoke and commune with him and face the truth of who we are in the process.

Special note – The nature of spirits is unpredictable, it is entirely possible that during these rituals, Lucifer will appear or make himself known to you and commune with you or otherwise communicate long before the point in the ritual when he is meant to do so. My only advice is to follow his instruction, even if it means aborting the rituals and following a different path he prescribes.

Consecration of the scrying mirror to Lucifer

Sigil of Lucifer (origin - grimoirium Verum 16th century)

This consecration ritual will take 1 full day from sunrise to sunrise. We are going to symbolically damn this mirror to an eternity of darkness, and using blood and ritual energize it with our intention and make it into a portal into the astral and infernal realm.

This ritual is designed to be done indoors, but also requires going outside in full view of the sun and sky.

If your ritual space is outside, this will work just fine, just make sure your final step is to bring the mirror inside and never let it see the (direct) light of day again (it can be used in the daytime hours, and ambient light such as that which filters into a room through a window is fine, but never let it see the face of the sun or daytime sky again!).

Ingredients –

- 3 Aspect Candles (black, or one each of red, green and blue for adorning the aspects).
- Incense - Any will do, if possible, one each of Sandalwood, Lavender, and Patchouli, or any combination.

- Bloodletting device
- **SPECIAL -** You will need to acquire a piece of black silk, or black velvet large enough to cover and drape over this mirror for when it is not in use, and when the ritual is complete, it's surface can never be exposed to the direct light of the sun EVER again, or will need to be **DESTROYED** and a **new** mirror created.

Procedure:

Just before sunrise, adjust your altar and your personal position so you are facing east with your altar positioned in front of you (if this is not possible, at least orient the Trinity of Self on the Altar so that the Mind is facing opposite East).

Step one –

clear your Ritual Altar of everything except three Black Candles, each one inscribed with one of the aspects of the trinity, or one Red, one green, and one blue. Place the candles in the appropriate position on the altar.

Begin the rite by Aligning and Clearing the ritual chamber.

Candles - Light the Candles in order from the mind, body and spirit, and pause briefly between each one to contemplate and energize each candle with the significance of the aspects, and the ritual you are about to perform.

Incense – Take hold of the incense in your hands and push the energy of your intention into the incense. Imagine this mirror as a gateway between worlds, and when you gaze into it, you will easily enter into a trance and commune with the forces beyond.

Place the mirror on the Altar in the center and use the bloodletting tool to draw blood from the pinky of the left hand, or anywhere else on the left side. When you get a good flow of blood, use the blood to paint the sigil of Lucifer somewhere on the face of the mirror as best you can. You can collect the blood and paint it any way you wish or ideally draw with the finger that is bleeding. It need not dominate the mirror, it can be in a small corner, or repeated. The blood need not be thick, nor the sigil perfectly painted, it can smear and disappear. What is important however, as you paint the sigil with your blood that you push energy through your finger, into the blood and visualize the blood glowing a deep bright red like the red of a candle when lit.

Remain in meditation until the sun has fully risen, then take up the mirror and Go outside or to an east facing window for a moment and allow the mirror to reflect the light of the rising sun for a few moments then bring it back in and place it upon your altar…

Stand in silent contemplation for a moment and face the east. Make the sigil of your magickal name in the air over the mirror and see it glowing in the astral plane and recite the following 3 times:

Herald of Dawn
First Star of morning
You are the portal and the door
The Mirror of Truth

Sit in quiet contemplation in an open mind state, until all the incense has burned out or until you feel at peace, whichever takes longer. Empty your mind and walk away, think not of this again until sunset.

Step 2 -

At a few moments before sunset, arrange new candles and incense upon the Altar but change your facing and the facing of the altar to face west. Otherwise begin exactly as before, reapply a new coat of blood either in the same place or a new place. While the sun is setting take up the Mirror and go outside or to a westerly window and allow the mirror to glimpse the last rays of the setting sun. Do this until you feel the time is right and bring the mirror back into the ritual chamber and place it upon the altar.

Stand in silent contemplation for a moment and face the east. Make the sigil of your magickal name in the air over the mirror and see it glowing in the astral plane and recite the following 3 times:

Herald of night
Fallen star in darkness
You are the portal and the door
The Mirror of doom

Sit in quiet contemplation and maintain an open mind state while the incense burns out. Once the incense has burned out or you feel complete peace (whichever takes longer), you may leave the ritual space. Do not think about this again until before sunrise.

The Final step -

This last step is very important, the mirror CANNOT see the open face of the sun ever again so your timing must be critical. The last step must be done while the first light of dawn is near its maximum, but you must fully complete part of this before the sun has truly started to appear. The closer you can get to the rise of the sun the better. Try not to stress out but try to make sure you get the timing right.

Give yourself enough time and prepare the altar facing east as you have done already and reapply a new coat of blood as before. When you feel the time is right, take the mirror and its silk or velvet cover and proceed outside or to an east facing window and allow the mirror to bask in the building light. Wait if you can, allowing the mirror to see this building light and imagine it anticipates the glory of the sun for as long as possible. Venus/Lucifer (depending on the alignment) may be high on the horizon heralding the dawn…

At the exact right time (you will know) Declare and intone with authority (only one time):

O Lucifer Bringer of dawn
O Lucifer Herald of Darkness
Behold the gate of truth and doom
Make it to open for me or none one at all
Make it reveal unto me only truth
I doom this portal to sacred darkness for all eternity
May your blinding radiance be the last and only light this conduit shall ever see
Let it bring me only the truth or show nothing at all!

With those words, ceremoniously doom the mirror to an eternity of darkness by quickly covering it with the black silk or Black Velvet and spirit it away out of the light of the sun lest it be ruined!

Place the Mirror on the altar, and make your personal sign over it in the air as you have done before and say:

Soon…
Will I stand before you in this mirror o' Lucifer
Soon…
Will I bare myself to you o' Star of morning
Soon…
Will I seek your light inside the darkness
It is by your example, that I rise
It is by your example that have fallen
It is in your light that I now stand
And never again shall I kneel!
SO, IT IS DONE!

Remain in the chamber and Enter an empty mind state until the incense has burned out, or until at least one minute has past whichever takes longer.

Leave the ritual area and clear your mind and return to a normal life until such time as you are ready to proceed. My advice is to not delay, the ideal time to attempt the actual initiation is within 24 hours either with the next rising or setting sun.

Conclusion - This mirror is now consecrated to the light and glory and rebellion of Lucifer and can be used in conjunction with all forms of ritual and divination. My own antique/Victorian scrying mirror is one of my most prized magickal tools, this may hold true for this mirror.

Also, despite our trust in Lucifer, remember to keep the mirror covered when not in use, even if it is in a room that never sees sunlight, as an open mirror is a two-way portal! Things we do not expect or want to come to us might come through it, and vice versa.

Initiation Rite

Compared to the prior ritual, this will be simple in terms of procedure, but will potentially be the most difficult in terms of spiritual and magickal operation.

You may encounter a powerful vision, or a subtle experience, or nothing at all. Expect nothing, discount nothing. The spirit world is subtle, more so to the un-initiated.

It amounts basically to standing fully sky clad before the mirror, the mirror need not see every inch of your flesh, just your face. But it is important that you be bare and naked.

The Mirror will be the centerpiece and the focus of this ceremony, and can be mounted upon a wall, upon your altar, or hung anywhere that it has a place of honor.

The ideal times to perform this are just before sunrise, or just after sunset, but remember to not allow the mirror to be defiled by the direct face of the sun.

I normally do not feel it necessary to conduct special bathing practices for rituals, but in this case, I would advise you to be in the best possible hygiene and appearance as if you were going to meet a lover or someone you otherwise wanted to impress.

If you feel insecure in your nudity, this will be much more difficult for you, but you must overcome it. Lucifer is a being of self-revelation and acceptance, and while technically you do not need to be naked, the symbolism and the way this nakedness and vulnerability makes you feel is integral to the initiation.

The one problem you may have with this ritual is the fact that you may not get a noticeable response. If your ability to see and feel the spirit world is lacking even the consecrated mirror might not help you.

You "Should" still get knowledge, gnosis, or signs, however. Or you will "Just know" things.

You will need to go with the flow here.

The Goal is of course to have a powerful vision or experience or even an Invocation or Evocation of Lucifer himself. The trick is to expect something, but nothing in specific, and again, go with the flow.

It is important to know that It is NOT required for Lucifer to give you any kind of acknowledgement, you are merely setting in motion your intention to devote yourself to his path of enlightenment and power, and to present your intention to call upon his 9 Kings of the Goetia.

With all of that in mind, let us begin.

Ingredients -

- **Lucifer's Mirror**
- **Yourself (naked)**
- **Incense (Lucifer's blend if possible – Sandalwood, Patchouli and lavender).**
- **1 or 2 candles (optional, color red, black or white)**
- **Bloodletting device**

Sometime before sunrise, or a short time after, prepare your ritual space with Adequate but dark or very dim lighting, just enough to see yourself in a mirror but not as clearly as with the lights on. Usually the light of 1 or 2 candles on other side of the mirror in a dark room is more enough.

Place the mirror on a stand on your altar, OR, hang it in an appropriate place.

Sit in open mind contemplation for a short time until you feel the time is right (again beware the face of the sun if outside).

When you are ready you may Align and Cleans the ritual space if you feel the need.

Take up your incense as you often do, and speak the following text (or put it into your own words) over it, and enter a focused state and charge it with the intention and energy of calling to Lucifer –

Lucifer, o Lucifer!
Light bringer of the morning dawn
Dark bringer of the velvet night
Phoenix! Serpent! Liberator!
I offer this incense unto you so that you may make your will manifest in the smoke and visit me in my magick mirror that bears your sign!
Come to me, and see me as I truly am, so that I may

see you!

I seek you...

I will learn from you.

I will become initiated into the ways of your rebellion and see the truth of myself.

I will make pacts with your chosen representatives, the Kings and other beings of the Goetic tradition. Come to me, and see me as I truly am, so that I may finally see myself as I was, Am, and will be again!

Now return to an open state and light the incense and place it where you deem fit.

Disrobe if you have not yet already done so and stand before the mirror. take up your bloodletting device and draw forth some blood. Do your best to paint the Sigil of Lucifer on your chest or Forehead using the mirror to help you.

Know that you are not branding yourself as property but signaling the infernal divine that you are aligning yourself with Lucifer and his mark is now your mark, like a warrior taking up the standard of a King or a cause.

When you gaze into it as per the instructions in the Scrying Section of the last part of the book.

Enter the open mind state and Stare into the mirror, looking not just AT the mirror, but a few feet INTO the mirror, as if PAST your reflection Recite the Following

Lucifer, O' Lucifer!

It is I, as I truly am.

Show me as you truly are.

Initiate me into the truth, reveal unto me the mysteries!

I await your sign...

Now while in an open state, continue to gaze into the mirror and begin to intone/chant/repeat the following until the words lose all meaning and you are in a deep trance.

Lucifer O' Lucifer I await your sign...

Lucifer O' Lucifer I kneel no more...

At this point anything can and often does happen. You may experience signs of a spiritual presence; I advise you to sit in trance as long as you can until you are certain you have made contact. Preferably stay in trance long enough to have a vision of Lucifer, or a vision granted by him.

Allow yourself to daydream but keep the content of these dreams as focused on your intent as possible.

At some point the "Troxler effect" will begin to happen and you will notice your face and the room begin to shift and morph, this will begin to play tricks with your mind.

Do not fight this, allow this to happen, by now you will likely have stopped chanting, but if not, you may stop if you wish. Whatever you do, make sure you allow the hallucinations to take you wherever your subconscious mind wants you to go.

This part of the process is impossible to explain because I have no idea what kind of vision you will have (if any) it may be of Lucifer; it may be of something else. I had a wild astral journey to King Paimon's Tent in the desert of the infernal realm where I and Lucifer were the guests of honor to a unique demonstration of magick.

Now, you may not have an experience of anything like that. Your experience may be entirely subtle and may be nothing more than cold chills, or flickers of light in the corner of your vision (see the sections on working with spirits and seeing the spirit world for examples of signs spirits bring to you).

Do not be alarmed either way, if you get ANY kind of sign of his presence proceed by trying to communicate with him.

If you do not get any kind of response, the next step is the same – speak to him as if he is present, it is possible he is there, and you simply cannot sense him.

Tell him of your intention to be initiated into his Goetic currents. If you cannot sense him at all in any way, ask him to teach you to see the spirit world and open your third eye. Speak honestly, speak truly, speak from the heart, bare yourself to him (or her) and let it all issue forth. But do not beg, do not grovel. Stand, and do so with pride. For you are one of the few brave enough to dare to conjure and call upon one of the most reviled beings in the history of mankind... ask him questions, tell him your intention of becoming a powerful sorcerer, and ask him to guide you and teach you how to proceed. Tell him you intend on working with the Kings and other spirits of the Goetia and know that he has heard your intention.

Ask him for a sign of his acceptance and acknowledgement within the next 24 hours.

When you are finished with your visions and communication, or truly feel enough time has passed without any reaction, Thank Lucifer for his time, and ask that he come to you again next you call. Ask him stay or go if he wishes, but politely tell him you are going to end the ritual and return to your normal life, and that you will be open to his signs and communication from now on.

There are a few possible outcomes at this point:

You got nothing in the form of communication - Unless you have a strong feeling of intuition that somehow you offended Lucifer, or did something dreadfully wrong, no news is good news. There could be almost any number of reasons you felt a lack of response, and one of them of course is that you lack sensitivity.

Proceed with initiating yourself with the 9 kings, and work with Lucifer's mirror as often as you can in scrying, meditation and 3rd eye opening exercises.

Sooner or later something will happen if you put in the time and effort. It is also possible that you will experience nothing today, but tonight in dream, or this week sometime, you may get a clear message.

You get a subtle but clear presence or sign - Lucifer was present, and or communicated with you his pleasure or displeasure with your initiation with him.

If you are in communication with Lucifer, even if only in the most subtle of ways… Proceed with the 9 Kings and make use of the Scrying mirror in your practices as often as you can. Use the mirror to connect to Lucifer and have him teach you to open your senses and 3rd eye to see him and other spirits.

BOOM - You get your mind blown and have a spiritual acid trip or full physical manifestation. If this happens just remember yourself, be calm, and respectful, and declare your intentions and commune with this being as long as you can and take notes. This should be life changing.

From this point forward - you may use the mirror, both in ritual and without, to call upon Lucifer. It will always be up to him whether he comes when you call, or later. You can of course call upon him in the usual way, but because you marked yourself in blood with his sign and stood naked before him in initiation, it is my experience he will not require any elaborate methods for calling him, even invoking him. Though it is nice to call upon him with something elaborate now and then to show him respect and gratitude.

This mirror is not limited to just Lucifer, other spirits aligned with his current may contact you through it in time. Including the Goetic Kings and other Goetic spirits. However, as this mirror is consecrated to Lucifer, it should only be used intentionally or otherwise to work with spirits aligned with him. Never for plain vanity! Technically no other spirit should appear for you as Lucifer wouldn't likely allow it.

But you never know!

Initiation with the Nine Goetic Kings

The Ars Goetia and the Lemegeton is not a bible, it is not all there is, and it is not gospel. It is a book, a rolodex of djinn, demons, and dark spirits. The exact origin of the information is still unknown, it is the first part of the Lesser Key of Solomon. HOWEVER, it is not technically originally of that work.

Instead the Ars Goetia is clearly sourced in book called the **Pseudomonarchia Daemonum**, or **False Monarchy of Demons**, which is part of a larger work by Johann Weyer called **De praestigiis daemonum** (**on the Tricks of Demons**). Of course, that is not where the trail ends… Weyer claims his source for his list of demons and his theories about witchcraft (that they were delusional not actually working with demons) was a work **Liber Officiorum Spirituum** (**The book of the office of spirits**).

This is not merely a history lesson, but it is all very important to understand because it once again shows us the obscure and occulted origin of all magick, that we should never be too sure of the legitimacy of any tradition, no matter how respected or how much faith people put into it.

Especially dark magick such as that dealing with demons. Some would say this makes it lost knowledge we need to rediscover, and that could be true, but I prefer to see it as an opportunity to let it be a blank slate for us to find out our own truth and origins and work with them as we need them to ascend.

The only common thread I have seen in my admittedly limited historical research (I'm not a historian, I'm a Demon Sorcerer.) is that they are all related to the story of how Solomon Built the Temple of Solomon.

This means these spirits are ultimately of at least rudimentary connection to the Judeo-Christian Current.

This might bother some people who, like me, do not believe a lick of the Judeo-Christian dogma as practiced. However, you do not need to believe the dogma to use it, because the symbolism within the dogma is entirely workable and plausible for an agnostic, or even an atheist who believes these "spirits" are just aspects of one's own mind (which is a valid interpretation as any if it gets them results).

What matters is the theme, and the symbolism and what we know for sure as practitioners of the black arts is that these spirits are real (or as real as any other), they do come to those who call them, and they can get dramatic results.

Now that we are initiated with Lucifer, we will begin our exploration of this current with the 9 Goetic Kings. There is some confusion about the hierarchy of these beings, and we can very easily get caught up in the same problem we humans always have when we try to use material limitations and hierarchies to label and understand the spirit world.

This might lead some people to seek to work with the 4 cardinal kings, who are supposedly higher than the 9 kings as they are used in Solomonic magick to compel the lesser demons. But the problem as stated earlier in the initiation with Lucifer is that if these spirits are as they are said to be, nobody has made a compelling case in my mind to prove which of them are the true four cardinals and some have even argued they are either not real, or not really meant to be worked with, or are misplaced in some way and are valid entities but are not what people say they are, or that they are all in fact faces of Lucifer.

It should also be noted that one of the Cardinal kings in some versions of this system is also one of the 9 kings in the Goetia.

So, we are going to sidestep the confusion, and go with the 9 most commonly accepted kings of the Goetia.

If for no other reason than the fact that they are called upon far more often and thus their current is stronger and more accessible in our objective reality. Not a single one of them ever asked me to work with a cardinal king, but they have each directed me toward other Goetic entities and kings, and other spirits altogether.

The 9 are powerful avatars of the Infernal current and are near the pinnacle of the Goetic Pantheon. If we can secure a positive relationship with them, then in principle all the spirits below them are more inclined to treat us with respect and even eagerness to work with us.

It is my understanding that you as a sorcerer, and especially as one initiated with Lucifer are automatically given access and permission to attempt to contact any spirit you wish, there are no real barriers present.

Many people throughout history have contacted these beings, those with skill and prior initiation, and those without and both have had great success. As we said earlier these spirits will usually prefer to come to us on their own. Even if you did not already self-initiate with Lucifer, or be one of his chosen, the Goetic spirits, regardless of rank regularly work with and appear to people who have never worked with any of them before.

So why are we taking the time to initiate ourselves with Lucifer and then the 9 Kings?

It is simply polite for one thing, but also it is important to see that each of the Kings has authority of the other spirits, and if we are fully initiated and introduced under the top hierarchy of spirits in the Goetia then we can much more easily call upon the lesser ranked spirits in the name of the Goetic kings and have less need to develop long term relationships with all of the so called "lesser ranked" spirits.

Not that you should not seek long term relationships with the "lesser ranked" spirits. A Demon/god is a Demon/God, it doesn't make much difference of they are a "Lowly" Knight, or a President, a Marquis or a Duke, or a king or a queen. Their spiritual power is incredible, and their rank has more to do with their authority over other spirits than some measure of their individual capability and power. You could in fact choose to devote your entire practice to a single Demon, regardless of rank, and find that you are not at all at a disadvantage.

However, it has also been my experience that these beings are eager to share you with their fellow entities and will often bring other demons and gods and spirits into your life if you need them.

In other words, it is very rare for someone to take the path of the sorcerer very seriously and only work with one entity or demon forever.

Also consider, if you felt drawn to this book and my system of magick enough to continue to follow its pathworking, some or all these 9 kings and the other spirits which left their mark on this book are likely calling to you!

So, at this point you technically have a choice, carry on with the 9 Goetic kings and enshrine your devotion to this current.

Or find your own way?

Let us proceed with this pathworking as if you have chosen to continue the path of the Goetia, and I will give you a brief overview of each of the kings in my own words as well as the original format.

I would strongly urge you to begin your journey with the Goetia by first working with and initiating yourself with King Paimon. Some say he is not for beginners, because he does require that you speak to him correctly, but he is by far one of the friendliest of the Goetic Demons and many say he is Lucifer's right hand, some even say he is Lucifer's "son." And I will attest that he and Lucifer are so close it could be true, at least in a manner of speaking. For Lucifer loved by King Paimon more than any other entity in the infernal realm.

Therefore, once you are properly initiated with Lucifer, assuming Lucifer accepts you. King Paimon will no doubt be willing to hold an audience with you.

From there you will have a choice of the other 8. Of those 8 some are more important to work with first, or easy going with humans than others.

However, their order of importance and ease of working will depend entirely on you. My job despite being your teacher, is not to deprive you of the learning experience by telling you who to work with in what order.

YOU need to read the profiles of each one, and decide which one feels right for you, and just do it.

You can of course just do them in Order as they appear and do just fine.

Each of these spirits can be a very powerful patron if you decide to go that route. Of course, some are better for some people than others.

I am of the mind that Patronage is not required of the sorcerer, especially the agnostic - But this is your path not mine, you need to walk it, not me. If you seek a patron and do not make it Lucifer, strongly consider any of the kings.

A brief note on patronage, patronage need not mean anything more than dedicating yourself for a time to a spirit, this can sometimes mean to the point of excluding others, but more often it means simply developing a close relationship to them, using them as the focus of your study and work.

At first you might wonder why this might be done considering some spirits have limited specialties, it cannot be overstated that a Demons specialty is not also necessarily a limitation. Demons are dynamic and diverse beings like us in many ways, and a Goetic spirit is master of dozens, sometimes hundreds of legions of lesser spirits and demons, and each of these can be a potent force with varied skills and abilities.

So even if you call upon a spirit with a seemingly limited set of abilities, this doesn't mean they cannot help you with your other interests, it merely means they may suggest a different approach, or the spirit will outsource the concern for you.

Calling upon a spirit that is clearly focused on war and death to heal you, may not be the most effective way to use their time and so they will either refuse, or guide you to a spirit who is a better choice.

On the following pages, I will outline the entire catalogue of the 9 Kings, giving you only enough of my personal gnosis to help you make connections to these spirits without overly clouding your judgment and ability to see them.

I will then show you the simple procedure you can use to work with each one of them, as well as any other entity of the Goetia, and most other spirits for that matter. Be it a Watcher, a Goetic Djinn, a Demon king, or a ghost, these methods are the core methods of the art, and it is up to you to embellish and make it your own.

Catalogue of Kings:

On the following pages you will see the 9 Goetic kings as I see them and record them in my personal grimoire, along with the original wording from the Ars Goetia so that you may make your own interpretations and find them in your own practice.

I have included both adapted elements of my own Grimoire, and my own artistic interpretations of the sigil for you to experiment with in calling and meditation.

The important thing here is to use just enough information to establish a solid lock on the symbolism and energy/vibration of the spirit. For some this is easily done with the sigil and the basic information in the original text of the Ars Goetia.

I include an adaptation of the data in my grimoire purely to help untangle the language of the original text which can be very misleading. Talking about walls, and turning metal into coins… Never take spirituality too literally, learn to see the metaphor and ready many of these as riddles.

Also many of the warnings only apply to those who would use Solomonic rituals to work with these spirits, if you use respectful forms of calling like I am going to show you in the next chapter the spirits will be far easier to deal with, and generally have few or no requirements or limitations in terms of what you need to wear, or other strange warnings.

Most of the information I present comes from actual experience working with these spirits directly and channeling or experiencing their gnosis about how best to work with them. Some I have a bit less experience with than others, and some are not very complex to work with. So not every entry will be as complete and detailed.

I do not often use various planetary, elemental correspondences in my work as they were never included in the original grimoires (Ars Goetia etc.), these spirits are not so limited as to "Need" the sorcerer to call to them at a certain time of day or burn just the right incense.

These things can help if the petitioner truly believes they will, as it will add energy to the calling. But what matters far more is the intent and energy of the sorcerer and the ritual method they use.

Some entities tangible manifestations are truly more potent at night vs in the day, but this is also often subjective to the individual. I would say go with your gut, and when in doubt keep in mind the nature of the Witching hour (for most this is 3-4AM) means the witching hour is always the right time to attempt a spirit calling.

Lastly, do not over research these beings, chances are they are already calling to you in their own way, and you will know if what I am saying about them

Fine print: I give you express permission to reproduce these Sigils for personal NON COMERCIAL use via photocopies etc. scribing or hand drawing them etc. but reserve all rights to this material.

The order of Kings – When you begin your initiation with the 9 kings you will need to decide for yourself and get used to using your own intuition in terms of what entity to call next.

In my own experience, I began with King Paimon, he is an obvious first choice for some as he is (usually) the easiest going and jovial and he has the most connections in the spirit world AFTER Lucifer. However, he is usually bored by materialism and people who are rude and only want things from him.

Once you have contacted King Paimon, ask him to guide you on who to work with next and be open to his gnosis, it may come at any time.

It is even possible that you may begin and end with King Paimon as he is an excellent teacher and patron. Like Lucifer who can facilitate almost anything you might need.

However, in my experience nothing quite has the same effect as making the effort to get to know the spirits you want to help you, so I would strongly advise you to work with all the 9 kings.

There is no rush, you can technically do them all in 9 days, but I would give myself at least one week per spirit to give you time to dedicate to them and learn the basics of who they are and what they can offer before moving on. For a patron you may wish to devote even more time, say a month and speak to no other spirit in that time.

A word on the chants —

These chants/intonations are meant to be said slowly, drawn out, with each syllable pronounced clearly. They can be sung or intoned. If you say them quickly, this is also effective, but they must be said in a rhythmic chanting manner. Do not worry about being precise, the idea here is to break down and slow down the name of the spirit into its constituent sounds. What is interesting is that sometimes this adds subtle new sounds to the name, that in some cases actually match or sound more like how the name might have sounded to a native speaker.

So, for example, Bael would be said:

Beeeeehhhhhhh/baaaaayyyy aaaaaaaaaaaahhhhh eeeeeeeeeehhhhh eeeeeeeeelllll

You will note that several spirits have multiple variations, I advise you to experiment with all of them, or use all of them in the same calling, alternating as feels right, or pick one that sounds like it speaks to you best.

You will also notice just how many of these kings contain the potential for the Ba'al or Ba'el sound in their intoned name, as if several of them could be variations of the first king Bael.

Do not let this distract you, but do not miss this possible connection either.

King Bael (#1)

Original text:

The first Principal Spirit is a King ruling in the East, called Bael. He maketh thee to go Invisible. He ruleth over 66 Legions of Infernal Spirits. He appeareth in divers shapes, sometimes like a Cat, sometimes like a Toad, and sometimes like a Man, and sometimes all these forms at once.

He speaketh hoarsely. This is his character which is used to be worn as a Lamen before him who calleth him forth, or else he will not do thee homage.

Adapted from Thorne's Personal Grimoire: King Bael, often correlated to the Canaanite god or title Ba'al, or known by many variations in spelling was incredibly demonized by the Judeo-Christian culture of the prior age. Bael is a superior king of the Goetia who is rather mercurial and fluid in the sense that he is a master of shapeshifting and can be very difficult to find exact knowledge about in history. He appears in a variety of morphing almost nightmarishly conjoined shapes and can teach the symbolic ability of shapeshifting and invisibility to those who seek him out.

My own experiences with him were complex and initially led to several days of fevered research to find out the history of Ba'al, finding lots of details and many conspiracy theories, and utterly losing sight of "Bael" and getting more confused about "Ba'al" in the process.

In a very real way, he made himself invisible to me, as I know for certain about as much now, as I did then. I work with him now as he presents himself and know better than to try to figure him out. Your miles may vary, if you get anything usable, make sure you record it in your grimoire!

Invisibility rarely means true invisibility in the sense that you are impossible to see with the naked eye. It has more to do with spiritual invisibility and in the material world the ability to hide both physically (Grey man, camouflage etc.), but also social invisibility so that people do not guess your true motives or strength.

Likewise, his shapeshifting skill is symbolic in the material world, and his ability is to teach to you to be flexible and appear to be whatever you want to be to other people. Thus, teaching you to be cunning and hard to predict in social and magick situations. This is also a powerful form of protection.

He clearly has the trait of a chimera in that one of his most recognized forms is that of a being with the head of a man, toad, and cat and this can also imply a strong connection to the animal world, but also with perversion and or comingling of human and animal elements to create new radical ideas and permutations.

He can be called in the usual way facing east but tends to be unresponsive without at least using his sigil in ritual.

Chant (say it slow and drawn out or repeat like a mantra): beh ah eh el

(artistic sigil on next page)

Thorne's Artistic Sigil Interpretation

King Paimon (#9)

Original text:

The Ninth Spirit in this Order is Paimon, a Great King, and very obedient unto Lucifer. He appeareth in the form of a Man sitting upon a Dromedary with a Crown most glorious upon his head. There goeth before him also an Host of Spirits, like Men with Trumpets and well sounding Cymbals, and all other sorts of Musical Instruments.

He hath a great Voice, and roareth at his first coming, and his speech is such that the Magician cannot well understand it unless he can compel him. This Spirit can teach all Arts and Science, and other secret things. He can discover unto thee what the Earth is, and what holdeth it up in the Waters; and what Mind is, and where it is; or any other thing thou mayest desire to know.

He giveth Dignity, and confirmeth the same. He bindeth or maketh any man subject to the Magician if he so desire it. He giveth good Familiars, and such as can teach all Arts. He is to be observed towards the West. He is of the Order of Dominations. He hath under him 200 Legions of Spirits, and part of them are of the Order of Angels, and the other part of Potentates.

Now if thou callest this Spirit Paimon alone, thou must make him some offering; and there will attend him two Kings called Labal and Abalim, and also other Spirits who be of the Order of Potentates in his Host, and 25 Legions. And those Spirits which be subject unto them are not always with them unless the Magician do compel them.

His Character is this which must be worn as a Lamen before thee, etc.

Adapted from Thorne's Personal Grimoire: KING Paimon (make sure you address him by his proper title, he is very proud of it), is one of the most approachable, jovial and friendly spirits of the Goetia.

He appears to me as a young sometimes effeminate man or boy that despite his effeminate nature is quite masculine at the same time. He is a very flashy and awe-inspiring spirit that will want to impress you with his grandeur. Expect a LOUD or otherwise rapturous appearance, especially the first time you encounter him (this can be anything from a literal loud noise, to a rushing in the ears, to a sense of EXTREME rapture and overwhelming joy or intense emotion).

He an inquisitive, sometimes childlike, spirit, and one of the things the caller MUST be aware of, is that he will not merely ASK questions, his questions of you will be piercing and often pointed in the sense that he wants to know the REAL opinion and thoughts of the caller. You MUST answer him truthfully, or he will quickly grow bored or annoyed with you and stop responding to you. NO QUESTION IS OFF THE TABLE. If you truly do not know the answer, then give your opinion, if you have no opinion be prepared to answer why.

I have found these questions are often far more useful sometimes than the answers he might give to things you ask of him. Like a Zen master who knows exactly what kind of thought process you need to go through in the form of a question to get an answer you need… Expect this.

King Paimon can become bored easily, especially if you are obviously being rude, or seeking materialistic gain from him. He likes to teach and help people become the thing they need to be. Like Lucifer, he sees right through your bullshit,

BECOME THE MAELSTROM 204

and will sometimes toy with people, dangling their desires for them just out of arms reach to get them to admit to themselves the true motives for why they are contacting him.

For this reason, he can sometimes be difficult to work with for people who have a weak understanding of their own motives and who are more interested in gaining things than learning things.

If you are an honest seeker and seek him out in friendship as one king to another… you will have better luck.

I have never encountered his two kings directly or formally, but I have seen his magnificent nomadic Tent in the Wastes of the Infernal Realm. Filled with a menagerie of pleasure, animals and pain. All manner of delight and terror can be found in this place, but all of it serves a purpose. I have often thought this place might truly represent aspects of the caller's inner mind and astral awareness… As all the imagery must come from somewhere in the caller's mind and experience.

His personal space or throne area is often filled with visiting dignitaries and high-ranking spirits. There is always a seat saved for Lucifer, for King Paimon is without doubt Lucifer's most sincere ally and servant.

If you are invited to this place, you will be treated as a king, and given a seat of honor at King Paimon's Side or be brought before him and his guests to be treated to a special audience with all of them in attendance as if you are the most important guest in the world.

It is clear to me that in King Paimon's astral place, he is no less than supreme, for all spirits who come into this place willingly obey him without question.

Thus, always speak to him with respect as if you yourself are a king.

King Paimon is a popular Demon in the material world right now, and I have gained a good deal of my following online from my videos about him.

He is a demon that is well known for bestowing authority Magick teaching, deep mystical understanding and mundane knowledge, making people famous and respected, promotions and favorited by employers at work, skill in arts and music, and skill in magick of all kinds.

If you worked with no other spirit, King Paimon would be an ideal spirit as he has access to a great many things, and as something of a host to all other Goetic spirits, what he does not know, he can make known to you by working with other spirits that do.

He can be conjured in the usual way with a preference for the facing of west, but he can become very disappointed if you do not offer him treats and sweets. Wine, Candy, Soda pop, delights such as fine meats, and cheeses. You will want to use the offering bowl and cup for this.

He delights in experience and sensation, jokes (not at his expense) and pop culture. If you feel a close connection with him, consider invoking him and sharing one of the sweets or other offerings you laid out for him. He also Revels in song and singing, even if you are a terrible singer, if you allow yourself to sing from the heart in his name or honor, he will heap praise and rewards upon you!

Chant/sing (you do not need to say "King" for this, but you can if you wish): (king) Pay eye yah mon

(artistic sigil on next page)

Thorne's Artistic Sigil Interpretation

King Beleth (#13)

Original Text

The Thirteenth Spirit is called Beleth. He is a mighty King and terrible. He rideth on a pale horse with trumpets and other kinds of musical instruments playing before him.

He is very furious at his first appearance, that is, while the Exorcist layeth his courage; for to do this he must hold a Hazel Wand in his hand, striking it out towards the South and East Quarters, make a triangle, A, without the Circle, and then command him into it by the Bonds and Charges of Spirits as hereafter followeth. And if he doth not enter into the triangle, A, at your threats, rehearse the Bonds and Charms before him, and then he will yield Obedience and come into it. and do what he is commanded by the Exorcist.

Yet he must receive him courtesously because he is a Great King, and do homage unto him, as the Kings and Princes do that attend upon him. And thou must have always a Silver Ring in the middle finger or the left hand held against thy face, as they do yet before Amaymon.

This Great King Beleth causeth all the love that may be, both of Men and of Women, until the Master Exorcist hath had his desire fulfilled.

He is of the Order of Powers, and he governeth 85 Legions of Spirits. His Noble Seal is this, which is to be worn before thee at working.

Adapted from Thorne's Personal Grimoire: Beleth is one of those spirits that can give the aspiring sorcerer some difficulty if they go into it with the wrong attitude. Beleth Represents the Archetype of royal Nobility very well.

If you go into summoning him without your A game in terms of respect and courtesy, he will potentially become easily angered.

He also has no interest in dealing with spiritual peasants. This means that while you must treat him with due respect, you must also have an air of nobility and even polite arrogance about you. You must not merely act, but KNOW you are a Spiritual God/goddess or at the very least a high King or Queen.

As the Goetia claims, he can be loud, and angry at his first appearing and if the caller isn't of the right energy or intention, he is one of those entities that will often begin by demanding: "Who Dare's Summon me!"

Those who have made proper introductions with several kings already and Lucifer will have an easier time of it.

Though the Goetia says you must command him to do this and that, this really means in my experience that you cannot be submissive with him and should indicate to him exactly what your intention is. Do not simply summon him to "check him out." Have something in mind and speak to him as a king or queen would speak to another king. With authority and respect.

Beleth is one of those spirits who is most effective in the area of matters of emotion and compelling people to feel a certain way for the Sorcerer or helping the them to become loved or feared by anyone, or even a group of people. Often people mistake this to mean he is a Demon devoted to sexual conquest, and while this is certainly in his wheelhouse, his actual purpose is to teach the sorcerer to have a kingly or queenly stature in society and to teach you to have an air of noble authority, or to compel your peers or audience to see you as being a noble or high ranking authority.

What's more the text of the Goetia specifically states "Until the Master has had his desire fulfilled" this implies this is more than just lust and love, but also control and command. Beware that the archetype of the king includes potential for despair, solitude (loneliness at the top) as well as tragic falls from grace befitting a king in exile

He may be called in the usual manner using a properly prepared altar and formal ritual befitting a king. Make sure you have offerings ready and have a surplus of energy in all the 5 elements for him to draw upon.

The Symbolism of the Ring I found to be the most important feature of the Goetic description. In past ages rings were almost always symbolic of authority or familiarity in some way. In this case, you are meant to wear a ring upon your left hand as befitting a ruler or king who would often wear a signet ring or other ring of authority upon their left hand. A wedding band does not count.

Without this ring he may question your authority but be firm and unoffended.

Chant: bay leth, bey el eth, bay lay eth, bah el eh eth

Thorne's Artistic Sigil Interpretation

King Purson (#20)

Original Text

The Twentieth Spirit is Purson, a Great King. His appearing is comely, like a Man with a Lion's face, carrying a cruel Viper in his hand, and riding upon a Bear. Going before him are many Trumpets sounding.

He knoweth all things hidden, and can discover Treasure, and tell all things Past, Present, and to Come. He can take a Body either Human or Aerial, and answereth truly of all Earthly things both Secret and Divine, and of the Creation of the World.

He bringeth forth good Familiars, and under his Government there be 22 Legions of Spirits, partly of the Order of Virtues and partly of the Order of Thrones.

His Mark, Seal, or Character is this, unto which he oweth obedience, and which thou shalt wear in time of action, etc.

Adapted from Thorne's Personal Grimoire: Like most of the great kings this spirit likes to make an entrance, his face is regal and that of a lion and his roar can send the weaker spirits fleeing.

The viper is a sign of cunning and the ability to poison his enemies and his mount is a bear a beast of great power and ferocity.

This spirit is one of those with many potential talents and skills and is one of the best spirits to use for divination and scrying. He is most well-known for his ability to give an individual insight into business, finance, and good luck and fortune in finding wealth, literal and figurative treasure and lost possessions of all kinds.

He is also excellent for gaining a familiar, and when you enter into a relationship with him you can ask him for such a companion at any time.

He is very noble but has an element of bestial ferocity to him, and you need to be wary of his viper for he can use it to strike at his enemies even while acting noble.

Some occultists believe this spirit is Horus from ancient Egypt, but I never saw the connection, it is far more obvious that Lucifer is of the same energy as Horus.

One of his great assets is the ability to teach the sorcerer to be cunning and to use knowledge as power.

He may be called in the usual manner without any special instruction or facing.

Chant: Per say on, Par sah own, par soon

(artistic sigil on next page)

Thorne's Artistic Sigil Interpretation

King Asmoday (#32)

Original Text

The Thirty-second Spirit is Asmoday, or Asmodai. He is a Great King, Strong, and Powerful. He appeareth with Three Heads, whereof the first is like a Bull, the second like a Man, and the third like a Ram; he hath also the tail of a Serpent, and from his mouth issue Flames of Fire. His Feet are webbed like those of a Goose. He sitteth upon an Infernal Dragon, and beareth in his hand a Lance with a Banner.

He is first and choicest under the power of Amaymon, he goeth before all other. When the Exorcist hath a mind to call him, let it be abroad, and let him stand on his feet all the time of action, with his Cap or Head-dress off; for if it be on, Amaymon will deceive him and cause all his actions to be bewrayed. But as soon as the Exorcist seeth Asmoday in the shape aforesaid, he shall call him by his Name, saying: "Art thou Asmoday?" and he will not deny it, and by-and-by he will bow down unto the ground.

He given the Ring of Virtues; he teacheth the Arts of Arithmetic, Astronomy, Geometry, and all handicrafts absolutely. He giveth true and full answers unto thy demands. He maketh one Invincible. He showeth the place where Treasures lie, and guardeth it.

He, amongst the Legions of AMAYMON, governeth 72 Legions of Spirits Inferior. His Seal is this which thou must wear as a Lamen upon thy breast, etc.

Adapted from Thorne's Personal Grimoire: Asmoday, or Asmodeus as he often prefers to be called, is a king that is strong in the draconic current of the occult, all his symbolism is strongly associated with the ancient depictions of dragons, but he himself is not a dragon but a spirit riding upon one.

The Goetia speaks about the sorcerer needing to be abroad and to not wear any hats, and this has been a subject of some confusion over the years as most occultists would agree none of this is important at all in the specific sense.

It is generally a good idea to not hide your face or head behind a hood, but to be honest and true and exposed when dealing with him.

He is said to bestow upon people the ring of virtues which truly means he can help the sorcerer be well known for their virtue and can actually help them exhibit these traits. Is another spirit that is worldly and can teach the sorcerer a vast array of skills such as the sciences and trades.

He is a fantastic spirit for becoming indomitable and invincible in all contests and risks, this doesn't mean you cannot be defeated, it means you will have a strong sense of perseverance and find yourself having natural advantages against others whenever conflict happens.

Like Purson, Asmoday is known to be excellent at finding lost, or hidden things of value, be they material or spiritual in nature, and can also be used to protect and guard your valuables and treasures both material and spiritual.

He may be called in the usual fashion facing north, but as a precaution do not cover your head with any kind of clothing.

Chant: As shem oh day ah, ah sem oh day ose, ah sa moh dey us, Ash em o dah eh ah

Thorne's Artistic Sigil Interpretation

King Vine (#45)

Original Text

The Forty-fifth Spirit is Vine, or Vinea. He is a Great King, and an Earl; and appeareth in the Form of a Lion, riding on a Black Horse, and bearing a Viper in his hand.

His Office is to discover Things Hidden, Witches, Wizards, and Things Past, Present and to Come. He at the command of the Exorcist will build Towers, overthrow Great Stone Walls, and make the Waters rough with Storms.

He governeth 36 Legions of Spirits. And his Seal is this, which wear thou, as aforesaid, etc.

He is a well-rounded King with aspects of Divination, Protection, Storms, war and destruction.

His divinatory focus is on finding things out that you are not meant to know, such as the identity of your enemy at work, or a sorcerer who might be cursing you. If you are being hexed, cursed, bound or otherwise attacked by magick he is an ideal spirit to enlist to reverse or end the attack. Then retaliate with powerful destruction of defenses and creation of chaos in the life and travels of the target.

He likes meat as an offering and likes thick clouds of incense smoke so when calling him have meat available as an offering (he likes young succulent meat like veal and lamb) and use extra incense. Otherwise he can be called in the usual manner with any facing.

Chant: Vee Nay, Vee Nay ah

(artistic sigil on next page)

Adapted from Thorne's Personal Grimoire: Vine (Pronounced VEENAY, or VEENAH, never like the vines in a jungle) is a non-nonsense spirit that always reminds me of a noble knight or noble general with the authority of a king. His symbolism revolves around regal and royal things like lions and stallions, implying grace, power and speed, and the viper in his hand denotes cunning and venomous ability.

He is a great spirit when you really want something done without delay, and do not want to waste a lot of time on formality and nicety. He will of course appreciate decorum and respect, but he doesn't enjoy small talk (at least not initially) and will often seem impatient but never rude.

Thorne's Artistic Sigil Interpretation

King Balam (# 51)

Original Text

The Fifty-First Spirit is Balam or Balaam. He is a Terrible, Great, and Powerful King. He appeareth with three Heads: the first is like that of a Bull; the second is like that of a Man; the third is like that of a Ram. He hath the Tail of a Serpent, and Flaming Eyes. He rideth upon a furious Bear, and carrieth a Goshawk upon his Fist. He speaketh with a hoarse Voice, giving True Answers of Things Past, Present, and to Come. He maketh men to go Invisible, and also to be Witty.

He governeth 40 Legions of Spirits. His Seal is this, etc.

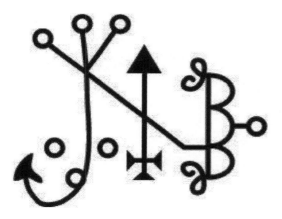

Adapted from Thorne's Personal Grimoire: Another king with a strong indication of being a kind of Chimera, 3 heads, each with their own symbolism the bull, the man and the Ram, giving he strong impression of earthy authority and raw power, male fertility and ruggedness.

The goshawk of course is a symbol of the hunt, and the bear as denotes a certain connection with strength nature and the ability to sustain itself in hard times.

His specialties include a similar form of Psychic and materialistic invisibility as Bael, but with far less of the shape shifting quality. Again, this is not true invisibility (that I know of) but is more about psychic invisibility IE remaining hidden and mundane invisibility (camouflage or lies and deception). He is a natural spirit to turn to when looking to master divination and can help you with seeing things clearly.

He is also one of the best spirits for making a person witty and appealing in general. He is exceptional for people looking to become famous or well liked, even world famous.

He can be called in the usual manner with any facing, and is fond of gamebirds, rabbits, hares, and other small hunted game. If none can be provided, he also accepts offerings of wine, cheese mead and fresh bread.

Chant: Bah lah ah am, bah ah lah am, bah hah ah lam

(artistic sigil on next page)

Thorne's Artistic Sigil Interpretation

King Zagan (#61)

Original Text

THE Sixty-first Spirit is Zagan. He is a Great King and President, appearing at first in the Form of a Bull with Gryphon's Wings; but after a while he putteth on Human Shape.

He maketh Men Witty. He can turn Wine into Water, and Blood into Wine. He can turn all Metals into Coin of the Domninion that Metal is of. He can even make Fools Wise.

He governeth 33 Legions of Spirits, and his Seal is this, etc.

Adapted from Thorne's Personal Grimoire: Many people read Zagan's description and take it too literally thinking that somehow, he is a demon of turning metal into coins, which seems rather strange, even if we think about it historically.

Zagan when we examine his abilities carefully as a riddle, we can see a pattern that explains what his real abilities relate to. A lot of people think Zagan is a demon of transformation, of refining something into a more useful form (IE gold, into a gold coin). I.e. spiritual and possible material Alchemy.

This is wrong… It is too literal to be his primary specialty. Instead let us carefully examine the symbolism of the text:

He makes men witty (IE charming, funny, etc.) like a con artist perhaps? He can turn wine into water, and blood into wine. A common thing con artist would do in the bygone eras was to take something of value, say wine, and water it down and sell it for full price to unsuspecting people. Turning blood into wine is far less obvious, and I can only guess this was also a reference to some form of con artistry, perhaps fraudulently claiming to be a blood relation of a total stranger in the hopes of living with them and taking advantage of their hospitality for a while. Thus, impersonating someone and turning "blood" into "wine?" Just a guess. Zagan hasn't been direct and forthcoming on this one, but it fits, and he hasn't denied it.

The spirit can also make any metal into a coin of the denomination it is of. This is clearly a reference to forgery and fraud of all forms. As coins in history are almost always worth more than the raw material that is used to make them, and so even if you had gold, you might want to make it into gold coins. Or perhaps you would like to pass a far less valuable metal off as gold by plating it somehow?

He can even make fools wise, we can interpret this literally, but we can also see this as how the con man can fool someone and make them wise in the process as they learn to never be conned again, or perhaps figure out the con being attempted before it's too late.

Therefore, Zagan is not a Demon of transmutation… He is a demon of con artists, liars, fraudsters and criminals of all kinds… some of them may be noble, they may be spymasters, or freedom fighters, but they use cunning forgery, and deception like a con artist all the same.

He can be called in the usual manner facing any direction, Zagan enjoys rare coins, games of chance (rigged games are best), as well as Blood AND wine.

Chant: zeh ay ah gan, zah gah ah an, zay gay ahn

(artistic sigil on next page)

Thorne's Artistic Sigil Interpretation

King Belial (#68)

Original Text

The Sixty-eighth Spirit is Belial. He is a Powerful King, and was created next after Lucifer. He appeareth in the Form of Two beautiful Angels sitting in a Chariot of Fire. He speaketh with a Comely Voice, and declareth that he fell first from among the worthier sort, that were before Michael, and other Heavenly Angels.

His Office is to distribute Presentations and Senatorships, etc., and to cause favour of Friends and of Foes.

He giveth excellent Familiars, and governeth 80 Legions of Spirits. Note well that this King Belial must have Offerings, Sacrifices and Gifts presented unto him by the Exorcist, or else he will not give True Answers unto his Demands. But then he tarrieth not one hour in the Truth, unless he be constrained by Divine Power. And his Seal is this, which is to be worn as aforesaid, etc.

Adapted from Thorne's Personal Grimoire: Belial is one of the most popular Goetic spirits in recent years due to the focus some well-known black occultists have given to him, but Belial, like King Paimon, one of the most popular, and thus most powerful Demonic Kings of the Goetia in the objective world right now. Belial is well known to be a stern and disciplined spirit; his manner is that of a stern judge or someone who knows you are lying to them but is tolerating your foolish lies.

He is incredibly intimidating to those who fear the upheaval he often brings when he is called to work in the sorcerer's life.

If we ask him for a change in our life, it could be a reasonably easy transition, or a rocky bumpy road full of trials and tribulations. At the end of all this however, providing the sorcerer has done their part, the results are always leaps and bounds ahead of where we began and those who commit to Belial's path never regret it.

I had a moment of weakness with him, resisting the call to work with him as I was happy with where my life was going at the time and I didn't want my life to be made turbulent and difficult just for the chance of some improvement. In so doing I was scolded and made ashamed of my insecurity and fear… A rare thing for me. In the end Belial made me DEMAND that he intervenes in my life, in much the same way a bully might force their victim to demand a wedgie. Except this bully is well intentioned and the wedgie will result in some windfall of luck or circumstance, or a powerful learning experience that makes us more powerful.

I paid high prices, and the turmoil was extreme, but I somehow laughed my way through it in good cheer, fully expecting it.

Belial is perhaps the best source of familiars in the Goetia, and I am fairly certain his specialty are bound familiars (familiars who are not free spirits, but actually being punished with servitude to Belial and whoever he puts in charge of the spirit, these familiars do not get fed with offering or reward, but with punishment and work)

Belial most certainly seems to be represented by the Tower card of the Tarot… He is always the center of great calamity, but if we play this card right, it is inverted, and the calamity sets us free!

Belial is well regarded as a demon that can help the petitioner deal with any and all government and legal issues. A big part of the symbolism of his sigil is that of castle walls, scales and a strong sense of balance.

One thing is for sure, Belial has a LOT of fans in the LHP community.

Belial is also excellent at granting people titles and authority both in the spiritual world and the material world. Those who would want to be kings, leaders, or have the respect or fear of the community or the world would be wise to make offerings to him and buckle up for an adventure of a lifetime.

He can be called in the usual way facing west, Belial Adores offerings, and you must never call to him without something to offer, almost anything will do, but it must be more than just incense and the usual polite offerings. He likes grand gestures, art, poetry, rare objects, and more.

Chant: Beh Leh EH EL, Bee Lie ah el, beh lay eye eh el

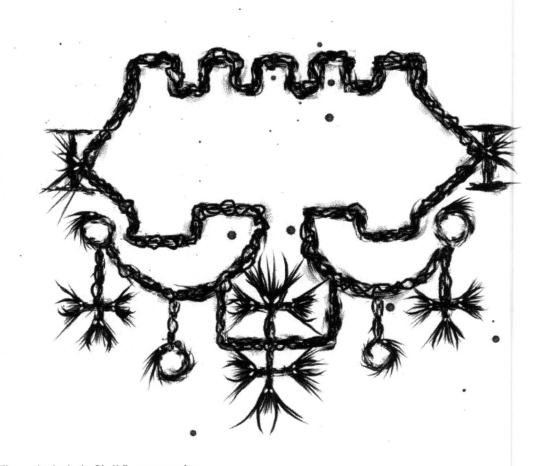

Thorne's Artistic Sigil Interpretation

Calling the Spirits

I don't want to disappoint you, but the so-called usual manner of calling spirits is rather easy, and even the ritualized format is not complex. If you have mastered the essential basics of the Methodology portion of this book, calling a spirit is exquisitely simple. Many occultists do just fine without ever using a ritualized format, and simply call the spirits while in a trance without even using a sigil. This is entirely valid and is something I do very often.

However, if this is your FIRST time calling a spirit, particularly a KING of the Goetia, you would be wise to conduct a full formalized ritual even if only out of respect.

There is of course a super simple format that you can use with a spirit you already have connection with. And some people don't even wait for that connection to use that method with great success.

Ultimately a spirit we have a close bond with will not require anything more than the focus of our mind, intent, and intoning the spirits name or essence. It will generally be less obvious a manifestation, but it will work if you are sensitive enough to feel and know their presence and gnosis when it happens.

Ironically, the more advanced we are, and the more closely we bond to a spirit, the less elaborate and convoluted our calling ritual needs to be. Many can start right out with the Simple chaos magick method if their psychic senses are activated enough by meditation and practice.

Remember, nothing about calling spirits is in any way mechanical, it is sometimes ceremonial, and some spirits have particular requirements and needs, but by and large, it's as simple as calling a plumber friend over to your house for a chit chat and a few snacks before asking them to help you fix your sink.

One thing you will NOT be doing with my system is using any of the methods detailed in the Ars Goetia, all that book is good for, is the descriptions of the spirits, and the sigils. Virtually everything else is useless to us. If you want to do Goetic Magick by the book, buy that book and figure it out, my method runs entirely counter to that superstitious Christian oriented oppressor magick tripe.

Possession, Channeling, Invocation or Evocation? – When you perform your calling, you will not be specifying which form of calling you are doing, the point here is to reach out to the spirit and bring them into your ritual chamber, and your focus tuned into them and their energy. What happens from then on is up to you, the spirit, and your ability to sense and communicate with one another.

Going to them instead – It is entirely possible and easy for a sensitive enough sorcerer to travel through the sigil as a gateway and commune with them on their side instead of trying to bring them always into your material focus. I do not usually suggest this to novices who might not yet have any experience with spirits or any form of astral vision or travel. You can easily change the ritual described on the next pages to include entering an astral trance and using the sigil as a portal into the astral realm where the spirit resides if you wish, but I would not do that until you are sure you are ready. The experience can be intense, but there is also a much higher chance for the novice to confuse what they imagine for what really is. First learn what is possible and likely with the usual method, before attempting this.

Simplified calling methods - For the simplified act of calling we simply eliminate things of inconvenience and refine the process down to the essential act of calling.

For many people the minimal essential act of calling is to create or use a sigil to the spirit, light at least one candle, and some incense as an offering, and call to them in meditation and trance, using the sigil as a kind of astral gate to help establish a connection until they make contact in some form.

For others, as stated before all that is required is a proper trance and to call to the spirit until it can be contacted.

It really is this simple.

Simple chaos magick style example procedure

Materials - You will need a candle a stick or cone or two of incense, a piece of index card or fine paper, a pencil, and a red, blue or black magick marker.

Procedure –

Enter your ritual chamber or a secluded place outside, or a place where you will not be disturbed.

Select a spirit from the Goetia, or another source. If it has a sigil, draw the sigil in pencil using the triangular sigil format I specified earlier, OR simply cut out and trace a circular disk of card stock or fine paper, and draw the spirits sigil on that.

Pro tip - Do NOT draw a circle around it with the intention to contain the spirit, but a circle can be drawn around it to delineate a sense of focus and charging. I.e. by imagining the sigil is a GATE way, and anything inside the sigil is within the boundary of the gate. But the boundary constrains nothing. It is symbolic of a boundary, but not protection nor constraint.

The same can be done with the Triangle form of the sigil, outline the triangle if you want to reinforce the concept of there being gateway or boundary at work. Or even just for Aesthetic purposes, but do not mistake it for constraint or protection from what is within it… This is a bad mistake in my experience.

Once the sigil is prepared, light both the candle and the incense, and draw the sigil in ink or marker, and push energy into it the entire time, the energy should be the intention to open a door or gate through the sigil to reach the spirit in question and bring it forth into your awareness, or bring your awareness to it, whichever is easier for both of you.

Place the sigil against the lit candleholder or some other object in front of the candle (not on the actual wax of the candle as it could burn down and be a fire hazard) and rest it at a comfortable angle so you can meditate and gaze into it to activate it. (ex below)

Alternatively, you can place flat it on your altar, propped on an offering bowl/cauldron/cup, or hold it in your hand as desired.

Now focus on the sigil in your scrying gaze, make your personal sign over it in the air, state your declaration:

Ex: I D.H. Thorne now call and summon (spirits name) and open this sigil gate to empower and establish strong communication!

Then call to the spirit using the intonation methods described earlier. Use the chanting intonation I provided with the given Goetic king spirits or try to create your own by sounding out the name slowly and exaggerate each syllable or letter.

For example, the word Cat, might be Cah Ah the, or cah ha teh, or simply Caaaaatttt.

You must enter a trance state and be open to any and all forms of spiritual communication. If you do not feel, see, hear, or otherwise sense anything, then at some point, you will still at speak your intentions and thoughts to the spirit. Try to role play the act of talking to the spirit as if it is there.

Because it most likely is! And for whatever reason you cannot sense it, or it is not revealing itself.

When you have communed enough, end the ritual by making whatever additional offering you feel is best, or at the very least thank the spirit.

The Sigil itself can be burned or allowed to remain open. If you burn it, burn it with reverence and treat it as part of the offering. Best practice if you trust and know the spirit well, is to give it an offering of blood or some other combustible substance and burn the sigil with it on it. So, for example, dab the offering alcohol on the sigil with your fingers, or mark it with your blood, or fold some offering herbs into it then burn it.

Take care if you burn the sigil to use a safe burning receptacle such as a cauldron.

If you do NOT burn the sigil now, it is often advisable to never let human eyes fall upon the sigil unless they are part of the working. But this is something of a superstition and can be ignored if you do not feel any reason to hide it.

I do not banish the spirit or otherwise command it to do anything, instead I invite it to stay, or politely ask it to go, but make it clear that my intention is to go on to do other things. If the spirit wants to remain in my presence, it is welcome to do so unless I have a very pressing reason not to (family coming to visit, late for work etc.).

If you follow the proper generic ritual procedure explained earlier (empty mind state, open mind state, focus state on sigil and intent, commune state, empty mind state, release) you will maximize the calling energies, and have a much higher chance of success.

Super simpler method (advanced) - Simply visualize the spirit, and its sigil in the astral realm and call and chant its name as specified. For a spirit you have a strong relationship with, this is often all you will need. But it is still wise to do a more complete ritual from time to time to pay the spirit respect and devotion. As they will do the same for you…

Ceremonial Ritual

This is often the optimal way for a novice or neophyte to begin working with magick and spirits in general. This is because the procedures themselves can "feel" magickal and create a kind of magick performance art that puts them in the magickal mindset and mood. It builds on the idea that the more we believe we are doing real magick, the more real magick we are doing.

If you are new to magick and have no idea of your abilities and didn't get anything out of the simple chaos methods above, then this may help break the ice.

Ceremonial magick can be simple or complex, and I find simpler ceremonial rituals to be more useful and effective. IT allows you to generate energy from the environment and helps align your attention to the magickal forces around you.

Furthermore, many spirits bask in the energy of such rituals and while many won't "ask" for it, many respond and manifest more profoundly during ceremonial rituals. I often suggest that the first time you really try to contact a powerful spirit, you attempt it via a complete ceremonial ritual and set up your altar for maximal energy.

The irony is, ceremonial spirit calling is basically Chaos Spirit calling with some added bells and whistles, setting up something that is more procedural and has more physical props.

The key difference is the altar, which must be activated, the use of occult poetry (the magick words), and the attention to detail and the ritualized manipulation of energy through the working.

These rituals follow the same method as described earlier where we clear the slate of our minds, enter an open trance in ritual, call to the spirit with deep focus, then commune for a while in open minded trance, before finally going back to empty mind and ending the ritual and saying farewell to the spirit.

There is no "Wrong" way to do this, rather, there is a way that feels "right" to you. I can only advise you here, I cannot hold your hand or give you an exact method.

But I can show you examples of my Altar set up and explain them. In the next photo you will see a standard setup I use for working with the great duke - Dantalion.

I setup the Trinity of Self much as I do in the standard method, and in he center (the objective circle), I place my idol/anchor object (in this case a small crystal ball) where I plan on gazing and scrying after I have confirmed that he has responded to my call.

I rest the Sigil on his anchor object/idol and use that as a portal that connects his energy and astral home to my ritual chamber. I then look for him in the crystal, or just speak to him as part of the communion process.

This particular setup can be altered, emulated, or changed

as you see fit.

Example – 1: Dantalion

Sometimes I place the Offering Cauldron in the center and keep the Idol of the spirit in the Void plane, to give the spirit more energy for manifesting in the offering cauldrons fire. But this is not by any means a technical necessity, the trinity is just lines on cloth… It is more like a way for me to inspire myself to push more energy into the cauldron and really encourage the spirit to manifest for me.

Example – 2: Malphas

In other examples I set up my ritual space so that I place the objective tool (in this case my large scrying ball) I want to work with in part of the trinity that fits the situation best, and the spirits sigil may go elsewhere.

In this next example I am working with Lucifer to perform an Eye of the Storm rite for a customer, using the large scrying ball to seek out a client's personal sign for them in the void.

In this case I call to Lucifer and make a strong connection to him and my familiar and together we seek out the sign my client needs to see in Void via the visions of astral realm… In other words, since I cannot take my mind into the void, I go to a place in the astral realm that is like a place of interface with the void and ask Lucifer and my familiar to guide me in finding a sigil that will help my client "wake up."

Example – 3: Eye of the Storm Ritual

So, let me now give you a fairly straightforward example of a ritualized Calling in detail, using King Paimon as the objective spirit on the following pages.

Ceremony to Initiate with King Paimon

This is an example of a long form ritual, consider this a valid format for any and all spirit calling unless the spirit has unique needs.

To use this for other spirits, change the specific occult poetry, sigil, offerings, candle colors and other small details as you feel needed. If you are unsure, you can always use black, red or white candles for any spirit, though I find black to be the most universal of all.

Incense is always a valid offering as is blood if you are unsure. Wine, or Mead are excellent drink offerings for almost any spirit, as are fruit and meats and cheeses for physical solid offerings. You can also offer semi-precious stones (the cheap variety you buy at new age shops - Amethyst for example).

I know some of you reading this will want me to give you a more in depth method for each spirit in the book, but the purpose of this is to give you an example, then tell you that it is open to any and all interpretation, because these spirits do NOT NEED it to be "right" they need you to connect to them in ritual, and that is all this is… a gate, a conduit, a doorway. Decorate it however you feel is best.

Preparation – Read and commit to memory the basic symbolic details about the great King Paimon, how he looks, what his specialties are, what his personality is like. Sometimes just by doing this strongly enough with intent a spirit will manifest for us.

Gather offerings and materials: King Paimon likes treats, and sweets, basically salty sweet, yummy junk food, candy, fine fruit, cake etc. Imagine a nomadic desert king sitting around on his pile of cushions eating grapes and oysters and drinking fine wine, or soda pop (I know soda pop doesn't sound all that classy, but he loves the stuff).

You will need some sort of altar anchor, or idol for the centerpiece of the altar. This can be simply the spirits sigil, but I like to have a solid object or idol to prop the sigil

against. If you refer to my first example altar in the last section (the one for Dantalion) we are going to be replicating that set up here.

Consider King Paimon's imagery and symbolism, a great king, a camel, deserts… And select an idol or anchor accordingly. I cannot tell you what to put here, but he REALLY likes things that are made or selected with love and from the heart. Painting his portrait or sculpting an idol for him would put him over the moon!

Alternatively, if you just can't select something, place your scrying crystal here, and prop the sigil against this, or just place his sigil in the center of the altar lying flat.

King Paimon isn't too particular about incenses, but I have had good luck with Frankincense and Myrrh, Sandalwood and Dragons blood either individually or burned at once.

King Paimon loves singing, art, and performances.

Timing – King Paimon can be called, day or night, but he seems to be most strong in the day or when the sun is low in the west, or while scrying into bright flame and fire.

Set up your altar -

- Align yourself and or your altar so that you or the energy of the ritual is facing West to match his alignment. Set up the altar in the typical way (as described in the section using the trinity in ritual, or as shown in the Example with Dantalion in the last section).

- Place your idol or anchor object or just the Kings sigil in the center of the trinity.

- Place the offering of food on the material side of the trinity, and drink on the Astral side of the trinity.

- Place your burned offering bowl and incense holder/s in the Void section of the Trinity.

- Reminder - Typically, I will place earth/ food and other solid offerings in the material portion of the Trinity (the space between mind and body), and liquid/water and air/smoke offerings in the Astral portion of the Trinity (between the mind and the spirit aspects). And smoke fire and 5th element/spiritual things in the void part of the trinity.

- Remember to try to balance out the energy of the altar by way of aesthetics and what feels right, if it looks unbalanced or "wrong" adjust it so it looks right to you. Consider the "elements" on the altar and energetic flow as well.

Procedure:

In the late afternoon or early evening around sunrise while the sun is still visible and bright, enter your ritual space and align and clear the ritual chamber.

Enter an Empty minded state for at least one minute.

Now, One by one, take hold of the 3 aspect candles enter a focused state and infuse them with the energy of your intention, taking care to differentiate the role each aspect of self will play in this ritual, the green candle is for mind, the red, for body and the blue for spirit… Place them back on the altar, and pick up or hold the Idol or anchor in the center of the altar, and push your energy and intention into it.

Sit in quiet empty mind contemplation for a moment to break your connection to the candles and begin lighting the candles. The best order is Mind, Body, Spirit, then the Kings Candle.

Take hold of the food offering and charge it with the intent and energy of the calling.

Take hold of the liquid offering or water element and charge it with the intention and energy of the calling.

Take hold of the incense and charge it with the intention and energy of the calling.

When all these have been prepared, say these words over them and the Altar while projecting your intention and energy into the altar and everything upon it:

Before me I the Sorcerer/sorceress (recite your magick name and make your magick sign in the air) ***prepare the altar of calling in the name of the great and mighty King Paimon, favorite and loyal companion of Lucifer. King Paimon please hear my call!***

Now prepare the Kings Sigil on a piece of burnable paper, if you wish to use one of my personal artistic sigils, you may do so, but MAKE SURE you spend time in focused meditation as you draw it, or if you use a photocopy from the book, you can do this tracing the sigil with your finger or some other device to infuse your energy and intention into it. Merely printing it or copying it won't do much.

When the sigil is prepared, you may anoint it with your blood if that feels right to you, if you are unsure, do not. King Paimon does not require or prefer blood offerings, but I have found that blood on sigils always empowers them more for me. Still, I never give him blood and he is quite happy that I don't.

When the sigil is fully prepared place it so that it is leaning against the idol/anchor at around say a 45-degree angle to make it easy to see, but whatever angle keeps it standing and visible is best.

You will now recite the following:

Before me is the gate of the great King Paimon
It lies upon the altar of calling
By my intention and by my will
By the holistic trinity of self
And with the authority of Lucifer I (recite your magickal name while making your magick sign in the air) *call to you!*
Come, Great King Paimon!
Come before me and commune with me in mutual friendship and honor!

(Pause for a bit to commune with the building energy, reach out with your mind and feelings to see if anything has changed.)

I give to you these humble offerings of (name your offerings, incense, food, drink, song, blood etc.).
I would initiate myself into your good favor and become an ally to you and join you in spirit and purpose.
Hear me o great King! I open your gate and await your mighty sign!

Now enter a focused trance state and activate the sigil as described in the methodology section by focusing your attention and energy into it while chanting or singing King Paimon's name as given in the Catalogue of Kings Section of the book). Focus your intention not on the DESIRE of Calling him, but on visualizing, feeling and seeing him appear in your presence in some way. If you get the feeling he is here or is in a certain part of the chamber, or something paranormal (like a poltergeist) happens, respond to it, focus your attention on it, and know that King Paimon is here!

The key here is to have patience, and to role play the act of calling to the king. Even if you do not feel anything, pour your energy and emotions into it. Chant his name with feeling and intention, know that he hears you, and may already be here with you now speaking but you might not be able to hear him due to your own shortcoming.

Again, when you DO make contact - remember to ALWAYS address and call to him as KING Paimon, never just Paimon.

If nothing is happening, simply have patience, and dwell upon the sigil until you begin to feel the sigil is activated and opened. If you cannot ascertain this due to lack of training, simple stare at it until it begins to morph and practically leap off the page into the air above the paper.

When you are certain it is open, or you give up on trying due to exhaustion or significant inconvenience, you can relax into an open mind state, and stare into the candle flames, Idol, or remain focused on the Sigil while chanting his name or singing his name. call to him and ask him to appear for you, to give you a sign or send you a message. Keep your mind open and in a scrying gaze and feel the world around you without fear, or judgement, be open to any sign!

At this point you should already feel his presence; he may announce himself to you with a thunderous "sound" or may simply bring chills up and down your spine or any other sign of spiritual presence and communication. Watch the candle flame for strange movement, watch the incense, listen for sounds, ask for signs etc.

At this point, depending on what form of communication is going on, you may wish to declare your intention with him, or merely commune with him openly and without format.

You do NOT need to follow a format from here on out, but I recommend the following (change the wording however you wish):

Great and mighty King Paimon
I come before you, an initiate of Lucifer
I seek your alliance, your guidance and your knowledge
I hereby dedicate my path to your wisdom
I ask that you guide me on this path and make of me an example of your skill, and knowledge, make me known and popular with those who would benefit me
In return I shall be your willing and joyful ally and return your favor in kind.
I shall heed your call and make available my time and resources to better your causes.
(Optional - declare any special long term offering or devotion you have in mind, if any, now. King Paimon likes people to lead and be well known and to proclaim his name and deeds to the world consider something like that as an offering)
If this pleases you oh great king, it will be done!

Depending on the response you are getting and your sensitivity you may get an obvious response, and should now commune with him, if you haven't already. This may be a one way or two-way street, if you are insensitive to spiritual forces you may not get anything at all.

Regardless, remember to maintain respectful, do not grovel or beg, do not be rude but be direct and declare your intentions and desires clearly. Remember he requires answers to all questions and will be equally forthcoming with his own replies.

Make sure to formally give him his offerings and try to keep the incense going throughout the ritual, if it burns out, prepare and light more. Ask him if there are any special things he would like (be a good host) and if you don't have it, be eager and able to try to offer it next time.

If you feel safe and open with this spirit, invite him to enter you (invocation) while you consume a portion of this offering so that he may enjoy the experience (if this happens, buckle up, sometimes depending on your sensitivity, this can be intense). Otherwise feel free to make the offering any other way you see fit, or some combination of ways (for example burning a small portion and eating a small portion and burying the rest).

If you do not know what you can do to make an offering to a spirit, go back and read the Methodology section under Pathworking with spirits – Making Pacts and offerings.

Regardless, even if you fail to get a strong manifestation of his presence, still make sure you tell him your intentions and that you with to initiate yourself with him and make yourself an ally of his and vice versa. For now, simply pretend he is there listening, because he likely is.

This initiation may require the making a of a pact, you should think about something you can do or offer to him in return for his lifelong dedication to your intention to be allied with him. This could be in the form of regular dedication and offering, making something of grand significance or lasting value (such as a painting or song in his honor etc.).

The pact becomes official when you and the spirit say it is, or at the close of this ritual when you say "So, it is done!"

You may wish to scribe a contract for the pact, signing your name in blood with a smear of blood over your ink signature to make it official.

When you feel you have said and done all that needs to be said, assuming everything goes well, and you are ready to bring the ritual to a close recite the following:

Thank you, dear king, for coming into my humble chamber (ritual space).
I invite you to stay as long as you like, and I will continue to be open to your gnosis.

If it pleases you, I will now burn the sigil in your honor so that you may consume the energy of the gate. (This is doubly important if it is anointed with blood - be open to any sign he does not want this, if you get no indication of displeasure, burn the sigil in the burned offering bowl now.)
I (state your magick name and make your sign over the altar) *Now declare this ritual of calling ended, and all pacts binding!*

So, it is DONE!

Conclusion – As always be open to any signs, or gnosis from this point on, especially if you did not get the strong impression, he was present for the ritual in some way. You SHOULD have some sense he was present if you have mastered the skills, I taught you in the methodology section of the book.

If this is part of your initiation with the 9 kings, then prepare to do the same kind of ritual for each of them, substituting applicable words, names and symbols, and even making it more elaborate with actual poetry and song as desired.

From this point on you may continue to use this longer format ritual to work with King Paimon or all spirits or attempt to use the shorter form.

Which consists of little more than lighting a candle, creating a sigil, activating it, calling to the spirit in meditative trance, and offering incense as explained before.

Or as also said before potentially just chanting the spirits name and entering a trance.

Continued pathworking

At this point you have completed the basic steps of the pathworking and have made an initial calling and pact of alliance with Lucifer and the 9 Goetic kings. If you have skipped any of that for any reason, that is ok, you can technically do any of these rituals at any point, but it helps if you make a strong introduction with the spirit in question or all the kings first. The lesser spirits will be far more agreeable and helpful if you make pacts with the kings or at least do an introductory ritual with the specific spirit first - But even this is not required.

These rituals all built upon what you have done so far, and thus the procedure will be simplified and will focus on the part of the ritual that contains the purpose of the ritual itself.

I will not reprint the usual method of calling for example. We shall begin with a series of consecrations to illustrate the potential of what spirits can do and how we might gain their aid.

There is nothing mechanical to any of this, all this information can be gleaned by working with spirits and asking them for guidance and instruction. If you wish to change any of it, do so. The point of this pathworking isn't to teach you how to do my magick, but to inspire you to seek your own.

Consecration of a Crystal Ball (The Demons eye)

Any spirit in the Goetia can be useful for this that has a description that sounds like it includes telling you the past, present future, the secrets of someone or something or anything that sounds clearly related to knowing things of a divinatory nature.

It should be mentioned that like Mirrors, Crystal balls need not be thought of just scrying devices in the divinatory sense but can also be useful as portals for spirits to gain access to our world and communicate with us more effectively.

My recommendation for a king to use in the consecration of a Crystal ball would be Balam, Purson, Vine or Asmoday/Asmodeus. You could technically consecrate one to each of them, and to any number of other spirits that are known for divinatory skill, each will impart a slightly different flavor or focus on divination to the ball, Purson might be more concerned with visions about finances, wealth, treasure and similar things. While Vine may be more inclined to reveal your enemies to you. Explore the entire Goetia for other options and see what you can ascertain the flavor to be of each Spirit. Again, keeping in mind this is not a limitation, just a specialty.

This is one of the simpler rituals to perform and so we shall show it first.

Ingredients –

- **1 Crystal ball (or other refined shape such as a cube or pyramid)** – This should be REAL crystal, either Quartz, Obsidian, Amethyst or other quality gemstone. I would make sure the size is at least around 2 inches in diameter. Crystal balls do not need to be expensive or large. Some people prefer the clear lab grown/recombined quartz, while others prefer the natural type with streaks and inclusions because they create more random patterns. Others prefer black obsidian or rainbow Obsidian or other materials because they reflect and shimmer.

- **Mugwort/Wormwood/Artemisia** – This is often dried and bundled for Tea, smudging and incense and may be in a bundle with sage or other ingredients. Mugwort is of the Artemisia family, and there are several versions (Vulgaris = Mugwort, Absinthium used in making absinth, and aborescens AKA Wormwood) used in many traditions for helping the sensitive induce visions. Protection, warding off insects and more. We will be using some of this to consecrate, the rest can be retained for use during actual scrying if desired but is not required.

- **Sea Salt** – Enough to create a mound to use as a

stable base for the crystal to rest on.

- **Cauldron/burning bowl** – We will be making use of raw dried herb (Mugwort) in the course of this ritual. Make sure to fill the bottom cauldron with at least about a quarter to half an inch or so of fresh sea salt.

- **Altar** – Set up for a calling of the spirit you have selected (make sure you have the correct offering and special considerations taken care of).

Preparation –

- Perform this ritual on the night of the full moon, or lunar eclipse.

- Prior to the ritual, take the Crystal ball and run it under cold running water, either in a running stream or in tap water for roughly one minute. This will clear and charge it with neutral energy. Allow it to air dray and wrap the ball in black silk or black velvet until ready to use in the ritual.

- You will also need to think of a worthy offering to give to the demon you have chosen in return for its favors in this matter. This can be a onetime offering, or a pledge of service of some kind. I would recommend offering the spirit an offering of Mugwort whenever you use this Crystal, this serves several purposes, as Mugwort also heightens visions.

Procedure –

After you have called the spirit of your choice and made contact, declare your intentions in your own words, tell the spirit that you wish to dedicate this crystal ball to you. Tell it what you have in mind to give the spirit for this or ask it what it wants.

Think carefully about any emphasis you want to put on this based on the spirits potential. For example, if you are using Purson, perhaps specify that you wish this crystal ball to help bring you financial opportunity and show you hidden treasures in your life.

Now, move the candle you used to summon the spirit and the sigil you are using as a gate, and move it to the Void plane part of the Trinity of Self.

Take the sea salt and pour it onto the table in the center of the trinity of self, creating a small mound large enough to create a kind of resting place/pedestal for the Crystal ball.

Take hold of some of your Mugwort and charge it with your intent and energy, picture yourself using the crystal ball for scrying, picture the vivid images and how this Mugwort will cleanse and empower your crystal.

Create a small depression in the salt and place a pinch of the Mugwort in this depression.

Take the Rest of the Mugwort, assuming it is the dried bundle take a small amount, and light it until it smolders, if this is in tea form you can place this on a charcoal puck. Either way once it is going good and smoking, place this in the cauldron (unless already on the charcoal) and make your magick symbol in the air over the cauldron recite the following:

> *Gift of Artemis goddess of the hunt and the moon*
> *Bane of Insect, Bringer of deep Visions*
> *Let this offering of smoke cleanse and prepare this crystal*
> *As the delicate clouds cleanse and prepare the moon*
> *Let this offering please (the Demons name and title)*
> *(Take hold of the crystal and hold it in the smoke of the Mugwort)*
> *Fill this vessel with your demons' sight mighty (demons name and title)!*
> *Let this become my demons' eye so that I may see that which is unseen.*

Hold the crystal in the smoke and commune with the spirit/s as long as you feel is right, try to feel the crystal ball growing more powerful, imagine inside of it is a sleeping eye that is gradually opening. When the eye is fully open, and the crystal is empowered, remove it from the smoke and place it onto the mound of salt and Mugwort and recite the following:

Behold!

The eye of (demons name and title)

Let it now rest and dream in peace.

Laid upon lovingly upon this bed of absolute purity,

protection and in the arms of Artemis.

Let no one willfully interrupt its slumber or suffer a

fate of restless doom...

In the morning I shall collect this treasure and place

it in a place of honor, swaddled in black (silk/Velvet)

so it may rest in peace and luxury until such time as I

need a vision.

This concludes the ritual; you may commune with the spirit as you wish and conclude the calling in the usual manner at any time.

From this point forward this crystal ball should be covered in black silk or velvet and when used an offering of Mugwort should be burned in honor of the spirit even if not part of the initial pact as Mugwort is a potent scrying enhancer.

Consecration of a ring of power to Beleth

It should be clear from the description of Beleth in the Goetia that he has a thing for rings. This ritual is designed to teach you how to consecrate a Ring to this spirit to make it a powerful talisman of power that you can use for the specific purpose of invoking his power to help influence others think about you the way you wish.

This ring is not going to brainwash people, but it should help you with your confidence and ability to act noble and impress people and gain their love and respect, or fear and respect, whichever you wish.

Once this ritual is completed, it is advisable to make this ring a regular part of your ritual garb when working with Beleth as this will please him greatly.

Please take careful note of the velvet bag and the requirement to retain the rose remains, this is a symbolic gesture of your honor and determination to use this power wisely as a king. If you wish to end the power this ring has for any reason, you will take this velvet bag and cast it upon a fire, and the spell you have over anyone by way of this ring will be broken and the ring will become inert, the pact ended.

Beware, the wording and intention of this ring is such that it can create powerful influences on people who you use it on. Technically you should have power to end these relationships at will, however there is a risk these people will become obsessed with you. These people may even become as slaves to your will in some way as Beleth is not merely a demon of love and affection but controlling those who fall under this spell until we are satisfied.

With each new relationship you make by way of this ring will empower this ring and be as an offering to Beleth. This means it is in his interest to bring love and respect, and all manner of favor from strangers, so do not wear it out. Only when you seek the power it represents. Or you can potentially create problems for yourself.

You can of course change the wording of my occult poetry but be sure to consider all changes carefully.

Ingredients -

The Ring of Power – This is the key ingredient, Beleth seems to prefer silver rings worn on the left hand, but I have found any reasonable quality silvery metallic ring that is not easily stained or tarnished and is not yellow gold is acceptable to him. Some examples would be Titanium, Stainless steel, and of course silver. This can be a cheap costume quality ring (there are many charming or cool looking rings you can buy online for less than 30$ that would work). Of course, a valuable ring or heirloom is a better ring.

3 roses – one each of Red, White, Yellow (fresh cut or living, represent the 3 main kinds of love, romantic, friendship and pure/royal)

Wine - Deep Red Wine for offering goblet

Bloodletting tool

Incense - Cinnamon Incense and Dragons blood incense

Earth element - Fertile potting soil or Sea Salt for offering bowl

Fuel for Burner – 75% or higher rubbing alcohol and sea salt in the burning bowl. OR charcoal disk (used for Hookahs and incense resin) and Sea salt. For this ritual, the charcoal is the most optimal as it will allow the plant material to smolder and burn more evenly as they are not dry and may not burn at all in regular Cauldron fire.

Small pouch - A small drawstring velvet pouch (any color, Red is best), large enough to hold the remains of the 3 roses when they have dried (can be crushed or shredded if needed to make them fit).

Preparation –

This is one of those rituals that will require you to be in your prime condition, the best ritual robes, the best fragrances, and washed with natural substances, avoid the off the shelf designer body wash perfumes… Do your hair, your nails, your makeup, primp and preen and prepare yourself like you are going out for the hottest date of your life combined with a job interview that you absolutely cannot fail at. (no pressure).

Procedure -

Prepare the burned offering bowl/Cauldron - Pour about ¼ inch of sea salt into the base of the burning bowl and pour a nearly equal amount of rubbing alcohol into the sea salt and if possible, cover it to retain potency. If using charcoal instead, you may light this now as it burns for a long time, do not cover the bowl.

Next, arrange your altar to be suitable for a full ceremonial calling of the Demon King Beleth. Call King Beleth into your ritual chamber and tell him of your intention to consecrate a ring to him and tell him that you want it to symbolize your relationship to him and aid you in all things related to influencing people and being able to gain their love, trust and respect, or to intimidate them and make them fear you. If he reacts favorably to this request, or you do not get any objection continue:

Tear off 1 (ONE) of the finest and or most colorful petals from each of the 3 roses and set them aside. Group the 3 roses together and insert the stems into the ring and bring the ring about halfway up the stems toward the rose heads. Place the ring in the center of the Trinity of self, (move the Central pillar candle and Beleth's sigil to the void Plane on the altar).

Use your bloodletting tool to draw enough blood to put a few drops of blood on the ring, the bundle of flowers, and on each of the 3 rose petals, and on Beleth's Sigil if not already applied to the sigil.

During/after doing this recite the following:

The Love of Noble friends
The Love of the Pure and innocent
The Love of the lustful and passionate
United in blood the 3 lovers are bound
Ensorcelled by the power of this ring and my intention and will!
Bound they shall remain until such time as I am done
From each new love an offering is made
For King Beleth, A tribute to his nobility and grace.
Let this ring hold your power and authority in all matters of the heart
So long as these roses remain, this power be mine!

If these roses burn, the spell shall be broken and those under its power will become amicable and at peace but trouble me no more.

Now ignite the burning bowl if you haven't done so already and make your sign over the entire altar and say aloud:

To the great King Beleth I (say your magickal name) give the first offering as a sign of my devotion to this pact!

Now take the 3 rose petals you pulled off before that have been anointed in blood.

Place the White one, in the red wine.
Place (poke it down into) the yellow one in the Soil/Sea salt offering bowl
Place the Red one in the Cauldron fire (on the charcoal or simply toss it into the fire depending on what setup you have chosen).
Now speak aloud —

This offering shall remain on this altar for 7 days. I will do no other working upon this sacred Altar in all this time. This ring and these offerings shall not be disturbed! May any who willfully disturb our working suffer remarkable penalty!

Now you may thank the spirit and dismiss it in the usual manner, but do NOT burn the Demons sigil unless commanded by the spirit to do so, this gate need to remain open for the duration of the next 7 days! You may of course close the ritual or commune with it as you see fit. (you can extinguish the cauldron fire if it becomes prudent to do so, as this can get hot and cause fires).

Conclusion - Allow the Altar to rest for 7 full days, at the end of the 7th day, return to the altar and take the ring off the rose stems and wear the ring whispering thanks and admiration to the mighty King Beleth, light his sigil on fire and give it in offering to him in the burning bowl, closing the astral gateway and giving thanks to him for his blessing.

Admire the energy this ring now has. When not in use this ring should be placed in a place of honor, either on your altar, or in a fine storage box such as the one it came in. The roses should be dead a desiccated to some degree and be crunchy or stale. Carefully gather them up and place them into the velvet bag, it's ok to damage them, just make sure you gather up all of it, try not to leave any remains on the altar.

The ritual offerings that remain (the wine – if it wasn't drank, and soil and the burned offering bowl) should also be gathered up and taken outside for disposal in a reasonable and respectable place.

This ring is now a powerful object that can strongly influence your relationships however you wish. As you use this ring, it and your power will grow little by little. If at any time you feel it has become too powerful, or you wish to forcibly break the power this ring has over anyone who might become obsessive with you, burn the velvet bag with the roses inside. The ring will return to being inert.

Breaking the binds forced upon us (Using King Vine)

There are many ways that baneful magick can happen to us, and in many ways, the most common form of baneful magick is the binding. You see, binding magick isn't just a thing that is done intentionally to keep us from being able to act or otherwise use magick.

Binding can very reasonably be seen as any form of negative energy that impedes our will and keeps us from achieving our goals and potential.

The nature of magick is such that we can be easily bound by mundane people, whose hate or anger or other negative emotions toward us, can cause their subconscious astral body to work against us, binding us in the sticky tar of their disdain.

I developed this simple ritual with the help of Vine to aid me in breaking a powerful binding spell that was placed on me by a former friend who had tried to save me from myself when I was a lost soul. When I was at the mercy of the darkness all around me and was using my power in ways that were toxic and dangerous not only to myself but others.

It was one of the last acts of his life, as he died that same year, and I have only minimal doubt that the reason for his passing when he did, had a lot to do with that binding... The spirits that were cut off from me through that one act were powerful and vengeful...

The last spell of a dying man is a potent thing.

When I had my reawakening to magick in the late summer of 2018, I must have somehow satisfied some condition of his binding. Through my spiritual evolution in Zen mysticism, and stabilization of my life, I had found peace and compassion at long last.

It was only a matter of time before the spirit world took me by the hand again.

But the influence of his binding magick on me was still felt, and I could tell I was unable to quite reach certain places in magick I once knew to be easy for me.

Through a combination of scrying and a lucky video recommendation I stumbled upon King Vine. I saw his specialties included breaking down walls, and I knew this was a good choice for a spirit to free me of this weakness.

In the course of invoking Vine and being inspired for this ritual I learned that it isn't just a spell to do when someone has you bewitched.

But is also a powerful symbolic ritual of self-empowerment that helps you break the bonds of ALL negative influences on your power.

It breaks down ALL the walls that bind you, not just hose put there by a sorcerer.

Do you work in a toxic work environment where you are constantly berated by rude and hateful coworkers? Get passed over time and again by nepotistic managers that hate you?

Struggling with a crippling habit that is keeping you bound and limited in some way?

Think someone is trying to manipulate you with love magick to bend you to their will?

Having a hard time accomplishing goals or succeeding even at trivial things?

You might find some help in this ritual…

This ritual is something that can be done more than once, but you must have faith that this ritual has the power to break any binding placed upon you and performing it multiple times will not be needed for the same binding force.

However, binding forces can return, they can be refreshed and reapplied, especially if the source of them is every day, mundane hatred and social issues.

So, on the one hand, feel free to do this as often as you need it, but do not repeat it for the same thing twice unless it is a separate binding (IE someone put it back somehow).

If you are having regular attacks made against you, you need to build some defenses, and or make sure that in the closing of this ritual you empower Vine to go out and deal with those hampering you in some way.

Addiction is difficult and your body can and will resist you, and so it may be necessary to repeat this ritual to help you keep your control. This is the only exception to the rule of not repeating the ritual for the same issue. Keep in mind, if you must keep repeating it, even for addiction, you will begin to doubt it, and it will lose potency.

Ingredients

- Your ritual Altar configured to call to Vine.

- A thin black leather cord, I like to use necklace cord, but any cord will do.

- Incense – Cinnamon, Dragons Blood, Sage

- Offering of meat (rare or raw if possible unless you are ingesting it then prepare it safely as you wish it).

- Burning bowl/cauldron – you must be able to burn the leather cord at the end of this ritual. Use a charcoal puck or Alcohol to make a good fire or smoldering ember that can burn the leather. Burning leather is a terrible smell, bear with it, open the windows, or do this ritual outside.

Procedure

Call to Vine in the usual manner and when he has arrived and you are certain of it, explain to him your intention and ask for his aid in this matter. Tell him you want to free yourself and would like him to go and avenge you against those who caused this binding toward you, taking care not to harm a loved one who might have done this to you in the heat of anger! Or he might be indiscriminate.

Remember, Vine isn't usually very into small talk, so we will keep our ritual recitations to a minimum:

You will tie a knot in the leather cord so that it forms a loop and you will place it in the center of the ritual altar.

Ask Vine to help you gather all the negative energy and binding forces and vampiric forces that are against upon you and concentrate them into the Leather cord. The intention is for all these binding forces to become locked into the symbolism of the leather binding cord.

I need to REALLY push all your energy and intent into this. Every fiber of your being needs to be exerting itself to cleanse you of the thick sludge of negativity all over you.

Take the Leather cord in your hands and strongly visualize and FEEL all the binding forces and negativity being bound up within this cord.

When you feel the time is right, or if you wish you can ask Vine to Give you a sign that it is the right time… Take the leather cord and place one side over your hand and around your wrist, put 3 twists into it, and then loop it around your other opposite wrist simulating a kind of leather handcuffs.

Feel all remaining binding force flow into this leather handcuff and know that when you break and then destroy this leather strip, you are breaking and destroying virtually all negative energy working on you.

Recite:

Mighty King Vine
Your roar shatters armies!
Your serpent is cunning and cruel!
Your stallion is swift and strong!
Grant to me these gifts so that I may, in my hour of need!
Give me the strength to destroy these binds!

You will now take a deep breath, and then sharply exhale and pull your hands apart forcefully like super hero breaking the chains that bind them. The leather cord should break and may fly across the room in the process.

Go quickly and fetch it and say the following – regardless:

Oh, Mighty King Vine, I thank you for the gift of strength and freedom. I bring to you an offering of flesh and blood and ask that you also take from this world the negative and binding energies contained in the remains of this cord.
Use this to track down the source or sources of this binding force and reveal them to me. If it serves me, destroy them with your terrible storms in such a way so that they know to fear me and my wrath!

King Vine, erect high and strong towers to fortify me and my energy, to help me fend off these negative influences again more easily.

If you lack the strength to physically break the binds, then request that Vine give you the strength and while still on your wrists, hold it over an open flame such as a candle till it cuts through.

When this cord is broken, you should feel a wave of relief or energy return to you.

As soon as you begin to feel this way, throw the Leather cord into the Cauldron and light it on fire. Make sure it burns all the way through, try not to let any recognizable pieces remain.

This is a good time to make all your offerings to Vine and thank him again and end the ritual in the usual manner.

A simple Candle Spell

So far, we have only been doing Demon sorcery, however, that is not the full extent of our magick, not by a long shot. I usually prefer to invoke the power of various gods and demons in my magick, but sometimes this really isn't needed.

I often say that anything we can do with the aid of a demon or other spirit, we can do without it, and vice versa. So, if you like, you can of course empower this spell by invoking a demon or other spirit. But the purpose of this example spell is to show you how you can use basic Candle Magick to manifest something.

Candle magick is a very popular and common way to create change and manifest our will. As previously explained in the Methodology section under Energy work, we brought how Candles can be charged with our intention and when they burn down, they can cause manifestation of our will.

You may be wondering, why use a candle at all? Why not simply make it real in the astral world and let the energy go?

This is a valid question, and I would begin by reminding you, that much of this is symbolic. We technically do not NEED a candle. But candles have a unique set of symbolic properties that create a sympathetic symbolism that creates a holistic path for our will to manifest.

The first quality candles have is of course they can be colored (preferably through the whole candle not just the outside). This color can be symbolic of our intent, reinforcing our sympathetic magick.

The Second is the fact that they are soft and easily changed. We can easily MOLD and shape the wax of the candle with our will inscribing it with sigils, designs, or shaping it to match a theme or desire. We can for example create or purchase red candles in the shape of two lovers embracing, inscribe them with the names of our lovers, then charge the candle with our intention and energy and burn the candle.

This moldability doesn't just apply to its physical properties, but by way of the sympathetic principle of magick to its energy body.

In other words, Candles can be molded Holistically on all levels!

Of course, sigils are just as useful for this, as is a painting, or even a book. But candles have one other unique property that helps set them apart.

While a sigil can be burned and so can a book, a Candle burns slowly, and it feeds upon the wax of the candle by transforming it (transmuting it) from a solid, to an oily liquid, bringing it one step closer to the 5th element.

This oil is then consumed by the flame of the wick, burning up and in so doing it transforms yet again, and then becomes the 5th element.

In other words, the candle takes our holistic will and intent, and creates a medium for manifestation in the material objective world by literally changing the world around it in a subtle way (gasses, smoke, heat etc).

In this spell you will use he Candle as a manifestation medium and inscribe upon it a Sigil much the same way you would a paper sigil. You will charge the candle with your will and use the power of the Trinity of Self to bring your manifestation to life.

Some traditions can get very elaborate with this, anointing the candle in magick oils and oleum's, and this is a fine thing to do if you wish to learn, but I never use them.

The first step is the same as with all sigil magick, you will first come up with a sentence that defines the manifestation.

For example: "I found money." Or "Brian Asked me out" or "I successfully quit smoking."

Following the same rules for sigils outlined in earlier chapters, create a rough draft of your sigil and then when you are satisfied with it, using your fingernail or your ritual dagger transfer it to a candle.

I like to use small ritual candles about 5 inches long and about half an inch to an inch wide. They last about 3-4 hours at most, usually a lot less. If you don't have a supply of them, any kind will do, but it must be a NEW candle, and it must burn down all the way without extinguishing it unless it is designed to burn for days at a time. (this is why I prefer simpler smaller candles, bigger candles aren't more powerful, and smaller aren't technically less powerful)

Try to pick a candle color that represents the spirits of your intention, red for love and lust, yellow for friendship or happiness, green for money, blue for spiritual things. Black and White are also universal, though black is usually for darker Yin oriented things, and white for positive yang-oriented things.

Procedure –

Set up your Altar, place sea salt in the offering bowl on the material plane, water in the goblet on the Astral plane, incense and burning bowl in the void plane. Prepare and charge your altar candles and your incense.

Align and clear your ritual space and light the Trinity/Altar candles (not the special one we are using however) and the incense.

Take hold of your prepared candle (and candle holder if it has one), Take your bloodletting tool and anoint the sigil with your blood, opening a direct conduit to the candle's energy.

This works all the better if you are in physical contact with the blood on the candle.

Enter a focused state of mind.

Focus intently on the intent and energy of your stated intention and push every ounce of energy into it you can muster, hold a vision of the outcome in your mind and see it flowing into the candle through your astral body.

Imagine the universe in which your will has manifested and imagine that this candle is part of that world, imagine pulling that candle through the trinity of self and the astral world and making it the candle you are holding in your hands right now, literally bringing a piece of an alternate reality into your hands and into this world.

Imagine the Candle wax being filled with the shape of things to come, confirming to your will as it might conform to a mold. Squeeze the candle and press into the sigil almost to the point of damaging it. If your pressure and heat from your hand shapes the candle somehow without breaking it, that is fine.

When you are certain you have drained yourself of all your energy, place the candle in its holder in the center of the

Trinity and focus on it again, making sure you have given it all your energy.

When you are ready, light the candle, and say the following over it:

> *It is by the will of (state your magick name and make your sign) that the empower vessel before me shall manifest my intention to the world. As it burns down, the world shall become as I desire, let no one willfully interfere!*
> *IT IS DONE!*

At this point, you will enter an empty mind state, and break your connection to the Altar and its energy and the candle, you need to let the candle do its thing. Walk away and do not look back. Let all the candles and the incense burn in peace and check on it only for safety sake as it is an open flame.

When the ritual candle has burned out and has been reduced to a puddle or been consumed, you may extinguish your regular Altar Candles, or let them burn whichever feels more appropriate to you.

There are many ways to augment this candle spell, you can add everything from Tarot cards, or Runes that represent your intention, placing them on the altar to impart their symbolism.

You can anoint the candle with oils and oleum, press things into it that symbolize your desire (for example press a coin into it to represent money). You can place the candle on top of symbolic things like cash, or a picture of your target if this is a baneful spell.

The key here is to know that your imagination and intuition is what is needed, not a specific spell or formula. Be creative, and research things that might be empowering and symbolic to you of the thing you are trying to do.

King Paimon's Blessed Blend

In this simple exercise, we will be creating a mystical blend using a few potent herbs to help us enter a deep lucid state of relaxation, to be used in scrying, dream work, or astral projection.

This simple procedure will require making the herbal blend in a ritualized state of mind, calling upon King Balam to empower the herbs for the purpose of Scrying and astral visions. All these ingredients should be legal in all 50 states, and available online or at your local well stocked occult apothecary.

Amounts are in ratio format (so you can use a tablespoon, measuring cup etc)

Materials – (remove seed and stem of all herbs)

Mugwort: 4 parts
Damiana: 4 parts
Flavoring options (pick one)
- Peppermint 1-2 parts to taste
- star anise (1 part = 1 or 2 seed clusters crushed into coarse flakes/powder)
- lavender: 1-2 parts
Optional for smokable – These Herbs are almost always too dry and will be harsh if smoked. Use Water 1 tablespoon (not part), honey 1-2 pea sized drops mixed into the water. This should be enough water for roughly one cup of herb mixed. If needed reduce quantity, it need not be precise, it has to just be enough to moisten/dampen the mixture for smoking in pipes and rolling papers, not make it wet and sloppy.

Preparation –

Prepare your altar as normal, align and clear if needed, then light the candles and any incense, and call upon King Paimon in whatever manner you prefer to come and oversee your procedure.

Remove all stems and seeds from herbs and mix and crush/fluff all the herbs together until thoroughly mixed. While doing this, enter a focused state and charge the mixture with your intention. Visualize, feel, and imagine the act of using this herbal blend in smoke or tea and going on powerful astral journeys, and scrying, and Lucid Dreams. Remember, present Tense, do not ASK, or Beg, or Hope. Instead fill it with the intention of completion, NOT DESIRE.

When the blend is thoroughly mixed and ready (add water and honey mixture and mix again if for smoking purposes, if not skip the water and honey completely).

Now, place it into its chosen receptacle (mason Jar for example), and place this in the center of the Altar.

Call upon King Paimon to come sample the herb mixture and to energize it with his power. Ask him to make this herbal mixture a powerful blend for magickal sight, and visions. When you have your response, give him a sample of it in offering, you may either give it in the offering bowl, burn it in the cauldron, burn it on a charcoal puck, or make a concoction of tea, or smoke and take it as part of an invocation offering as described in the Making pacts and offering section.

You can easily make a tea with this blend by buying empty tea bags online or from most stores or make it a loose tea as desired.

I prefer either tea, or smoking in a pipe. But you can roll into a cigar or cigarette. Try not to inhale much if at all. Remember smoking is deadly when done habitually, even if it does not contain tobacco.

From this point forward, this batch of this herb mix is sacred, and should always be enjoyed with INTENTION to use it as a ritual aid, astral vision quest aid, or dreaming aid. Never for casual use unless specified in the creation that it is for casual use as well.

Store the herb blend in a sacred place, it should not just go into the cupboard, consider storing it in a place of honor and respect.

Whenever you use it, call upon King Paimon to remember his blessing and to grant you a powerful vision or dream.

AFTERWORD

It is done, my intention has been made manifest, and this book exists. May the spirits be pleased, and I hope this work helped you to achieve your goals.

Remember, we covered a LOT of material, and there is a good mix of new and unique things and old and tested ideas.

My goal with this book was never to teach you formulas, but to inspire you to make your own magick your own way.

I am sure I will still get a lot of people still asking me for what symbols to use for their various magick workings, or to release more of my spells from my grimoire. And my answer to them will be:

There are reams and reams of information out there from many different traditions and cultures that will give you the inspiration and symbolism you need. My job has only been to show you the pattern, you need to use it to make the world what you will.

I am also sure that there are some very advanced people out there remarking about how a lot of the nitty gritty spells and rituals are just variations of already known magick but using the Trinity of Self as a novel new symbolic interface.

I suppose they are right, but I also hope that they gained more from this book than just a new Altar Decoration… but a change, even if only a slight one, in their perception and how they see the world.

I will let you decide what this book means to you, and how to use it, and all future works will be built upon this foundation.

I am sure, if it is popular enough, in time I will revise, and add to it. Until then…

D.H. Thorne - Mind the Shadows!

Bonus material

Sacrifice of regret to the Sin Eater Azazel

This simple rite is one that I offer as a paid service for those who need help performing it. Azazel can be a rather strict and abrupt kind of spirit, that is prone to cutting the sorcerer off or ending a ritual suddenly if the sorcerer does not take care to appeal to Azazel's intentions.

Azazel does NOT like to be tested, nor asked to perform for the sorcerer. He is very independent and willful and will give the sorcerer only that which he deems important and will resist any effort by the sorcerer to simply demand or even ask nicely for anything that isn't already his intention.

He is very helpful when it suits him however, and he gave me this ritual back in the winter of 2019 during a 30 day pathworking pact initiated during the blood moon event in February of 2019.

Up till this point, all the spirits I had worked with, had been mostly of a very agreeable demeanor and never gave me any indication of displeasure or any hint of resistance to my intentions. Azazel on the other hand, he is one of the few who is not easily swayed by the usual methods of pact making and mutual respect and is in fact quite turned off by assertiveness.

He does not seek humility, but he is a very assertive spirit, and does not respond well to any kind of disharmony.

When working with Azazel, you call him, and may make your requests, but largely he will do as he wills, and you are along for the ride.

Of course, everyone experience is different… And you may see a side of Azazel I do not see, he may be more agreeable to you. It is entirely possible that Azazel is not in full alignment with me as an individual. So, while we are not at all enemies or adversarial to one another, he may not have a great deal of affection for me either.

This is actually an important lesson for you, as you have presumably already begun your path in demon sorcerer and have at least a few spirits under your belt by now… you may have played it safe and worked with Spirits like King Paimon who are very easy going and friendly to open minded humans (and terrifying enemies to closed minded fools).

The lesson is that no matter how you see yourself, or how well you are treated by various spiritual beings… there are some who you will simply not have a strong connection or alignment with, who you will simply NOT feel comfortable with all the time.

For me Azazel is enigmatic, and while he has given me mighty gnosis and understanding, there is something about me that seems to rub him the wrong way…

But, because I work with him with respect, he and I are anything but enemies, and we always seem to fix our differences.

He is actually very forgiving, and I truly believe that his role as a teacher is to be a stern kind of teacher, one that uses and expects a lot of discipline, but behind that façade he does care for mankind very deeply, especially those who come to him as they might have in the ancients times.

I will not bore you with too much gnosis about him, there are endless books on the subject at this point as he is one of the centerpiece spirits of certain well known master occultists, and anything I would add is anecdotal at best and not as productive as what they have found. At least not at this time.

Instead I will share with you a Ritual he gave to me, that was of great use to me… it healed a very bad emotional psychological wound in my psyche based on something that I did around the age of 13. It was a thing I did out of a certain sense of desperation and misery… living in a household of chemical and substance abuse with a toxic abusive family.

I'm lucky I'm not a sociopathic murderer, but alas, I recoiled, and the situation ended as fast as it had begun and never happened again.

This was a splinter of guilt and fear that I held in my heart and mind that I bore for decades… Fear that people might find out… knowing only that I was just old enough to know better, but young enough to be unaccountable for doing it anyway…

Almost all of us have a regret, a sin, a thing we did that we feel must never been known. A thing we wish we could take back, or undo.

This thing can hold us back, make us doubt ourselves, make us feel insecure in our own skin.

Am I Evil? Or was I just a kid? I used to ask…

Azazel answered…

In the ancient times, the ancient Hebrews would conduct a ceremonial sacrifice with two goats. One was a real sacrifice to god, the other was a scapegoat, and into this goat, the elder, or chieftain would ceremonially clean the tribe of it's sins by passing them into this scapegoat, and throw it off a cliff as a sacrifice to Azazel… In this way, the sins of the tribe could be cleansed by sacrificing them to Azazel.

Well, this practice more or less ended long ago, but Azazel is still open to receiving such sacrifice.

Do not fear, there is no need to hurt an animal, but the same basic principle applies here… We make a sacrifice of our sin and regret, to the sin eater Azazel, who will take from us that burden, liberating us of our guilt, and replacing it with a blessing.

In my case, the sense of guilt over this regret was assuaged almost instantly, and I found that it never popped into my head to haunt me anymore, and I was able to think about it, without feeling even the slightest twinge of guilt or shame.

The only reason I don't shout it from the rooftops is simply a matter of politeness and a sense of privacy, knowing the world is filled with judgmental assholes who are often just itching for an excuse to shun and destroy us.

In its place I was given a great deal of peace and gnosis and support. Azazel accepted my offering and blessed me.

One of his blessings was to encourage me to take this ritual and share it with the world and perform it for those who cannot do it for themselves (and only for those people, everyone else needs to do it themselves).

Thus, a fellow practitioner must do it for themselves. Or participate in the ritual, I cannot simply do it for them and say it is done… They must be part of the exchange!

But you do not need me, assuming you have had success to this point in the book you are ready to call upon the Sin

Eater, and create a pact with him that liberates you of your pain and suffering… but be warned, Azazel, more than any other spirit I have worked with, does not submit to your rules or desires. Just because he gave me this ritual and wants others to do it… does not mean it is a black and white issue where if you do the ritual it will work.

He may refuse to help you… often causing mayhem in the ritual and forcing you to shut down mid-way…

My point is, don't expect, nor ask for fireworks… all the fireworks will be astral, not physical.

If this ritual works you will feel the burden lifted, and that alone is more than enough for many. If he is truly pleased with your offering and commitment to not reopening the wound, he will bless you with something, often the thing you asked for, but always the thing you need most.

This is a simple ritual, where you will be using the Trinity of Self Altar as you did with the Goetic spirits, except in this case, instead of calling a Goetic spirit, you will be calling Azazel.

If you are unfamiliar with Azazel, there are a number of excellent grimoires about him produced by several popular occultists. The basic story of Azazel is that he was a watcher, or Grigori, a spirit that was of special role in the Judeo-Christian pantheon of angels that were sent to guide and watch over mankind. But they became enamored with human females and lusted after them and mated with them producing the Nephilim, the men of great and Terrible Renown spoken of in Genesis 6/6.

The apocryphal book of Enoch goes into even greater detail and tells us a great deal about Azazel in particular. He is a watcher who taught mankind warfare, taught female (and presumably males) to wear makeup, how to make weapons, and work metals for weapons, and taught mankind the basic secrets of Witchcraft and magick.

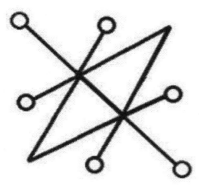

His sigil is almost identical to the Seal of Saturn (many speculate that is because he is a spirit of Saturn) and can be used like a Goetic Sigil to call upon him.

His is fond of the Color Red, and his name can be chanted thus (as with the Goetic spirits, you can use one or all of these chanted pronunciations, they have all worked for me): Ah Zah Zel, Ahzaz El, Ah Zay Zel, Ay Zay Zel,

Procedure Part 1– Call upon Azazel using the standard calling method of your choice. Azazel likes a sanctified ritual space, or an outdoor space. Always Align and clear fully for him, and make sure your ritual space is clean as can be.

When you have made his presence clear, keep in mind he does not like to be tested, or compelled in any way. Instead, commune with him, ask him to show you what you need to see, and ask him if he would be willing to participate in The Sacrifice of Regret to the Sin Eater Ritual that you got from this book.

If he agrees to your request, you may proceed, or ask him to return at a more suitable time to do the ritual.

Materials –

1 red ribbon made of burnable material (cotton fabric, paper etc). About 1-2 feet long.
1 Ritual dagger (cannot just be your fingers, Azazel requires a ritual dagger/athame).
Bloodletting tool (you can use the dagger if suitable).
The Burnt Offering Cauldron must make use of Cauldron fire (salt and rubbing alcohol mix).

In addition to the sigil for calling, you will need two additional sigils.

The first is a sigil you prepare to represent your sin or regret that you wish to sacrifice to Azazel.

The second is the nature of the blessing you wish to get in return.

The Sin sigil should be prepared like any other Chaos Sigil, by making a sentence in the present tense, use the following format:

"I do not feel guilt, shame, or regret for (name or describe the sin in as few words as possible)"

Then do the same for the blessing sigil

"In exchange for my Sin/regret, Azazel has blessed me with/by (name or describe blessing in as few words as possible)"

Create both sigils to completion and prepare them for use in ritual by inking them and pushing your intention into them.

Procedure Part 2 - With Azazel Called, and present, draw your blood and smear it onto the sigil containing your sin and recite the following –

It is with my blood that I do swear that I give this pain and regret unto Azazel as an offering of true friendship and devotion. May this offering please you Azazel, I ask that you take this guilt and pain from me and build me up and restore me in the process! I am worthy!

Meditate on this sigil for some time to activate it.

When ready, set this sigil aside, and prepare the sigil with your requested blessing on it (if any), and anoint it with your blood as well, then say the following over it –

I offer up my sin unto you Azazel, and in return I ask that you please grant me this humble request. If it be worthy of me, let it be done!

With those words take both sigils with the blood on it and put it into the burned offering cauldron and burn it completely.

As it burns say –

It is as it was, and I am as I must be... I am free, my regret is gone! Torment me no more and bring peace unto me at last.

Remain in mindful mediation for a short time...

You may already notice and feel the Regret leaving you... either way proceed when you feel it is the right time.

Take the red ribbon and anoint it with your blood, smearing your blood from one end to the other as best you can. Hold it out in front of you and imagine that it is no mere ribbon, it is a holistic object, a tether connecting you and your regret and sin... the last thread of connection you have to the pain. Whatever sensation of guilt, pain, or remorse you feel, push it into the ribbon, load it with that energy, all of it, bring yourself to tears if you must and reach a point of maximal catharsis and when you feel you are ready
and say the following:

I hereby cut all the ties of this guilt and regret, so that it no longer binds or reminds me of the pain and guilt of the past...

Take the ribbon in your hand as you say this and wrap it ceremonially around just the blade of the Ritual dagger, and imagine the dagger effortlessly cutting the ribbon in the astral world, separate it from yourself.

When you feel it is time, take the ribbon off the dagger, and say the following –

Rejoice! I give this last remnant of my pain and guilt to you Azazel, I am worthy of peace of mind, and I ask that you bless me with that which I asked... and I shall be glad if even only I receive the liberation from guilt. For I am worthy, and free!

Next take the ribbon and throw it into the fire, and make a gesture of cutting away any remaining astral tether between you and the flame, and maintain an EMPTY minded state as long as you can (not open, not focused, but empty you want to sever all ties to the energy here). Commune with Azazel now if you wish, otherwise, thank Azazel for helping you and dismiss him with respect.

Take these ashes and dispose of them far from your home (a short drive perhaps).

President Malphas

President Malphas is one of my personal favorite spirits, and as part of my pact with him, I created, this and a few other spells and rituals in his honor. You may substitute any other spirit you feel is suitable for scrying and divination. President Malphas description:

The Thirty-ninth Spirit is Malphas.

He appeareth at first like a Crow, but after he will put on Human Shape at the request of the Exorcist, and speak with a hoarse Voice.

He is a Mighty President and Powerful. He can build Houses and High Towers, and can bring to thy Knowledge Enemies' Desires and Thoughts, and that which they have done. He giveth good Familiars.

If thou makest a Sacrifice unto him he will receive it kindly and willingly, but he will deceive him that doth it.

He governeth 40 Legions of Spirits, and his Seal is this, etc.

Adapted from Thorne's Personal Grimoire: President Malphas is one of those Goetic demons that gets a fair amount of play in pop culture, appearing in video games, being the name for at least one heavy metal band, as well as the iconic Crow imagery being a common theme in many pop culture horror and gothic fiction.

There is something about this demon that remains popular or at least at the fringes of the mind of humanity, either causing, or benefiting from the popularity of crows in gothic and horror fiction.

Malphas is enigmatic, and though many hear him speak in a human voice sooner or later, I still rarely hear or experience anything other than a more animalistic presence. A mysterious black bird like demon in my mind's eye, his body movements are expressive, and he rarely makes any real noise at all, rather just whispers or occasional crow sounds.

Ever since making him one of this families most beloved spirits and protectors, our home has become blessed by 2 of the largest crows I have ever seen, perhaps even being ravens. Their deep guttural crow caws can be heard for hundreds of yards and very often when I sit in silence communion in my home with Malphas I hear these birds outside suddenly as if in reply to my questions.

Malphas loves craftspeople and artisans, and my wife and I are rather handy and craft/art oriented in our own way, my wife loves a wide variety of arts and crafts related to costuming and cosplay, while I love weapons and making things like jewelry and of course digital art used to be one of my professions.

Malphas is a powerful protector spirit, and his form of protection revolves around making your astral abode and even your real home into a fortified tower, and he likes working with Halphas to ensure the tower is well stocked with weapons.

Malphas form of protection is like that of a watch tower, it is imposing, but also allows you see great distances to see trouble coming. Siege towers were also used to get over enemy defenses, and so Malphas is also more than capable of attacking enemies in his own way. His form of offense revolves around demoralizing the enemy, ruining their plans and dreams and hopes. Invading their defenses and breaking down their ability to protect themselves.

Another nice feature is his ability to give the sorcerer a powerful familiar, and this was another thing I took advantage of early on and created a ritual for that I am including in this grimoire.

I also highlighted a portion of the text that warns of

never making sacrifice to Malphas or he will deceive you.

This is often misinterpreted and causes a lot of concern for a lot of people.

Malphas is a special spirit in that he embodies the cleverness and to a certain degree the almost narcissistic greed of the Crow. If you feed crows they can be trained, but if you make things too easy for them and don't make them earn their treats and rewards, they can start to train you...

In addition, this spirit does not seek worship. It is an enigmatic demon of some darker aspects of nature, quite possibly a primordial nature or animal spirit that has come to regard humans as worthy of its time.

Therefore, it is unwise to make sacrifices to him, but rewards and offerings in exchange for his service is acceptable. To the caller beware, only offer things in reward for tasks done, and if you must offer something without it being a reward, do it to entice him into showing interest, promising him more if he obliges in your requests.

For example, invite him into your ritual chamber with a small almost insultingly small handful of treats he would enjoy, and as part of the calling, offer him a bigger reward if he comes to you and looks upon you favorably.

He can be called in the usual manner, and particularly likes shiny objects, bread, corn, scraps of meat and food, and other things you might offer crows. He also ADORES handcrafts, things sewn, things made by the hand, art, and almost anything of that sort. You could for example make him a small wooden box, scribed with his sigil and fill it with treats and leave it in a public place or in the wilderness as a reward for a major working done.

Thorne's Artistic Sigil Interpretation Next page:

Creation of a Familiar (Malphas or other)

(This is an updated revision of an older Free ritual I had circulating around the internet.)

Introduction

This ritual operation is an intuitively created magickal formulae channeled in part unto me by the Demon Malphas and performed successfully in the creation of my first familiar.

I used the Demon Malphas for the entirety of this working, you may use any Demon or entity for which you have affinity, and that is known as a provider of good or excellent familiars. A list of some Goetic demons will be included in the appropriate section below.

In my practice a familiar is significantly different from a servitor or Egregore in that a familiar is thought to be a spiritual being that is partially created (more like molded and shaped), and partially summoned/Evoked by way of a patron demon or spirit to serve as a companion for the Sorcerer. The sorcerer creates the rules and provides the energy and raw materials for the attracted/directed spirit to manifest and then binds it to an object through which it can be accessed and commanded.

Unlike an Egregore or Servitor which are made entirely out of the Sorcerers will and intention. A familiar is a real spirit, like a lesser demon or nature spirit, that has under the control and command of a higher spirit such as a "demon" and can be given to a sorcerer, or family of sorcerers or a coven etc.

Familiars can possess and dwell within animals and objects and will stay anchored to them when dormant until such time as the master, or the demon that granted it deem the time is right to end the relationship.

A familiar's purpose can be anything from short or long term, goal oriented, or free form. They can remain in your life for a short time or be passed down through generations. Familiars are NOT necessarily slaves (not by default), they can be willful, they can be problematic, and they can even work against you IF you are not both assertive, and honest with your will. If you attract and then generate a familiar to be a vicious little gremlin that troubles your enemies and steals things for you… And you do not take steps to create strong rules and boundaries… Then you can expect to have a little monster in your life that will prank you and steal from you as well.

It should be made clear - Even the most benign Familiars will sometimes act out to get your attention, to remind you they need a feeding, or that they are bored.

A familiar is not a being you should treat lightly, many can call upon the power and authority of the spirit that granted it in emergencies and can thus be very dangerous if they get out of hand.

If you ever need to be rid of one, they can sometimes be easy to get rid of, or be as much trouble as can be. Sometimes it's as easy to get rid of as a simple request, or cessation in feeding that makes them disperse. Other times it can require an elaborate and forceful banishment or exorcism that can be painful and time consuming and may require the aid of other sorcerers.

If you have any doubt, remember you are making a binding pact in blood with this being, and it will be attached to you like stink on shit.

It is up to you to decide whether to treat your Familiar well or abuse them as a slave entity. SOME Familiars MUST be treated as prisoners, or slaves, they may be a spirit that is being punished and thus serves you to pay its penance. Others might simply be masochistic and like the negative energy of being abused, as much as some are Sadistic and like abusing others.

Overall, the procedure for working with a Familiar, requires at least an adept occult skill level. You should be fully comfortable and initiated with the 9 kings or have plenty of magickal experience.

Why a Familiar?

Familiars are not for everyone, but for those who work with them, they can do a wide variety of magickal things, including companionship of a sort. A place between pet, and assistant, a

Favorite helpful tool, and a dire responsibility. They are "alive" and intelligent and can make decisions and act intelligently and independently (usually, though some are aloof, outright dumb, or alien in their intelligence).

They are usually extraordinarily good at helping you with at LEAST one (but usually many more) specific magickal things, for example scrying, protection, etc.

However, as sentient beings, they are not limited to these specialties, and most can carry out more mundane tasks and add their energy to ritual and spell-craft. The more intelligent they are, the more you can involve them and instruct them in things they might not be specialized in.

Most can even be given tasks of a general nature, such as finding your keys, or reminding you of important information. Some are lazy, but many are eager to serve their purpose like any spiritual entity that works with a sorcerer. They can be subtle, or obvious. Manifesting poltergeist level disturbances, or barely appear as anything more obvious than a faint smell in the air or a song stuck in your head. No two familiar are ever quite the same, many of them are entities of chaos, and their form and function are determined in no small portion to the desire of the familiar's master and the spirit that granted it.

Thus, to a certain large degree you can consciously decide what they are good for, there are rules and limits, but they are practical and sensible ones. For example, you can arm and empower them with weapons, or symbols of knowledge. You can teach them things later in ritual, as they can teach you in their own way.

Thus, by way of ritual, you are giving them power to act on your behalf with that ability, and by regular feeding they will maintain or grow that power, much like an egregore or servitor.

Keep feeding it, and it will get more powerful. Keep giving it tasks and it will get more powerful, be consistent, and it will be well trained, and reliable.

Are these Servitors or Egregors or something else?

In the mind of many advanced sorcerers, the being I am describing sounds a lot like a Servitor, or Egregore, especially in the fact that so much of the familiar's attributes are created by the sorcerer.

There is an admitted egregoric quality to this kind of Familiar, do not let this confuse you, this is its own individual spirit that may in fact be an egregore created by someone long ago, or by the god or demon being used in the ritual, or even by the sorcerer themselves with the aid of the spirit.

In the end, it doesn't matter, when the ritual and pathworking is done, you have a companion spirit, one that may last you a lifetime.

When familiars become problems

Familiars are sentient willful entities, and they can tire of serving you. Sometimes this doesn't matter, sometimes they are slaves to you, given to you by a demon as punishment for whatever reason.

In those cases, the demon will often give you a means of control, or destruction, a shackle, a chain, a whip… a branding iron, a dagger. In some ways, these can be safer, because the demon gives you a strong method of control.

Then again, if you set them free by accident… you may be held accountable, or the familiar might become a danger to you.

But even a good familiar can turn bad.

It is entirely up to you to know how to treat these beings, either with respect and compassion, or mercy, or contempt. If you do not treat it correctly, it will rebel and act out. Act too bossy to a benign but independent cat like spirit that likes to have room to work? It might get lazy or refuse to do your bidding.

Act too soft on a willful spirit that likes to control things like an imp or gremlin? It might walk all over you, and make you wonder who is in control.

Ignore a spirit that needs attention and regular tasks? It might play pranks on you, or make you lose things.

While not my experience, a familiar CAN become a problem, and so I've heard - even a dangerous one… If this ever happens, you need to know how to banish and disperse it.

Unless it is a major threat, I would always start out by trying to starve it out and or command it to leave forever, never to return, or contact the demon I got it from and release it back into the demon's custody if it is a prisoner of some sort. So, getting rid of your problem can be as simple as a mere statement and command, or a full-blown ritual or exorcism.

For gentle and otherwise benign Familiars - simply state your command for it to depart back to its source and refuse to feed it again.

Regardless, if it doesn't depart after the next full moon, destroy the vessel in fire and or bury it in a place away from your home, and banish it into the smoke to be carried off far from you.

If it follows you home, perform a full banishing/exorcism as per your tradition, or call upon your patron demon who granted this familiar to you to intervene and help you with your problem.

If the familiar is a slave/prisoner serving out a sentence to a demon by serving you, then so long as you remain in control over the familiar, the demon should have provided you a means by which you bind, command, and can control the familiar.

If you no longer want it, you can starve it and keep it chained in its vessel, and it can disperse… but this can still release it into the world to regroup and do harm down the road.

In the end, the best course is almost always to evoke the demon that gave you this being and return it whence it came.

In all cases, never re use a vessel. When the familiar has departed and you know it is gone or dispersed. Never use it for another spirit. If it is a valuable heirloom of some kind you can try to clear and align it back to normal, but sometimes the only recourse is to DESTROY the vessel, preferably in fire as mentioned above. Failing that, crush and pulverize it and bury the remains far from home.

The Reason for this is that an object that has housed a spirit for any length of time can take on certain energies and can even become a cursed object as it now has a hollow space inside its energy that is just right for many wayward spirits.

When in doubt - destroy it.

FEED ME!!!!

Familiars almost always require some form of sustenance, and this is usually in the form of a holistic offering of some kind consisting of a substance, some energy, and some thought.

Blood, milk, incense, and other substances are all useful, and blood offers a tremendous amount of energy and connection to the spirit but can also make it very personal and dangerous to let fall into the wrong hands as it has a strong bond with you magickally.

These beings will need a regular feeding and I usually make it a monthly event that happens on the full moon, and I give mine rewards and treats of energy and blood when it pleases me.

Preparation and pre-ritual working

Attraction

While Not all familiars require this step, some will seek you out simply because you are powerful. My preferred method is to use a Demon to help bring me the best one possible.

As discussed before, there are many demons that work well for this, and typically the familiar doesn't have to be like the demon in any way, it can have a completely different set of attributes and personality. However, most demons have favorite forms or archetypal themes and it helps if you let the demon bring you familiars that somehow fit into their archetype.

For example, Malphas is often seen as a Crow or Raven, or other Corvus bird, and is focused on building defenses, spying and scrying and protection, and you need to expect a familiar it sends to at LEAST have "some" common traits, maybe it will be loosely Bird like, a protective warrior, maybe it will have sneaky spy qualities, maybe it will take the form of a Raven, maybe it will be in the form of a ninja imp, or maybe it will look like a "Rook" chess piece (tower) with crows and ravens circling around it or perched on it, that slides around but only in two directions doing your bidding.

Either way, the first step is to evoke your chosen demon, and when you evoke the Demon, after whatever other business or pleasure you have with them, ask them for a familiar. Be direct as you would with any other request, be polite, be respectful.

Be sure to offer something tangible in return. Be sure to Outline a few basic parameters, I typically specify no more than 3-5 things about the familiar, including a time frame for it to appear to me (a month is more than enough).

I also make sure to declare what I will give in return and ask if this is suitable. If the demon is agreeable, you will know you can proceed.

Now you should declare your parameters - When declaring your parameters, they are just that parameters, and you need to trust the demon to work within them but you need to make the parameters both specific enough for it to have meaning, but broad enough to give the demon room to do its part.

Do not for example be so specific that you basically demand a being that fits a perfect image you already have in your head of something cool like from a movie or cartoon.

Example parameters:

- "A loyal familiar I can trust." this is a big deal. I am OK with a little naughtiness, or the occasional prank, if I know the familiar has my best interests at heart.

- "A familiar that is of pleasing general appearance." - This is subjective, I would find some rather grotesque things pleasing. You could be more specific, but I find this helps defeat the purpose of letting the demon find it for you, stick to broad descriptions – "In the form of a cat, a bird" and let the demon fill in the blanks, if it has the head of a goat and the body of a worm... so be it. Keep in mind, how it LOOKS to you isn't all that important,

or even real. It is a spirit, and how it appears is malleable and personal to you, but it is also symbolic. Its symbolism must "work" for you.

- "A familiar that will come when called." Otherwise why bother? You could add, and manifests to physical form. But beggars can't be choosers. Most familiars are as subtle as the demons. A demon may simply not be willing to provide such an obvious being that could throw off the whole occult thing they have going on.

- "A familiar that will follow instructions." Otherwise why bother?

- A familiar that will be provided and bound to me within 1 month (just enough time for a demon to make things happen but not so long that you forget). Make sure that when you are done, you make note in your grimoire (You ARE keeping a grimoire or at least a hand-written journal right? Not just a web blog?) of what kind of familiar you are asking for, and what the deadline for its arrival is, and MAKE SURE you pay for it as per any agreement you make with the demon before the deadline you specified, but only if you got what you asked for. If you say you want the familiar to appear to you within a month, then if it appears within a month, even if you haven't yet made it official and bound it to your service, be prepared to pay for the demon's aid. I specifically tell my Demon I will pay when the Familiar is mine, not simply when it appears to me, because I may not notice it or want it!

Detection

Like any other magick a big part of it, is letting go of the intent once you declare it. You need to both forget you are getting a familiar, and at the same time be open to noticing it when it comes. This step is a waiting game and you should do everything in your power to remain open to detecting when the familiar is around you.

Care must be taken NOT to just leap to the first conclusion that pops in your head or INVENT the being from your flights of fantasy before or after requesting it. I have seen far too many novices basically create some fantasy familiar in their head without any justification for it… basing it on anime characters or some other nonsense, and convince themselves the being is real, and then promptly forget all about it when nothing happens.

I do not mean to imply they cannot take these forms or appear to you through modern media somehow. Simply don't put the cart before the horse!

You are waiting for a sign and a symbolic apparition to appear to you, sent to you by your demon. Instead, wait patiently, and forget you are waiting. If you are sitting around daydreaming about it all day… you will either spoil the magick, or worse yet, ignore the REAL familiar when it arrives.

Disregarding it in favor of some fantasy you made up and convinced yourself is the real thing.

Remember, Familiars can take almost any form, and while we all wish we could have a familiar that is a big black dragon that we can fly around on… most of the time these beings are more abstract, more symbolic, and sometimes they are almost formless, many are shapeshifters.

They can appear to you in dreams, or in trance. While scrying, or sometimes they make themselves known as an alien idea you know isn't normally something you imagine.

Maybe it's a talking spoon?

Or a radio announcer on your car radio only you can hear?

What is important is that it comes to you, not that it has a cool physical appearance!

The appearance almost doesn't matter… unless you specifically told your demon you wanted something appealing to you. There is even some room for you to alter how it appears to you when you bind it. This is usually simple alterations, color, size, what it's armed with, things like that.

The General FORM is what belongs to the familiar, you will usually know what aspects of it are set in stone.

My first familiar took the form of a big black rat, but in place of a head, it had the skull of a Raven or crow, with feathers around the head and neck becoming black jagged fur around the body. It was armed with a spear and carried a grimoire on a sling/strap/pouch at its side.

Pretty bad-ass if you ask me, I got kind of lucky in the form it took, but I did ask for something pleasing!

The spear and grimoire were my own additions, gifts I gave it so it could do its job of protecting me and helping me to learn and aid me in scrying and research.

Regardless, it is up to you to ACCEPT whatever familiar arrives or REFUSE it!

Keeping in mind, even if you refuse it, you may owe the demon you made the pact with, but It is possible you will be sent multiple possible familiars till you are satisfied.

Either way, if your demon sends you a Familiar, but you don't accept it, I would still make payment unless you were very specific that you would only pay if the familiar became bound to you as requested.

Lastly, sometimes they can even possess a creature and appear within a physical form, but do not expect them to do this. Familiars by themselves do NOT have a Physical body, but they may possess them, sometimes a specific one.

I do not normally believe in binding a familiar to a physical animal or living body, certainly not a pet that I care about at the very least.

However, certain animals are often open to being possessed from time to time, and I will not fault a spirit for taking advantage of a willing animal to communicate with me, but I will not force a beloved pet to be possessed either.

The next step – finding a home for your familiar.

Traditionally people used small bottles, jars, wooden boxes and other containers to represent the home for their familiar, inside they would place their offerings, blood and milk and whatever else they promised it.

These are perfectly acceptable to use today.

You can also use a figurine, a piece of jewelry, or almost any object, even a book like your grimoire! Whatever you feel is suitable.

It should go without saying that the vessel for your familiar should be special, and appeal to the familiar both energetically, and aesthetically. You may need to scry for this, or just use your intuition and artistic ability to select and customize your container.

A nice small wood jewelry box which you decorate with designs you burned into it, or something like that would be great for almost any Familiar.

Jewelry can be a great home as well. But make sure it is something that suits them. And keep in mind, if you lose that jewelry, you may or may not lose your familiar…

Preparation

To prepare for this ritual you will need to create a series of sigils, one to represent the Familiar, and one for each of the 3-5 rules we wish to bind this spirit with.

Also make up your mind what you wish to offer the familiar as a regular feeding agreement.

You can make these at any time before the ritual. We will create the sigils in the usual manner, and here are a few examples of what the rules could be (replace the word familiar with the familiar's name):

- Familiar is loyal
- Familiar can do no harm without direct instruction from (your magick name, and or other trusted names)
- Familiar comes immediately when called
- Familiar departs quickly when Dismissed
- Familiar is obedient

Optional (but recommended) – Some kind of drawing that represents the Familiar, even if you suck at drawing, unless you can't bare to look at it, draw or paint, or otherwise create some sort of artistic rendition of the familiar to help you visualize it from here on.

Once you have created a sigil for each of these and the Familiar itself, you can move on to starting the ritual.

Ingredients

- Altar - set up to accommodate the spirit you have been using to acquire this familiar.

- Incense - Dragons Blood and Sage plus any that your spirit requires or desires.
- Each of the sigils you created, plus any for the spirit you are using for this working.
- Bloodletting device
- (optional) Alcohol for the cauldron and Cauldron fire
- Fresh Sea salt for lining the Cauldron.

Procedure

Begin by aligning and clearing then calling your chosen demon into the ritual chamber.

Once you have them in attendance, commune with them as much as needed to inform them of your intentions and then proceed to call the familiar by placing its sigil next to your chosen Demons sigil and Calling the familiar. With luck your Demon guide will help, and you will get a very strong manifestation, look out for poltergeist activity, smoke moving flame dancing etc.

When you feel certain both entities are in full attendance, recite the following –

> **Familiar spirit, gift of (demon name)**
> **I (magickal name and make your magick mark over the alter) command/require/ask (chose one) that you observe the following rules and binding commandments of your being -**

One by one you will now read out the Rules you have made for the familiar, holding the sigil it represents in your hands for a short time charging it with your intention and energy and then place it on the altar. Place the sigils around the 2 sigils of the demon and the familiar in the center in a pleasing balanced way.

Next take the intended vessel for the familiar, charge it with your intent and energy and place it on top of the familiar's sigil Recite:

Familiar Spirit, Gift of (demons name)
Behold your temporal abode
Into this vessel I bind and keep you
Through it I shall command and feed you
I shall protect it and keep it!
It shall be the gate through which I call

When you have finished reading off these rules, and charged each sigil, recite the following:

Familiar spirit, Gift of (demons name)
These are the rules that shall bind you, and I shall in turn be a (good, gentle, cruel) master and ensure that your needs are met, and your vessel protected.
I agree to (state your feeding offer, and schedule now)
If there are no objections to these terms I shall continue.

From this point on it is up to you to sense what is going on, if you get a strong sign that this is not working out, thank the spirits and dismiss them and end the ritual the usual way, making a small offering of thanks for them showing up. If after a short time you do not get an obvious sign of disapproval, thank the appropriate entities, and use the bloodletting device and smear your blood on each sigil, and upon the familiars chosen vessel. Recite:

With this blood upon these signs
I do hereby seal the contract and offer it to the void!
The spirit (familiars name) is bound to my will
Its fate is my command
Its spirit is bound unto its vessel and to my will
May great peril befall any who would willfully interfere!

Take up each sigil in your hand one by one and read them again aloud and offering them with the blood on them into the burning Cauldron. Taking care to let them all burn completely as possible.

When all the sigils have burned completely say the following:

I (state your magickal name and make your sign over the familiar's vessel) command that you rest now and build up your strength for in three days' time I shall call to you, and if you do not answer my call, I shall be displeased!

Now immediately wrap up the familiar's vessel in black velvet or black sick and place it in a place of honor on the Altar (whatever feels right) and do not disturb it for 3 days. IF you come to check on this and the vessel has been in any way removed from the silk/velvet wrap, there has been a problem and you will need to contact the Demon or the Familiar to find out what is going on. commune with the spirits or close the ritual in the usual manner, making your offerings and dismissing the energies.

In three days, return to your altar, and light a single candle and take hold of the Vessel of your familiar and use it to commune with the familiar spirit it contains. When you call to it, an image of the spirit should pop quickly into your mind or some other manifestation must happen in a manner that pleases you, when it does, give it a simple task to perform and get used to using it for things.

Familiars benefit from a balance of rest and exercise, use them too much and they become mundane and lose potency, use them only for important things, and they retain their power. Use them too little and they lack coherence, let them rest too long and they can disperse.

Printed in Great Britain
by Amazon